ASK A LAWYER
Landlord and Tenant

ASK A LAWYER

LANDLORD AND TENANT

Steven D. Strauss

W · W · NORTON & COMPANY

NEW YORK   LONDON

For information about permission to reproduce selections from this book, write to: Permissions, W. W. Norton & Company, Inc., 500 Fifth Avenue, New York, NY 10110.

The text of this book is composed in Berkeley Book, with the display set in Futura. Desktop composition by Chelsea Dippel. Manufacturing by the Haddon Craftsmen, Inc. Book design by Margaret Wagner.

Library of Congress Cataloging-in-Publication Data

Strauss, Steven D., 1958–
    Ask a lawyer. landlord and tenant / Steven D. Strauss.
       p. cm.
    Includes index.
    ISBN 0-393-04585-4. — ISBN 0-393-31730-7 (pbk.)
    1. Landlord and tenant—United States—Popular works. I. Title.
KF590.S77 1998
346.7304'34—dc21   97-33617
                                                  CIP

W. W. Norton & Company, Inc. 500 Fifth Avenue, New York, N.Y. 10110
http://www.wwnorton.com

W. W. Norton & Company Ltd., 10 Coptic Street, London WC1A 1PU

1 2 3 4 5 6 7 8 9 0

This book is dedicated to my great bruhddies, Spencer and Larry, and to my wonderful sis, Robyn.

I would like to thank Seymour Fagan for everything he has taught me, legal and otherwise.

CONTENTS

INTRODUCTION: ABOUT THIS BOOK AND THE *ASK A LAWYER* SERIES

A person usually needs an attorney either to act as an advocate or to get advice. While there are many books on the market that endeavor to teach people how to be their own lawyer-advocate, this is not one of them. This book, and the *Ask a Lawyer* series, focuses upon the second function of an attorney—dispensing helpful, useful, and needed legal advice.

Few can afford to pay $250 to sit down with an attorney for an hour in order to get legal help. The *Ask a Lawyer* series is designed to give people the advice of an attorney at a fraction of the cost. Helping people understand the law and their rights; explaining which of several options may work best for them; giving insights, tips, and helpful hints; in short, giving readers the type of assistance they would expect if they sat down with an expensive lawyer, is the purpose of this book and this series.

Landlord and tenant law in particular is an area of the law that requires good, affordable legal help. As this book explains, there are many problems that can arise in this particular relationship; problems that can often cost either party a lot of money if not handled correctly. This book will help you figure out how best to resolve such issues. How do you handle a landlord who refuses to return a security deposit? What do you do with a tenant who continually fails to pay rent on time? How should an eviction be handled? Read on.

This book will sensibly walk you through landlord and tenant rights and responsibilities, caution you about possible pitfalls, explain in simple terms important aspects of the law, and guide you toward a sensible solution to your particular problem. It is organized to make this often complicated area of the law quite easy to understand. Each chapter has its own table of contents, so that once you turn to a chapter of interest to you, you can quickly find the specific area with which you need help. If, for example, you have a question about who should fix a leaky faucet, flip to Chapter 14, "The Duty to Provide a Habitable Home and Repair the Premises," and look under "The duty to repair necessities." Each chapter ends with "The Important Legal Concepts to Remember" so that you leave the topic understanding exactly what it is you need to know.

Appendix A lists many common landlord and tenant questions, along with sensible, simple answers. Any **boldface** word in this book can be found in the glossary, Appendix B.

Unlike many other areas of the law, resolving landlord-tenant disputes usually does not require the assistance of an attorney. Since this book easily explains each side's rights and duties, the need for a lawyer to resolve a dispute is eliminated. No book of this type can come with a guarantee, and no book can substitute for the advice of an attorney familiar with your particular problems and issues. However, absent many hours with high-priced legal counsel, this book is just about the next best thing.

1

BEFORE YOU
RENT

A NOTE TO LANDLORDS AND TENANTS

The landlord-tenant relationship
Landlord-tenant law in general

Compare this scenario:

> Ari had lived in a home owned by Raphael for three years. Ari had always been a good tenant and Raphael a good landlord. However, when the house's fence fell down after a big storm, Raphael refused to fix it. He claimed that Ari's tomato vines, which had climbed the fence for years, were the cause. Raphael therefore claimed it was Ari's responsibility to fix it. Ari believed that since Raphael was the landlord, he should fix it.
>
> Tempers flared, and neither party would budge. Ari stopped paying rent. Raphael threatened to evict him. In the end, Ari *was* evicted for his failure to pay rent. However, in the meantime, Raphael fell behind on his mortgage due to the lack of rent, and the fence was never fixed by the time the bank foreclosed on the house.

with this scenario:

> After the fence fell down and the yelling had subsided, Raphael realized that he needed to solve this problem lest

he be faced with a much larger one. He sat down with Ari one day over a cup of coffee and said, "Listen, Ari, I need your rent and you need a place to live. If I buy the lumber, would you be willing to put up a new fence?" Ari knew that an eviction would make finding a new home very difficult. "Sure," he said. "That's a fair compromise."

THE LANDLORD-TENANT RELATIONSHIP. Before you arm yourself with laws, statutes, and other ammunition to hurl at your **landlord** or **tenant**, it is important to understand a *nonlegal* concept: the landlord-tenant relationship is, first of all, a relationship. Like all relationships, it can be positive or negative. It can be friendly or adversarial. It can be mutually beneficial or mutually detrimental. It is up to the parties in the relationship to determine the quality of that relationship.

Yes, knowing your rights will undoubtedly help to solve a problem. Yet no knowledge of the law can be more effective than this basic rule of landlord-tenant relationships: *Nothing beats a good working relationship with your landlord or tenant.* A friendly, personal call by a landlord to a tenant whose **rent** is tardy is often more effective than a hostile threat of **eviction** backed by rules and statutes.

So, this is your first tip: try to cultivate a positive, working relationship with your counterpart in this relationship. Be fair and responsible. You will find that it will be much easier to get what you want if that person likes and trusts you than if he dislikes and resents you. In that sense, the landlord-tenant dance is just like any other—work together or someone will step on the other's feet.

LANDLORD-TENANT LAW IN GENERAL. Try as you might to get along with your dance partner, it is not always possible. Some people are simply too mean or too stupid or too irresponsible or too bureaucratic to work with. When faced with people or institutions like these, it is best to come armed instead of friendly.

In the context of landlord-tenant law, that means knowing your legal rights and the other party's legal responsibilities. A tenant who knows that she is not normally legally responsible for a fallen fence will not be bamboozled so easily. A landlord who knows that he is not normally legally responsible for a tenant-created problem will not be so quick to open his wallet. So, this is your second tip: know your rights.

Tenancy is the term used for the period of time that a tenant rents a unit from a landlord. A tenancy can last any length—a week, a month, a year, or more. A tenancy can be created in writing or by verbal agreement. No matter the type of arrangement, any rental creates a tenancy. What is important to understand is that the creation of a tenancy simultaneously and automatically creates rights and duties on both sides.

And just what are those rights? Prior to the 1960s, landlords held all the cards in the legal deck. Tenants had very few rights, and landlords had many. Although it is well known that the consumer rights movement of the 1970s drastically changed the rights of consumers, what is less well known is that it had an equal, if not greater, effect on landlord-tenant law.

Whereas landlords in previous eras could collect rent without having to provide little more than a roof in return, today they are obligated by law to provide safe, clean, and **habitable** dwellings. Landlords are now prevented from **discriminating** in housing, **rent control** has taken effect in many communities, and landlords in most **jurisdictions** are forbidden from raising rent, shutting off utilities, or evicting a tenant in retaliation for some minor dispute.

Yet, while the scale has definitely tilted in favor of the tenant, landlords are not without protections. A landlord is, after all, still the owner of the property and law itself was created to protect property rights. If rent is late or a tenant becomes a problem, expeditious evictions are available. If a tenant harms the property, the **lease** can be terminated. If a tenant uses the unit to break the law, a landlord can immediately end any agreement.

Landlords and tenants are mutually dependent upon one another. Landlords depend upon their tenants for rent, and tenants need landlords for a place to live. So, although everyone is now legally armed with rights, responsibilities, and **remedies**, remember that it takes two to tango.

The Important Legal Concept to Remember: It is a lot easier to be friendly to your landlord or tenant if you know your rights. If kindness fails to solve a problem, the law will.

BEFORE THE TENANT MOVES IN

What the tenant should look for
How to find the right tenant
Discrimination in housing

Before a lease is ever signed, before the cat is deemed accept-able, before the fence ever falls down, the wary landlord and the prospective tenant first must meet. Renting an apartment or house from or to someone you do not know is a risky venture. A landlord needs proof that the tenant is responsible. A tenant needs proof that the unit is habitable.

WHAT THE TENANT SHOULD LOOK FOR. Any tenant wanting to rent space from a landlord needs to inspect the premises thoroughly before any agreement is reached. The first thing to do is to check out the neighborhood and speak with some neighbors. It would be especially helpful if you could speak with other people who rent from the same landlord.

Although she liked the apartment her potential landlord, Paul, had shown her, Anne decided to speak with some neighbors before signing the year-long lease. She was glad she did. It turned out that Paul had a reputation for being difficult, and rarely fixed problems in a timely manner. Anne found a similar apartment with a good landlord instead.

Besides the neighborhood and the neighbors, be sure to check out thoroughly the condition of the unit too. This is especially important in order to discover any defects on the premises. If, for example, the unit has a window pane that is broken, it would behoove the prospective tenant to bring it to the landlord's attention so that the landlord does not later try to blame the new tenant for the old problem.

If the unit you are looking at has some of the problems listed below, either the landlord should fix them first or you should not rent the space. As explained in Chapter 6, implied in *every* **rental agreement** is something called the **implied warranty of habitability**. That warranty means that every residential landlord is obliged to provide every tenant with a dwelling that is livable. If the unit lacks basic necessities *before* a tenant ever moves in, make no mistake about it, it certainly will not have them later, no matter what promises are made.

- *Plumbing:* Be on the lookout for leaky faucets, water around the base of the toilet, drains that don't drain, and rusty-colored water. Make sure that the hot water works.
- *Kitchen:* Does the stove work? Is the sink clean? Does the refrigerator door close? Try sticking a dollar bill in the door; the harder it is to pull out, the better.
- *Structure:* Is the unit weatherproof? Look for water stains and excessive caulking near windows, and stains on the ceiling and down the walls. Be sure too that any linoleum floors are not curling, since **liability** could be a problem if someone trips.
- *Heat and air:* While laws mandate that a rental unit must have adequate heat, air-conditioning is not usually required by statute.
- *Fire safety:* Most cities require smoke detectors to be installed

in rental units. Stairways, hallways, and storage areas should
be free of combustible materials.

After the inspection is complete and the landlord wants to
rent to you, be sure to list on the rental agreement all problems that you found with the rental. Moreover, make sure to get
in writing any promises the landlord makes, such as assurances
that he will fix a leaky faucet or repaint before you move in.
That way, there will be no misunderstandings.

HOW TO FIND THE RIGHT TENANT. Needless to say, finding
the right tenant is critical to the success of a landlord's business.
When looking for a tenant, a landlord needs to be quite careful.

Of course, he must find a tenant with a good rental and credit history—that is a given. Equally important, though, legally
speaking, are the many laws that apply to landlords when they
are looking for tenants. Probably the most important laws to
know about are antidiscrimination statutes, which dictate that
a landlord cannot discriminate when renting out his property.
When advertising for a prospective tenant, the smart landlord
should not mention race, sex, age, national origin, or religion.
Discrimination in rental housing is forbidden and such ads
can be misconstrued (see below).

Once a landlord has located some prospective tenants, he
should have them fill out a rental application and list their
rental history, credit history, and references. He must make sure
to call the references, including previous landlords. What is
necessary to know is whether a possible tenant has a history
of paying rent on time, if he has ever been evicted, and whether
he caused problems previously. It is also a good idea to verify
the employment and income of any prospective tenant.

It is also wise to run a credit check on the possible tenant.
Charging the tenant a nominal **fee** (say, twenty-five dollars)
for the time and expense of running the credit check is legal in
most states, and advisable. If you use the report to deny an
application, federal law mandates that you notify the applicant

and tell him the name and address of the credit agency upon which your decision was based.

Many landlords choose not to interview or rent to potential tenants who have pets. While perfectly legal and understandable, they may want to reconsider that position. Pet owners tend to be more stable and better occupants than tenants without pets. Many will pay higher rents and large **deposits** just to have a place where they can have a pet. They also are more reluctant to leave since finding a new rental that accepts a pet is often difficult. The upshot is that renting to a pet owner means a landlord may get a tenant who will pay more, leave a larger deposit, and probably will not leave too quickly. Not a bad deal.

DISCRIMINATION IN HOUSING. If you are faced with two equally qualified tenants, it is legal to pick one over another for no other reason than that you liked one better; there is nothing discriminatory about that. However, if you have a pattern of not choosing African-Americans, women, or other minorities, you leave yourself open to an expensive discrimination lawsuit, even if you never actually intended to discriminate against anyone.

Regardless of whether you are the manager of a one-hundred-unit apartment complex or the owner of a small duplex, federal antidiscrimination laws apply to you, as may several state and local ordinances. The federal Civil Rights Act and Fair Housing Act prohibit landlords from discriminating on the basis of race, ethnic background, national origin, religion, and sex. It is also illegal to discriminate against families with children. The Americans with Disabilities Act (ADA) effectively prohibits discrimination against someone with a disability.

Not only are landlords forbidden from denying a tenant a unit because of her race, religion, or sex, but it is also illegal to provide inferior housing, or to state that a unit is unavailable when that is not so. In essence, a landlord cannot reject a prospective tenant, or allegedly discriminate against her in any way, for any reason other than "legitimate and valid business reasons." Whereas denying a woman a unit because you do not like her religion is flatly illegal, denying her the place because she has a poor credit history is not. The bottom line: a landlord must have a valid business reason for any potentially discriminatory act.

The only time a landlord can legally discriminate against a family with children (assuming, of course, that the unit is large enough to accommodate such a family) is if the complex is designated "seniors only." A landlord does not, however, have to rent a two-bedroom place to a qualified applicant who has five children. Reasonable occupancy standards are expected and permissible.

The only time discrimination is legally permissible is when the unit is "owner-occupied"; that is, if the owner and the tenant will be sharing a house, for example, or otherwise may be sharing kitchen and bathroom facilities. In that case, antidiscrimination laws do not apply since such arrangements are not considered a business venture, and these antidiscrimination laws apply only to businesses.

Even if he is not discriminating, a landlord should be equally concerned with the *appearance* of discrimination. If you have a complex occupied only by whites, for example, then you may appear to be discriminating, even if you are not. The key to minimizing that risk is to set up some objective, legitimate business criteria when looking for new tenants and to stick to them. What you must do is to look *consistently* for things such as two positive references, stable employment, and a good credit history. Treat people equally and use the same criteria in every case. It may even be wise to write down your criteria and keep it on file. Above all, *be consistent, and document your reasons for denying someone a unit.*

If you do discriminate, the affected person can **sue** in state or federal court, or can file an administrative complaint with the Department of Housing and Urban Development (HUD). If you are found to have violated federal antidiscrimination housing laws, the ramifications can be severe. Authorities can order you to rent the unit to the person discriminated against, as well as force you to pay **damages** (i.e., money). Such money damages may not only include the out-of-pocket expenses of the **plaintiff**, but also money for pain, suffering, humiliation, and attorney's fees. Punitive damages, if applicable, can bankrupt a person.

The Important Legal Concept to Remember: Both landlords and tenants need to do their homework and check each other out before any agreements are signed. Landlords must treat all prospective tenants equally.

A CRASH COURSE IN LEASES AND RENTAL AGREEMENTS

Month-to-month agreements

Leases

Understanding written leases and written rental agreements

Written month-to-month rental agreements are usually best for landlords

Why fixed-term leases are best for tenants

There are two types of rental arrangements that a landlord and tenant can enter into: periodic tenancies and **fixed-term agreements.** A fixed-term agreement is popularly known as a **lease.** The more common name for a periodic tenancy is a **month-to-month agreement**.

MONTH-TO-MONTH AGREEMENTS. The first thing to understand about a periodic tenancy is that the period can be any length of time; a month is only the most common (and, therefore, is used most often in this book). Landlords and tenants can agree to any length of time; it all depends upon how often rent is due. If rent is due once a month, then it is a month-to-month agreement. If it is due every week, then it is a weekly agreement. The period corresponds to the frequency of rent payments.

The length of time of the period is critical. The second, and most important, thing to know about periodic tenancies is that the agreement can change on *very short notice*; again, depending upon how often rent is due.

> Claire entered into a month-to-month agreement with her landlord, Howard. Rent was set at $750 per month. After living in the unit for only two months, Howard gave Claire thirty days' notice of a rent increase. The new amount of rent was to be $1,500 a month. Claire's only two choices were either to pay the grossly inflated increase or to move.

Almost any change is permissible with a periodic tenancy, as long as proper **notice** has been given. Rent can be raised. The agreement can be **terminated**. A tenant can be told that a pet will no longer be welcome. Again, the amount of notice required to change the terms of the deal corresponds directly to how often rent is due. If rent is due every thirty days, then the amount of time required to change the terms of the agreement is also thirty days. If rent is due weekly, then the agreement could be terminated on seven days' notice. So, the important thing to know about month-to-month agreements is that *thirty days is all that is required to change the agreement*.

The agreement, while month-to-month, can actually *last* any length of time—a month or five years. It depends on what the parties want. As long as a tenant pays rent on time and cares for the unit, and as long as a landlord lives up to his duties, there is nothing stopping them from keeping the agreement going as long as they want to.

Month-to-month agreements can be made either verbally or in writing; there is no legal requirement that the arrangement has to be in writing, although it is a very good idea (see below). Changes in the terms of the agreement also do not have to be in writing. A landlord can give a tenant thirty days' notice to vacate over the phone.

LEASES. The second type of agreement that landlords and ten-ants can enter into is called a fixed-term agreement, common-ly known as a lease. A lease is different from a month-to-month agreement in that it fixes all terms of the agreement for a spe-cific period of time, typically, but not necessarily, one year. Whereas a monthly rental arrangement can change on thirty days' notice, *no changes* can occur in the terms of the lease while the lease is in effect. Rent cannot be raised. A landlord cannot give notice and force a tenant to move on thirty days' notice. It is because the contract does lock in the terms of the agreement for a fixed period of time that a lease is known as a fixed-term agreement.

And just as the landlord is obliged to allow the tenant to stay in the unit for a year, the tenant is obliged to pay rent for the full year. If a tenant has a year-long lease and moves out after nine months, he is legally obliged to pay the remaining three months' rent, whether or not he is living in the dwelling. A lease is a year-long **contract** obligating both sides.

Another important thing to realize about a lease is that, unlike a month-to-month agreement, it ends *automatically*. No notice needs to be given to terminate a lease. When the lease term ends, that is it. The tenant is supposed to move out that day, unless the lease has been renewed.

Whereas a month-to-month arrangement can be made either verbally or in writing, a lease *must* be in writing due to some-thing called the statute of frauds. That statute mandates that certain types of contracts must be in writing to be valid. Under the statute of frauds, agreements that last a year or more, and that pertain to land and real estate, like leases, are required to be in writing to have any legal effect. If they are not, it is as if no agreement was ever made. An oral lease that purports to last longer than a year is **void**.

UNDERSTANDING WRITTEN LEASES AND WRITTEN RENTAL AGREEMENTS. As indicated, when a landlord and a tenant enter into a month-to-month agreement, that agreement can be either verbal or written. Verbal monthly agreements are a very bad idea for everyone.

A landlord can promise a tenant the moon, but if it is not in writing, it will be very difficult to get those promises enforced. A tenant can promise to take care of the yard in return for a lower monthly rental payment, but if it is not in writing, there is no way to prove the agreement. Moreover, people may have different perceptions about what was agreed to. Memories fade over time. There are simply too many areas for disagreement when an oral contract is entered into. So, it is an altogether better idea to get any rental arrangement in writing.

When a month-to-month arrangement is memorialized in writing, it is called a rental agreement. When a fixed-term agreement is memorialized in writing, it is called a lease. (Thus, a lease really has two meanings: it is both the *term* for the type of agreement the landlord and tenant have and also the *name* of that agreement.)

A written rental agreement looks very much like a written lease. Both state who the parties to the agreement are and where the unit is located, and list the amount of rent. Both likely contain many boilerplate legal provisions that tend to favor the landlord. Not knowing the difference however, can have severe ramifications.

Upon graduation from college, Bill found an apartment that he loved for $1,000 a month and signed what he thought was a month-to-month rental agreement. When he was let go from his new job two months later, he gave thirty days' notice and intended to move home with his parents for a while. His landlord informed him that he had signed a lease and was responsible for the entire year of rent. Bill ignored him. Bill's landlord sued Bill for $10,000 ($1,000 x 10 months) and won.

While many such written rental contracts indicate clearly whether it is a yearly lease or a monthly rental agreement, some do not. A landlord has no problem distinguishing a lease from a rental agreement; he or she uses them all the time. How can a tenant tell them apart? The important thing to look for is a provision that *allows the agreement to be terminated, or rent to be raised, on thirty days' notice*. Such a clause means that the agreement is a month-to-month tenancy and not a fixed-term lease.

Neither leases nor rental agreements can legally include provisions that attempt to circumvent rental laws. Tenants have the right to habitable dwellings, to **privacy**, to use the place in **quiet enjoyment**, to minimum-notice requirements if they are being sued, and to a speedy return of deposits. Any agreement containing clauses that attempt to force tenants to **waive** (forgo) these rights is flatly illegal and unenforceable.

Either agreement can be intimidating; they are seemingly written in stone. But the truth is that they are changed all the time. Any written rental arrangement, be it a lease or a rental agreement, is a contract. Like any contract, both sides must agree to it. If a landlord wants to add an extra provision and both sides agree, then that provision can be added. If a tenant wants to delete a questionable clause and the landlord agrees, then it can be crossed out, and the change initialed and dated. Neither tenant nor landlord should ever sign an agreement that he does not agree with. That is why it is called an agreement.

Tenants especially may think that changing a lease or a rental agreement offered by a prospective landlord is practically impossible, but it is not usually as difficult as they may think. Landlords are in the business of renting their property. Unrented property is lost money. By the time a tenant is reading and ready to sign a rental agreement, his potential landlord has already concluded that he is the best available prospect. The landlord wants to rent to this tenant. Believe it or not, that tenant is in the power position.

Norman wanted Robyn to move into his vacant unit. Robyn was interested, but really wanted to bring her cat along, and Norman normally did not allow animals in the apartment.

Robyn knew that the space had been empty for a while, and she also knew that her previous landlord would give her a great referral. She insisted that she be allowed to bring her cat. Since Norman really wanted Robyn as a tenant, he agreed to the cat, changed the lease, and had Robyn put down an extra $200 cleaning deposit.

WRITTEN MONTH-TO-MONTH RENTAL AGREEMENTS ARE USUALLY BEST FOR LANDLORDS. Written monthly rental agreements are best for the tenant who does not plan to stay in the unit too long because the arrangement allows him to move on little notice. They are bad for the tenant who wants some security.

While they are sometimes good for tenants, written monthly rental agreements are often better for landlords, as these agreements keep power in a landlord's hands. First of all, it is the landlord's form. The landlord either buys the form (written by attorneys for landlords) from a stationery store or legal bookstore, or has his attorney draft it, or drafts it himself. In any case, the agreement protects the landlord at the expense of the tenant.

Even more important, these agreements permit changes on short notice—that is the very nature of a month-to-month agreement. This fact almost always helps a landlord. If a tenant becomes a problem, he can be out upon thirty days' notice. If a variable-rate interest mortgage on the unit suddenly increases, rents can be raised on thirty days' notice. This simply is not true with a lease. Leases lock everyone into the agreement for the entire term of the agreement. Month-to-month agreements let landlords make changes quickly if needed, and that is a great advantage.

Really, from the landlord's point of view, the only downside to using a monthly rental agreement is that it provides less security. Knowing that a house will be rented for a year is seemingly a great comfort. *Seemingly.* Leases are broken all the time. Unpaid rents are a fact. Security may be a myth. In most cases, the flexibility of a shorter-term agreement usually outweighs any perceived security of a lease.

WHY FIXED-TERM LEASES ARE BEST FOR TENANTS. Whereas a written monthly rental agreement favors the landlord, a fixed-term lease is often in the best interests of a tenant. First of all, a lease does give a tenant security. She knows that unless she gives the landlord **good cause** to evict her (such as ruining the apartment or not paying rent), she will have a place to live until the term expires. She also knows that her rent will not go up during that period.

Maybe best of all from the tenant's perspective is that she can probably break the lease without repercussion, if need be. This gives her the security of a lease with the flexibility of a monthly rental agreement. That is a hard combination to beat.

Under normal circumstances, a tenant is obliged to pay the entire year's worth of rent, even if she does not stay in the unit the entire time. That is the price one pays for the security that comes with a lease. If a tenant leaves with six months remaining on her lease, she is technically obliged to pay those six months of rent, with one very important caveat.

That is this: under contract law, landlords have a **duty** to try to rerent the unit as soon as is feasible. This is called **mitigating** one's damages. A landlord must take reasonable steps to reduce any damage he may suffer as a result of a tenant's breach of the lease. Renting the unit again in a reasonable amount of time to a qualified tenant would be a landlord's mitigation. In the case of the tenant who leaves with six months left on the lease, if a landlord rented the place again in three months, then his actual monetary loss would only be the three months that the house was vacant. The tenant who moved early would be obliged to pay her landlord only for those three months.

Even more problematic for the landlord is that collecting that lost money is often difficult and not worth the time and expense it would take.

Alice signed a year-long lease with Stephen. She was to pay $500 a month in rent. Six months into the term, Alice was offered a better job in a different city and moved out. It took Stephen three months to rent the place again. Although Alice was legally obligated to pay Stephen $1,500 ($500 x the 3 months that the place was vacant), Stephen knew in reality that he would never see that money. Alice didn't live there anymore. Stephen did not even know where to find her. Alice never paid the money and Stephen never even asked for it.

Leases are broken—that's a fact—and most often by tenants. Tenants really have little to lose by breaking a lease. A sad but true fact is that tenants usually do not have much money. People without many assets are known to lawyers as "empty pockets." No lawyer wants to sue an empty pocket. Accordingly, a landlord may not even go to the effort to sue over a broken lease, and even if he does, he may have a hard time collecting on any **judgment** he may eventually get.

Thus, not only is the landlord legally obliged to mitigate his losses when a tenant breaks a lease and moves early, but suing the tenant is usually not worth the landlord's effort. Since most landlords know this, a tenant can usually break a lease without consequence, if need be.

Accordingly, *a tenant should almost always get a lease if at all possible.* It obligates the landlord, prevents him from raising rent, and stops him from terminating the agreement unless good cause exists. A lease gives a tenant security without, in reality, any of the anchors.

The Important Legal Concept to Remember: Rental agreements vary greatly. Landlords should usually try to get their tenants to enter into written rental agreements, and tenants should almost always try to get a lease.

COMMON LEASE AND RENTAL AGREEMENT PROVISIONS

Common provisions
Provisions to be wary of if you are a tenant
Which provisions landlords should be most concerned with

COMMON PROVISIONS. The following are the ten most important sections in any lease or rental agreement. As a lease or rental agreement can be changed before it is signed, if any corresponding provision in your agreement is vague or unclear, make sure to clarify it. If and when a dispute arises, it will be this agreement that everyone will look to—judges especially—when determining who did wrong to whom.

1. *Identification of the parties and limits on occupancy:* The agreement must name the landlord and the tenants. A tenant who anticipates that his girlfriend may be moving in within two months should get her name on the agreement at the beginning of the term to avoid any confusion or later cause for eviction. If the agreement states that the unit is limited to four people, then the unit is limited to four people.

2. *Rent:* The agreement should clearly spell out when, where, and how much rent is due. It should also indicate if there is a grace period and any penalty for late payment of rent.

3. *Term:* Is this a month-to-month tenancy or a lease? Again, leases end automatically at the end of the term. Month-to-month tenancies normally end upon thirty days' notice. If the document allows modifications on thirty days' notice, it is a month-to-month rental agreement.

4. *Deposits:* The deposit clause should clarify how much deposit is required and to what it will be applied. The custom is to use the deposit for cleaning, unpaid rent, and damage above and beyond normal **wear and tear**. **Last month's rent** may be included in the **security deposit**, as long as it is clear that that is the case. That money can thereafter be used only to pay the last month of rent. The amount of a security deposit is often limited by state law; the equivalent of two months' rent is common. (For more information, see Chapter 10, "Security Deposits and Last Month's Rent.")

5. *Pets:* It is the landlord's right to allow or not to allow pets. If a tenant plans on bringing in a pet, even something as innocuous as a guinea pig, it is best to get the landlord's permission, again to avoid confusion or cause for eviction. A landlord cannot legally prohibit an animal that is used to assist someone who is blind, deaf, or disabled.

6. *Subletting and assignments:* **Subletting** is when the renter allows someone else to move into the space and pay the rent, but remains liable under the lease. An **assignment** takes the original tenant out of the agreement altogether; the new person takes over all obligations under the contract. Assignments and sublets may or may not be allowed under the agreement, but they usually are as long as the landlord first approves of the proposed change. The landlord cannot unreasonably withhold approval. (See Chapter 18, "Getting Out of a Lease Early.")

7. *Utilities:* The agreement should specify which utility bills are part of the rent and which are the additional responsibility of the tenant. Landlords usually pay for garbage, and tenants usually pay for phone, gas, and electric.

8. *Attorney fees and costs:* This clause states that the loser of any lawsuit must pay the legal fees and costs of the winner. As landlords win most eviction lawsuits, this clause effectively shifts the legal cost of eviction from the landlord to the tenant. This section is legal, and if a tenant is evicted under an agreement with such a provision, the tenant will be liable for all of the landlord's legal costs.

9. *Entire agreement:* This clause states that the document is the entire agreement between the parties, and that any previous oral promises are superseded by this contract. If your landlord or tenant made any promises to you earlier, you had better include them in this document, as they will be of *no effect* once the agreement is signed.

10. *Inspection notes:* A smart tenant will closely inspect the premises prior to signing the agreement and will note all defects.

PROVISIONS TO BE WARY OF IF YOU ARE A TENANT. Since leases and rental agreements are written by or for landlords, more often than not they favor the landlord. This is not to say that all landlords are unscrupulous; most certainly are not. Rather, it is a word of caution to the overzealous landlord and the too-trusting tenant—there are provisions in some rental agreements that are illegal and that may either harm the tenant or render the agreement altogether void. The most onerous are the following:

· *Waiver of the tenant's right to privacy:* This sort of clause endeavors to allow the landlord to enter the unit on no notice and without the tenant's permission. Since every residential rental agreement has implicit in it a tenant's right to privacy (called the **implied covenant of quiet enjoyment**), this clause is illegal and unenforceable.

· *No liability for damages or injuries:* This clause attempts to protect the landlord from having to pay money if the tenant is injured due to the landlord's negligent maintenance or upkeep of the property. Such provisions are also illegal and unenforceable.

· *Waiver of legal rights:* A **waiver** is a voluntary relinquishment of a known right. Although a contract may attempt to have the tenant waive certain rights, some rights are simply nonwaivable, no matter what the contract says. For instance, although the right to a jury trial for an eviction proceeding is guaranteed by many states, some rental contracts endeavor to have the tenant waive this right. Similarly, clauses that allow the landlord to evict the tenant without proper notice, that force the tenant to waive the right to appeal a court decision in an eviction action, that waive refunds of security deposits, or that waive applicable rent control ordinances are blatantly illegal and unenforceable.

· *Repairs:* Landlords are almost universally obligated to make major repairs. This is due to another rule implied in every residential agreement, called the implied warranty of habitability. This warranty means that it is up to the landlord to ensure that the dwelling is livable and that it is his responsibility if it is not. A lease provision that attempts to circumvent this rule is most likely void.

Tenants faced with agreements that contain provisions such as these have two choices: fight or do nothing. Of the two, doing nothing is, surprisingly, probably preferable. Think about it. Getting into a dispute with a landlord before he is even your landlord is a good way to ensure that he will never be your landlord. If you simply say nothing, comfortable in the knowledge that illegal provisions are void and unenforceable, then you will get the place *and* have a lease without the questionable provisions.

Richard's landlord, Frederick, had a lease that stated that Frederick would not be responsible if Richard were ever injured due to Frederick's negligence. Richard later sued Frederick after he was scalded by a faulty water heater that Frederick was well aware of. Richard won the lawsuit, and the questionable lease provision was completely ignored by the judge.

Remember, such provisions are unenforceable—no judge will make you pay for major repairs not of your creation, no matter what the contract says.

Aside from these illegal provisions, there are other provisions that, while legal, are at least negotiable. For instance, a prohibition against subletting or assignment without the landlord's permission is certainly negotiable. A pet restriction is often worth discussing. Whereas reasonable late charges for tardy rent are permissible, unreasonable penalties (say, 10 percent of the rent) are not and should be changed.

WHICH PROVISIONS LANDLORDS SHOULD BE MOST CONCERNED WITH. There are two aspects of lease and rental agreements that landlords need to be concerned about. The first are the provisions listed above, which are clearly illegal. Landlords need to be careful not to load up their contracts with too many illegal or questionable provisions. A principal of contract law is that some contracts are interpreted *against* the maker. That is, a court looking at a rental agreement drawn up by a landlord may likely analyze that contract in a light that favors the tenant. An agreement that contains too many questionable clauses may be disregarded in its entirety.

Even if a contract does not contain any illegal sections, the cautious landlord will want to protect his interests by making certain aspects of the agreement nonnegotiable:

- *Limits on occupancy and use:* You certainly do not want your tenants inviting their in-laws and cousins to move in after the agreement has been signed. Note, however, that it is normally perfectly legal for a tenant to bring in a spouse and children later without a landlord's consent. Also, a residential unit should be limited to that purpose only. While local zoning laws may prohibit businesses from being run out of the unit, it is a good idea to limit use specifically (if that is your desire).

- *Rent:* For the most part, the amount of rent, when and where it is due, charges for late rent, and bounced-check charges should not be subject to negotiation.

- *Prohibition against assignment and subletting:* This clause normally prevents the tenant from replacing herself in the middle of the term with another tenant whom you do not know and may not approve of. While an outright ban on sublets may be illegal in your area, a clause requiring your express written consent of the new person is not, as long as that consent is not unreasonably withheld.

- *Condition, alteration, and damage to the premises:* Sometimes appearing in separate clauses, this section limits the landlord's liability for damage to the unit caused by the tenant. A landlord is responsible for repairing items that break due to normal wear and tear (such as a leaky faucet or an old refrigerator that finally dies), and the tenant is responsible for damages that he or his guests create. Make sure this is spelled out clearly in the agreement. Should he so choose, a landlord can restrict alterations to the unit, such as building bookcases or painting.

Here is one more thing to consider: as indicated, most standard agreements permit the winner of any lawsuit to collect attorney fees and court costs from the loser. Landlords should think carefully about whether they really want this clause in their agreement. The first problem with this is that a landlord might end up paying a tenant's legal expenses. And if that were not bad enough, the clause may actually encourage a tenant to fight, given the possibility that she will be reimbursed should she win.

The Important Legal Concept to Remember: Like any contract, a rental agreement is completely negotiable. Try to
get as many helpful clauses inserted into the contract as
possible. Landlords should be especially conscious not to
add in too many questionable clauses that would make the
agreement unenforceable.

TENANT RIGHTS, DUTIES, AND SOLUTIONS

THE TENANT'S RIGHT TO POSSESSION

Understanding the right of possession
When the landlord can enter
Fixtures

When a landlord rents property to a tenant, certain rights and responsibilities come into effect as a matter of law. What is important to realize is that these rights are *automatic*. They exist *whether or not they are mentioned in the agreement* and are created whenever a tenant moves into a unit. The first of these rights is called the right to possession.

UNDERSTANDING THE RIGHT OF POSSESSION. A rental agreement is a contract. As with any contract, both sides make promises. The tenant promises to take care of the unit and to pay the rent in full and on time. The landlord promises to let the tenant live in the property to the exclusion of everyone else. Although the landlord owns the dwelling, by entering into the rental contract with the tenant, he is foregoing his right to possess the property in lieu of the rent money received.

> Hannah lived in a lovely home for many years. While she lived there, she cultivated a beautiful garden in the backyard. When she inherited some money, Hannah decided to buy a

bigger place and rent out her house. She found what she thought to be the perfect tenant in Jenny, and leased it to her for a year. After Hannah moved out, she told Jenny that she would be coming back to the house once a month to clip some flowers from the garden. Jenny correctly informed Hannah that the house was now hers and that Hannah was not welcome.

The reason why a landlord cannot enter is because once a tenancy is created, so is the right to exclusive possession. Both a month-to-month tenancy and a lease give the tenant the exclusive right to control the premises.

This right to exclusive possession extends to the entire property.

Although Hannah had been out of the house for six months, she never emptied the garage, despite Jenny's repeated requests for her to do so. Finally, Jenny sued Hannah in small claims court, and the judge awarded Jenny $500 as compensation for not having use of the garage attached to the house she rented.

Had she wanted to, Jenny could have voided the lease, moved out, and not paid another penny in rent. This is due to a concept known as **constructive eviction**. If a landlord takes possession of all or even part of the premises without permission, the tenant can cancel the lease and leave. (See Chapter 18, "Getting Out of a Lease Early.")

Thus, the right to possession means that once the unit has been rented to the tenant, it is hers to possess, to the exclusion of everyone, including the landlord. However, some landlords do not know the law. They think that because they own the premises, they still have the right to enter the unit whenever they want to. This is just not so. Once the landlord delivers the unit to the tenant, the tenant has the sole right to possession. After the tenant moves in, her home is her castle.

This point should be underscored. Even though the landlord may own the property, even though the landlord pays the taxes and is responsible for maintenance, and even though the landlord has a right to exclusive control of the property *before* it is rented, once occupied, it is the tenant who has the right to exclusive control of the property.

WHEN THE LANDLORD CAN ENTER. This right to exclusive control is not absolute, however. There are times when the landlord needs to enter the unit, even if the tenant may not want him to. In the situations listed below, landlords retain the right to enter the unit:

- *Showing the unit to prospective tenants:* If the landlord will soon be renting the unit to a new tenant, he has the right to show it to prospective tenants. Again, he can do so even if the tenant in possession does not want to let him in.
- *Repairs:* If repairs to the unit are needed, the landlord can enter in order to make those repairs.
- *Court order:* If a tenant has been evicted yet still refuses to move out, a landlord has the right to enter, although he should consider bringing the sheriff or a police officer along.
- *Emergencies:* Should an actual emergency, such as a fire or a medical crisis, warrant it, a landlord may immediately come into the unit without any notice whatsoever. A trumped up excuse, such as "I thought I heard the water running for too long," will not do; it must be a real emergency.

Absent an emergency (when he can enter the unit immediately), a landlord is required to give his tenant "reasonable" notice of his intent to enter. In most cases, twenty-four to forty-eight hours is considered reasonable. After proper notice has been given, the landlord should enter only during normal business hours. If the landlord does not give proper notice, ironically enough, he will be considered a **trespasser** on his own land.

FIXTURES. Once a tenant has exclusive control of the unit, he may want to improve the property by building a bookcase or a deck, for example, or by painting a room. Normally, the landlord's permission is needed before such improvements can be made, since even though the tenant has possession, the landlord remains the owner. In most cases landlords do not object to such changes since the property will likely be improved.

Tenants are warned that they should undertake such improvements with caution since they may inadvertently be giving their landlord a gift by doing so. A **fixture** is an improvement on property that is fairly permanent in nature. Improvements that attach to the building and cannot be easily removed become fixtures. Decks, built-in bookcases, and toilets are all fixtures. The rule to be wary of is this: a tenant is not legally allowed to remove a fixture when she moves out. Thus, *fixtures become the property of the landlord.*

If, however, the improvement can be fairly easily removed, such as a chandelier or a satellite dish, then it is not a fixture and can be taken when the tenant moves. It is sometimes difficult to determine whether an improvement is an immovable fixture or a removable addition. If the improvement can be easily detached without harming the building, then it is not a fixture.

The Important Legal Concept to Remember: Once a tenant moves into a unit, the place is hers, and *everyone* needs her permission to enter. Because of the rule of fixtures, it is probably unwise for tenants to make major improvements to the property.

THE IMPLIED WARRANTY OF HABITABILITY (THE TENANT'S RIGHT TO A HABITABLE HOME)

Understanding the implied warranty of habitability
What the warranty means
Solutions for breach of the warranty of habitability

UNDERSTANDING THE IMPLIED WARRANTY OF HABITABILITY. It is a tenant's worst nightmare. He moves into a seemingly beautiful garden apartment and nothing works. The hot water runs cold. The cold water does not run. The refrigerator leaks. What is he to do? He should call the landlord and demand that everything be fixed, pursuant to the implied warranty of habitability.

The implied warranty of habitability is a clause implied in every residential rental agreement. Basically, the warranty mandates that a landlord must make the unit fit for residential occupation, and that he maintain and repair all problems that make the place unlivable.

The name says it all. First, the warranty is *implied*. It is part of every rental agreement, whether or not it is specifically mentioned. It is part of month-to-month agreements as well as year-long leases. It covers all residential rentals. In fact, it is highly unlikely that your lease or rental agreement will even mention the warranty.

Yours may actually say the opposite. A clause that states something like "This lease expressly repeals the implied warranty of habitability" or something to the effect that the unit is being rented "as is" or that the landlord is relieved of any duty to maintain the premises is illegal and unenforceable. It is legal only in commercial (i.e., business) agreements, where there is no warranty of habitability. In all other cases, the warranty is implied in every rental contract, despite what the contract says. Because it is implied in every rental agreement, *this is probably the only time when you can absolutely ignore what the agreement states*. The warranty is implied in every contract, no matter what the contract says.

Next, notice that it is an implied *warranty*. A warranty is a statement or representation that something is true. In essence, a warranty is a promise. By renting the apartment to you, your landlord is making certain promises. What is he promising? That the unit is *habitable*—the third part of the equation.

"Habitable" means that the unit is fit to live in. It means that it is safe and sanitary. That it is structurally sound. That there is heat and hot water. That the toilet and plumbing work. It means that the windows are not cracked, and that the doors lock. Rats, rodents, cockroaches, and insect infestation are absent. It means that all building and health and safety codes are being met. This is not an exhaustive list by any means; any condition that makes the premises uninhabitable is covered. Habitable means that the unit is fit to live in.

Because every residential unit is covered by the implied warranty, any problem that affects the habitability of the home becomes the landlord's responsibility. This would include such items as a broken heater, refrigerator, or toilet, as well as something like a frayed electrical wire. Less severe things—normal wear and tear, as it were—may also be your landlord's responsibility to repair, depending upon the circumstances. (See Chapter 13, "The Duty to Maintain and Repair the Premises.")

After Marla had lived in her apartment for two years, the carpet had become a bit matted. She demanded that her landlord recarpet the place pursuant to the implied warranty of habitability. Her landlord refused, stating that carpet had nothing to do with habitability. Marla then withheld part of her rent in protest, and her landlord sued to evict her. The judge agreed that carpeting was not a habitability issue. Marla had to pay her landlord more than $2,000 in back rent, fees, and costs.

WHAT THE WARRANTY MEANS. The implied warranty of habitability means that the landlord must offer the dwelling to the new tenant in good shape. Before a tenant moves in, the unit must be fit for human habitation. It should be clean, sanitary, safe, and functioning. After a tenant moves in, the unit must be kept that way.

Sometimes, very rarely, a habitability problem will arise that is not the landlord's responsibility. This occurs only when the tenant, or someone the tenant knows, has created the habitability problem. Alternatively, if the problem was created by someone unknown to the tenant, then it is the landlord's job to fix it.

Denise was out shopping one day. When she came back to her apartment, she found the front window broken and her TV stolen.

Clearly, a broken window goes to the habitability of the apartment. Since it is fairly obvious that a stranger broke the window, it is Denise's landlord who is responsible for its repair.

About a month after the window was repaired, Denise's son was playing ball in front of the house. Not surprisingly, the ball went through the new window.

In this case, it is Denise's responsibility to repair the window, as it was her son who broke it. The landlord is liable for "third party" damage only if the third party is a stranger. The landlord is not responsible for problems that are caused by the tenant's **negligence**. If a tenant's child or friend causes the problem, it is up to the tenant to fix it. In all other cases, the duty to repair falls upon the shoulders of the landlord.

SOLUTIONS FOR BREACH OF THE WARRANTY OF HABITABILITY. The first thing a tenant must do is to figure out if the problem actually makes the dwelling *uninhabitable*. There are several factors that go into this determination:

1. When health, safety, or sanitation are in question;
2. When there has been a violation of a building, housing, or safety code;
3. When a vital part of the dwelling is affected;
4. When a consistent problem has not been fixed in a reasonable amount of time.

If a tenant suspects that the implied warranty of habitability is being violated, the next thing he must do is to notify the landlord of the problem and give him a reasonable amount of time to correct it. A landlord certainly cannot be held responsible for a problem he does not know about.

If the landlord refuses to fix the problem, the tenant should call the local authorities. Every city has some type of housing authority or health and public safety agency whose job it is to make sure that landlords are following the law. A call from them will certainly get your landlord's attention.

There are many other **remedies** that a tenant can also choose to use. The first is to withhold rent. This is called **rent abatement**. If a landlord is not living up to his end of the bargain, then the law allows the tenant to change the other end of the bargain. That is the theory behind rent abatement.

Here is how to utilize rent abatement: after you have determined that there has been a breach of the warranty of habitability, notify your landlord *in writing* of the problem and give him adequate time to fix the problem. If he does not fix it in a reasonable amount of time, notify him again *in writing* that you will be withholding rent the next month.

To withhold all of the rent or part of the rent—that is the question. The rule is that a tenant is allowed to withhold enough rent to make up for the problem. What is an apartment in New York worth in the winter without heat? Not much. The key is to pick a reasonable amount and stick to it.

After you withhold all or part of your landlord's rent, he will either fix the problem or **serve** you with an eviction notice. If he tries to evict you, it will ultimately be up to a judge to decide the proper amount of rent that should have been withheld. Sometimes keeping the entire rent until the problem is fixed is permissible, sometimes it is not. It all depends upon the severity and length of the problem. *Be sure to put whatever money you withhold in the bank.*

Maria's apartment lacked heat. She notified her landlord, Maggie, of the problem, but Maggie was too cheap to fix it. The next month, after proper notification, Maria withheld her entire $1,000 rent. Maria had put two months' rent in her savings account by the time Maggie's eviction lawsuit went before a judge. The judge ordered Maggie to fix the problem, but stated that Maria had no right to withhold her entire rent. He then ordered Maria to pay back Maggie $250 per month.

Had Maria spent that $2,000 instead of holding on to it, she likely would have had a difficult time paying Maggie the $500. If she failed to pay it, she would have been properly evicted.

The next option is often the best one. It is called **repair and deduct**. Repair and deduct operates on the same principle as rent withholding. The tenant keeps part of the rent in order to compensate for a **breach** by the landlord. However, instead of waiting to go to court and having a judge order the landlord to fix the problem, the tenant uses the withheld money to actually fix the problem himself (or he hires someone to fix it).

Mike had complained about his cold-running shower for a week, and still his landlord, Kevin, refused to fix it. Mike decided to solve the matter himself and called a plumber. The plumber came, fixed the problem, and charged Mike $85. Mike deducted the amount from his rent the next month.

Before a tenant decides to repair and deduct, it is incumbent upon him to notify the landlord of the problem and allow a reasonable amount of time for repair. Once the landlord fails to fix it, the tenant can remedy the problem without any authorization from the landlord. When rent time rolls around again, the tenant should send his landlord the deducted rent along with the receipt for the repair. The two together should equal one rent payment.

There are several limitations to this solution. First, a tenant cannot deduct more than the cost of the repair. That is why you must document everything you do with letters, receipts, and invoices. Also, again, repair and deduct cannot be used if the problem was created by the tenant. Some states also limit the use of this remedy to once or twice in a twelve-month period. In many states, the cost of repair cannot exceed one month's rent.

Sometimes the problem is so severe that the tenant does not want to fix it. She just wants out of the apartment, out of the lease, out of the whole deal altogether. In that case, the best remedy is to **vacate and sue**. Like any contract, if one party to a rental arrangement substantially breaches the agreement, the other party has the right to cancel the rest of the contract. Thus, once a landlord has been notified of a problem with the unit that impairs its livability and he fails to remedy the situation, the tenant has the right to move out, *even if* he has a long-term lease.

Another term for this right to cancel the contract and move is constructive eviction. Because the landlord has failed to fix a substantial problem, the law presumes that he is, in essence, evicting his tenant by his inaction. The tenant has been "constructively" evicted. The tenant can move out without repercussion.

A tenant may also, but does not have to, sue his landlord. Should he succeed, he would be entitled to a rebate for rent paid while living in an unfit unit, monetary compensation for substandard housing, and moving costs. (See Section V, "Lawsuits.")

The Important Legal Concept to Remember: Every residential tenant has an absolute right to a habitable home.

7

THE IMPLIED COVENANT OF QUIET ENJOYMENT (THE TENANT'S RIGHT TO PRIVACY)

Understanding the implied covenant of quiet enjoyment
How the covenant may be breached
Solutions for the breach of the covenant of quiet enjoyment

UNDERSTANDING THE IMPLIED COVENANT OF QUIET ENJOY-MENT. Once a tenant moves into his new rental unit, he has the right to be left alone in the "quiet enjoyment" of his home. This is called the implied covenant of quiet enjoyment. The covenant essentially states that a tenant has the right to use the premises without interference by either the landlord or other tenants.

Basically, this means that neither the landlord nor anyone under the control of the landlord can disturb the tenant's right to enjoy the unit quietly. Whereas the right to possession means that the tenant has a right to privacy in his home, this implied covenant states that he is entitled to live there peaceably. That is what quiet enjoyment means.

Sherri lived in a ten-unit apartment house, and her neighbor Spencer just loved to play Broadway musicals loudly at all hours of the day and night. Although Sherri complained to her landlord, Chris, he refused to discuss the matter with Spencer, and allowed the racket to continue. Accordingly, Chris has breached the implied covenant of quiet enjoyment.

Like the implied warranty of habitability, the implied covenant of quiet enjoyment too is found in every lease or rental agreement, whether or not it is specifically mentioned. That is why it is called an "implied" covenant.

This implied covenant goes further than the implied warranty of habitability. While the habitability promise applies only to residential tenants, the covenant of quiet enjoyment applies equally to both residential and business tenants. It is very important to realize, however, that unlike the implied warranty of habitability, the implied covenant of quiet enjoyment can be *waived* in the rental agreement. That is, while the implied warranty of habitability is *always present,* no matter what the lease states, the implied covenant of quiet enjoyment can be nullified if the rental agreement so states. Tenants should beware of this in the "fine print."

HOW THE COVENANT MAY BE BREACHED: There are many ways a landlord can breach the covenant of quiet enjoyment. The first is by refusing to control other tenants in the building. This implied promise of quiet enjoyment is intended to give hard-working people who pay rent the right to be left alone. A landlord who refuses to rein in an out-of-control tenant violates the covenant of quiet enjoyment since loud, boisterous, or obnoxious tenants are the responsibility of the landlord.

But the problem must be severe for the landlord to be held liable. A merely annoying neighbor does not constitute a breach, nor does the wrongdoing of a neighbor across the way who does not rent from the landlord. The landlord must have control over the premises *and* the tenant, *and* the problem must be substantial for the breach to be attributable to the landlord.

Here are some other examples of breaches by the landlord of the implied covenant of quiet enjoyment:

· Preventing the tenant from using an allotted parking space.
· Attempting to fix a problem in the unit, but failing to finish the job in a reasonable amount of time.
· Interfering with the tenant's business.
· Terminating the lease without just cause.
· Entering the unit repeatedly without authorization.
· Allowing tenants to harass other tenants.

Finally, the covenant can be breached in a manner similar to a breach of the warranty of habitability. If the landlord's action, or failure to act, is so substantial as to make the unit unfit to live in, then the covenant of quiet enjoyment as well as the warranty of habitability have been violated. A broken heater is a good example. Lack of heat clearly makes the unit uninhabitable, but it also certainly interferes with the tenant's quiet enjoyment of the apartment. While it may be a technical point of law, it is still good to know. The more ammunition a tenant has, the better.

SOLUTIONS FOR THE BREACH OF THE COVENANT OF QUIET ENJOYMENT. Several remedies that are available for a breach of the warranty of habitability are not applicable to a breach of the covenant of quiet enjoyment. First, repair and deduct is not a viable option since usually there is nothing to repair. Nor is calling the authorities relevant; loud landlords or noisy neighbors usually do not constitute a violation of a statute or housing code.

If you are a tenant whose privacy is being invaded, the first possible remedy is rent abatement; withhold a portion of your rent for a short period of time. This is especially effective if the interference is fairly minimal. Try withholding a small portion of your rent for a month or two. Your landlord will probably try to solve the problem.

If the interference is more severe, you can also try withholding a more substantial amount of rent. This, though, is a risky proposition; an eviction lawsuit will inevitably soon follow, and a judge may not be sympathetic to your cause. Whereas a tenant without heat who withholds rent is both a legally and emotionally sympathetic plaintiff, the same cannot be said for a tenant who "merely" has a loud neighbor. What seems to you to be a clear breach of the covenant of quiet enjoyment may be considered nothing more than a petty annoyance to a judge. If you gamble incorrectly, you will likely end up having to pay your landlord's legal and court costs.

That is why the final option is sometimes the best option: move out and sue your landlord. As with a tenant whose unit is uninhabitable, a tenant whose quiet enjoyment has been interfered with can allege constructive eviction, terminate the lease, and sue. If a judge agrees that the tenant has been constructively evicted, the tenant is owed the difference between what she paid for the unit and what it was actually worth with the problem, along with other incidentals.

Debbie was unable to use the second bedroom of her rented home for six months because her landlord "never got around" to moving his belongings out of it. An exasperated Debbie finally moved out and sued her landlord for a breach of the covenant of quiet enjoyment. The judge awarded Debbie $4,000.

Here is how that was calculated:

Rent per agreement:	$750
Value of the unit with the problem:	$500
Number of months with the problem:	6
SUBTOTAL	$1,500
	($250 a month x 6 months)
Moving costs	$1,000
Deposit	$1,500
GRAND TOTAL DUE DEBBIE:	$4,000

Since the amount that a tenant can likely recover is fairly small, you are advised to file your claim in **small claims court**. Small claims cases are expeditious (a month or two from filing the suit to trial) and relatively inexpensive. (See Chapter 21, "Small Claims Court.")

The Important Legal Concept to Remember: Tenants have a right to be left alone.

THE DUTY TO PAY RENT

Payment of rent

Late rent payments

When payment of rent is excused

When can a landlord raise your rent?

Illegal rent increases due to retaliation or discrimination

Rent control

Many tenants resent paying their rent every month. Aside from
the financial burden, they believe that their hard-earned cash is
nothing but pure profit for their greedy, rich landlord. Unfortunately for the landlord, that is rarely the case.

While knowing where your money goes will not ease the
financial pain that paying rent often inflicts, it may ease the
emotional resentment. Your landlord likely spends your
monthly rent as follows: 20 percent is paid in taxes, 65 percent is paid to the bank for the mortgage on the property, and
12 percent is spent on costs and upkeep on the rental unit.
Probably only 3 percent of your monthly rent is considered
profit. If your rent is $500 a month, that means that only $15 is
your landlord's actual profit. So, have some compassion, if at all
possible. When you are late with your rent, the bank may be
breathing down your landlord's back and he may be cranky
for a reason (although he may just be cranky altogether).

PAYMENT OF RENT. *Paying rent is the first and foremost duty of any tenant.* Excuses do not pay the mortgage, nor do bounced checks. Irresponsible roommates are not a reason not to pay rent, and neither is the need to buy a new mountain bike. The only reason a tenant even lives in the house or apartment, which is owned by the landlord, is because he promised to pay rent. Failure to pay rent in full consistently and on time will get you evicted. Paying rent is the first and foremost duty of any tenant.

Rent is normally paid monthly and is due on the first of every month, although a landlord and tenant can actually agree to any arrangement that they want. If you get paid on the fifth of every month, there is nothing preventing you and your landlord from agreeing to your rent being paid on the sixth. Some landlords want rent paid every two weeks. This too is legal.

If the day for paying rent falls on a weekend or a holiday, then it is typically legally permissible to pay it on the next business day. Note that while many landlords offer a three- to five-day "grace period" for paying rent, they are not required by law to do so.

Similarly, if you bounce a check to your landlord, he is not required to charge you a bounced-check fee and continue the relationship. Some landlords simply begin eviction proceedings (since a bounced check means that rent has not been paid), especially if there is a pattern of bounced checks. A tenant must pay rent—it is as simple as that.

Here's a good tip if you know you are going to have a difficult time paying rent one month: tell your landlord about your situation, and offer to make a partial rent payment. That is far better than possibly bouncing a check and hoping for the best. It is always far better to treat your landlord with respect, communicate well, and try to get along with him than to be a pain in the neck. You will find that your landlord will be far more willing to work with you when needed if you are a good tenant and normally pay your rent on time. If your landlord does agree to accept a partial rent payment one month, get the agreement in writing.

LATE RENT PAYMENTS. Landlords are well within their rights to charge a fee for a late rent payment. Fees for late rent are perfectly legal, although excessive fees may not be. What is "excessive"? That is a good question without a definitive answer. There are few laws that actually regulate the amount a landlord can charge for late rent. While $50 may be legal, $150 may not be.

If you think that your landlord charges too much in late fees, here's a trick that might work: any contract (not just a landlord-tenant agreement) that includes *grossly excessive* fees may be deemed **unconscionable** by a court. Unconscionable contracts, or sections of contracts, are unenforceable. You can always take your landlord to small claims court and get a judge to rule that the fee is excessive. But while such a decision could save you some money, it would also likely alienate your landlord. As with the rest of your relationship with your landlord, be aggressive, know your rights, but don't be stupid. Pick your battles wisely.

WHEN PAYMENT OF RENT IS EXCUSED. As indicated, paying rent is the most important duty a tenant has. There are, however, two times when failure to pay rent may be legally excused.

As explained in more detail in Chapter 6, "The Implied Warranty of Habitability," rent may be temporarily excused when a tenant elects to utilize the remedy called repair and deduct (you pay someone else to fix a problem and deduct that amount from your next month's rent).

The other time rent payments are possibly excused is when there is a substantial flaw in the unit and the tenant utilizes the remedy of rent abatement, withholding all or part of the rent. A judge will later determine whether the tenant had the right to withhold the rent. Other than repair and deduct or rent abatement, there is no other situation in which failure to pay rent is legally justifiable.

WHEN CAN A LANDLORD RAISE YOUR RENT? Whether your landlord can increase your rent depends upon the nature of your agreement. If you have a lease, your landlord cannot raise your rent, not even a penny, during the course of the agreement. From a tenant's point of view, that is one of the advantages of having a lease. If at the end of the lease you want to stay and your landlord wants you to also, then she can legally raise your rent at the beginning of the new term.

If you have a month-to-month agreement or some other sort of periodic tenancy, then your landlord *can* raise your rent, but only after giving the proper notice. The amount of notice required corresponds to the payment of rent. If rent is due every thirty days, then thirty days' notice is required to raise your rent. If it is due every two weeks, then two weeks' notice is all that is needed to raise rent.

There is no set limit as to how much a landlord can charge for rent. She can charge whatever the market will bear. If she raises rents too high, her tenants will move out and she will have a problem re-letting the space. The only time a rent increase is prohibited is when rent control (also known as rent stabilization) is in effect or if the increase is either retaliatory or discriminatory.

ILLEGAL RENT INCREASES DUE TO RETALIATION OR DISCRIMINATION. It is illegal for a landlord to raise a tenant's rent simply because the tenant has exercised some legal right.

> Rebecca could no longer wait for her landlord to fix the oven in the house she rented. She finally hired a handyman and had the appliance repaired. She deducted the amount of repair from her next month's rent. Rebecca received a termination notice the following day.

Rebecca's landlord's actions are patently illegal. Raising rent because a tenant organized a tenants' union, for example, is illegal, as would be any increase directly related to a tenant utilizing a legal landlord-tenant remedy.

In a similar vein, a landlord cannot raise a tenant's rent

because of that tenant's race, ethnicity, religion, sex, etc. It violates federal and state civil rights laws, and is just another form of illegal discrimination. Any rent increase based upon a discriminatory purpose is illegal.

Proving retaliation or discrimination is not always easy, but a tenant who feels that she has had her rent increased for improper reasons should not let the increase go by without some sort of retaliation of her own. A variety of remedies are available:

- *Complain to the proper authorities:* Often, complaining to the proper local, state, or federal housing authorities will put enough fear into a landlord to reverse the illegal rent increase. When you do complain, make sure to send a copy of your letter to your landlord.

- *Organize a rent strike:* A **rent strike** is an organized effort on the part of tenants designed to put financial pressure on the landlord by withholding everyone's rent. Few landlords can afford to go without their rent for more than a month. (See Chapter 11, "Other Tenant Solutions.")

- *Sue:* If you are being treated unfairly and illegally, you can always sue in either state or federal court. A federal antidiscriminatory suit is called a civil rights suit. It is expensive both to pursue and to defend. (See Chapter 22, "Superior Court.")

A final option is simply to refuse to pay the increase. When that happens, your landlord will try to evict you. It is important to know that legally it is your landlord's responsibility (called his **burden of proof**) to prove that the increase was not discriminatory or retaliatory. In fact, in many cases, the law presumes that an arbitrary rent increase was improper. Your landlord will have to present sufficient evidence that the increase was reasonable, and not spiteful.

RENT CONTROL. The basic intent of rent control (laws that restrict the amount of rent a landlord can charge) is to slow rent increases. Rent control does not mean that a landlord cannot raise rent at all. What it does mean is that the amount he can raise it is regulated by statute. In some cities, landlords are permitted to raise rents yearly, but the amount that rent can be raised is limited. Typically, rents in these places can be raised between 4 and 9 percent each year. In other cities, landlords are required to go before a local rent-control board to get permission before rent can be raised. In cities with ordinances like these, rental increases are usually tied to inflation and interest rates. Tenants who are covered by rent control need to get a copy of their local ordinance and acquaint themselves with the law so that they can know what type of rent increases are legally permissible in their area.

If you believe that your rent has been increased more than is legally permissible in your city, you need to take your complaint before your local rent-control board. A rent-control board hearing is not all that much different from a hearing before a judge, albeit you will be presenting your "case" before a panel of people rather than a single jurist. The key to both is to be well prepared and to be able to prove your case with **evidence**—witnesses, letters, documents, receipts, etc. Make sure to read Chapter 21, "Small Claims Court," to get a better idea about how to approach such a hearing.

The Important Legal Concept to Remember: Renters must pay rent; nonpayment is rarely excused.

THE TENANT'S DUTY TO BEHAVE REASONABLY

The duty to keep the unit in good condition
The tenant cannot commit waste
The tenant cannot be a nuisance
The tenant cannot use the rental for unintended purposes

There are, unfortunately, too many tenants who push the limits of acceptable behavior. Tenants who know that they can stop paying rent and still stay in the unit until a judge tells them they have to leave. But there are consequences to such actions. Many jurisdictions allow a landlord to collect money damages, as well as attorney fees and costs, from the tenant who violates the standards set forth below.

THE DUTY TO KEEP THE UNIT IN GOOD CONDITION. The law imposes upon landlords the responsibility to maintain and repair normal wear and tear in the unit, and this makes sense. If a dryer breaks after ten years of normal use, it should not be the unfortunate tenant who needed to dry her laundry one day who should pay for it. Landlords repair normal wear and tear.

But they do not have to fix problems not of their making. Any extraordinary damage to the unit is the tenant's duty to fix.

Larry and his college roommate Tim were wrestling in the den one day. Larry threw Tim against the wall, the wall broke, and Tim fell through. It is Larry and Tim's responsibility to fix the wall.

It would also be Larry and Tim's responsibility to repair the wall if it were broken by someone they knew. Problems caused by tenants and their guests are the tenants' responsibility.

THE TENANT CANNOT COMMIT WASTE. A tenant not only has a duty to repair whatever significant problems he creates, but has a further duty not to allow the unit to fall into disrepair. This is known as the doctrine of **waste**. Although a tenant has exclusive control of the unit, it is still the landlord's property. Accordingly, a duty is imposed upon the tenant by law that says that he cannot decrease the value of the property.

Tom loved to fix old cars. As time went by, he collected several on the front lawn of the home he leased, none of which worked. Neighbors started complaining. His landlord demanded that the cars be removed. Tom was committing waste.

Waste means that a tenant has an obligation not to let the property fall apart. While this may seem to contradict the rule that a landlord has a duty to repair the premises, they really are two different things. The duty to repair means that the landlord must keep the unit habitable. The duty not to commit waste means that the tenant has an obligation not to harm the property. While a landlord might welcome a new coat of paint on the house he is renting out, he might not if the tenant paints it purple. That is waste.

THE TENANT CANNOT BE A NUISANCE. As indicated earlier, all tenants have a right to the quiet enjoyment of their rental property. Not only does this mean that they have a right to privacy but it also means that they have a right to live in relative peace and quiet. A tenant who disturbs another's quiet enjoyment is a **nuisance**, and a landlord has a right to rid his property of any nuisances. The tenant who stays awake at all hours blasting his stereo will be facing an eviction in a short amount of time.

Many different types of actions can constitute an illegal nuisance. A tenant cannot, for example, allow his trash area to become unsanitary. A tenant cannot allow her garden to grow so out of control that her neighbor cannot use his driveway. Any action or inaction that significantly impairs another tenant's use and enjoyment of her dwelling would be considered a nuisance.

THE TENANT CANNOT USE THE RENTAL FOR UNINTENDED PURPOSES. A landlord has a right to have his property used for its intended purpose. For example:

- A tenant cannot allow six more family members to move into her two-bedroom house after she has moved in. A landlord has every right to expect that a two-bedroom home will house no more than four or five people.
- A tenant cannot normally run a business out of a residential property unless she has the express prior written approval of the landlord. The intended purpose of a residence is to reside.
- A tenant cannot participate in any illegal activity in the space. Selling drugs and prostitution are definite no-no's.

A tenant who violates any of these duties will give her landlord just cause for eviction.

The Important Legal Concept to Remember: With rights come responsibilities. If a tenant is irresponsible and behaves in an unreasonable manner, the law will protect the landlord's right to get rid of the tenant.

10

SECURITY DEPOSITS AND LAST MONTH'S RENT

Security deposits in general

The important differences between deposits, fees, and last month's rent

How to make sure your security deposit is returned

If the deposit is not returned

SECURITY DEPOSITS IN GENERAL. A security deposit is money paid by the tenant and held by the landlord to make sure that the tenant performs all obligations under the lease or rental agreement. In that sense, security deposits are like a form of insurance. If a tenant fails to live up to certain obligations under the agreement, the deposit (or a portion thereof) is forfeited to the landlord to pay for these things. Generally, security deposits can be used only to clean the unit, to repair damage to the unit above and beyond normal wear and tear, or to pay for unpaid back rent.

It is important for both tenants and landlords to understand that a security deposit is the *property of the tenant*. Yes, it is held by the landlord. Yes, the landlord has the right to keep part of it if the tenant acts improperly. But until the end of the tenancy, and until the landlord can justify keeping all or part of it, the deposit is the tenant's money.

By definition, then, a security deposit is refundable. As long as the tenant pays rent, keeps the premises in good condition, and leaves the place clean, the deposit should be fully refunded. Any agreement that states that the deposit is nonrefundable is illegal and unenforceable against the tenant. *A security deposit belongs to the tenant and is refundable.*

Different localities set different amounts that can be charged as a security deposit. Usually, the amount of the deposit will equal between one and three months' rent. Deposits for more than that amount are probably illegal, although, again, it depends upon where you live.

For many tenants, paying the security deposit on top of rent often makes moving into a new rental unit difficult. Here's a method that allows tenants to pay a large security deposit more easily while also permitting landlords to collect the maximum deposit allowed by law: allow the tenant to pay the deposit over a period of several months.

Eve wanted to rent a house from Francesco. The problem was not that Francesco wanted $500 a month for the place; instead, it was that he wanted a $1,500 security deposit, which was permissible in the city they lived in. Rather than lose a potential good tenant like Eve, Francesco offered Eve the option to pay the deposit over a six-month period. For her first six months in the house, Eve paid her regular $500 monthly rent payment, along with an extra $250 a month toward her security deposit.

This plan gives the tenant some breathing room and allows the landlord to collect the maximum possible deposit allowed by law.

THE IMPORTANT DIFFERENCES BETWEEN FEES, DEPOSITS, AND LAST MONTH'S RENT. You should know the difference between fees, security deposits, and last month's rent, as they are three distinctly different animals.

Fees are payments for a service, and requiring a fee for a service rendered is normally legal. A credit-check fee, for example, is usually permissible. As opposed to a deposit, a fee belongs to the landlord and is nonrefundable, although it is illegal to charge a fee for something that is already covered by a security deposit. A common abuse occurs when a landlord requires a security deposit and also asks for a "cleaning fee." Since security deposits cover cleaning costs, charging an extra fee for cleaning is prohibited in most jurisdictions.

Last month's rent is different too. While a security deposit can be used for a variety of things when a tenant moves out, last month's rent can be used only to pay the last month's rent. That is it. A landlord who is holding a $500 security deposit and $500 in last month's rent actually has only $500 to rectify any problems the tenant may cause. Legally, that other $500 can only be applied to a last rent payment.

Laws in most cities restrict the total amount of money a landlord can hold, whether it is called last month's rent or security deposit. So, even though a prepaid last month's rent is not a refundable deposit, if a landlord collects last month's rent he limits the total amount of security deposit he can also collect. For landlords, the problem with that is if something major goes wrong, a landlord cannot legally use the last month's rent money to fix the porblem. So, here is a critical tip for landlords: *The smart landlord should always call all retained money a security deposit so that the money can be used for any legal purpose.*

Jay rented an apartment from David. When Jay moved in, David required $500 in first month's rent, $500 in last month's rent, and a $250 security deposit. Jay lived there for six months and then gave proper notice of his intent to move. He did not pay his last month's rent pursuant to the agreement, and then moved out. After Jay left, David learned that Jay's cat had ruined the carpet and it needed to be completely replaced. The $250 deposit hardly covered David's costs.

Had David asked for a $750 security deposit instead of $500 in last month's rent and a $250 security deposit, Jay would have paid rent that last month, and David would have had enough money to pay for the new carpet.

It is also good practice for a landlord to get as much money up front as is legally permissible. Not only will this give him enough money to fix almost any problem that may arise, but it will also induce the tenant to be as good as possible since she will want to get her money back. Tenants with small deposits have little to lose by breaking the rules.

HOW TO MAKE SURE YOUR SECURITY DEPOSIT IS RETURNED. Again, the security deposit is owned by the tenant, even if it is rarely treated that way. A landlord cannot keep it without justification. Tenants, then, should give their landlord no reason to keep their money.

Any tenant who wants his security deposit returned is advised to abide by the following five rules:

Rule 1. *Give proper notice of your intent to move:* Your landlord can keep deposit money for lost rent if you move without giving proper notice. If you have a month-to-month rental arrangement and you give less than thirty days' notice, you should fully expect your landlord to keep part of the deposit. So, don't do it.

Rule 2. *Pay all rent due:* If you do not pay your last month's rent, your landlord can legally keep as much of your security deposit as necessary to make up for it.

Rule 3. *Fix what you broke:* Since your landlord can legally retain part of your deposit to repair damage to the unit that is not considered normal wear and tear, be sure to make all needed repairs.

Rule 4. *Leave the unit spotless:* Your landlord can subtract deposit money to clean the premises. If you make sure to clean it thoroughly before you leave, this will not be necessary.

Rule 5. *Document what you have done:* After you have fixed and cleaned everything, be sure to document that you have left the unit in good condition. Photograph or videotape the unit after you have moved everything out. It is also a good idea to have a walk-through with your landlord on the day you leave. To be really safe, bring a friend along; if you later have to sue your landlord to get your deposit back, your friend will be an invaluable witness.

Aside from rent, cleaning, and repairs, your landlord cannot use your deposit for any other reason. In most localities, landlords are obliged to return the deposit to the tenant within a fairly short period of time, usually four weeks. At that time, if any of the deposit is withheld, as it usually is, landlords are obliged to give their tenants an itemized statement of how the money was used. By following the five rules above, you stand a far greater chance that your entire deposit will be returned.

IF THE DEPOSIT IS NOT RETURNED. Many places require a landlord to return the security deposit with interest, but it is the lucky tenant indeed who ever sees a security deposit returned with interest. It is not unusual for a landlord to keep all or part of a security deposit without reason.

If your landlord has not returned what you believe to be enough of your money, you have two options. You can either sue him in small claims court (or "housing court," if one exists in your area), or you can try to threaten him with a demand letter, which, surprisingly, works if done correctly.

Attorneys write demand letters all the time. The reason lawyers find these letters successful is because recipients decide that the financial consequences of not doing as demanded are not worth the risk. A person who receives a letter from a lawyer demanding $100 often decides that it is simply cheaper to pay the money than to hire an attorney and fight back. The lawyer's letter induces fear. Yours can too.

Your letter to your landlord must explain in simple terms why you are entitled to a return of your money. Set forth the facts of what happened simply and without emotion. Then let your landlord know that you know the law. Explain why you are legally entitled to a return of your deposit—the unit was left clean, you paid your rent, nothing was broken, etc.

If your letter is to be at all effective, you must also create some fear in your landlord. Tell your landlord that you have *proof* that the unit was left in proper condition. Tell him that you have photos and witnesses. Tell him that if he does not return your deposit within three business days, you will sue in small claims court. Tell him that not only will he then have to return your money with interest but he may get hit with a fine as well.

It is this threat of a credible lawsuit that may return your money. You have to be correct—you have to have left the place clean, paid all rent, etc. If there is a legitimate dispute, your landlord will probably decide to take his chances and let a judge resolve the matter. But if you are right, and if you can show your greedy landlord that you can prove you are right, he may just decide to return your money. Without a credible threat based upon facts in your favor, do not expect to see your money returned by using this method.

If the letter does not work, sue him. Chapter 21, "Small Claims Court," explains how to prepare and present a case in small claims or housing court. That is what you will need to do if you are to get your money back.

The Important Legal Concept to Remember: A security deposit is the property of the tenant and must be returned unless there are good reasons to keep it.

11

OTHER TENANT SOLUTIONS

Negotiations and mediation

Lawsuits

Tenants' unions or associations

How to organize

Your final options

When it gets to the point where a tenant feels she must take some action against her landlord in order to rectify a problem, there are a variety of legal tools available. Happily, many of these solutions do not require the assistance of an attorney. Please note that if the problem you face has to do with a breach of either the warranty of habitability or the covenant of quiet enjoyment, solutions to those particular issues are dealt with in Chapter 6 and Chapter 7, respectively.

NEGOTIATIONS AND MEDIATION. The very easiest, least adversarial, most inexpensive solution to many landlord-tenant problems is simply to try to work things out with your landlord. In fact, it is often in his best interest to work things out with you. Landlords know that tenants now have a variety of legal solutions they can employ. They also know that a disgruntled tenant or a vacant apartment means no rent. There are few things landlords like less than no rent. Accordingly, you may find that your landlord may be far more willing to replace that refrigerator than you think.

Negotiations with a landlord need not be intimidating. The key to a successful negotiation is twofold. First, be reasonable. Try to be nice and accommodating. Listen to your landlord and try to give him something. If he wants rent paid on time, then promise to really try to pay your rent on time. Acting reasonably costs you nothing and generates goodwill.

But goodwill all by itself rarely works. It is when you add a credible threat to your reasonableness that good solutions appear. Make sure your landlord understands that you know your rights, and that you will utilize your rights if necessary. This means that he knows that you may withhold rent and possibly sue if things cannot be worked out. Conveying a viable threat that will hit him in the wallet will give your landlord a great incentive to settle with you. A new refrigerator is far less expensive than three months' lost rent.

Sometimes a more formal approach is needed. If your chat with your landlord failed to produce your desired results, another option is mediation.

Liz was three months into a year-long lease when a dispute about her rose garden erupted with her landlord, Dan. They fought for months. Liz really liked the house and wanted to renew the lease when it ran out, yet she knew that Dan would never do that until the "rose war" ended. She swallowed her pride, called Dan one day, and asked, "Do you want to go to mediation to see if we can resolve this problem?" Dan was happy to agree.

Mediation is a nonadversarial process that attempts to bridge gaps, find common ground, and resolve differences. Mediators are neutral individuals whose job it is to assist the parties in creating an agreement that works for everybody. And, while permissible, attorneys need not be present.

Mediation works. It is a flexible process that can be used to settle major wars or minor skirmishes. Mediation is also a confidential process. Whatever is said to the mediator will be kept private, and whatever results are reached (good or bad) will also remain confidential. It should also be fairly inexpensive. Many communities have free, or at least very inexpensive, mediation and dispute-resolution centers. Look in the phone book under those topics or call a local law school.

After finding a mediator, a mutually acceptable time for the mediation will be set. The mediation may take an hour or a day—once the issues involved are made clear to the mediator, he or she can estimate how long it will take.

Most mediations will proceed something like this: at the scheduled time and date the mediator will likely bring both parties and their attorneys, if they have any, into one room for an opening session. This beginning session allows each party to state his or her point of view about the situation and provides the mediator with necessary background information.

The mediator will probably next put each party in a separate room and continue the process by conducting a type of "shuttle diplomacy," whereby he goes back and forth between the rooms, prodding, cajoling, pulling, and sometimes yanking the parties toward a resolution based upon compromise. If successful, the parties will agree to resolve their differences and end their dispute.

LAWSUITS. If meditation and negotiations have failed, then things are pretty dire in your neck of the woods. At this point, you essentially have three choices left. First, you could give up and move. Second, you could form a tenants' association (discussed below). Finally, you could opt to use the most commonly thought of solution to most legal problems: filing suit.

There are two types of lawsuits that a tenant can file against a landlord. If the problem is relatively minor and the amount in dispute is less than, say, $5,000 (the amount depends upon which state you live in), then you should file suit in small claims court.

If the dispute is more serious and the amount in controversy exceeds $5,000, then you need to file suit in a **superior court** (also known as municipal court, county court, or district court). Small claims actions can be done without the aid of an attorney, while a superior court lawsuit necessitates legal counsel. Both are discussed in detail in Section V, "Lawsuits."

TENANTS' UNIONS OR ASSOCIATIONS. When all else fails—when after negotiations, mediation, and rent abatement a significant problem still exists—it is time to consider forming a tenants' union, and then using, if necessary, probably the most potent tool in the tenant arsenal: a rent strike.

A tenants' association or union is not unlike a labor union. It is a group of people acting together to effectuate change. The concept is the same, only the actors change. Labor unions are in existence because individual laborers sometimes have a more difficult time negotiating with management than does a group of employees acting together. Similarly, tenants may find their landlord more responsive when twenty of them show up together with the same grievance.

There is great power in uniting, acting, and negotiating as a single unit. It is much more difficult for a landlord to lie, break promises, and bamboozle his tenants when they are sharing information and acting together. If your building lacks substantial necessities, such as proper lighting, heat, smoke alarms, or hot water; if your landlord takes too long to fix a problem (if he fixes it at all); if the complex is unsanitary; or if you simply feel that the building needs to be run more professionally, then forming a tenants' union makes sense.

The central heat and air-conditioning unit for the Meadowview apartments broke one November day. It was not the first time this had happened. The management did nothing to fix it for several days. Bob was fed up and knew that withholding his rent alone would provide little incentive for the management to fix the heater. Instead, he printed up some flyers and organized a tenants' meeting. About half of the tenants showed up. He suggested that they *all* threaten to withhold rent if the heater was not fixed in a day, and he convinced the angry yet skeptical crowd to go along with his plan. Everyone there signed a petition to that effect that night. The heater was fixed the next day.

Rents are the lifeblood of a landlord's business. While an individual rent withholding or repair and deduct might be annoying, it certainly does not threaten the landlord's business. But in the case of the Meadowview, if an average rent payment is $500 and fifty tenants threaten to withhold rent, the owner stands to lose $25,000 *that month alone*. A landlord could go out of business and lose his building very quickly if a rent strike went unchecked. Rent strikes level the playing field.

HOW TO ORGANIZE. Organizing is a labor-intensive endeavor. It will require a lot of work at first, and a lot of work later on. But it should be worth it.

Organizing usually begins when there is a problem that everyone is aware of but no one is doing anything about. If you are interested in starting a tenants' association, here is one way to do it: begin by talking with a few people you know well and see if they want to help organize a general meeting to discuss the problem. Go door-to-door and try to get at least ten to fifteen people to come to the meeting. Hold the meeting in your apartment.

This first meeting is informal. It is a chance to share ideas, explain the benefits of organizing, and get to know one another. As the host, you should speak first. Explain who you are, your history at the building, and your perception of the problem(s). Everyone there should do the same. Compare notes, share experiences, and come up with a tentative game plan. If everyone agrees to continue, then plan the second meeting.

Between the first and second meeting two things need to

occur. First, the rest of the complex needs to be made aware of what happened at the first get-together and should be encouraged to show up at the second meeting. It is critical to get as many people involved as possible. You cannot have too many members, but you sure can have too few; the strength of organizing is in the numbers. In a small building, you need virtually every tenant to join the union for it to be effective.

If at all possible, you should also try to find a representative from another tenants' union in your area to come speak at the second gathering. Tenants' unions are hard to find—they do not advertise or make much noise outside the complex. Go to a few well-established, large apartment complexes in your area and see if you can locate a union. Call some local tenant attorneys. Contact a local labor union. Legal-aid offices and media outlets may also be good sources for locating tenants' unions in your city.

The second meeting is used to set priorities, elect officers (president, vice president, secretary), and spread the gospel. What is the purpose of the union? Stopping frequent rent increases? Improving sanitation? Getting a specific problem fixed? It is imperative to try to get some sort of consensus. If you have a representative from another union there, have her explain how her union began. Depending upon the circumstances and size of the union, collecting dues may even be warranted. Dues are used to hire competent legal counsel.

Besides officers, section leaders should be elected for each floor or section of the building. These officers help to keep everyone informed and energized. The keys to a tenants' union are strength in numbers and *solidarity*. You must act together and stay unified. That is where section leaders come in. They are your troops.

Make sure that no members of the building management or their employees come to this meeting, or to any of your meetings, for that matter. This is your union—management need not apply. Management should, however, be informed of the existence of the union and its officers. At the conclusion of the second or third meeting, your landlord should be advised to expect a list of issues to be discussed.

After the union has been organized, the next meeting or two should be used to come up with a formal list of demands. You cannot begin to discuss issues with your landlord until you know exactly what you want, and how far your group is willing to go.

It is a very tense situation when you get to a place where a rent strike is looming. Is everyone prepared for that? Are they willing to live with the stress? As mentioned several times previously, it is the credible threat that often induces change. Unless your group is willing to go all the way, your threat of a rent strike, which should induce fear, may instead seem hollow.

The officers, or a standing committee, should be empowered to negotiate with management on all the tenants' behalf. It is then time to go meet with your landlord.

Have the officers or negotiations committee take the list of demands to your landlord to see if a compromise can be reached. Be friendly, but not too friendly. Be serious, but not bombastic. Make sure your landlord understands that if your demands are not met, a rent strike will be forthcoming. It is the credible threat that will force him to take you seriously.

At the same time, be sure to contact the appropriate government agency. Health departments and building departments have staff ready to investigate your complaint. It is also a very good idea to send a press release to local television, radio, and newspaper news departments.

YOUR FINAL OPTIONS. If negotiations fail to solve the problem, then the final two options are either to collectively repair and deduct or to collectively withhold rent. In a repair and deduct situation, part of each member's rent money is paid to the union instead of the landlord, and the union spends the money to fix the problem. The advantage of a community repair and deduct is that when large amounts of money are collected, large items can be fixed.

It is critical to keep immaculate records. Members of the union as well as the judge who may eventually review what has happened will want to see what the union did with the money it received.

When one person withholds his rent, it is called rent abatement. When an entire building withholds rent, it is called a rent strike. It is the tenants' ultimate weapon. A rent strike is a very serious matter and should not be attempted by the faint of heart. It should be used only as a last resort, when all else fails. By the time the union is contemplating a rent strike, it needs to have hired a good tenants' attorney to help it through the crisis.

Participating members should pay their entire rent to the union instead of their landlord, and the union should then deposit the money in its bank account. As all or part of that money will eventually need to be paid to the landlord, it is critical that your members do not just go and spend their rent one month instead of paying it to the union.

The ultimate goal, whether it is reached by negotiations or by a rent strike, is a written agreement between the landlord and the union. This is sometimes called a collective bargaining agreement. The agreement will recognize the union as the legitimate bargaining entity for the tenants. It will also spell out what the landlord has agreed to do and when he will do it.

Finally, recall that retaliatory evictions are illegal. A landlord cannot evict any tenant merely because the tenant joins or participates in the union or its activities.

The Important Legal Concept to Remember: While it is usually better for everyone concerned if problems can be resolved amicably, that is not always possible. It is the credible threat that most often induces change.

LANDLORD RIGHTS, DUTIES, AND SOLUTIONS

LANDLORD RIGHTS

Ensuring that rent is paid
The right to have reasonable tenants
The right of entry
The right to change rental agreement terms

It is important to understand that when rights are mentioned, be they landlord rights or tenant rights, duties soon follow. Rights and responsibilities are flip sides of the landlord-tenant coin. When, for example, it is said that a landlord has a right to have reasonable tenants, it follows that tenants have a corresponding duty to behave reasonably. When a tenant has a right to a habitable home, the landlord has a responsibility to make sure it is habitable. That is the very nature of landlord-tenant law. Rights and duties go hand in hand.

ENSURING THAT RENT IS PAID. The first right a landlord has corresponds with a tenant's foremost duty—the duty to pay, and the right to receive, rent. Renting property is a business, and the purpose of business is to make money. The money a landlord makes comes from rent. No tenant would expect to be able to walk into a store and leave with a new pair of pants with only a promise to pay "real soon." That simply does not happen. Landlords have every right to expect that rent will be paid in full and on time. If it is not, the tenant will not be living in the unit for long.

It is good practice for a landlord to have a firm policy to ensure that rent is paid promptly. Rent should be due on the first of the month. It should be considered late no later than the fifth. Failure to pay by the fifth should result in a **Notice to Pay Rent or Quit**. (See Chapter 16, "Landlord Solutions.") While there is nothing wrong with working things out with a tenant you like, it is usually far better to have a firm policy to deviate from when need be instead of having deviation be the norm.

Here are three other ways to make sure rent is paid promptly:

1. *Late fees:* This is a simple and well-known policy that tenants do not like. The landlord sets the date for rent payments, sets the date when rent will be considered late, and sets the amount the tenant will pay if rent is late. If you decide to use this method, make sure it is made part of your rental agreement so that no one is surprised when the late fee is assessed.

2. *Discounts for timely payments:* This is a more user-friendly approach. Here, the tenant gets a discount of, say, $20 if the rent is paid on time. The key is to *add $20 extra into the price you would normally charge for rent* initially so that you are not really giving a discount at all, although your happy tenant will feel like you are.

3. *Evictions:* If word gets around the complex that you evict rent scofflaws, you soon won't have many.

A landlord also has a right to raise rent as he or she sees fit. Again, as long as there are no rent control laws prohibiting rent increases, as long as tenants are willing to pay the higher rent, as long as no lease is involved, and as long as proper notice has been given, there is nothing improper about a rent increase. Raising rent should not be taken lightly, though. Many landlords dislike rent increases; tenants get mad and vacancies occur. If a rent increase is necessary, be sure to do the following:

- *Give ample warning:* Let your tenants know informally that rent will have to be raised and when the increase will likely take effect. Here's a way to make this act more palatable: when you tell your tenants about the possible raise, inflate the amount by 10 percent. When you do raise the rents, and do so at a price that is 10 percent less than your tenants feared, it will not seem as bad.

- *Give proper notification:* All rent increases should be in writing, and should state the name of the tenant and the number of the unit, the amount of the old and new rent, and the date when the increase will be effective. Try to hand-deliver the notification if at all possible. As improper notification is cause to disregard the increase, at least for a month, be sure to give more than enough lead time. Six weeks is a good idea.

THE RIGHT TO HAVE REASONABLE TENANTS. Landlords have a right to expect that tenants will behave in a reasonable fashion. Even though a tenant has exclusive possession of the unit throughout the tenancy, he cannot treat the unit in a way that will harm it or decrease its value. In legal terms, that means that the tenant cannot commit waste. He cannot harm the structure, paint it purple—that sort of thing.

Acting reasonably also means that the tenant cannot use the apartment for anything other than its expected use.

J.J. signed a residential lease with Leonard. After he moved in, J.J. started to run his photography business out of the duplex. People were constantly coming and going from the house, picking up pictures and sitting for photo sessions. After warning J.J. several times, and even though the lease had eight months to run, Leonard served J.J. with an eviction notice, and the eviction was upheld in court.

The right to reasonable tenants also means that landlords have a right to have tenants who do not disturb the quiet enjoyment of other tenants. Constant loud parties, daily band practice, and nightly shouting matches are all examples of inappropriate tenant behavior that violate this right.

Finally, it is patently illegal for a tenant to participate in illegal activities in the rental. Selling drugs, engaging in prostitution, and the like, are activities that are legally outside the bounds of reasonable behavior and are justifiable grounds for eviction.

THE RIGHT OF ENTRY. Although a house is a tenant's castle while she lives there, even a castle sometimes needs attention. The right to exclusive possession and quiet enjoyment of a home is thus not an unconditional right. As the owner, the landlord retains the right to enter the premises when necessary, albeit in a limited capacity. Generally speaking, there are three times when a landlord can enter the premises:

1. *With permission:* A landlord can always enter the unit when given permission to do so by the tenant. There are any number of reasons why a landlord may need to enter the unit: for maintenance purposes or to show the unit to a prospective tenant are two examples. In some states, the landlord does not even need permission to show the place to a possible tenant; only reasonable notice of intent to do so is necessary.

2. *To make repairs:* Most states allow the landlord to enter the unit without permission to make necessary repairs. Normally, all a landlord is required to do is give reasonable notice. It is good practice to give notice in writing and to keep a copy of the notice in your files. *You never know when such proof will come in handy.* After proper notice has been given, a tenant cannot legally deny access to the landlord.

3. *In an emergency:* In a real emergency, such as a fire, burglary, or medical crisis, the landlord can enter the unit immediately, without notice and without permission.

If you have given proper notice or made a proper request for entry and your tenant unreasonably refuses to let you in, you still can enter without the tenant's express authorization. It is your property, and the law recognizes that fact. Again, be sure to have put your request in writing. If forced to enter a unit after a tenant has denied you permission to enter, it is smart to bring along a witness when you do enter. After you have entered and done what you needed to do, and if your agreement is a month-to-month one, simply give thirty days' notice to terminate the tenancy and get rid of the problem tenant.

THE RIGHT TO CHANGE RENTAL AGREEMENT TERMS. Whether a landlord can change the terms of the agreement depends upon the agreement. A fixed-term lease (normally, but not always, for a year) cannot be changed. The terms of the agreement—rent, amount of security deposit, etc.—are, in fact, fixed while the lease is in effect. Once the lease ends and the tenancy terminates, a landlord is free to change the lease terms.

Unlike a fixed-term lease, most aspects of a month-to-month rental agreement are subject to modification. The landlord is free to change the terms as long as he adheres to proper notification requirements (usually thirty days). Provided that the change is legal, almost any alteration is permissible. A tenant can be told that pets will no longer be allowed, that rent will be raised, or that garbage fees will be assessed. If a tenant is unhappy with a proposed modification of the terms of the agreement, he or she can move.

The Important Legal Concept to Remember: Do not ever forget that it is the landlord who owns the property and that law was created to protect property rights. While tenants today have many rights, none trumps the rights of the property owner.

13

THE DUTY TO MAINTAIN AND REPAIR THE PREMISES

The duty to maintain
The duty to repair necessities
What the landlord does not have to do
Renter's insurance

THE DUTY TO MAINTAIN. As discussed in detail in Chapter 6, "The Implied Warranty of Habitability," every tenant has a right to a habitable home. This right creates a corresponding duty on the part of the landlord to provide and maintain a clean and safe dwelling for the tenant. While this right to a habitable home is implied in every rental agreement, most states have enacted housing and health codes that delineate exactly what a tenant should expect and what a landlord must provide.

In most states a landlord has a responsibility to provide and maintain running hot and cold water, heat, plumbing, a structurally sound building, a dwelling that is free from rodent or insect infestations, and clean and safe common areas—garbage facilities, lobbies, elevators, meeting rooms. These items are the duty of the landlord alone. A lease or rental agreement that attempts to put responsibility for these things on the tenant is illegal and unenforceable.

THE DUTY TO REPAIR NECESSITIES. The upshot of this duty to provide habitable premises is that the landlord is equally responsible for the repair of these items. If any are in need of repair after the tenant moves in, it is the landlord's responsibility to fix them.

A landlord must know about the problem before it can be fixed. Once the tenant has made the landlord aware of the problem, it should be fixed quickly. The tenant must cooperate and allow the landlord into the premises to fix the problem. If he does not, the landlord should give the tenant notice that he will enter the unit without permission, give a time and date for the entry, and then come in and fix the problem.

A landlord who fails to keep the dwelling in good repair should expect a timely visit from local housing authorities or the health department. A savvy unhappy tenant is usually not reticent to turn in a scofflaw landlord. Most building inspectors have the right to fine a landlord whose property is below statutory standards. Some communities even give building inspectors the power to close down a building that is in violation of safe housing laws.

Besides repairing necessities, in many cases a landlord has a responsibility to repair other, nonnecessity items that break due to normal wear and tear. For instance, if a faucet starts leaking, it is the landlord's job to repair it. The reason is that a tenancy is based upon a contract. The landlord's end of that deal is essentially that he will provide a nice place for his tenant to live. Therefore, a tenant whose paint finally fades after living in an apartment for many years probably has a right to have the place repainted. Normal wear and tear is the landlord's responsibility.

WHAT THE LANDLORD DOES NOT HAVE TO DO. While landlords have a duty to fix problems that threaten the habitability of the home and items that break due to normal wear and tear, they are not required to do more. Landlords certainly are not required to fix problems created by tenants or their guests.

Furthermore, landlords are not liable for criminal acts that could not be anticipated.

> Patty rented a nice house in a quiet neighborhood from her landlord, Stan. The house had a garage that had been converted into a studio, so Patty parked her car on the street every night. One morning she came out to go to work and found that her car had been vandalized; the stereo was missing and the driver's side window had been smashed. Stan is not responsible for Patty's loss.

While landlords do have a responsibility to keep the dwellings they rent safe (see next chapter), they are not insurers; landlords are not, and cannot be expected to be, responsible for criminal acts they cannot anticipate. And in most cases, a landowner's insurance policy will not cover such a loss.

Landlords are also not required to replace the personal property of a tenant if the tenant's property was destroyed by what the law calls "an act of God." Storms, hurricanes, tornadoes, earthquakes, floods, and the like are not, despite what some tenants may think, a landlord's responsibility.

For example, if the pipes in a house freeze and then burst one December night, a landlord is not responsible for any damage to the personal property that a tenant may suffer. Yes, the landlord must repair the unit and make it livable again, but the cost of property replacement and new lodgings while the place is being repaired is the tenant's responsibility.

RENTER'S INSURANCE. Because of this, it is a very good idea for tenants to buy renter's insurance. The cost is really quite minimal, and the dividends can be huge. The policy would cover and replace all the belongings of the tenant that are damaged or destroyed due to an act of God, as well as the court costs and legal fees should the tenant ever get sued.

Jim's teenage son was practicing target shooting in the backyard one afternoon when he accidentally hit the neighbor's prize horse. Jim's renter's insurance picked up the cost of hiring a lawyer as well as the $5,000 settlement.

If you own a lot of personal property, then a renter's policy is a necessity. Note that these policies vary greatly. If you live in a hurricane area, the policy may not pay for hurricane damage. For a small extra charge, the policy could cover expensive computers or family heirlooms. So, check with a good insurance agent and make sure that you buy the kind of policy that will cover any realistic possible loss.

The Important Legal Concept to Remember: Inside the rental, landlords are responsible for habitability and normal wear and tear, but nothing more. Renters are strongly advised to buy renter's insurance.

14

THE LANDLORD'S LIABILITY FOR CONDITIONS ON THE PREMISES

Common areas under the landlord's control

Negligent repairs

Crime

The need for insurance

Outside the four walls of the unit, landlords have other obligations. These responsibilities revolve around a general duty to keep the entire building safe and in good repair for the tenants. What a prudent landlord needs to understand is that if he fails in these broader responsibilities, the potential financial liability is hefty indeed.

COMMON AREAS UNDER THE LANDLORD'S CONTROL. It is the landlord's job to maintain, repair, and keep safe the common areas in a multiunit dwelling. Common areas are places under the control of the landlord and not any one tenant. Common areas include hallways, entryways, lobbies, stairs, elevators, yards, porches, meeting rooms, and any other area designated for the use and benefit of tenants.

The Bellvue apartments had a playground area for the children. After many years of use, the swing broke. In fact, the entire playground needed to be refurbished. The management tried to assess a fee on all tenants for the repair of the area. The tenants refused to pay, citing the rule that common areas are the landlord's responsibility. The tenants prevailed.

If a landlord fails to keep these common areas in good repair, *and* if a tenant is injured as a result of the landlord's omission, then the landlord will likely be held legally liable for any injuries suffered by the tenant.

Even though the management of the Bellvue apartments knew of the broken swing, it did nothing to warn its tenants of the problem. Unfortunately, before it was fixed, five-year-old Michela climbed on the swing and started to play. When the seat collapsed, Michela fell and broke her leg. The Bellvue's insurance company settled the claim for $30,000.

Almost any injury that can be traced back to a landlord's act, or failure to act, can constitute liability. In the language of the law, this is called a **tort**—a harm caused by another. In everyday language, this is called a personal injury. A broken stairway causing an injury, a defective electrical box causing a fire, or a rotted ceiling that collapses, harming someone, are all examples of a landlord's possible **negligence**.

NEGLIGENT REPAIRS. Landlords must keep common areas safe. That is the rule. That means that they must repair whatever is wrong with these areas—whether or not it applies to habitability—and that such repairs must be done properly. Negligent repairs are as much a source of liability as the original problem.

After the swing broke, the Bellvue hired a handyman to fix it. Instead of bolting the swing's seat back onto the chain, the handyman merely tacked it back on with an ill-fitting screw. Any injury resulting from his shoddy work would be the Bellvue's responsibility.

These responsibilities—to keep the complex in good repair and to fix any problems promptly and properly—should not be underestimated. Failing to live up to these responsibilities could result in a damage award to a tenant ranging into the *hundreds of thousands of dollars*. The owner of a duplex could easily lose his building if he is found liable in a personal-injury suit resulting from his negligence or that of his employees.

The question a judge will ask if you are ever in the unenviable position of having to defend a personal-injury suit is "Did this landlord act like a reasonable and prudent landlord under the circumstances?" This question is called the reasonable-person test. As a broad but useful generalization, a landlord who is said to have acted like a prudent, reasonable landlord would have under the same or similar circumstances will not be found to have been negligent. A landlord who is said to have acted unreasonable, either by omission or commission, will be held liable for a tenant's injuries.

There are many things a landlord can do to act reasonably and thereby to minimize his potential for liability. Have frequent inspections. Let your tenants know that you want to be notified as soon as possible of any problem. Post appropriate warning signs. Anything you can do to identify and rectify a potential problem will go a long way to help exonerate you should the unfortunate need ever arise. *You cannot be too cautious.*

CRIME. Another area landlords need to be concerned with is with regard to crime. Dwellings obviously need to be outfitted with locks (and probably deadbolts, to be "reasonable"), windows should have security features, although providing a security alarm is probably not necessary. Many localities have specific requirements regarding security, and it is best to find out what they are in your area.

In any case, the key again is to behave reasonably and do what a prudent landlord would do given the likelihood of crime in your complex. In higher crime areas, the landlord's duty increases correspondingly. While no landlord can guarantee total safety, what he must do is what would be reasonable under the circumstances.

A local gang of thugs had been hanging out around the Bell-vue apartments for a month. Although the management knew about it, they did nothing to stop it. One of the residents was finally mugged, and she sued the Bellvue. The court found in favor of the resident. The court noted that the reasonable thing for the complex to have done under the circumstances would have been to hire a security guard for the building.

Almost anything that contributes to crime can be a possible cause for liability, such as inadequate lighting, a lack of security gates, or no security guards. While no landlord can insure against crime, he can and should take every possible precaution within the bounds of reason and economic reality to ensure that his tenants are as safe as can be expected.

THE NEED FOR INSURANCE. What with tenants who are willing to sue over almost any perceived problem and personal injury lawyers only too willing to take their cases, the landlord's potential for liability is great.

In order to minimize this risk, financially speaking, landlords should have plenty of insurance. **Comprehensive General Liability Insurance** (or CGL) is an insurance policy that serves two purposes. First, if you are sued, the policy will pay for the cost of the defense. If you have ever had to hire an attorney, you do not need to be told how helpful this aspect of the policy would be.

Second, if you are found liable, the policy will pay the damage award (in most cases) up to the policy limits. But think about that. If you have a policy with $100,000 in coverage and you get hit with a damage award for $300,000, then it is you, the landlord, who will be stuck paying the other $200,000. If your property is worth that much, you could lose it. That is why, although CGL coverage is not inexpensive, you should buy as much as you can afford. Liability insurance is a necessity for any landlord.

The Important Legal Concept to Remember: Be overly cautious. Inspect often. Fix problems properly and quickly. Get plenty of insurance.

LANDLORD REMEDIES I: PROHIBITED REMEDIES

Retaliatory evictions and rent increases
Preventing a retaliation allegation
Self-help evictions
Lockouts, seizures, and utility shutoffs

Almost all states have enacted laws that delineate exactly what actions a landlord can take against a problematic tenant. Such statutes can generally be divided into two sections: prohibited actions and permissible actions. Prohibited actions are explained here. Permissible actions are dealt with in the next chapter.

The gist of all prohibited-action statutes is that landlords cannot engage in **self-help**; they must follow the rule of law in order to rid themselves of an unwanted tenant.

RETALIATORY EVICTIONS AND RENT INCREASES. A landlord who has a tenant who constantly calls the health department, seemingly without reason, may understandably want to rid himself of that tenant. But if that landlord attempts to evict his problem tenant, he will lose. If a landlord can point to nothing more than an overzealous tenant, a judge will throw the eviction out and award the tenant attorney fees and costs.

A landlord cannot retaliate against a tenant who chooses to

enforce his legal rights. He cannot raise a tenant's rent for joining a tenants' union. He cannot evict a tenant for complaining to housing authorities. He cannot shut off the utilities of a tenant who is late with his rent. He cannot illegally retaliate.

Yet, while retaliatory evictions are illegal, they do occur, and are often successful. This is especially true when a tenant has a month-to-month tenancy since it can be terminated on thirty days' notice for no reason. After all, it is quite difficult to prove that a landlord's intent was retaliatory when he can terminate the agreement at any time anyway.

In order to rectify this abuse, many states have enacted "presumption of retaliation" laws. These laws state that when an eviction fairly quickly follows a complaint or other legal action on the part of the tenant, it is the *landlord's responsibility to prove that the action was not retaliatory*. A tenant doesn't need to prove anything; the law presumes the eviction was retaliatory and the landlord must disprove it. Thus, all a tenant often needs to do is to get a copy of his local presumption of retaliation statute and bring it to court.

In contrast, a retaliatory eviction is easy to prove when you have a year-long lease. In that case, a landlord essentially can evict a tenant only if he stops paying rent or harms the property. Absent proof of that, any eviction following the use of a legal remedy is likely retaliatory.

Retaliatory rent increases are equally illegal. If a landlord has more than one unit, then proving retaliation is actually quite easy. Unless the landlord wants to raise everyone's rent at the same time (and he usually does not), then all the tenant needs to show are two things. One, he must be able to prove that he recently utilized a legal landlord-tenant remedy. Two, he must show that his rent alone was increased when others' were not. The tenant wins. The landlord is fined.

PREVENTING A RETALIATION ALLEGATION. Here is how a landlord can avoid a false (or true) charge of retaliation:

- *Fix the problem:* If a tenant has a legitimate beef, resolve it quickly, and do not forget to document what you did. If the problem is imaginary, document that too.
- *Have a good reason to evict:* Landlords need a reason to evict a tenant, such as nonpayment of rent. Without good cause for the eviction, a retaliation charge will stick.
- *Wait:* If you do want to get rid of a tenant and your reason is in fact retaliatory, that is fine. It is still possible to avoid a retaliation allegation, *but only* if the tenant has a monthly rental agreement. If he does, then just wait a while. Wait five or six months, and then give notice to terminate the tenancy. It would also help if you could find some other, non-retaliatory reasons for the termination notice.

The same is true for retaliatory rent increases. Fix whatever problem the tenant complained about, wait a while, justify a rent increase, give plenty of notice of the proposed increase, and then raise his rent. He will leave.

SELF-HELP EVICTIONS. It should be no surprise that a landlord cannot evict his tenant without giving her proper notice and a day in court. It is illegal in almost every state for a landlord to enter the unit and physically evict a tenant and her belongings. Landlords simply must go through proper procedures. A landlord who resorts to illegal self-help evictions opens himself up to a nasty lawsuit in which he could end up owing his tenant a lot of money. That is a dumb landlord.

LOCKOUTS, SEIZURES, AND UTILITY SHUTOFFS. Even if they have done nothing to warrant retaliation, some tenants are just a pain. Some are more than a pain and are a liability risk. While you may be tempted, even justified, in wanting to take immediate action against such tenants, don't. *Self-help is illegal* and only gives a troublesome tenant ammunition.

One action that a landlord may contemplate is a **lockout**:

changing the locks while the tenant is gone, and either moving his stuff out or seizing his property. Lockouts are illegal in almost every state. Instead of locking out the problem, landlords must use the statutory eviction process. In fact, it is because evictions are now so streamlined that lockouts are illegal. Like it or not, agree or not, every tenant gets his day in court. Even if the lease states that lockouts are permissible, they are not. Such lease provisions are illegal and unenforceable.

A tenant facing an illegal lockout should take the following actions: First, call the police and tell them that your landlord is illegally trespassing on your property (which he is). The police may or may not act. The next step is to sue. A good attorney can get a court order permitting you back into the dwelling. A small claims action will allow you to recover monetary damages.

Just as lockouts are almost universally illegal, so are utility shutoffs. An angry landlord cannot shut off his tenant's utility service, period. Not paying the bill and causing the utilities to be shut off is also illegal.

The Important Legal Concept to Remember: Landlords cannot take the law into their own hands.

LANDLORD REMEDIES II: PERMISSIBLE REMEDIES

Working it out
Give notice to vacate or raise the rent
Notices to perform

Neither landlords nor tenants like evictions. Landlords lose rent and tenants lose homes. While sometimes necessary, there are many other options short of eviction that a landlord can try first to resolve conflicts with tenants.

WORKING IT OUT. It is a good policy, and certainly a less expensive one, to first try to resolve differences with your tenant informally.

Karen's tenant Bill had developed a bad habit of playing his saxophone around 10:00 P.M. most nights and she was getting a lot of complaints about him. Rather than simply giving Bill thirty days' notice, she went over to his apartment one night while he was playing. After visiting with him for a few minutes, she asked to hear him play. She complimented him on his style and then explained her problem to him. Karen told Bill that she liked him and wanted to keep him as a tenant, but that she really needed his help. Bill agreed that the music would stop by 9:00 P.M.

It does not matter whether the problem is late rent, loud noise, or parking in the wrong space, if you have kept an open-door policy, hopefully there is room to try one of these techniques:

- *Talking it out:* You might be surprised to find out that your tenants are more reasonable than you think. Most lawyers know that it is almost always smarter to negotiate amicably before getting nasty. Landlords should do the same. Be nice. Understand your tenant's dilemma. Try to find a fair solution.

- *The veiled threat:* If a reasonable compromise does not seem possible, then tell your tenant that you sure do not want to evict him, but you may have no choice. Sometimes all it takes is this kind of threat for a tenant to understand the seriousness of the matter and to then take action to correct the problem.

- *Friendly persuasion:* Here's a great trick: if eviction is a realistic alternative and therefore a credible threat, you can often avoid having to go through that process and get your tenant to move on his own accord by sweetening the pot. Tell your tenant that if you have to evict him, he will likely get no money back from his security deposit, but that if he voluntarily moves now, you will give him his entire deposit back, no questions asked.

GIVE NOTICE TO VACATE OR RAISE THE RENT. If these less formal techniques do not work and the tenant has a month-to-month tenancy, you can always change the terms of the agreement and see if that works. Raise rent or give thirty days' notice to vacate.

Raising rent often results in the tenant deciding to move on his own. The only thing to be cautious of is a possible retaliation allegation, if applicable. If it is, simply wait a few months before raising the rent. A more direct method is just to give the tenant notice to vacate. If your tenant refuses to move, you will then have to evict him.

NOTICES TO PERFORM. As a last resort, prior to filing an actual eviction action, you can always serve your tenant with a formal notice of your intent to take further action.

A Notice to Pay Rent or Quit is the first step in an eviction lawsuit. It tells the recalcitrant tenant either to pay the rent in a prescribed number of days or to leave the premises. The number of days varies, depending upon the state, but is usually quite short—three to five days is typical.

It is critical that the notice is filled out correctly, that the correct amount of past-due rent is stated, and that it is served properly. Since this notice begins the eviction process, it will be scrutinized by a judge to make sure it is complete and accurate, should it come to that. If it is not, then the entire eviction could be at jeopardy. If you do not know how to fill out the form correctly or calculate the past-due rent accurately or serve it properly, hire a lawyer or an eviction service. It will save you money in the long run.

Tenants are typically quite intimidated by Pay Rent or Quit Notices, and the need to actually continue the eviction process often dissipates after the tenant gets the notice. Many tenants are so terrified by the official-looking notice, which can be purchased at most office-supply or stationery stores, and so worried that they will be evicted the day after the notice expires (which is not true), they will beg, borrow, or steal the money needed to get caught up with rent.

If you really want to get your tenant's attention, here's a good idea: hire the local sheriff or an off-duty policeman to serve your tenant with the notice. You can rest assured that your tenant will not sleep well that night and that your past-due rent will be shortly forthcoming.

It is important to understand that a tenant does not have to leave at the expiration of the notice—that is not how the process works. You will still have to serve him with an eviction complaint and follow through with the eviction process. What this notice does do is tell your tenant that the jig is up. Remember, self-help is illegal. You must go through the proper channels to get rid of your problem tenant.

Another notice that may apply is the **Notice to Perform Covenant or Quit**. A covenant is a promise to do or not do something. Whereas a Notice to Pay Rent or Quit is used when tenants are late with rent, this notice is used when a tenant breaks some other type of promise in the lease or rental agreement.

> David rented a small flat from Louie. After living in the place for a few months, David had his girlfriend move in, even though his lease specifically stated that he was to be the only tenant in the unit. Louie did not approve of the arrangement, and immediately served David with a Notice to Perform Covenant or Quit. The notice specifically stated that David's girlfriend had to move out within three days or David would be evicted. David's girlfriend reluctantly moved.

> Similarly, if a tenant is keeping a pet when the lease forbids it, a Notice to Perform Covenant or Quit would be appropriate. These types of notices are very effective because tenants immediately realize that there will be dire consequences for continuing to break the rules.

The Important Legal Concept to Remember: The intimidation factor of a threatened eviction can often be the quickest and least expensive way for a landlord to get a tenant back in line.

TERMINATING
THE TENANCY

WHEN THE AGREEMENT ENDS

Month-to-month tenants who refuse to leave

Fixed-term lease tenants who refuse to leave

How to get out of paying last month's rent

How landlords can ensure that last month's rent is paid

Returning security deposits

How to get a security deposit back

Most tenancies end simply. The lease runs out and the tenant moves. Either party gives thirty days' notice and the tenant moves. But sometimes things are not so simple.

MONTH-TO-MONTH TENANTS WHO REFUSE TO LEAVE. A monthly tenant who stays on after the term ends is called a **hold-over tenant**. Some of these tenants offer to pay rent again, while others stay on with no intent of ever paying rent again. When faced with a hold-over tenant, a landlord can either begin eviction proceedings or accept rent if proffered by the hold-over.

Landlords should be *extremely wary* of accepting rent again once a tenant holds over. Here is why: the tendering of rent is, in actuality, an offer to enter into a new rental contract. The acceptance of rent is an acceptance of that offer. Contracts are created by offer and acceptance. Once a hold-over tenant pays rent again, a *new rental contract* is created by operation of law. You are back at square one with your tenant.

> Shelly rented a duplex from Bob on a month-to-month basis. Shelly was not a great tenant, and Bob finally gave her thirty days' notice on August 1. On September 1, she failed to move out and officially became a hold-over tenant. A week later, when she realized that she would have a hard time finding a new place, Shelly sent Bob a check. Bob really needed the money and cashed the check. By cashing the check, Bob agreed to allow Shelly to stay. If he wanted to evict her now, he would have to wait until October 1 to give her a new thirty-day notice, and she would not have to leave until November 1.

By accepting Shelly's rent, Bob created a new rental agreement with her. This would be true for any landlord who accepts rent from a month-to-month tenant who holds over. It is generally a very bad idea, then, to take the money.

FIXED-TERM LEASE TENANTS WHO REFUSE TO LEAVE. A year-long lease that starts on January 1 ends *automatically* on December 31 of that year. Neither tenant nor landlord needs to give any notice whatsoever.

Once the lease expires, there are four possible scenarios. The most common is that the tenant moves out, as he should. The second is that both parties decide to renew the lease, and rent begins again. The third is that the tenant holds over and does not pay rent. In that case, the landlord needs to evict him.

The fourth possibility is that the tenant holds over, offers to pay rent again, but signs no new lease. As in the case of a hold-over monthly tenant, a landlord can either accept or reject that offer of rent. If he accepts it, as in the case of Bob and Shelly above, a new rental agreement is created. However, instead of creating a new lease, as they did, the acceptance of rent from a lease-holding hold-over tenant creates a new *month-to-month* agreement. The lease expired, and the new rent does not revive it. All the new rent does is create a new monthly rental arrangement. So, be sure you want this tenant around for a while before you accept his rent after the term has expired.

If the landlord refuses the rent, then the tenant is still a hold-over. The landlord needs to evict him as he would any other tenant who does not pay rent.

HOW TO GET OUT OF PAYING LAST MONTH'S RENT. Whether you have a lease or a monthly rental arrangement, the thorny questions of security deposits and last month's rent are usually equally applicable. Often, a tenant will want to use the deposit as last month's rent and the landlord will not want him to. If the entire deposit is called a security deposit, the landlord is not obliged to apply any of it toward last month's rent. He can if he wants to, but he does not have to. It is the landlord's decision.

Do not be dismayed if you know that your landlord does not intend to apply a portion of your security deposit toward last month's rent. It is still possible to use part of that money for a last rental payment. Here's how: when you give notice, simply add to your written notice a few sentences telling your landlord that you will not be paying last month's rent and to apply the deposit (or a portion thereof) to rent. Of course your landlord will be unhappy, and may even give you a Notice to Pay Rent or Quit. That is fine. It will still take your landlord at least a month or so to evict you, so there is little he can actually do about it since you will be gone by the time you would have been evicted.

This trick works best if your deposit roughly equals your rent. Why? Your landlord is holding your money. Once she is mad at you, she will find every reason to keep the rest of your money. If your security deposit equals your last month's rent, then there will be nothing to keep.

HOW LANDLORDS CAN ENSURE THAT LAST MONTH'S RENT IS PAID. If a tenant decides not to pay rent the last month and tells his landlord to use the deposit instead, in reality there is not much a landlord can do. Eviction takes time. Try this instead:

> Amy owned a small house that she rented out on a month-to-month basis. It was her policy, as explained in her rental agreement, to allow tenants to move on *two weeks' notice*. Her tenant Anne lived in the house for a year. When Anne decided it was time to move, she had *already paid rent* that month. Since Anne knew that she needed to give Amy only two weeks' notice, she did not think to try to use her deposit as rent.

There is nothing illegal about requiring less time than required by law for tenants to give notice. If you require only two weeks' termination notice, then your tenant will likely have paid her rent by the time she gives notice. Try it, it works.

RETURNING SECURITY DEPOSITS. Landlords are required by law to itemize deductions and return security deposits promptly. In order to avoid confusion and ensure that they do not get sued in small claims court, landlords should follow these simple rules:

- *Require notice:* Require written notice of your tenant's intent to terminate the arrangement, and make sure that this requirement is part of the original rental agreement.
- *Offer guidelines:* Give tenants written guidelines describing what you require to refund a deposit in full. Have this notice explain that rent must be fully paid up to date, that the unit must be thoroughly cleaned, that all property must be removed, and that all keys need to be returned on the last day of the agreement.

- *Be honest:* Do not deduct for those items for which the tenant is not legally liable. Normal wear and tear is your responsibility; damage caused by the tenant is not.
- *Be timely:* Return deposits on time.

HOW TO GET A SECURITY DEPOSIT BACK. A tenant who wants her entire deposit back should do the following:

- Have your entire rent balance paid in full at the time you give notice.
- Pay your last month's rent on time.
- Give enough notice.
- Fix anything you broke.
- Leave the place spotless.
- Document the condition of the place (photographs, video-tape) after you have cleaned it.
- Return all keys promptly.

The Important Legal Concept to Remember: When the tenancy ends, tenants should leave and their deposits should be promptly returned. Failure by either party to live up to his obligations upon termination can be very costly.

18

GETTING OUT OF A LEASE EARLY

Getting out early when the other side breaches the agreement
Surrender, abandonment, and mitigation
Assignments and sublets

GETTING OUT EARLY WHEN THE OTHER SIDE BREACHES THE
AGREEMENT. A lease obligates both parties. The landlord is
required to allow the tenant to possess the dwelling for the term
of the lease and the tenant is obliged to pay rent for that
amount of time.

> Bill rented an apartment from Mark on a yearly lease basis
> at $500 per month. After eight months, Bill moved out with-
> out reason. Mark sued Bill for $2,000 ($500 x the 4 months
> remaining on the lease) and won.

If either party violates his obligations, he is in breach of the
agreement. In that case, the *negatively affected* party has the
right to simply call the whole deal off.

> Rather than suing Bill, Mark just wanted to find a new ten-
> ant as soon as possible. He therefore terminated the lease
> and found someone else to rent the unit. Bill owed Mark no
> extra money.

Tenants too can terminate the lease if the landlord has substantially breached an obligation. Remember that landlords are obliged to deliver possession of a habitable unit and are required to ensure a tenant's quiet enjoyment of that dwelling. If a landlord fails in either of these duties, the tenant can void the remainder of the lease.

For example, when a landlord physically prevents a tenant from entering his home, he has committed what the law calls an actual eviction (although eviction here has a different meaning than the court procedure discussed earlier). Actual evictions allow tenants to move immediately, regardless of any binding lease. An example would be when a landlord padlocks the door of the unit if his tenant is a few days late with the rent. That is an actual eviction and the tardy tenant could simply end the lease and leave.

Even if a landlord is not foolish enough to actually evict a tenant, there are many other ways that a landlord can violate his obligations and negate the lease. Many of these breaches will result in what is known as a constructive eviction. Constructive evictions too permit the tenant to cancel the lease and leave.

Stacy's apartment was without heat for three months. She called her landlord several times, but to no avail. Finally, she moved out with six months remaining on her lease, claiming a constructive eviction. She was right.

Besides a lack of heat, other violations that may be cause for constructive eviction are

· *Breach of the warranty of habitability:* If a landlord continually fails to repair a major item—one that affects the habitability of the home—then a tenant can safely claim constructive eviction. Note, though, that the item must relate to the habitability of the home; a broken tile will not do. So too the landlord must be given a reasonable chance to fix the problem. A solitary phone call is insufficient.

· *Breach of the covenant of quiet enjoyment:* If a landlord continually interferes with a tenant's quiet enjoyment of the unit (by playing the tuba at all hours, for example), then the tenant can move due to a constructive eviction. Also, and this is an important point, if another tenant is too loud, *and the landlord has done nothing about it*, a tenant can claim a constructive eviction and terminate the lease.

Using constructive eviction to get out of a lease is a double-edged sword. The upside is that it is not difficult to make an argument that your landlord has violated some lease provision or implied covenant, and therefore you are justified in terminating the lease. The downside is that you had better be right. If you leave in the middle of the term and your landlord sues you for lost rent, you can be sure that a judge will carefully scrutinize your reasoning. If you are wrong, you will end up owing your ex-landlord a lot of back rent.

Finally, if the dwelling is destroyed, a tenant may terminate the lease and incur no further rent obligations. While that may be self-evident, the following may not be: if only part of the unit is destroyed, say, the garage, it still may be possible to terminate the entire lease. The key is to be able to prove that the garage was essential to your use of the dwelling, and that the lack of the garage materially impedes your enjoyment of the unit. If that can be proved, a tenant can get out of the lease. If it cannot, then the tenant is obliged to honor the agreement, despite the lack of a garage.

SURRENDER, ABANDONMENT, AND MITIGATION. Another way for a lease to end early is for the tenant to move out and give the unit back to the landlord, regardless of any breaches of the agreement. If this is done with the landlord's consent, it is called **surrender**; if it is done without it, it is called **abandonment**.

A surrender occurs when both parties agree to end the lease early and release each other from any further obligations. A surrender is often in the best interests of both sides. For the landlord, it saves the likely expense of suing the tenant for unpaid rent. For the tenant, it precludes possibly having to pay any more rent. If one side wants out, surrender is often a good choice. To be effective, the surrender must be in writing.

Abandonment, on the other hand, occurs when the tenant vacates the premises without agreement or permission and defaults on payment of rent. In that case, the landlord has two options. He can either do nothing and sue, or "accept" the abandonment.

While doing nothing and suing for lost rent sounds nice, the truth is, financial danger lurks for the landlord who makes that choice, due to a legal axiom known as mitigation. Mitigation means that a party to a breached contract must do everything possible to minimize any future financial loss he may suffer. In the case of a breached lease, it means that a landlord is required, in most states, to try to re-lease the unit in a reasonable amount of time.

> Leslie moved out of her leased home three months early and left the place spotless. Her landlord, Tim, knowing he was required to mitigate his damages, was able to find a new tenant in just two weeks. Instead of being liable for three months of lost rent, Leslie was responsible for only the two weeks of lost rent incurred by Tim.

Even if it takes a landlord some time to repair, clean, and rent the unit again, he still will likely have to sue his tenant before he sees any of the back rent. And even then, the tenant may unfortunately be "judgment proof." Judgment proof is a term that brings tears to the eyes of lawyers and landlords alike. It means that even if found legally liable, the defendant does not have enough money or assets to pay the judgment (i.e., the court order to pay the amount due). A judgment that cannot be collected is a judgment that is worthless. Thus, suing for lost rent is not as easy as it sounds.

The other option, while not as emotionally satisfying as "suing the bastard," is sometimes the best one. That is to accept the abandonment and attempt to re-let the unit as soon as it is feasible to do so. In light of the duty to mitigate, and the cost and difficulty in obtaining and collecting a judgment, accepting and rerenting is often the most cost-effective solution.

ASSIGNMENTS AND SUBLETS. These are two final ways for a tenant to get out of a lease obligation before the lease ends, and without the baggage or risks associated with many of the options above. An assignment or a sublet allows someone else to take the tenant's place and finish the obligation for him.

If you are the tenant, an assignment is the better way to go. The reason is that an assignment allows the new party to take over a tenant's lease obligations completely. Basically, an assignment means that the new tenant's name will be written into the lease, the old tenant's name will be taken off the lease, and the old tenant's security deposit will be returned. All of the old tenant's legal obligations under the contract cease. If the new tenant defaults on rent, the landlord *cannot* come after the old tenant. To be valid, the assignment must be in writing.

Sublets are a bit different than assignments, and have substantially different legal consequences, even though they look the same. Both allow someone new to come in and live in the unit instead of the original tenant. However, whereas an assignment permits the original tenant to legally evade further obligations under the lease, that is not true of a sublet.

The key legal aspect of a sublet is that the original tenant *remains legally liable* to the landlord for all obligations under the lease. If the new tenant defaults on rent, it is the *original tenant* who is legally liable to the landlord. It is, therefore, a risky proposition for a tenant to sublet his unit. The original tenant gets none of the benefits of the lease (a place to live), yet still has all of the responsibilities. Accordingly, sublets are best used when a tenant may be gone for only a short period of time (say, for two months over the summer).

If you do sublet, realize that it is an agreement between the tenants only. Although the original tenant may need her landlord's consent to bring the new tenant in, the **sublease** agreement itself really has nothing to do with the landlord.

David had a great apartment overlooking the beach. When he got a job requiring a lot of travel, he decided to sublet his place. His sublessee, Steve, agreed that he would move in, pay rent, and vacate the place for a week every other month or so when David was back in town. This worked for six months. When Steve left the last time, David decided not to leave again. Steve was out of luck.

Almost all leases require the landlord's permission before a tenant assigns or sublets the lease to someone new. Normally, a landlord cannot "unreasonably" withhold his approval. Unfortunately, since determining what is reasonable is what makes lawyers rich, an uncooperative landlord can often withhold approval without repercussion.

Here is a trick that may get your landlord to approve your proposed transfer: find someone who is willing to accept the assignment or sublet and who would be willing to extend the length of the current lease. One reason landlords like leases is that they give a level of security—landlords know that the place is rented and will be until the end of the term. They do not have to think about cleaning and renting it again. Finding a new tenant who will extend the lease length dovetails with a landlord's desire to keep the place rented.

The Important Legal Concept to Remember: There are many ways to get out of a lease before it ends, although some are better than others. The best of all possible options is an assignment.

V

LAWSUITS

EVICTION LAWSUITS

CAUSES FOR EVICTION. Evictions occur after a tenant has been asked to move out and has refused to do so. With a month-to-month tenancy, a landlord ostensibly needs no reason to give thirty days' notice, since, by the very terms of the arrangement, either party can terminate the agreement on thirty days' notice. It is when a tenant has not moved on the thirty-first day that an eviction lawsuit is necessary. Eviction is a process that utilizes the assistance of the courts to put the landlord back in possession of the dwelling.

> Clarence rented an apartment from Bruce and had a year-long lease. Bruce wanted to rent the unit to his brother, and therefore gave Clarence thirty days' notice to vacate. Since Clarence had a lease, and since he knew that Bruce could not legally give him thirty days' notice, Clarence did nothing. When Bruce tried to evict Clarence, the judge threw the case out of court and made Bruce pay all of Clarence's legal bills.

The critical question to be answered by the courts is whether a landlord has a justifiable reason to possess the property again.

If a tenant has an ongoing lease and has done nothing wrong, a landlord has no right to possess the property until the lease is up. A landlord like Bruce will lose his eviction lawsuit because a court will decide that he has no justifiable reason to gain possession of the property again. His tenant did nothing wrong.

So, the issue is this: has the tenant given the landlord a legally justifiable reason for taking the property back? A tenant who has properly withheld a portion of her rent to fix a broken shower has not given her landlord just cause for an eviction. A tenant who has withheld a portion of her rent because she thinks her landlord charges too much rent has in fact given her landlord just cause for eviction. In the former case, the law allows for repair and deduct. In the latter, there is no right to unilateral, unjustifiable rent withholding. Is the law on your side? That is the question.

Just cause for terminating a tenancy includes all of the following: nonpayment of rent, expiration of the term, the tenant is disturbing other tenants, the tenant has damaged the property, the tenant has violated a term of the agreement (e.g., a no-pets clause), or the tenant is breaking the law in the unit. Any one of these would likely result in a victory for the landlord.

THE PROCESS. Once it has been established that a landlord has a valid reason to evict a tenant, usually, but not necessarily, for nonpayment of rent, he does so by initiating a lawsuit, usually called an **unlawful detainer** or a **forcible entry and detainer** action. Unlawful detainer actions are expedited court processes, typically taking anywhere from *one week to two months, from start to finish.*

Evicting someone is not the type of thing one should attempt to do without the assistance of a professional. Eviction services run by **paralegals** are available at a small fee, but you get what you pay for. Paralegals are not attorneys and cannot give legal advice. They also cannot go to court with you. If you can afford it, it is much smarter to hire an attorney.

The eviction begins when the landlord, or his attorney, files a **complaint** against the tenant. The complaint identifies the **parties**, states the reasons for the action, and requests that the tenant be evicted.

After the complaint is filed (by the party called the plaintiff), it must be **served,** along with the **summons,** on the tenant. Although each state has different rules, service is usually accomplished by either (1) personal delivery by a sheriff or registered process server, (2) tacking the summons and complaint to the door of the rental, or (3) certified mail. Since improper service constitutes grounds to dispute the eviction, *be sure the tenant is served properly*.

In an unlawful detainer action, the person being sued (named as the **defendant**) has a very short amount of time to file a response with the court and the other side, and some states do not even require a formal response. Tenants are advised to read the summons carefully; it will state whether a formal written response is required, and, if so, by when. If a written response is required and the tenant fails to respond in time, then the landlord can save the time and expense of a trial by filing for a **default** judgment. By defaulting, a tenant forfeits his right to go to trial. The landlord wins automatically.

If the tenant does respond to the suit, it will go to trial in a very short amount of time. A landlord may find his tenant trying to forestall an eviction trial, and thereby stay in the unit even longer, by filing some sort of **motion** with the court (see next chapter). If a landlord has acted properly, then such a motion is nothing but a delaying tactic.

TRIAL. Eviction trials vary depending on state law. Some states allow for jury trials, others do not. Some eviction trials are notoriously quick, lasting no more than fifteen minutes or so; others may last half a day. The issues are whether the landlord acted properly, filed suit properly, gave notice and served the tenant properly, and whether he has a right to retake the unit. Similarly, the judge will want to know why the tenant did whatever he did, and whether he had any justification for his actions or inactions.

Again, if you can afford an attorney, it is best to hire one. Trials are complicated, and if you do not know what you are doing, the judge will quickly stop you. Judges do not suffer fools lightly.

Whether or not you have an attorney, you still must act appropriately in court. How you behave will have a significant impact on the outcome of your trial. Dress nicely. Exercise decorum and self-restraint. Do not overreact. Do not argue with your tenant or landlord. Present yourself well, and speak only to the judge. Do not chew gum. Be on time. Do not whisper. Be respectful.

The key to being believed when testifying is to be honest. Your testimony must be credible, make sense, and have the ring of truth to it. Judges instinctively know when someone is lying. Speak up. Be calm. Do not memorize answers. Listen to the question, and answer only the question asked. If you do not understand a question, ask for it to be repeated. Do not avoid the truth, even though it may be unflattering. Be clear, concise, and honest.

In order to win, not only must you act appropriately but you must also have the law on your side. If you are a tenant and have not paid your rent, you had better have a legal justification for your inaction, such as repairing and deducting. You also need to come to court well organized, with documents and witnesses who can help you prove your case. The party who comes in unorganized, ranting and raving, with no proof, loses.

EVICTION. Assuming, not illogically, that the landlord won the eviction trial, the tenant must usually move within a matter of days. In some states, tenants have one day to move; in others, twenty-one. California, for example, gives a tenant five days to leave after trial.

Tenants should leave peacefully before the deadline. If by the deadline they are not gone, the police will physically evict them. Their property will be immediately removed. Again, it is best to avoid this ugly scene and just move before the deadline.

The Important Legal Concept to Remember: Landlords usually win eviction lawsuits because they know what they are doing and have done it many times. Unless a tenant truly has a reason that can stand up in court, it is best for everyone concerned if the tenant just moves out when served with the suit.

20

DEFENDING AN
EVICTION LAWSUIT

━━━━

Defending against an eviction

Other Options

It is not easy for a tenant to defend an eviction action. Landlords usually have more resources (i.e., money and lawyers), as well as a justifiable reason for bringing the suit. Many tenants do not even bother to show up for the trial, knowing that the outcome is almost predetermined.

Yet it need not be so. There are two different possible avenues a tenant can take once served with an eviction complaint. The first option is to assert a legitimate affirmative defense. An affirmative defense is a defense that, if applicable to you and can be proved, will enable you to win in court and stay in the dwelling. The second option is to utilize a legally permissible procedural motion, which may also buy you some time.

The first course of action—asserting an affirmative defense—should be used if you really believe that you have done nothing wrong and should not be evicted. The second option—using legal procedure—is used when you suspect that your landlord has a good reason to evict you, but also think that he may have improperly handled the eviction proceeding. A positive by-product of filing a procedural motion is that it may allow you to stay in the unit a bit longer, if that is your desire.

DEFENDING AGAINST AN EVICTION. If you believe that the landlord should not be evicting you, the first thing to consider is whether you want to hire an attorney. It is possible to get very inexpensive legal help. Try the following:

- *Yellow Pages:* Look under "Legal Aid," "Legal Services," or "Legal Clinics." All of these are headings for nonprofit groups that specialize in helping poor people out of legal pickles.
- *Law schools:* Most law schools have clinics, run by attorneys, that teach law students how to become lawyers. Assisting in landlord-tenant disputes is often their specialty.
- *Local bar associations:* A **bar association** is an organization of lawyers found on local, state, and national levels. Many have voluntary legal-assistance programs. Call the local bar association in your city.

Next, whether or not you have an attorney, you need to decide which defenses to assert. These defenses are asserted both as part of your "response" to the complaint (if so required in your state) and at trial. They are the basis for your argument that you should be allowed to stay in the unit. There are many such defenses, depending upon the reason for the eviction. For example:

- *For nonpayment of rent:* If your landlord is evicting you for nonpayment of rent, the first and obviously best defense would be to be able to prove that it was, in fact, paid. Absent that possibility, there still are several viable defenses. Asserting and proving that your landlord breached the warranty of either habitability or quiet enjoyment would also work. Why? Because the law allows you to withhold rent when your landlord has breached these implied promises.
  Another possible defense is that your landlord failed to perform other obligations under the agreement. For exam-

ple, if your landlord failed to keep the common areas clean and safe. In essence, you need to be able to prove that you had a legally justifiable reason for not paying rent. Excuses, unjustifiable reasons, or an inability to pay will not suffice.

· *For nonpayment of a rent increase:* If you refused to pay a rent increase, a particularly good defense, if it can be proven, is that the increase was either retaliatory or discriminatory. Asserting these defenses are particularly effective as they turn the tables; your landlord will be on the defensive and will have to prove that the increase was not made for an improper purpose. In legal parlance, these defenses shift the burden of proof from you to your landlord. Remember that merely asserting retaliation will not do; you must be able to prove retaliation or discrimination with witnesses or documents, preferably both.

Another defense to a rent increase is that you were not given proper notice of the increase. A tenant with a month-to-month tenancy deserves at least thirty days' notice of the increase. Anything less is improper and therefore solid grounds to defend the action.

· *For any other reason:* There are a variety of other reasons that a landlord may assert as reason for eviction. Almost all of the defenses listed above apply equally to many of these causes. For example, say your landlord is evicting you because he says you had a boyfriend move in, in violation of the lease. Proving that he did not actually move in, but merely spent the night sometimes, would be quite effective. It would be especially helpful if you could get some neighbors to testify to that effect. Be creative and tell the truth.

These, then, are your basic defenses: rent *was* paid; retaliation or discrimination; the landlord failed to perform an obligation, thereby causing you to withhold rent; breach of the warranty of either habitability or quiet enjoyment; use of repair and deduct; improper notice of a change in the terms of the tenancy; or a defense on the merits (e.g., you never had a pet—you were only pet-sitting for a friend for a few weeks). If any of these apply to you and you can prove it, then by all means defend yourself.

OTHER OPTIONS. If none of these defenses applies to you and you have no real justification for doing whatever it is your landlord is angry about, it is better just to move. The only reason to stay would be if you think that the eviction was handled improperly. If so, use one of the options below. While they will not save you, they may at least buy you some time.

The first tactic is to file a motion with the court. Previously, it was stated that a tenant sometimes needs to file a response to the complaint, normally *within a matter of days of service of the complaint*. Usually this response is an **answer**—a document that essentially denies that the tenant did anything wrong. Yet an answer is not the only answer. There are two other possible responses that you can file instead. It is important to understand that these responses, called motions, *must be filed in good faith*. Filing a frivolous motion (one that cannot be supported by any facts) is a sure way to get monetarily sanctioned by the court. As each of the two motions listed below serves a very specific purpose, be sure that your case has similar facts before filing either one.

The first is something called a **motion to quash**. A motion to quash is used when you believe that you were not served correctly. Service of the eviction lawsuit normally must be accomplished by personal delivery, certified or first-class mail, or tacking the complaint on your door. If your landlord never served you with the summons and complaint personally, but just shoved the documents under the door while you were gone, then a motion to quash would be appropriate.

Realize that a motion to quash is a fairly technical motion. It is a good idea to go down to your local courthouse and get a copy of one, or to find a book that has one. Copy it, fill in your facts, file it with the court, and serve it on your landlord. If the judge determines that you were not served legally, then your landlord will need to start the eviction process all over.

The other possible motion to file instead of an answer is something called a **demurrer**. A demurrer tells the court that your landlord has no *legal* justification for the eviction.

> Brian had a year-long lease with his landlord, Jeff. Halfway through, Jeff served Brian with a thirty-day notice to vacate. Brian refused to move, noting that he had a lease. When Jeff then served Brian with an eviction complaint, Brian filed a demurrer, arguing that it is legally impossible to evict some- one on thirty days' notice when he has a lease. The judge agreed, and Brian stayed in his home.

Whether you should file a demurrer really depends upon the facts of your case. Grounds include improper notice of a change in the tenancy or termination of the tenancy, improper use of a Notice to Perform Covenant or Quit, and filing the complaint too soon, among others.

If you are contemplating a demurrer, understand that you are entering a very, very technical area of the law. It is really an area that only lawyers should tread. But if you want to file one and you do not have an attorney, the first thing to know is that a demurrer tests the *legal* sufficiency of the case, not its *factual* sufficiency. A demurrer is not the place to say that your land- lord is a slumlord. That is a factual issue. It *is* the place to say that he filed suit against you before ever giving you a Notice to Pay Rent or Quit, as he is legally obliged to do. Again, get a copy of a demurrer to use as a prototype, and change the facts accordingly. As a demurrer is so specialized, do not expect to win.

Another option, and one that might buy you some time, is to ask for a **continuance**. This is made before the trial, by filing a written request with the court. A continuance is granted only for good cause—an important witness will be out of town or you cannot get off from work that day, for example. If granted, this might give you another two weeks.

Another possible way to delay moving is to cut a deal with your landlord prior to trial. Your landlord really does not want to go to trial either, surprisingly enough. Trials cost him money in legal fees and continued lost rent. They are also risky; your landlord could possibly lose.

Your landlord may be willing to work with you if you can assure him that you will pay him what you owe him and will move out on a certain date. Especially if you let your landlord know that you have the procedural tricks outlined above up your sleeve, he may be far more likely to negotiate with you. Remember, you are still in possession of his property and are therefore negotiating out of a position of strength. Cut a good deal and get out already.

The Important Legal Concept to Remember: Tenants who know they deserve to be evicted should save their money and move out before trial. Those who feel justified in fighting the suit must be prepared to prove to a judge that their actions were legally justified.

21

SMALL CLAIMS COURT

Lawsuits in general
Small claims or superior court?
Filing suit in small claims court
How to present your case

LAWSUITS IN GENERAL. There are many reasons why a landlord or tenant may want to sue the other. Unpaid rent, an unreturned security deposit, discrimination, injury—the list is probably endless. Often, the most pressing reason is emotional—one party is just so mad at the other that a lawsuit seems like the best way to get back at him. And it often is. And, it often is not.

When faced with a problem that cannot be solved in a manner to your liking, and you are determined to get a different result, then your only option is to sue the person or entity who is aggrieving you. For better or for worse, lawsuits are just about the only legal method society has developed to resolve such disputes.

There are distinct advantages to filing suit. First, it puts your foe on notice that you are not to be taken lightly. It tells him that you have been harmed and that you refuse to take it anymore. Suing someone also puts him on the defensive. Indeed, throughout the suit you will be known as the plaintiff and he will be known as the defendant.

Filing suit also will (eventually) allow a neutral third party—the judge—to decide who is right and who is wrong. If you are right and can convince the judge, then you will be financially rewarded for your troubles. Except in the rare cases when a restraining order or similar legal device is required, money is all the law offers.

Kelly nearly died when she went for a swim in the pool at her apartment complex and discovered that it had been overchlorinated. Throughout her long suit, she demanded a public apology from the management of her complex. She told the judge the same thing. The jury awarded her $10,000. She never did get that apology.

The law cannot heal a broken leg or mend a broken heart. It cannot bring back a dead parent or comfort a traumatized child. However crude, money is all the law has to offer.

SMALL CLAIMS OR SUPERIOR COURT? Once you have determined that you want or need to sue someone, the next question to answer is whether to bring your suit in small claims court or superior court.

For most landlord-tenant disputes arising out of unpaid rent or a security deposit that was not returned, small claims court is the way to go. Small claims court is an informal, inexpensive, expedited process that is designed to settle disputes over small amounts of money. In Vermont, the most you can sue for is $3,500. In California, the limit is $5,000. In Georgia, it's $5,000, and in South Dakota, the maximum judgment is $4,000. Each state is different.

If the money you feel you are owed exceeds these limits (for example, if you suffered a physical injury or were discriminated against), then you will need to bring suit in a superior court (depending upon where you live and where you file, such courts are also called district courts, county courts, municipal courts, courts of common pleas, and the like). Whereas small claims court is quick and inexpensive, just the opposite is true for superior court. Cases often take years and hiring an attorney is a necessity.

The old television show *People's Court* was nothing more than glorified small claims court. While some states allow you to hire an attorney to represent you, it is not necessary. In fact, one of the great advantages of small claims court is that you are able to represent yourself without having to resort to hiring expensive attorneys.

FILING SUIT IN SMALL CLAIMS COURT. Bringing an action in small claims court is easy. Simply go down to your local courthouse, fill out the appropriate forms, and pay the fee. It should be somewhere around fifty dollars. When the form asks why you are suing, write in "breach of contract" or whatever your reason is.

Do not sue for more than you are legally entitled. In the case of a security deposit that was not returned, a tenant is entitled to the amount of the deposit plus interest, and any possible fines. Time for missed work, baby-sitters, emotional distress, and the like, are normally not compensable and will only weaken a case. The same is true for back-rent lawsuits.

The court will probably mail the necessary notices to both parties, informing everyone of the date and time of the hearing. It usually takes less than three months to get into small claims court.

HOW TO PRESENT YOUR CASE. The key to winning in small claims court is the two P's: preparation and proof. You must be able to *prove* to the judge that what you are telling her is true and that your opponent's version of the facts is false. You do so by being *prepared*.

Preparation means that you are fully organized and ready to present your case before the judge in a short amount of time. It is safe to assume that you will have about ten minutes to tell the judge your side of the facts. In order to do so, you need to have already organized your case.

Have your witnesses prepared and ready to testify. Speak with them beforehand and let them know where and when court will be. Call them the day before your hearing and remind them of the court date. Be sure to make an outline of your case. Before you get to court, you also need to have made copies of all relevant receipts, letters, and other documents. Like a Boy Scout, be prepared.

Sam found a nice house for rent, filled out the application, and gave his new landlord, Larry, a $500 security deposit. Sam lived in the place for seven months before deciding to move. He gave Larry thirty days' notice. Before he left, Sam thoroughly cleaned the house. Because he had had many problems with Larry in the few months he lived there, Sam decided to take a few photographs of the place before he left. He also had his pal Ron walk through the unit with him before he returned the key. Predictably, Larry never returned Sam's security deposit, even after Sam wrote a demand letter.

Even more important than preparation, though, is proof. Sam must be able to prove that he is entitled to a return of his security deposit. If he had no pictures, evidence, or witnesses, and simply told the judge his version of the facts, he would likely lose. A landlord is a businessperson who owns real estate. In the legal world, that carries weight. Tenants are often seen as less responsible. In many cases a judge will likely side with a landlord if a tenant simply goes in with her word against his. That is a sad but true fact.

So, you need evidence. Have extra copies of your lease and demand letter ready. Pictures and a videotape are indispensable. Witnesses must show up on time and be ready to testify succinctly. If you don't have any evidence, you are wasting your time and money.

When you get your day in court, dress professionally. As the plaintiff, you will get to speak first. One thing your judge will not want to see is a lot of emotion. The law in these types of matters is fairly clear-cut. Hot tempers and hurt feelings carry little weight with judges. What does carry weight is a clear, simple explanation of why you are legally entitled to money. Organize your case something like this:

1. *Give a one- or two-sentence description of the dispute.* "I lived at 1800 Mariposa Lane for eight months. I gave my landlord, the defendant, Larry Brooks, a five-hundred-dollar deposit, and he refused to return it to me when I moved out." Show the judge the receipt for your deposit.

2. *Explain why you should get your money back.* " I left the unit in the exact same condition as I found it. In fact, it was probably cleaner when I left than when I moved in. I also paid all of my rent, and I can prove it, Your Honor."

3. *Prove it.* Show the judge whatever photographs you have. Have your witnesses testify that you did, in fact, leave the place clean and in good repair. Show any receipts or canceled checks you have to prove that all rent was paid. Show your demand letter. Explain that you tried to be reasonable.

After the plaintiff presents his case, the defendant will have a chance to give his version of the facts. Do not interrupt him, as you will get another chance to rebut whatever he says. Proper decorum is critical in a courtroom.

Do not be surprised if the defendant lies. People lie in court all the time, plaintiffs and defendants alike. If your landlord says that you broke the refrigerator, you must be able to prove that you did not. If your tenant says that he paid all of the back-due rent, be ready to prove otherwise. The side who can prove his version of the facts will win.

After the defendant has presented his case, the plaintiff will have one more chance to speak. The first thing to do is to rebut what the defendant said. Then explain again in an abbreviated form why you should win. *Do not* try to present your entire case again. You will be told to be quiet.

The judge may render a judgment right there, or he may tell you that it will come in the mail in a week. If you win, congratulations. If you lose, you may have a right to appeal, but then it starts to get costly. Be sure you are right before you appeal a loss.

The Important Legal Concept to Remember: You have a much better chance of winning your small claims case if you remember to use the two *P*'s: preparation and proof. If you do, then you do not have to be bullied—a small claims judge can get your money back for you.

SUPERIOR COURT

Why you should be wary of large lawsuits
Finding a good lawyer
How the case proceeds
How the case may end
Trial

WHY YOU SHOULD BE WARY OF LARGE LAWSUITS. If your problem is more complex, then suit will need to be filed in your local superior, district, or county court. Such courts are where disputes over large amounts of money are resolved. A superior court case is needed when, for example, a child was seriously injured due to a landlord's alleged negligence, or a tenant allegedly suffered discrimination.

A lot of consideration is needed before bringing such a suit. Unlike small claims cases, superior court cases are very lengthy, very time-consuming, and very expensive. So, before threatening a landlord or tenant with a big, fat lawsuit, you had better understand that these sorts of lawsuits are clumsy and lengthy, and emotionally and financially draining.

When you sue someone in a district court, it is called litigating a case. **Litigation** is war. In fact, in most law firms, the place where the lawyers keep exhibits, motions, and evidence, and where they prepare for trial, is called the "war room." What does that mean? It means you should expect that your opponent will do whatever is necessary to win—spend money, hire experts, locate evidence, and so on. You can rest assured that the other side will be just as willing as you are to say and do almost anything in order to win. Again, this is war.

Tenants especially need to be careful before they give an attorney a large **retainer** since, in most cases, landlords have more money than they do. As such, a landlord is normally better able to pursue or defend a case aggressively, and may eventually wear down the tenant to the point where the tenant simply can no longer financially afford to continue the suit. In most cases, the only time a tenant is on a level playing field is when he has an attorney who is doing the case on a **contingency** basis (see below).

Now, it is true that 95 percent of all cases settle. That does not mean, however, that 95 percent of all cases settle in the plaintiff's favor. Defendants countersue, and sometimes the settlement is in their favor. Sometimes the plaintiff simply quits; that too is a form of settlement. It is only when the defendant clearly harmed the plaintiff, *and* it can be proven, *and* the plaintiff can afford to go to trial, that a settlement will probably occur in the plaintiff's favor.

But what if things are not so clear? In that case, the suit *will* go to trial. Trial too is an inherently dangerous proposition. The problem there is that judges, by nature and law, do not take sides. Their job is to be independent, fair, objective, intelligent, rational, and law-abiding. A judge may allow favorable evidence in, or she may not. While you may be positive that you will win, in the judge's mind your chances are at best fifty-fifty. The old legal axiom, learned the hard way by many a litigant, is *You never know what a judge or a jury will do*. Remember, one jury acquitted O. J. Simpson while another did not. You never know what a judge or jury will do.

Therefore, unless you are willing to commit fully the time and resources necessary to see the case to fruition, it is best simply to forget the suit, however difficult that may be.

So, now you heard the bad news, and, yes, there is some

good news. While litigation and trial are cumbersome under-takings, they are also worth it, *if you win*. Because if you win, you will likely win a substantial amount of money. And when you have been harmed, there is a lot of satisfaction in getting money from the one who harmed you. So, if you are prepared to take this arduous journey, read on.

FINDING A GOOD LAWYER. The first thing to do is to find a good attorney. The very best place to find one is from a satisfied customer. Word-of-mouth advertising will tell you far more about a lawyer than a dozen television commercials. If you know someone who has had success with a lawsuit recently, find out how she liked her attorney, how long the case took, whether the lawyer returned phone calls promptly, how much money she spent, and whether she was happy with the result.

Similarly, if you have a friend who is a lawyer, ask him, but do not hire him. There are more good lawyers than good friends around. If you do not know any attorneys, and don't know anyone who knows any, then finding one gets a bit more difficult. Try to stay away from any referral services aside from that sponsored by your local bar association. Other referral services, found in the phone book, usually have but one requirement of the attorneys they recommend—money. Any lawyer who pays the fee required by the referral service will probably be recommended by that service. The local bar association is an organization of local lawyers, grouped by practice area, who often have a referral service based upon expertise, not profit.

The final option is advertising. Almost all attorneys, good and bad alike, now advertise. If a Yellow Page or television ad catches your fancy and the lawyer practices in litigation, sched-ule an interview and go speak with him.

As indicated previously, if you are the potential plaintiff, it is best if you can find an attorney who will take the case on a contingency basis. Contingency means that the attorney will not ask for any money up front, but instead will take a per-centage of any settlement or judgment—33 to 40 percent is typical. The added advantage is that you will quickly find out if your case has any merit. Contingency lawyers carefully review the facts of the dispute as they cannot afford to take a case that is not likely to succeed.

The one big drawback to contingency agreements is that they normally only work when there has been a personal injury. Attorneys do not usually accept contingency cases for other types of disputes. If you are in the unfortunate position of having to defend a suit, no attorney will take your case on contingency.

> Stuart had a three-year lease with his landlord. Eight months into the lease, Stuart's company decided to send him to Tokyo for a year. Stuart subleased his apartment to Abby, but never told his landlord. After Stuart left, his landlord found out about the sublease and evicted Abby. When he returned, Stuart found a stranger living in his flat and all of his possessions, worth in excess of $20,000, missing. After speaking with three different attorneys, Stuart gave up on the idea of suing his landlord since none of the lawyers would take the case on contingency and he could not afford the $5,000 retainer each required.

HOW THE CASE PROCEEDS. A lawsuit begins when one side files a complaint against the other. Typically, the defendant has thirty days to file an answer.

The next phase of the suit is spent conducting **discovery**. Discovery is the formal process that allows both sides to discover information from the other. How much property does the landlord actually own? Has this tenant filed similar lawsuits in the past? Was he really hurt, or is he faking it? Does the landlord have a history of discriminating? That is discovery.

The filing of the complaint and the response and the discovery process can take as short as a few months or as long as a few years. It depends upon the attitudes of the parties, the complexity of the issues, and the amount of money involved.

As a general rule, the more money there is at stake, the longer the case will likely take.

HOW THE CASE MAY END. Any lawsuit can end in one of four ways: (1) the parties agree to a settlement; (2) the parties cannot agree on anything and the case goes to trial; (3) either the plaintiff or the court dismisses the case (the defendant cannot dismiss a case); or (4) the defendant fails to answer the complaint and loses by default.

Settlement and trial are the most common outcomes. If one side clearly has harmed the other, then a settlement is more likely. Because taking a case all the way to trial is such an expensive proposition, a party that is obviously in the wrong will usually want to settle the case to avoid that expense.

It is when the issues and facts are more complex and liability is less clear that a case will go all the way to trial. You can expect that your case will take one to three years before it ever gets there.

TRIAL. There are essentially four parts to a trial: opening statements, the plaintiff's case, the defendant's case, and closing arguments.

Notice that a trial begins with an opening *statement* but ends with a closing *argument*. They are quite different. Argumentative interpretation of what happened in your case is reserved for the conclusion. The beginning of the trial is a chance for the plaintiff's attorney to tell the judge or jury what she intends to prove during the trial. The attorney will likely give a brief overview of the case and explain her theory of why her client should win. The defendant's attorney will then do the same.

After each side has given its opening statement, the plaintiff will present her version of the facts. The lawyer will call witnesses intended to back up the theory of the case. If the issue is discrimination, the plaintiff's lawyer will call witnesses who will show that the landlord has a history of discriminatory practices.

The most important witness in your case will be you. After being called to the stand, your lawyer will ask you a series of questions. This is called direct examination. You and your attorney should have gone over these questions many times; you should not be caught off guard by a question your attorney asks. Answer the questions directly and honestly.

In cross-examination, the opposing lawyer will attempt to discredit you and your testimony. He will be very aggressive, even hostile. Expect incidents in your past to come up that may cast doubt on your integrity. Also, expect facts to come up that contradict your testimony. Do not expect to be treated with much respect.

There are two important factors that determine how a judge will rule in a case—law and facts. Laws are subject to much interpretation, and each lawyer will, throughout the course of the trial, argue as to why a certain legal interpretation should apply to a certain set of facts. The bulk of the trial will be taken up with what happened during the tenancy—the facts of the case. When contradictory facts are introduced, it is up to the jury (or, if you have no jury, the judge) to decide who is telling the truth and what the real facts are.

After the plaintiff presents her case, the defendant will get a chance to do the same. Witnesses giving a very different interpretation of what happened will be called. Facts about the plaintiff that are unflattering will come out.

After all witnesses have been called, closing arguments are made. Although the members of the jury may have made up their minds by this point, these arguments are important. It is a chance for the lawyers to put forth their best interpretation of the case, as proven with the evidence presented. After both sides have concluded their arguments, the judge or jury will rule on the case.

The Important Legal Concept to Remember: Ever risky, lawsuits are nevertheless one of the only retribution options society offers to harmed individuals. If you have been injured and are willing to commit the necessary resources to see your case through, then sue. Don't say you weren't warned, though.

APPENDICES

COMMON QUESTIONS AND ANSWERS

BEFORE YOU RENT

Can a form lease or rental agreement be changed?
Yes. A form contract is still a contract. And, like all contracts, it takes two to tango. It is not called an agreement for nothing. Although a form contract looks imposing, it is easy to change. Simply agree with the other side as to the changes needed, strike out the offensive language or clause, and have both sides initial the change. That's it.

Do I have a right to inspect the unit before I move in?
No, you have no "right," per se, to do so. However, you certainly have every reason to want to have a thorough walk-through before signing any agreement so that any flaws in the dwelling can be noted. If your potential landlord refuses to let you inspect the particular unit you will be renting, you do not want it anyway.

TENANT RIGHTS, DUTIES, AND SOLUTIONS

Can I change the unit after I move in?
It depends upon whether your lease or rental agreement forbids it. If it does, and you make changes anyway (paint, put up bookshelves, etc.), then you have breached the lease and can be evicted. If there is no clause preventing you from doing so, then you most certainly can make changes. Be aware, however, that you cannot decrease the value of the unit, and that if you make

fairly permanent changes, they will become the property of the landlord due to the doctrine of "fixtures."

Although my unit is rent-controlled, my landlord just raised my rent. What should I do?

Rent control is not the same as rent freezing—landlords can raise rent under the right circumstances. The first thing to do is to check the local rent-control ordinance or call the local rent-control board to see whether your landlord had a legal right to do what he did. If your landlord did raise your rent illegally, first try to work it out informally with him. If that fails, file a complaint with your rent-control board. If all else fails, hire a lawyer.

My landlord just told me that I cannot have my girlfriend spend the night anymore. Can he do that?

Probably not. It really depends upon how often she stays. Your landlord agreed to rent to you, not to you and her. If she has basically moved in, your landlord is right. If, however, she is there only a few nights a week, he is overstepping his ground. You have a right to be left alone in the quiet enjoyment of your own apartment. Your landlord cannot violate this right without also violating the law.

My landlord wants to sell the house I lease. He can't do that while I am still living there, can he?

Yes, he can. It is, after all, his property. This does not mean that you are without rights. First of all, your landlord will need to give you reasonable notice before he or his realtor shows the house to anyone (twenty-four hours is appropriate). Also, whoever buys the house will have to honor your lease. You can continue to live there until the lease term ends. You should also make sure that your landlord transfers your security deposit to the new owner. Get it in writing that he did so.

My roommate just moved out without paying rent this month. Who is responsible?
It all depends upon the lease or rental agreement. If both of your names are on the contract, then your ex-roommate is solely responsible to your landlord for her rent. If your name alone appears on the agreement, get ready for a rude awakening. You alone are responsible for the entire rent.

Can I sublease my apartment?
You can, unless your lease forbids it. Remember, though, that if you do, it is your name that is on the lease, not the new tenant's. If she fails to pay rent, you alone are liable to your landlord for rent. If you want out of this responsibility, you need to "assign" the contract to the new tenant. In that case, her name will go on the lease instead of yours, and all future liability will be hers alone.

My lease is about to expire. What happens if I don't move?
There are two possibilities. First, your landlord can accept rent from you, in which case you would have a new month-to-month agreement. Second, he can reject your offer of rent and evict you.

Do I need a lawyer to defend me in my eviction lawsuit?
It is almost always better to have a lawyer defend you in such situations. The real question is, can you afford one? If you think you are being evicted without justification and you want to stay in the unit, it may be worth your money to hire an attorney. If you know that your landlord has just cause to evict you, in which case he will likely win, don't waste your money.

LANDLORD RIGHTS, DUTIES, AND SOLUTIONS

Is there a limit as to what I can charge for rent?
Unless you are restricted by a local rent-control ordinance, the only limit is what the market will bear.

Can I pass on the responsibility to maintain and repair the premises to my tenant in the lease?
If your unit is a residential one, the answer is no; if it is commercial, you probably can. Remember that the warranty of habitability is implied. That means it is in every rental agreement, whether or not the agreement says so. In many states, it is illegal to try to transfer this duty to a residential tenant. In contrast, most states allow a commercial landlord to pass on this responsibility to a business tenant. The reason is that the law assumes (rightly or wrongly) that business leases are negotiated by equal parties, whereas residential landlords are usually considered to have the upper hand.

Can I increase the amount of the security deposit after the tenant has lived in the unit for some time?
Once again, it depends upon the type of agreement you have. Month-to-month tenancies can be altered on thirty days' notice. Since security deposits are a function of rent, they can be increased, but only if rent has been increased, and only if proper notice has been given. If your tenant has a lease, the security deposit can be increased only after the lease is up, *and if* you decide to renew it and charge more rent.

Can I get in trouble if I continue to use a lease form that I know contains several illegal provisions?
If the contract contains too many questionable or illegal provisions, a court may decide to void the entire agreement. In especially egregious situations, aggressive state's attorneys have been known to prosecute landlords who blatantly break the law. It is probably altogether wiser just to get a new form.

Do I have a right to object to the roommate my tenant wants to bring in?
What does the lease or rental agreement say? If the agreement limits the number of tenants or otherwise requires your permission, then, yes, he does need your permission. The impor-

tant thing as far as you are concerned is whether this person would make a good tenant. Interview and investigate him just as you would any new tenant, but do not unreasonably withhold your approval. If you do agree to let him in, be sure to add his name to the present agreement and have him sign it.

Am I liable for the acts of my apartment manager?
You most certainly are. Your manager is your "agent." As your agent, most illegal acts that she performs will be attributable to you as long as she was acting within "the course and scope" of her assigned duties. This means that you could be financially responsible for such things as acts of negligence that cause injury, acts of discrimination, or theft. Because of this, it is imperative that you hire highly qualified help.

My tenant refuses to pay his utility bills and I am forced to pay them. Can't I have them turned off?
Shutting off utilities or causing them to be shut off is usually an illegal form of "self-help." If, however, your agreement with your tenant requires your tenant to pay these bills and he does not, there is certainly nothing illegal about allowing them to be shut off.

TERMINATING THE TENANCY

My landlord wants to deduct the cost of new paint from my security deposit. Can he do that?
Probably not. If the paint is simply old, that constitutes normal wear and tear and is your landlord's responsibility, not yours. On the other hand, if you painted a room purple, then that is not normal wear and tear and you will have to bear the cost.

After the fact I, read my lease, and it says that my security deposit is nonrefundable. Is that legal?
No. Security deposits are just that—deposits. If you comply

with all the terms of the agreement and leave the place in good condition, you should get most, if not all, of your money back. If you do not, take your landlord to small claims court.

I just signed a lease with a new tenant and my old tenant refuses to leave! What can I do?
First, you must evict the old tenant. That means hiring an eviction attorney or service and paying the necessary fees and costs. You also face potential liability with the new tenant since you are required to deliver possession of the rental unit to him on time. In order to avoid this problem in the future, insert a clause into your standard lease that states something like "Occupancy is expressly contingent upon the present tenant vacating the unit." That way, if this happens again, the new tenant cannot sue you.

LAWSUITS

My tenant is suing me in superior court. I know I did nothing wrong. Do I have to defend the suit?
You really have no choice but to defend the suit. If you do not, your tenant will win by default. So, the very first thing you must do is to hire competent legal counsel. Having to defend a lawsuit when you feel you are without blame is a terrible thing since it is very expensive, emotionally draining, and quite time-consuming. But you have no choice.

GLOSSARY

Abandonment: The unilateral voluntary surrender or relinquishment of property. If both sides agree to the vacancy, it is called a surrender. If the tenant acts unilaterally, it is called an abandonment.

Answer: A written response to a lawsuit whereby the defendant denies the assertions made in the complaint. It also sets forth the grounds of the defense.

Assignment: A transfer of an agreement that permits a new party to assume completely the rights and responsibilities of the original party.

Bar Association: An association of lawyers found on local, state, and national levels.

Breach: The breaking or violating of a law, right, obligation, duty, or contract.

Burden of Proof: The duty to prove a fact in dispute. For example, in a criminal case, the burden of proof is on the government to prove guilt beyond a reasonable doubt.

Complaint: The papers that initiate a lawsuit. A complaint sets forth the parties, the jurisdiction of the court, and the grounds upon which the suit is based, and requests that the court solve the problem by granting relief.

Comprehensive General Liability Insurance: A type of insurance that covers the cost of defense as well as any damages the insured may have to pay as a result of a lawsuit.

Constructive Eviction: Any disturbance by the landlord of the tenant's possession of the rental whereby the premises are rendered unfit or unsuitable for occupancy. This allows the tenant to surrender the unit without repercussion.

Contingency Contract: A fee arrangement in which the attorney is paid only from the proceeds of a successful lawsuit. Typically, a contingency fee is anywhere from 33 to 40 percent of any money received.

Continuance: The postponement of a hearing or trial to a subsequent day or time.

Contract: An agreement between two or more parties based upon an offer, acceptance of that offer, and an exchange of money, goods, or services. A contract creates an obligation by both parties to do or not do a certain thing.

Damages: Financial compensation awarded to a person who was injured by another.

Default: Failure to answer. When a party who is being sued fails to respond to the complaint, he is in default. A party who defaults may lose the case.

Defendant: The party who is sued.

Demurrer: A motion filed by a defendant that states that the complaint against him is legally lacking.

Deposit: The delivery of money that is entrusted to another. The person receiving the money is legally bound to keep it, preserve it, and return it, unless there is legal justification to retain it.

Discovery: The pretrial process of discovering what the other party knows about the facts of the case.

Discrimination: Unfair treatment or the denial of normal privileges based upon race, creed, color, age, sex, physical ability, nationality, or religion.

Duty: A legal obligation to conform to a particular standard of conduct. Landlords usually have a duty to behave as a reasonable person would under the same or similar circumstances.

Eviction: The legal process a landlord must go through to deprive a tenant possession of the landlord's property.

Evidence: The use of witnesses, documents, records, or exhibits to prove a fact at trial.

Fee: A fixed charge for a service rendered. As opposed to a deposit, a fee is nonrefundable.

Fixed-term Agreement: A contract that gives a tenant exclusive possession of the landlord's property for a set amount of time, usually a year or more. Also known as a lease.

Fixture: Personal property that has been attached to real estate in a permanent manner so that it loses its status as personal property and becomes part of the real estate. Fixtures cannot be removed when a tenant moves.

Forcible Entry and Detainer: An expedited legal process for returning possession of land to the owner. Another term for an eviction proceeding.

Good Cause: A reason based upon substance.

Habitable: Suitable for living. It is a unit that is free of serious defects that would adversely affect health or safety.

Hold-over Tenant: A tenant who retains possession of a rental unit after the lease or month-to-month agreement has been terminated.

Implied Covenant of Quiet Enjoyment: A promise implied in every residential rental agreement that a tenant has a right to use and enjoy the property without interference.

Implied Warranty of Habitability: A promise implied in every residential rental agreement that a landlord has a duty to keep the unit in livable condition.

Judgment: The official and final decision of a court.

Jurisdiction: The geographical location of a court. A jurisdiction could be a city or a state. It also sometimes refers to the power and authority of a court to decide certain cases.

Landlord: The owner of real estate who rents property to another.

Last Month's Rent: When a tenant moves into a rental unit, it is money paid that must be applied to rent for the last month the tenant is to live in the unit.

Lease: A contract that gives a tenant exclusive possession of the landlord's property for a set amount of time, usually a year or more. Also known as a fixed-term agreement.

Liability: Penalty for failure to act in a manner as prescribed by law.

Litigation: The adversarial legal process whereby one party sues another to right an alleged wrong.

Lockout: The act by a landlord whereby the tenant is immediately put out of possession of the unit, usually accomplished by changing the locks in the tenant's absence. Lockouts are illegal.

Mitigation of Damages: The duty of an injured party to exercise reasonable diligence to minimize his damage. In landlord-tenant law, it is the requirement put upon a landlord to re-let his unit as soon as it is feasible to do so after a tenant has illegally moved out.

Month-to-Month Agreement: A rental arrangement that can continue indefinitely but can be terminated or otherwise changed on thirty days' notice.

Motion: A request made before a court that asks the court to rule on a matter in a certain way.

Motion to Quash: A motion that seeks to throw out a lawsuit because the defendant was improperly served.

Negligence: The failure to do something that a reasonable person would have done, or taking an action that a reasonable person would not have taken.

Notice: Informing someone of a necessary fact. Depending upon the circumstances, a person can be said to have notice if he actually knows of the fact or should know of it.

Notice to Pay Rent or Quit: A written notice given by a landlord to his tenant that states that the landlord intends to repossess the property if rent is not paid in full in a specific number of days.

Notice to Perform Covenant or Quit: A written notice given by a landlord to his tenant that states that the landlord intends to repossess the property if the tenant fails to take certain actions in a specific number of days.

Nuisance: The unreasonable, unwarranted, or unlawful use by a person of his property that interferes with another's use and enjoyment of his property.

Paralegal: A person who has some knowledge of the law, but is not a lawyer and cannot give legal advice.

Party/Parties: The people involved in a lawsuit. Each person or entity is a party to the suit; collectively, all plaintiffs and defendants are the parties.

Plaintiff: The person who initiates a lawsuit by filing the complaint.

Privacy: The right to be let alone.

Quiet Enjoyment: The right to use and enjoy property in peace and without disturbance.

Remedies: Options that the law offers to redress a wrong.

Rent: Money paid (or sometimes services rendered) for use and occupation of property.

Rent Abatement: Rent withholding. A remedy option for tenants whereby they withhold all or part of their rent in response to a violation of the law by their landlord.

Rental Agreement: An agreement between a landlord and a tenant that sets forth the terms of the tenancy. Most rental agreements create a month-to-month tenancy.

Rent Control: Laws enacted on a city-by-city basis that dictate the amount of rent landlords can charge tenants.

Rent Strike: An organized undertaking by tenants in which rent is withheld until grievances between the landlord and tenants are resolved.

Repair and Deduct: A legal remedy that permits a tenant to deduct a portion of her rent to pay for repairs that the landlord has refused to make.

Retainer: Money paid to an attorney that creates an attorney-client relationship.

Retaliatory Rent Increase: An illegal rent increase imposed by a landlord because a tenant utilized a legal remedy that the landlord did not like.

Security Deposit: Money deposited by the tenant with the landlord to ensure performance by the tenant of the terms of the agreement. It is refundable unless the tenant fails to pay rent, harms the premises, or otherwise violates the terms of the agreement.

Self-help: Taking the law into one's own hands without following legal procedure.

Serve/Service: The delivery of a legal document upon a party.

Small Claims Court: A special court that provides informal, quick, and inexpensive resolution of small matters. The limit is usually under $5,000, although it varies from state to state.

Sublease: An agreement between an old tenant and a new tenant whereby the new tenant agrees to move into the unit and pay the rent. The old tenant remains liable should the new tenant fail to live up to the rental agreement with the landlord.

Sue: To commence a legal proceeding.

Summons: The legal instrument initiating a lawsuit. Delivered to the defendant with a complaint, it notifies the defendant of the suit.

Superior Court: The court where disagreements over substantial sums of money are resolved. Sometimes also known as municipal, county, or district court.

Surrender: The giving up of property before the term is over. If both sides agree to the vacancy, it is called a surrender. If the tenant acts unilaterally, it is called an abandonment.

Tenancy: The period of a tenant's possession of the property. It can be either for a fixed amount of time, usually a year or more, or for a shorter period, usually month-to-month.

Tenant: One who rents and pays for property.

Terminate: Legally ending a rental agreement.

Tort: A private or civil wrong or injury caused by another.

Trespass: The unlawful interference with another's property rights. A landlord can trespass on his own property if he has rented it to someone else.

Unconscionable: An agreement that is so one-sided as to oppress one of the parties. If found unconscionable, a court will throw out the objectionable clause or contract. Courts look to the relative sophistication of both parties when making this determination.

Unlawful Detainer: An expedited legal process for returning possession of land to the owner. Another term for an eviction proceeding.

Vacate and Sue: A remedy sometimes available to tenants that allows them to end a lease early, move out, and sue their landlord.

Void: Null; ineffectual; having no legal force or effect.

Waive/Waiver: Knowingly giving up some right.

Waste: Abusing, destroying, or allowing property to fall into disrepair.

Wear and Tear: Ordinary and reasonable use.

INDEX

determining deductions from, 101,
141
guidelines offered for, 100
notice required for, 100
timeliness and, 101
security deposits, 22, 56–61, 99, 140,
148
landlords' retention of, 56, 58–61
payable over time, 57
as refundable, 57, 59–61, 141–42
return of, 100–101, 141
as tenant's property, 56–57
transfer to new owner, 138
seizures, 89–90
self-help, 87, 89, 94, 141, 148
selling rented property, 138
"seniors only" housing, 11
serve/service, 39, 113, 148
settlements, 121, 129, 132
Simpson, O. J., trial of, 129
small claims courts, 46, 52, 60, 61, 64,
100, 122–27, 148
filing suit in, 124
presenting case in, 124–27
vs. superior courts, 123–24, 128
statements, opening, 132
strikes, rent, 51, 63, 65–66, 68–69, 148
subleases, 22, 106–7, 139, 148
original tenant's liability under, 106,
139
prohibition against, 25, 26
sue, 11, 148
vacate and, 149
see also lawsuits; litigation
summons, 113, 119, 148
superior courts, 51, 65, 128–33, 148
vs. small claims courts, 123–24, 128
surrender, 104–5, 149

taxes, 47
tenancy, 5, 149
tenants, 4, 149
bargaining power of, 17–18
hold-over, 97–98, 145
identification of, in lease, 21
inspection of premises by, 7–9

pet owners as, 10
rental history of, 9
tenants' associations, 64, 65–69
organizing, 66–68
tenants' duties and responsibilities, 7,
37, 47–55
to keep unit in good condition,
53–54
not to be a nuisance, 54–55
not to commit waste, 54
not to use the property for unintended purposes, 55
to pay rent, 73–75
of reasonable behavior, 53–55
tenants' rights, 5–6, 31–46, 63, 73
habitability, 35–41
possession, 31–34
privacy, 42–45
quiet enjoyment, 42–47
tenants' unions, *see* tenants' associations
terminate, 14, 16–17, 149
terms, 22
third party damage, 38
torts, 83, 149
trespass, 33, 149
trials, 113–14, 129–30, 132–33

unconscionable, 49, 149
unintended purposes, 55
unlawful detainers, 112, 149
use, limits on, 25–26
utilities, 22
utility shutoffs, 89–90, 141

vacate and sue, 40, 149
void, 149

waiver/waivers, 17, 24, 149
of tenant's rights, 23–25
waste, 54, 75, 149
wear and tear, 22, 26, 36, 53, 56, 59,
79, 101, 141, 144
witnesses, 132–33
expert, 129

zoning laws, 26

est hits playing in the background. Crochiere delivers enough humor and surprises to keep the reader eagerly turning pages and enough heart to make this one memorable and satisfying journey."

—Stephen McCauley, author of *My Ex-Life*

"With a charming cast of characters, as well as intrigue, adventure, and touching mother-daughter relationships, *Graceland* sparkles from start to finish."

—Sonya Lalli, author of *A Holly Jolly Diwali*

"I can't help falling in love with this hair-raising road trip to Graceland! I was hooked on page one of this bighearted laugh-out-loud debut. Secrets, unexpected turns, and a mother-daughter-grandmother trio show that sometimes the right way can't be found on any map."

—Rachel Barenbaum, author of *Atomic Anna*

"A fun, warmhearted story with fresh and original passengers, *Graceland* is a new spin on the family road trip, complete with a love-story mystery at its center. I loved it!"

—Laurie Petrou, author of *Stargazer*

"*Graceland* is an utterly enchanting update of the American road story. Combining classic madcap antics with an up-to-the-minute look at family dynamics and forgiveness, the novel is at once funny and probing, personal and political, full of both youthful verve and the wisdom that comes with age. Imagine getting to hear slim Elvis and fat Elvis crooning together in harmony—that's how fun it is to read this book!"

—Michael Lowenthal, author of *Charity Girl*

"If a book could be a Cadillac convertible taken out for a joyful spin by three generations of strong-minded women, *Graceland* is it. With twists and turns aplenty, this warmhearted comic novel will leave you believing that love really does conquer all."

—Holly Robinson, author of *Folly Cove*

GRACELAND

GRACELAND

A Novel

NANCY
CROCHIERE

AVON
An Imprint of HarperCollins*Publishers*

GRACELAND. Copyright © 2023 by Nancy Crochiere. All rights reserved. Printed in the United States of America. No part of this book may be used or reproduced in any manner whatsoever without written permission except in the case of brief quotations embodied in critical articles and reviews. For information, address HarperCollins Publishers, 195 Broadway, New York, NY 10007.

HarperCollins books may be purchased for educational, business, or sales promotional use. For information, please email the Special Markets Department at SPsales@harpercollins.com.

FIRST EDITION

Designed by Diahann Sturge

VW Beetle illustration © Angie Boutin

Library of Congress Cataloging-in-Publication
Data has been applied for.

ISBN 978-0-06-328843-0

23 24 25 26 27 LBC 5 4 3 2 1

For Paul—my copilot, my compass

We find after years of struggle that we do not take a trip; a trip takes us.
—JOHN STEINBECK

Truth is like the sun. You can shut it out for a while, but it ain't goin' away.
—ELVIS PRESLEY

GRACELAND

Boston, MA

Chapter 1

Hope

Two days before my mother and daughter disappeared, my mother did something entirely out of character. She asked for my help.

She took her time, of course. Say what you want about my mother, the woman won't be rushed. Even after I'd rinsed our lunch plates and tucked the leftover pad thai into her fridge, she refused to explain the message she'd left at my office saying she needed to see me urgently. It wasn't until I'd sunk deep into her overstuffed sofa, and she'd handed me a sloshing cup of tea, that I fully appreciated her genius. My only escape would be to sip my way out.

Finally, though, she seemed to be coming to the point. I could tell because she'd moved to the window.

My mother never plays a scene without using light and shadow to her advantage. If you Google old episodes of *The Light Within*, you'll notice how before delivering a key line, she lifts her chin and cocks her head toward the light. For years, my father and I debated whether her movement was instinctive or if she blocked it out in advance. Either way, whenever Olivia Grant is about to deliver a showstopping line, a window is invariably to her right.

And so, with her signature chin lift and head tilt, my mother shared what was so urgent.

"Before I die," she said, "I want to see Graceland again."

I didn't mean to snort. Never in my forty years had I made fun of my mother's obsession with Elvis—at least not to her face. She'd simply caught me off-balance, and I laughed to cover my panic. Graceland? *Graceland* for God's sake? Just the thought of Memphis made my stomach churn. Leave it to my mother to ask for the one thing I absolutely couldn't do.

"Which part do you find amusing, Hope?" she asked. "Graceland? Or my dying?"

"Mom," I said, determined to steer the conversation away from Memphis, "you're not dying."

She turned and, as if on cue, the green tube connected to her oxygen dispenser caught on the edge of the coffee table, yanking the cannula from her face. I had to give her points for that one. Effective use of props.

"We're *all* dying," she said, repositioning the prongs under each nostril. "I'm just doing it faster than the average seventy-nine-year-old." With the afternoon sun backlighting her profile, my mother was still stunning: snow-white hair pulled back into a chignon, nose long and thin, with a hint of distinctive crookedness. I started to protest, but she waved me off. "No, no, this isn't self-pity. I'm explaining why we need to do this Memphis trip soon. Right away, in fact."

I bent forward and gulped the tea, scalding my mouth. I

needed to end this conversation—quickly, decisively, for all time. My mother didn't realize what she was asking.

"I understand you *want* to see Graceland again, Mom," I said, substituting "want" for "need," the way I did with my daughter, Dylan, when she *needed* Lady Gaga tickets. "I just can't take you anytime soon. Work is out of control." This wasn't the real reason but had the advantage of being true. The entire marketing department at EduLearn was putting in crazy hours. I couldn't afford time off—not after I'd missed a key meeting two weeks ago when Dylan pulled that stunt at school. "Let's plan a trip for later this year," I said, not specifying where. "Maybe in the fall."

My mother clapped a hand to her forehead. "You're missing the point! It's getting harder for me to travel now that I'm tethered to this"—she wagged a finger at the tubing circling her face—"this . . . cannoli."

"Cannula." She knew the word. It was her idea of a joke.

"Whatever." She flung a hand into the air, as if playing to the folks in the mezzanine.

My mother had smoked three packs of Camels a day for most of her life, despite my father's pleas for her to quit. She'd known the risks. And yet when her new specialist at Mass General repeated that she needed the oxygen day and night, even in the shower, I'd watched her close her eyes as if betrayed. *Et tu, nicotine?*

She wandered to her mahogany end table and lifted the photo I knew well: the framed black and white of her with Elvis the night of his 1970 Los Angeles Forum concert. In it, the King's sweaty face is framed by enormous sideburns, and a silk scarf hangs in the V-neck of his jumpsuit. He has one arm around my mother, the young soap star, with her jet-black bouffant. My mother was thirty-three at the time and—as she will be quick to tell you—often mistaken for Sophia Loren. The photo was reprinted in hundreds of newspapers and magazines and appeared in *Life*'s "The Year in Pictures." One columnist even called it the pop-culture image of the decade, pairing the King of Rock 'N' Roll with the Empress of Evil, the nickname given to my mother's villainous character, Andromeda, on *The Light Within*. When I was little, and my mother still lived with my father and me in Memphis, she kept the picture locked in a glass cabinet and let me hold it if I sat quietly on the sofa.

My mother wiped a speck of dust from the glass and replaced the photo on the table. "I need your help with this, Hope." She draped the red scarf Elvis had given her over the top, letting it puddle around the base. I waited. My mother was a master of the dramatic pause. "I've never asked you for much."

Hard to argue with that. For decades, the two of us had lived on different coasts, keeping a continent tucked between us like a pillow between uneasy bed partners. Even this spring, when my mother's health had forced her to move from LA to Boston to be closer to Dylan and me, she'd barely consulted me before hiring a real estate agent, leasing an apartment, and shipping her few belongings. I'd picked up the phone one day astonished to learn she'd arrived.

Since then, I'd stood ready to help. Shopping, errands, doctors' appointments. Whatever she needed. But not this. Not Memphis. My mother had no idea why I'd fled from my hometown almost eighteen years ago, though that wasn't her fault. I'd never told her.

I picked at a loose thread in the sofa cover. My mother was a trained reader of faces, and mine hides nothing. Instead, I pointed to the green tubing that snaked around the floor and connected to her liquid oxygen concentrator, a machine resembling R2-D2. "Mom, how can you even consider flying again? You said it was a nightmare."

"Oh, I refuse to fly." Her tone said I should know better. "Besides, how would we get around Memphis? We'd have to rent a car. Too expensive." My mother could pinch a penny until it squeaked—lucky, given that her last lover had drained her bank account and fled to Argentina. "We'll have to drive," she concluded.

"Mom, you've got to be kidding. That would take, what, two days?"

"Dylan could help."

"Right," I laughed. She couldn't be serious. My daughter drove like she did everything—impulsively, angrily, full throttle. Since getting her license, Dylan had scored two traffic tickets and taken down half our neighbor's fence.

I was done discussing this. Lowering my teacup to the floor, I dug furiously in my purse. "I think that's my phone."

My mother huffed, "This trip is for you, too, Hope. You need to get back to Memphis."

"Sorry, Mom, gotta go," I lied, pretending to read the imaginary text while heaving myself out of the sofa. "My manager called a meeting." Grabbing my bag, I pecked my mother on the cheek and made a beeline for the door.

"We can discuss this more tomorrow," she said.

I halted, my hand on the doorknob. I needed to put this

subject to rest. "No, Mom, we can't. I'm happy to take you shopping, or to the MFA, or a Pops concert, but I simply can't do this Graceland . . . thing."

She was peering out the window again. "You have issues with Memphis."

Her words raised the hair on my scalp, but I kept my voice steady. "I have no idea what you're talking about."

"Really, Hope?" And there it was again. The dramatic pause. Flawless. "I think maybe you do."

OUTSIDE, THE JULY humidity was like breathing water. Another Uber wasn't in my budget, though, so I headed for the nearest T stop. By the time I'd reached Allston Street, sweat dripped down my back, and my pencil skirt clung to my legs. I plunged down the stairs, nearly missing a step as daylight turned to soothing darkness.

The train wasn't crowded, and I collapsed into a seat in a far corner of the car, flipping my phone's camera to selfie mode to use as a mirror. Just as I feared—my cheap mascara was fleeing down both cheeks, making me look like Alice Cooper's less attractive sister. Rummaging through my purse, I unearthed a rubber band and the remains of a granola bar but no tissues, so I spit on a CVS coupon and wiped under my eyes, then yanked my hair back into a ponytail. Not cover-of-*Vogue* material, but good enough for my office.

I ran through the excuses I could offer my new boss for my grossly extended lunch hour and settled on a doctor's appointment. That would work. If anything shut Gary up, it was the fear of too much medical information from a woman. Scrunching down, I rested my head on the hard vinyl seat, hoping the vibration of the train would clear my mind. Instead, I kept replaying my mother's words.

You have issues with Memphis.

Where had that come from? Was it possible she knew something?

I couldn't imagine how. When I'd hightailed it out of Tennessee nearly eighteen years ago, in the late fall of 1998, my mother hadn't questioned my lies about wanting to travel, trying someplace new. My father had died earlier that year, and Mom and I weren't speaking much anyway. I sent her a postcard after I landed in Boston. When I realized I was pregnant, though, I didn't tell her for five months, and I waited until Dylan was six weeks old before sending a newborn photo. Was it possible my distracted and self-absorbed mother had done the math? No, almost certainly not. And even if she had connected my pregnancy with Memphis, she couldn't know more than that. Not the truly shameful part.

Across the subway aisle, a toddler in a Red Sox shirt scrambled onto his mother's lap and kissed her nose. She blew raspberries on his cheek.

I longed to please my mother. Always had. In one of my earliest memories, I'm perhaps three or four, and Mom is bathing me, rubbing a warm, rough washcloth across my belly. I press my nose to the bottle of baby shampoo, breathe in the sweet scent. When I look up, though, she is staring right through me, her eyes dull and sunken. Even at that young age, I knew I didn't make my mother happy.

This past spring, when my mother moved to Boston, I fantasized that the two of us might enjoy a late-in-life bonding, a new détente. We'd share things normal moms and daughters did—confidences, long hugs, favorite Netflix shows. So far, nothing had changed.

The train barreled to a stop and a burly, bearded man plopped down next to the young mother and toddler. The woman took one look at his baseball cap, which loudly proclaimed his pick for president, and scooted herself and child to the other end of the bench. Tensions were running high in that early summer of 2016, made worse by the heat. Both political parties were gearing up for their national conventions. I refused to talk about the election, told people at the office I hated politics. That hadn't always been true. I'd been enamored for a brief time—if not of politics, at least of a politician. Aaron's warm voice, disarming grin, the intense way he held your eyes when he listened. Lately, anytime I turned on the TV, there he was: revving up crowds, providing commentary, dismissing rumors of his own ambition. I kept the TV off.

Since fleeing Memphis as a distraught twenty-two-year-old, I hadn't ventured farther south than Philadelphia. An overreaction? Probably. I'd agreed never to return to Memphis, not to split the country Civil War–fashion, taking the North and ceding Aaron the South. Somehow, though, this felt safer, cleaner. My world and his world, with the Mason-Dixon line between. I planned to keep it that way.

As I CLIMBED the steps from the T station, shading my eyes from the assault of sunlight, I heard quacking. I swiveled toward the Public Garden, but no, the duck noises were coming from my purse. Dylan had changed the alert for my text messages again. A few weeks earlier, she'd switched my ringtone to a car horn, scaring the crap out of me as I'd crossed Beacon Street.

I took refuge under the awning of the Heal Within yoga studio to read her message: "Why won't you take Olivia to Graceland?"

Had my mother even waited until I'd left the building before complaining to my daughter? I dialed Dylan's cell.

"Since when do you call your grandmother Olivia?" I asked.

"She said 'grandma' made her feel like an old fart."

"She is an old fart."

"Well at least *she* doesn't act like one."

A late bloomer in most respects, my daughter hadn't begun snipping at me in earnest until almost a year ago, around her sixteenth birthday. That's when it all started: the military clothes, the neon pink hair, and her kamikaze, take-no-prisoners activism. "Where are you?" I asked. In the background, I could hear loud voices and an odd clanging sound.

"My question first. Why won't you take Olivia to Graceland? She says it's urgent."

A motorcycle roared behind me, and I leaned my forehead against the yoga studio's window, shoving a finger in my ear. "Trust me, honey, there's nothing urgent in her desire to see Elvis's microwave . . ."

"Hold on," Dylan interrupted. "Someone's beeping in."

"Dylan!"

My forehead still pressed to the glass, I noticed two women behind the desk of the yoga studio staring at me. I stepped back and, for show, tried a deep, cleansing breath, but caught an updraft from the subway and gagged. I hurried off down the sidewalk, phone to my ear.

Why was my mother calling Dylan? For years, she and my daughter had ignored one another. My mother had visited us maybe four times since Dylan was born, and only then if she was traveling to New York for an audition. Dylan had grown up seeing her grandmother on Viagra commercials more often than in person.

After my mother's move to Boston, I'd begged Dylan to spend time with her grandmother. This past weekend, I'd finally wrestled my shame to the ground and bribed her. Dylan had pocketed the twenty, but as soon as we got to my mother's apartment, I wondered what in God's name I'd been thinking. My mother took one look at Dylan's hot-pink hair and quipped, "What's with the clown hair?" Her eyes trained on her grandmother's white updo, Dylan had shot back, "What's with the Q-tip?"

At some point that afternoon, though, the two of them bonded. I'd left them alone while I picked up our Indian takeout, and when I returned, neither of them even looked in my direction. I had the odd sense that the teams had realigned, and I hadn't been picked by either side.

Dylan's voice on my cell brought me back to the present. "Sorry," she said. "Where were we?"

"Can't recall," I lied, pressing the crosswalk button too many times. "I may have dialed you by mistake."

"Oh, yeah, Graceland. Olivia said this was, like, her dying request. She's not dying, is she?"

"Of course not. Your grandmother loves hyperbole."

"That fake lettuce?"

I made a mental note to get my daughter tutoring before the SAT. "Dylan, bottom line, a trip to Memphis isn't possible right now. I can't afford to take time off work."

"That's bullshit, Mom, and you know it."

I stopped abruptly. A cyclist swore and swerved around me. "I beg your pardon?"

"You were just talking about the two of us going to Cape Cod. Remember?"

Crap. She was right. I'd been longing for something Dylan and I could do together and floated the Cape idea. I missed the days when we'd lay our towels side by side at Nauset Beach, dig our toes into the hot sand, and brave the frigid, salty surf. At night, we'd order pizza and share a single fleece throw as we watched *The Princess Bride* for the hundredth time. When recently I'd suggested a week in Provincetown, though, Dylan had scrolled through her phone and said, "Whatever." After checking the price of Airbnb rentals, I'd let it go.

I'd reached my building and was scouring my bag for my security badge. "Memphis is different, Dylan. It's too far."

"What do you have against Memphis, anyway? You lived there half your life, but you won't even talk about it."

I stopped searching. "What?"

"If I ask you anything about Memphis, you make this face, like I asked about your last gynecologist appointment or something."

Did I? This was news to me. Through the phone I again heard yelling, and that same clanging sound. "What's that noise?" I asked, desperate to change the subject. "Why are people shouting?"

The pause was so long, I thought I'd lost her. Finally, Dylan gave a long exhale. "You won't like it."

"I already don't like it."

"We're protesting."

"Dylan, no!" I yanked my hair. It was a bad habit.

"Mom, we have no choice. This bakery in town won't make wedding cakes for gay couples."

She launched into an explanation that I could only half hear over the now-chanting protesters. Dylan and her Gender-Sexuality Alliance group had set up a table in front of the bakery to sell their own, rainbow-colored cupcakes. I had to admit it was creative, and I felt proud of Dylan for fighting for what she believed in. The problem was, she was in such deep shit already.

Last month, my daughter had been so enraged by a lacrosse player who was bullying her friend Emma and Emma's girl-friend on social media, Dylan slashed the tires on the passenger side of his Chevy Malibu. When the kid tried to gun it out of the school parking lot, he'd careened into a construction trailer holding half a million dollars' worth of windows for the school renovation project. Now Dylan had a suspension on her record, not to mention a court date.

When I reminded Dylan of that, she cut me off. "Mom! This protest is nonviolent. We'll be fine."

"Please," I begged, "just don't do anything foolish."

"I can't possibly!" she yelled. "I'm chained to a bike rack."

Inside the building, I slapped my security badge against the sensor and boarded the elevator, punching the seventh-floor button and collapsing against the back wall.

Dylan had always been headstrong, and I'd worried her teen-age years would be tough. What I hadn't expected was the anger. Her rage simmered nonstop, just below the surface. She had every right to be furious about the inequities and injustice of the world. What frightened me was how much anger she directed toward me. Nothing I said was right. Sometimes I'd try to talk to her, and she'd turn away. I wanted to ask what the problem was but didn't. I was scared she'd tell me. I was scared it *was* me.

And now, Dylan and my mother had formed this . . . club . . . behind my back. Honestly, I shouldn't have been surprised. The two of them were cut from the same genetic cloth—stubborn, outspoken, dramatic. This past weekend, as I'd returned to my mother's apartment with the takeout, "Blue Suede Shoes" was blasting on the stereo, and Dylan twisted on one heel and then the other. Seated in her wingback chair, my mother pumped both arms in the air.

"What are you doing?" I called out, grinning.

"Trying not to have a stick up my butt," my mother shouted back. That was my daughter's favorite criticism of me. Apparently, they'd been sharing.

When we were getting ready to leave and Dylan used the bathroom, I'd prodded my mother. "You and Dylan seem to have hit it off."

"She has good taste in music. She's coming around to Elvis."

"I'm surprised it took this long to discover your common interests." It was my backhanded way of saying "You've never paid the slightest attention to my daughter." My mother didn't miss the dig.

"I accept your criticism," she said, boxing up the leftover chicken vindaloo. "I'll admit I've been somewhat preoccupied with my career."

"Somewhat?" I fake coughed into my hand.

"Oh, for heaven's sake, Hope." She'd pivoted to face me, her eyes narrowed, a takeout carton in each hand. "Can't people change? Is there no redemption in your worldview?"

Her outburst made me want to suck back my words. "Of course, Mom." I gave her a quick hug, awkwardly working around the cartons. "Of course. I apologize."

Dylan emerged from the bathroom, and my mother hurried over to give her the remaining vegetable curry. I'd stayed in the kitchen, clinking forks and knives into their separate bins, listening to them make plans to see some new documentary.

I'd said nothing at the time, but what I'd longed to ask my mother was this: If you're looking for redemption, Mom, why not start with me?

THE ELEVATOR DOORS opened to EduLearn's glass entrance, and I crept past the gray cubicles of editorial to the marketing department. At one time, sneaking back late from lunch would have sent my colleagues' heads popping over their cubes like the critters in a giant Whac-a-Mole game, but this day, the only sign of life was the clicking of a lone keyboard and the scent of a microwave burrito. Half our department had been let go in April because of slumping sales. College students were no longer buying new textbooks. They rented them or bought them used.

My boss, Gary, a dead ringer for John Goodman before his weight loss, was hired after the layoffs. Gary came from sales and ended his emails with the words "You've gotta believe!" even if the subject was fixing the coffee maker. He adored extroverts, schmoozers, and people who shouted out ideas in meetings, and I was none of these things, so we'd gotten off to a rocky start. The day Dylan was arrested for vandalizing that boy's car, I'd left the office in a panic and missed an important meeting. Gary had, by all accounts, been apoplectic. I hadn't been able to bring myself to explain.

I no longer enjoyed my job but couldn't afford to lose it. I desperately needed to win Gary over. A few days earlier, he'd asked for ideas in combatting the used-book problem and I'd mulled it over, wondering if I could save my skin by taking the lead on this issue. Lunch with my mother had strengthened my resolve. How better to prove—if only to myself—that I was too busy for a goofy road trip?

I planned to march into Gary's office and wow him with my initiative, but I never even made it to my desk. My cell rang. The Stoneham police. I needed to come get my daughter.

ONCE DYLAN AND I were belted into my ancient Corolla, she slunk down in the passenger seat and made a big show of inserting her earbuds. Message received. We weren't going to talk about this.

The cop who'd released Dylan said she'd hurled a projectile at a police officer. Dylan explained the projectile was a cupcake, and it wasn't hurled, but tossed to the officer so he could try one. "Waste of perfectly good Funfetti," she grumbled.

I believed my daughter. Dylan didn't lie. It was a policy she'd adopted around the same time she became an activist and vegan. Like everything Dylan did, though, she took it to extremes. She brooked no exception for "kind" lies. When Emma had asked her opinion of a new haircut, Dylan told her it looked ridiculous, and that was that.

Now, as we drove home, a sliver of sunlight danced over Dylan's fluorescent pink hair, a sharp contrast to her gray hoodie, gray camo T-shirt, and black shorts. Occasionally, she scraped at the floor mat with the badass, shit-kicking boots she'd begged for last Christmas. A phase, I kept repeating to myself about the clothes. Only a phase.

As I pulled into our driveway and turned off the ignition, I considered the paint peeling around the windows of our tiny ranch and wondered if I could do the touch-up myself. I'd almost forgotten Dylan was in the car.

"Know what your problem is?" she said, removing her earbuds, her eyes fixed on the glove compartment.

"I'm sure you're about to tell me."

"You don't want me to take risks."

I hesitated, trying to guess where this was headed. "Not exactly. I'd like it, though, if you stopped to think before you act."

"You want me to be cautious."

"Y . . . e . . . s," I said, cautiously.

"Like you."

Dylan's gaze was direct, taunting.

She unbuckled her seatbelt. "Because what if I'm not like you? What if we're just really different people?"

"I'm sure we are, in many ways."

"No, I mean, what if I'm not like you at all? What if I'm like my father?"

I looked out my window, as if the answer might be found on our neighbor's picket fence.

Dylan threw open her car door and got out before leaning back in. "Guess I'll never know, will I?"

"No," I replied. "You won't."

IT WAS TWO days later when I got the phone call that my mother had gone missing. That Wednesday was a disaster from the get-go. Like the coffee that spilled across my desk while I stuffed Kleenex in its path, bad luck seeped into the cracks of my day and finally poured over the edge.

Since our lunch, my mother had phoned three times to talk about the Graceland trip, as if we were seriously discussing such a thing. I'd begun letting her calls go to voicemail. That morning, though, she tricked me by calling from a number I didn't recognize.

"Quick question," she said after I told her I was busy. "Are you truly, intractably opposed to Memphis?"

"Yes, Mom. Truly, madly, intractably."

She sighed. "As you wish."

I had no time to ponder this. As soon as I'd hung up, the history editor was motioning me into her cubicle. She confided that Gary had called my marketing plan "pedestrian" and been furious when he couldn't find me to talk about it. I frantically revised the document and approached Gary's office several times that afternoon. He was tied up with budget meetings and—from what I could glimpse through the narrow window—in a foul mood.

In between stalking Gary and obsessively revising my marketing plan, I tried to reach Dylan, who wasn't responding to my calls or texts. We'd had a little disagreement the night before on the subject of college (I for, she against). I knew I should give her space, but after hours of silence, I longed for something, even a curt text. Even one asking for money.

By the time I packed up to leave at five thirty, I was wound so tight my neck crackled like a bowl of Rice Krispies. I needed to unload on someone who understood the cast of characters—Gary, my mother, and Dylan. I went where I always did in times of need: to George.

As I PULLED into the parking lot for Robinson Repair, my cousin George poked his head around the raised hood of a Prius and waved. At six feet five, George Robinson was a gentle giant whose curly black hair and cherubic face made him seem a decade younger than his forty-eight years. He wiped his hands on his coveralls and ambled over, squatting to examine the worn treads on my Corolla. I rolled down the window.

"Hope, these tires are dangerous. They're balder than Bruce Willis." Despite his years in Boston, George had never lost his warm Memphis drawl.

"Two weeks?" I asked, sheepishly. I needed another paycheck.

"I'll do it this weekend. Pay me whenever."

"I don't deserve you, George."

"No." He shook his head, grinning. "No one does, really."

When I'd fled Memphis in the fall of 1998, I'd had no destination in mind, but somehow my car had steered itself to George. Eight years my senior, George had been my favorite cousin and an adored babysitter. He'd run the service department in my father's East Memphis Toyota dealership until he was twenty-five, when my uncle Vern had kicked him out of the house for reasons no one would explain to me. "Lifestyle differences" was all my devastated father would say. George had moved to Boston and started his own auto-repair business.

George had let me crash on his sofa until I could get back on my feet. After I decided to stay in Boston, he helped me rent a room near him, in a suburb called Stoneham. ("You don't pronounce the *h*, Hope. It's 'Stow-num.'") Over the years, George had become my closest friend. He doted on Dylan and rolled his eyes at my mother's eccentricities. We shared a love of old, escapist movies like *The Wizard of Oz* and *White Christmas*.

George opened my car door for me. "You look like you need a beverage."

"Or maybe a life overhaul. Do you rewire crazy mothers? Adjust teenagers?"

"You can't afford my rates for those things, darlin'. Let's start with a beer."

THE DIVE IS nobody's first choice of where to eat in Stoneham. Rectangular and gray, it looks like it was picked up by a Kansas tornado and dropped in small-town New England. The picnic-style tables are set with a tiny dish of popcorn, and much of it ends up on the floor, where the staff crunch it into submission rather than sweep it up. It's rarely crowded, though, and they serve a plate of sweet potato fries so good I want to lower my face into them and roll it from side to side.

George and I had our pick of tables on a Wednesday night. We ordered our favorite craft beers. And the fries, of course. Always the fries.

I told George about my mother's Graceland request.

"My goodness," he said, his mouth full of popcorn. "That woman loves Elvis more than Jesus." He reached over to swipe another bowl from a nearby table. "Will you take her?"

"Can't. My job's nutty right now." It wasn't the real reason, but even George didn't know everything about why I'd left Memphis. "What's annoying is she's framed it as some kind of dying request. I feel guilty."

"It's okay to say no, Hope. You're such a people pleaser."

"Yeah, well, pleasing my mother has never been my strong suit." The waitress brought our order and we clinked glasses. The cold beer running down my throat felt heavenly. "She seems to have bonded with her granddaughter, though. She even had Dylan lobbying for her."

"Then you may as well throw in the towel. If Dylan wants it, you know you'll cave."

"That's not fair. I said no to Dylan . . . once."

I reached down to grab my phone, which was buzzing softly in my purse, and scanned the unfamiliar caller ID. I almost didn't answer, then remembered how my mother had called earlier from that odd number.

"So, this is Gus? From Air Systems?" said a confused-sounding young man. "You're the emergency contact for Olivia Grant?"

I pressed a hand to my chest. "Yes, I'm her daughter."

"I haven't been able to deliver her oxygen tanks. We tried three times this afternoon. No one answers the door, and the phone is disconnected."

"Disconnected?"

"Like, those three beeps and a recording?"

I hung up and speed-dialed my mother. I pictured her on the floor, unable to reach her landline. I'd lobbied hard for her to get a cell, but she refused to spend the money. The phone rang once, then the tones. "The number you have dialed is not in service."

Nothing made sense—not the dead phone, not being away from her apartment all day. Her portable oxygen tanks lasted only a few hours. George asked if we should call the police.

I said I'd drive over first and groped for the check. George grasped my trembling hand.

"I'll drive," he said, tossing some bills on the table.

I didn't argue. I was too afraid of what I might find.

I'D NEVER USED my key before, and it wouldn't turn in the lock. I tried twisting it both ways, yanking the doorknob in and out while kicking the door and shouting that we were coming. By the time George managed the correct combination of pull, key twist, and hip check, I was hugging myself to stop shaking.

My mother wasn't there. I chased around her apartment, checking behind her bed and shower curtain, until George called me over. He unpeeled a Post-it from the kitchen counter and handed it to me.

Hope,

Sorry you chose to miss out on the fun. We'll call you when we get to Graceland.

Mom

I slid onto a stool, read it again, and dropped my head into my hands.

"Who's 'we'?" George asked, picking up the note. "Does she have a boyfriend?"

It was a fair question. In the years since my father died, my mother had rarely lacked for male companionship. At one time, she'd kept lovers in both LA and New York so she could flit to auditions on either coast without paying for a hotel. As far as I knew, though, that had all ended with Rafe, the Argentinian who'd taken her money.

"She hasn't mentioned any new love interests."

"I wonder how that would work." He'd opened my mother's refrigerator and scanned the shelves.

"What? Driving?"

"No, sex." He squinted at the expiration date on a tub of yogurt. "All that tubing."

I'd wandered over to my mother's landline and lifted it. "What the hell?" The phone was unplugged, the cord wrapped around the base. I circled the small apartment again, throwing open closets. Her oxygen concentrator was gone, of course. Her rolling suitcase. The red Elvis scarf and photo.

George called after me. "What about that little guy who hangs out in the solarium?"

"Weebles?" Weebles was a little garden gnome of a man, five feet tall with a large belly and baldpate. Someone had named him after those egg-shaped toys I remembered from my youth. "Definitely not Mom's type."

"I wasn't suggesting she was dating him. You said he knows everyone's business. Maybe he spoke with her."

We took the elevator to the first floor, where Weebles was tucked into a striped armchair, jabbering to the woman next to him, whose head drooped forward to her chest.

"Hi, Mr. . . ." I realized I didn't know his real name but barreled on. "I'm not sure if you remember me. I'm Olivia Grant's daughter."

"Yep, your mom introduced us." He tapped a liver spot on his head. "Still got it."

"My mother seems to have taken off . . ."

"Midmorning," he agreed. "I noticed they brought her oxygen concentrator."

"They?"

"She was with the pink girl."

My breathing stopped. "The . . . pink girl?"

"The one with that gorgeous pink hair." He looked confused. "I thought she belonged to you."

Fairfield, CT, to Harrisburg, PA

Chapter 2

Dylan

Fuck, it was hot. Gobs of sweat ran down my back. When I cracked open the driver's-side door, a tractor trailer thundered by, inches away. I could have reached out and touched the damn thing. It made the Bug shake like that rickety roller coaster at Canobie Lake Park.

So what was I supposed to do? I was trapped in the breakdown lane. Step out of the car and I'd be roadkill. Stay inside and I'd be boiled like a little pink shrimp.

In the rearview mirror I could see Olivia pace, her head thrown back, hands on her hips. Around the collar of her white blouse, the red Elvis scarf fluttered like an emergency flag. Mom had been right about one thing—my grandmother was a drama queen. She'd barely waited for the Bug to coast to a full stop before throwing open the door, yanking out her oxygen cart, and stomping off down the road. Olivia was pissed, all right. Big time.

"Not my fault," I sang into the mirror. "Not. My. Fault."

Sure, I'd been aware of that clicking noise the Bug made. I'd even asked the girl who'd sold me the car, Bree-Sarah. She insisted it was harmless, a random quirk of old VWs. And if you can't believe Bree-Sarah Navarette-Smith, who can you trust? That girl was in the honor society and student government, both! I don't know much about those clubs, but I'm pretty sure kids get kicked out for lying.

And in the end, what did it matter whose fault it was? We were fucked. Broken down in the middle of East Bum Nowhere. By the time we got the car fixed, Wednesday would be toast, and we hadn't even made it out of Connecticut. Olivia said we had to get to Memphis by Friday if I wanted to meet my father.

That word stopped me. I whispered it out loud. *Father.* I loved the breathiness of it, the way your tongue touched your top teeth and lingered. So much cleaner, less muddy than "mother."

All my friends had fathers, even the ones whose parents were divorced. They coached their kids' soccer teams, taught them to roll gnocchi, and whipped their butts at Catan. Every year on Father's Day, while other families grilled hot dogs and held cornhole tournaments, I stayed home, curled up under my comforter, and read *A Wrinkle in Time,* about a girl whose father is missing.

My parents were never even married. According to Mom, my father had already traipsed off to Alaska to live in a yurt by the time she discovered she was pregnant. They'd broken up and she had no way to contact him. Later, she'd learned through a friend that he'd died.

I believed what Mom told me, that my father was dead, but that didn't stop me from creating a fantasy world where he wasn't. I dreamed he'd knock on our door one day, out of the blue, bringing apologies and gifts. That rumor that he'd died? It had been a mistake, a misunderstanding. No one was to blame.

What an incredible idiot I was. It never occurred to me until recently that my mother wasn't mistaken. My mother was a liar.

In the rearview mirror, I watched Olivia bat away a cloud of road dust, then bend over, hacking.

Shit. Not good. What if Olivia freaked out? What if she called Mom to come pick us up? That couldn't happen. After the lies Mom had told me, I'd die before I got in a car with her. I didn't want to see my mother for a long time.

I slapped the steering wheel with both hands, let fly a string of f-bombs. I wasn't big on apologizing, but I'd suck it up, make nice with my grandmother. We simply had to keep moving. Somehow, we had to get to Memphis.

Checking the side mirror, I waited for a line of cars to whiz by, then launched myself out and ran around the back of the Bug to where Olivia was standing. She didn't turn around. I stood behind her, digging the toe of my camo-print sneaker into the gravel.

"What do we do now?" I asked.

Olivia threw up a hand. "Find us a towing company," she said. "Use the Google."

I didn't even make fun of her for calling it the Google. I figured it wasn't the best time.

It had been only Saturday—just four days earlier—when Olivia had leaned forward in her wingback chair and said, like she was asking about the weather or something, "So tell me what you know about your father."

I nearly spit out my gum. We didn't speak about my father in my house! If Mom had been there, she would've shut that question down in a hot minute. Mom wasn't there, though. Olivia had hustled her out the door to pick up some Indian takeout that she didn't even bother to order until Mom left.

"Why?" My face felt hot. My father was a secret obsession. I didn't discuss him with anyone.

"Just curious what your mother told you about the man," Olivia said.

I studied Olivia, still getting used to the cannula under her nose. I barely knew the woman, hadn't laid eyes on her since I was twelve. The year before, Olivia had threatened to spend Christmas with us but canceled last minute, worried the cold would "wreak havoc with her rosacea." After hanging up the phone, Mom had exhaled loudly. "Of course. Olivia first. Always."

What little I knew about Olivia came from watching clips from her soap opera on YouTube and that Christmas movie where she played the grandma who got run over by a reindeer. Oh, and those horrifying commercials about old men with erectile dysfunction. They were the worst. When my friends learned the lady playing the surprised-but-satisfied wife was my grandmother, they were brutal.

I stood and moved to the window to watch for my mother's car. "I don't know much about my dad," I admitted. "Whenever I ask about him, Mom answers in as few words as possible and rushes off with some lame excuse—she's left the iron on or needs to change the water in the goldfish bowl. So all I have are little scraps of information."

"Such as?"

"They didn't date long. After Mom broke up with him, he

moved to Alaska to protest some pipeline or other. He lived off the grid, in a yurt. No phone, no mailing address."

Olivia peered into the iced-tea glass, brows knit, as if searching for something she'd lost. I had to agree—the story didn't entirely track, especially the breakup part. If Mom had been the one to dump my father, she couldn't have been deeply in love. So why was it so hard to talk about the man? Why all the squirming, the hasty answers?

Olivia sipped her iced tea, offering nothing.

I shrugged. "And then he died."

Olivia coughed. "Did he, now!"

Geez, how could Olivia have missed that fact? Granted, Mom never spoke about the man, but still. "He was part of a protest. Tried to force his way on some Russian whaling ship. Mom didn't tell you?"

"She did not."

Was it possible Olivia had that dementia thing? I chose my words carefully. "Maybe you . . . forgot."

"I do not forget," Olivia snapped. "Your mother is very stingy with information." She put down her glass. "If you're interested, though, perhaps I can find out more about your father."

I fought to keep my voice casual. "That'd be great."

"In exchange, I'd like a favor."

Olivia wanted to visit Elvis's home, Graceland, and thought I could convince Mom to take her. She showed me the famous photo of her and the King and offered to let me hold the red scarf he'd given her. After the concert, she said, the scarf had been dripping with Elvis's sweat, so I gripped it between thumb and forefinger, like it was a dead rodent. Luckily, I couldn't detect any lingering Eau de King.

I told Olivia I'd talk to Mom, but I knew it was useless. No way could I get her to drive to Memphis. Mom hardly ever took time off work, and as far as I could tell, she hated her hometown. But, whatever. I'd do my best. If it meant learning more about my father, even just a photo, I'd try anything.

OVER THE NEXT three days, Olivia called me seven times. For the most part, I didn't answer. I had nothing to report. Mom wouldn't budge.

By the eighth time, late Tuesday, I was in a horrible mood. The Pride bumper stickers I'd ordered had arrived a month late, and the damn things stuck like Gorilla Glue. I was trying to scrape one off Mom's kitchen counter when my cell rang. I kicked the box of stickers across the floor.

Enough. I'd suck it up and give Olivia the bad news.

Olivia, though, seemed unfazed. "No worries," she said. "It was a long shot. We'll simply move to Plan D." She waited, and when I didn't ask, added, "The Dylan Plan."

"Like the name," I said. "No clue what it means."

"We go ourselves. You and I."

"Wait. To Graceland?"

"That's what we're talking about, dear," Olivia said. "Do try to keep up."

I lowered myself onto a counter stool. I'd lost interest in Graceland after Googling it and discovering it didn't have a single roller coaster. But this idea was different. Taking my Bug on the open road? That would be bomb. "Sounds cool. When?"

"We need to leave tomorrow."

"*Tomorrow?*" I checked my phone. Almost five p.m.

"I know, unexpected. Something has come up. I can't explain now. I will once we're underway."

Apparently, Olivia doled out information like other grandmothers did hard candy, breaking it into little bits to make sure you didn't choke. I scrolled through my iPhone calendar to check my waitressing shifts for the weekend. Emma could probably cover them.

"Dylan?"

"Thinking!"

"It's your choice, of course," Olivia said. "Perhaps I've assumed too much."

"Well, a little heads-up wouldn't have hurt."

"Forgive me. I thought you'd *want* to meet your father."

I pulled the phone from my ear and frowned at it. "Olivia," I said, trying again, patiently. "We discussed this. My father is dead."

Olivia let out a long exhale. "I'm sorry to be the one to tell you this, Dylan. Your father is definitely not dead. Perhaps your mother had reasons for lying to you. I don't know . . ."

"So hold on. You think my father is alive? *Seriously?*"

"Yes. And in Memphis, but only for a few days. It's an amazing stroke of luck. The perfect convergence of plans. We need to go right away."

"I'm confused. I thought you wanted to see Graceland."

"Of course we'll go to Graceland! As I said, there are several reasons for the trip."

"But . . ." I waved my hand wildly, trying to get back to the part that interested me. "I don't understand. When did my father get back from Alaska?"

"He was never in Alaska."

I leaned both elbows on the counter. "How—"

Olivia cut me off. "It's a long drive to Tennessee, Dylan, and we'll have an abundance of time to chat. I'll tell you everything I know. But if we're going, I need to pack."

I pressed my fingers into my forehead, struggling to focus. "I don't think Mom knows this. If you're right, and my father is alive, I don't think she knows."

Olivia paused for so long, I wondered if she'd had a stroke. Finally she said, "Dylan, your mother knows everything about your father. What she doesn't want is for you to know."

I fiddled with one of the studs in my right ear, twisting it. At one time, I wouldn't have believed my mom would lie to me, but that had changed a year ago, the morning I'd asked about my father's name. I ran my finger along the line of studs, touching each one in turn. Only the first piercing hurts. You steel yourself for the rest.

"Okay," I whispered. "I'm in."

"Excellent. Meet me here at eight tomorrow morning. And pack light. July in Memphis will be hotter than Hades."

"Wait!" My mind was still reeling. "What am I going to tell Mom? Do you really think she'll let us go?"

"Well," Olivia said in a duh voice, "not if we *ask* her."

WHEN OLIVIA ANSWERED her apartment door the next morning, she was yelling at someone on the phone. She glared at her watch and then at me. Yes, I was like an hour late. Two, at most. As a peace offering, I'd bought Olivia a Dunkin' Donuts coffee in a reusable cup. She accepted it, then marched over to the sink and dumped it out. A little extra if you ask me.

Luckily, Olivia was even angrier with the person on the phone. Her oxygen company hadn't delivered her portable tanks, and she was ripping the guy a new one. She demanded they re-route the tanks to a hotel in Memphis and pushed the disconnect button hard, like the guy could hear that.

"Incompetents!" Olivia railed.

I blinked, suddenly aware of the obvious. "You have an iPhone!"

"I gave those airheads the new number. How many times did they plan to call a dead phone?"

Her old phone was on the counter, the cord wrapped around it. "You disconnected your landline already?"

"I'm only one person, Dylan. Why would I need two phones?"

Olivia's foul mood didn't improve even after I'd hauled all her bags and oxygen gear to the car. We'd barely turned out of the apartment parking lot before she complained, "Good Lord! Does your car always make that clicking noise?"

"Old VWs do that. Bree-Sarah said so."

"Then heaven knows, I'm reassured," Olivia said. "I mean, if *Bree-Sarah* says so."

I wasn't appreciating the sarcasm but kept my mouth shut. I didn't dare piss off Olivia if I wanted to hear about my father. When we stopped at the next light, I put on the Elvis songs I'd downloaded. "That's All Right (Mama)" played first, and the corners of Olivia's mouth curled up a bit. As with a cat, though, you weren't sure that meant she was happy.

Once we were outside Boston, I turned down the music and cleared my throat. "I never asked you about my father because you lived in LA. I didn't think you knew him."

Olivia lifted her travel mug of iced tea. "I didn't. Never met the man."

"So . . . Mom told you about him?"

"Oh good heavens, no. Hope doesn't share anything with me." Olivia shook the cup, rattling the ice cubes. "And certainly not with regard to your father. When she told me she was pregnant, Hope made it clear she wasn't going to say more." She took a sip from the mug. "I didn't press."

"Then . . ." I struggled to find the right question. "How do you know who he is?"

"I added two plus two."

"But which two? You just said you didn't know anything."

Olivia pulled down the sun visor. "I can't tell you everything right now, Dylan. You have to trust me."

A car behind us honked. I'd been drifting across the lane line and jerked the wheel back. Was it possible Olivia knew nothing about my father? Had she tricked me into coming on this trip because she needed a ride to Graceland? Olivia didn't drive, and Mom had often hinted that her main criterion for her LA boyfriends was that they own a car.

I tried a different angle. "Why would Mom tell me my father was dead?"

Olivia freshened her lipstick in the visor mirror. "Clearly she didn't want you trying to find him." She twisted her face side to side, satisfied. "I keep meaning to ask. Did Hope ever tell you his name?"

My mother had, and this was a sore spot, because her story had changed. The original was the one I believed. "I only know his first name. When I was five or six, she told me it was Aaron." I'd had a kindergarten friend named Erin and thought it weird that my father had a girl's name. I glanced sideways at Olivia. "Is that right?"

Olivia dropped the lipstick in her bag and said nothing.

"No offense, but you're not acting any different from Mom. You're not telling me anything."

"What I'm doing is very different, Dylan. First, I'm not lying to you. Second, I'm taking you to meet him. If I can't say more right now, it's for the best."

"But . . ."

"No 'but.' Just twenty hours ahead of us or one going back. You choose."

I closed my mouth. The *click, click, click* sounded louder. I turned up Elvis.

At a rest area, we grabbed lunch, and I offered Olivia iPhone lessons. When I showed her how to dictate text messages, Olivia clapped a hand to her mouth in amazement. After that, we got hysterical with Snapchat filters: my face with a Dalmatian nose, Olivia's with flames coming out of her mouth.

As we drove, I sang along to "Hound Dog," trying out an Elvis impersonation. Olivia laughed so hard, she wiped away tears. Then we sang together, Olivia correcting me on the lyrics, until I knew all the words to "Don't Be Cruel" and "Shake, Rattle, and Roll."

The clicking noise, though, was getting louder, and after Hartford, I felt the car vibrating. Neither of us mentioned it, but I sensed Olivia felt it, too. Then, after a sign for Darien, the car began shaking like Mom's old washing machine. Olivia shouted to take the next exit, but I'd seen a sign for Dunkin' and thought another two miles wouldn't matter.

Okay, so not my best decision.

Chapter 3

Olivia

A dust storm. Now that's what every person suffering from emphysema lives for! I turned away, covering my face with the Elvis scarf as a convoy of eighteen-wheelers thundered past, pelting my legs with tiny stones and leaving my mouth tasting of dirt. I surveyed the heavens for help. Not a single cloud in the sky—not one! Normally, I adore sunshine, but that afternoon, if the dust didn't kill me, sunstroke surely would. How had the girl managed to break down in the only unshaded stretch of road for fifty miles?

Dylan was keeping a safe distance from me, probably afraid I might throttle her. She leaned back against that absurd tin can of a car, poking at her phone, trying to find us a tow company. If she succeeded, it would be a bloody miracle. The first thing she hadn't screwed up all day.

The girl hadn't been my first choice for the trip. It was Hope who needed to return to Memphis, to face her demons there. But, whatever. Dylan could drive—more or less. And once the girl came, Hope would surely follow. With Dylan on board, I could lure Hope back to Memphis.

Unfortunate that everything had to happen so quickly. I'd just learned the day before that the politician was in Memphis for the weekend. With the campaign in full swing, who knew when he'd be back? I couldn't wait another month. I might not be able to climb stairs. No, the timing was critical for both goals—the one for Hope, and also my own plan for Graceland.

The traffic momentarily quiet, I tilted my face to the sun. My Graceland plan was a bold and brilliant scheme if I did say so myself. I'd conceived it several months earlier on that most horrible of days, the Afternoon of the Screaming Boy.

No DENYING IT, my final months in LA were a nightmare. I was dragged to the ER several times, barely able to breathe, once calling an ambulance at two a.m. and then collapsing on my condo's brick walkway. I refused to go on the damned oxygen. Fought the doctors tooth and nail. In the end, though, what choice did I have? My own body had turned traitor.

When that UCLA pulmonologist strapped the infernal tube around my face, I had to tamp down icy stabs of panic. The minute I got home, I phoned my agent. I needed Sylvia to tell me everything would be okay.

"Holy fuck" is what Sylvia said.

Well, that's LA for you. Kick you when you're down. And Sylvia, of all people! I *made* that woman. After I won my second Daytime Emmy, Sylvia hadn't lifted a finger. The offers poured in: commercials, voice-overs, Hallmark Christmas movies.

Once, when I joked about retiring, Sylvia pitched a nutty. "Don't even think about it! You're my gravy train."

And now? When I needed a little boost? Sylvia acted like I had some kind of . . . disease.

My tubing caught on the chair, and I jerked it free. "Sylvia, I'm still the same actor. Surely you can find parts for a 'mature' woman who happens to use oxygen."

I heard the flick of Sylvia's lighter. God, how I could have used a cigarette. Going forward, I couldn't light a candle without risking spontaneous combustion.

"Livvy," Sylvia said after a long exhale. "I don't know, babe." I waited. Sylvia wasn't a woman who lacked for words—though admittedly a fair number were curses. "Do you have to wear that thing all the time? I mean, you know, the part on your face?"

"Only if I want to breathe."

"Shit."

I pictured Sylvia rubbing her eyes, removing the rose-colored Anna-Karin Karlssons that my career had paid for. "Book me a medical show," I said. "What could be more convenient? I come with my own props. Or a crime series, like *Law & Order*. The witness is always an older woman, a shut-in with twenty cats."

"Livvy, you know this business . . ."

"Sylvia, you've said it a hundred times: the TV-viewing population is aging. People want characters who look like them. Think *The Golden Girls*. Think Kirk Douglas, in that movie after his stroke. Think . . ."

"*Harold and Maude*."

"Yes!" At least Sylvia was paying attention, not doing her online shopping. "Sure, it'll be a bit of tokenism at first. The way the Black best friend or gay neighbor was thirty years ago.

But I promise you, Sylvia, it will happen. Oxygen will be the new Black!"

"I just don't want you to get your hopes up, Liv. What are you now, seventy?"

I was nearly seventy-nine, but even my agent didn't know that.

"I mean, it's something to consider. Maybe it's time."

It took three weeks and countless phone messages, but Sylvia booked me a tiny part in a Lifetime movie. The role was Dying Grandmother. All I had to do was lie there and look serene while the family gathered round. An insult for someone of my stature. A cakewalk.

And it would have been, if not for the Screaming Boy.

All the little non-SAG brat had to do was kiss his bedridden grandma on the cheek. Instead, he screamed like I was Freddy Krueger. Perhaps the cannula frightened him. Perhaps his real grandmother was a pervert. Who knew? Regardless, in take after take, he let loose the same bone-chilling shrieks.

I couldn't tolerate screaming children. It stemmed from an incident long ago I didn't like to think about. The boy's shrieks felt like someone was scraping my nerves with a fork. Finally, I couldn't endure it any longer. Throwing off the blankets, I grabbed my portable oxygen tank and told the director I was done.

He had a complete hissy fit, of course. The scene was a one-day shoot. If I left him hanging, my reputation would be toast.

It didn't matter. I had no choice.

BACK AT MY apartment after the Screaming Boy fiasco, the top of my head felt like it was being pried off with a can opener.

I put Elvis on the stereo. The ballads. I didn't bother removing my makeup. After scouring the freezer for an ice pack, I
grabbed what I could find—a Lean Cuisine—and pressed it to
my hairline. I lay on the sofa, a glass of Scotch at my side.

I understood what this meant. My career was over. The
fabulous career that had rescued me—first as a young woman
fleeing from her mother, and then, later, as a young mother
fleeing from herself. Sylvia was already ignoring my calls. Soon
my friends in the business would follow suit. I'd watched it
happen countless times—that quiet slide into obscurity. Even
been party to it. For years, my former costar Rose had sent me
holiday cards with a pathetic scrawled note: "If you hear of any
parts . . ." I never replied.

My time had come. Best to admit it. I refused to end up like
those crumbling, Botoxed, has-beens who shuffled across the
Emmy Awards stage on someone's arm, smacking their lips,
mangling their teleprompter lines. That's not how I'd go. I'd
lived a great life and owed my fans a great ending. Robin Wil-
liams had it right: take your leave while people will still miss you.

It wouldn't be easy. Nothing worth doing was. But I'd go
out on my own terms, thank you. Not pushed around the
grounds by some aide or hooked up to machines in a hospital.
Not like . . . I shuddered, repositioned the Lean Cuisine. No, I
wouldn't repeat my father's mistake.

I lay on the sofa a long time, staring at the famous photo
of Elvis and me, until a new idea began to take shape. A tad
absurd, but also brilliant, if I did say so myself. A plan worthy
of my body of work and the reach of my fame.

I would end my life at Graceland. I would die in Elvis's bed.
My final act would link me forever with the King. News-

papers around the country—perhaps the world—would reprint the iconic photo of us together. Never would there be another tour of Graceland without whispers of my name.

I glanced at my oxygen tank. The only question was how to pull it all off, given my challenges. I'd need help. And it had to be soon, while I could still navigate a few stairs.

Then the phone rang, and it was Hope.

Later, I couldn't even recall why my daughter had called. I hadn't truly listened to anything she'd said. I was focused on one thing: how to get Hope to take me to Memphis.

It would be an uphill battle, for sure. Hope had a long-standing grudge against her hometown. From what I could piece together, something had happened with that politician, the girl's father. Whether he'd broken Hope's heart, or she'd broken his, it hardly mattered. She needed to move on.

I drained my Scotch and poured myself another. The more I thought about it, the clearer it seemed: Hope needed my help. Hope had always been a hider, but in the years since she left Memphis, she'd drawn inward even further. Hanging onto that damn secret forced her to keep everyone at arm's length. Dylan. Me. Even other men. Hope hadn't managed to hold down a romantic relationship in eighteen years.

Well, I could help her move beyond that. I hadn't been a rock-star mother, but it's never too late to make amends. This trip to Memphis would be my gift to Hope.

And if, in the process, I got what I myself wanted—well, where was the harm in that?

THE GIRL JOGGED back toward me, her tank top soaked with sweat, her pink hair ablaze in the afternoon sun. That hair! At first I'd found it an eyesore, but I was getting used to it. Pink was Elvis's favorite color, after all.

The towing company she had on the line could help us, but not for an hour.

Should've known better. Never send an extra to do SAG work. I held out my hand and she passed me the cell.

"Yes, this is Olivia Grant, grandmother of this stranded and traumatized child. And your name is? Ron? As in Reagan?" Pause. "Oh yes, a hero of mine, too." I jerked a finger toward my mouth and Dylan snorted. "Ron, I'm wondering if you recognized my name, Olivia Grant? No? Well if you can't get a truck here in under fifteen minutes, the headline in tomorrow's newspaper will read: 'Legendary soap star dies as towing company ignores her desperate pleas.' It's ninety-eight degrees out here, Ron. I'm elderly, I'm on oxygen, and I have ten thousand followers on Facebook. Send a truck *now*." I squinted at the screen, poked the red button, and handed the phone back to Dylan.

"Does that work?" Dylan asked.

I shrugged. "Runs about sixty/forty. We'll see."

The tow truck arrived fifteen minutes later, driven by a pimply teenager who clearly had no idea what he was doing. As he struggled to hook up the car, a police cruiser glided into the breakdown lane.

"Shit!" Dylan yanked on my sleeve. "Do you think Mom put out an Amber Alert?"

"It's two thirty, Dylan. Your mother hasn't figured out whether she can sneak out for lunch yet, never mind what you're up to."

I was right, of course. The cop offered us a ride to the repair place, where we waited until the Bug arrived. By the time the grease-covered mechanic informed us we needed a new drive shaft, it was four thirty and the shop closed in half an hour. He could get to it tomorrow afternoon.

"We need it done now!" Dylan shouted, slapping her hands on the counter.

I gripped Dylan's arm and guided her to the door. Closed it after her. Then I did what Elvis had taught me to do. I took care of business.

When I emerged from the office with news the car would be ready by eight a.m., Dylan's mouth hung open.

"There are three ways to get what you want, Dylan. Charm. Threats. Cash. Always use them in that order."

Still, the cost of greasing that man's filthy palm hadn't been insubstantial. I refused Dylan's plea for a hotel with a hot tub and "one of those minibars." No, I'd been considering our options since we'd broken down. I had old show-business friends in Fairfield, a city we'd passed not twenty minutes earlier. I'd even considered meeting Rose and Rudy for lunch if we hadn't gotten such a late start. Rose and I had a complicated relationship, and I'd thought, more than once, how it might be nice to mend that fence on the way to Graceland.

Rudy answered my call and—just as I'd hoped—insisted on putting us up. He was out doing errands and could get us in a flash.

"Great," Dylan moaned as she maneuvered my oxygen concentrator out of the Bug. "Tell me again who these people are?" Subtext: Are they at least famous?

Rose, I explained, had been the original star of *The Light Within*. She'd played the blond, kindhearted Krista, while I, an unknown, had been cast as her scheming, dark-haired cousin. "The show really took off when they introduced Andromeda," I said. "Nothing like an evil character to boost ratings." I tossed the Elvis scarf over my hair, fastened it under my chin. "In the early seventies, I left the show to marry your grandfather, and without my character, the ratings tanked. *Light Within* was canceled. A decade later, though, they resurrected it, and this time, I got top billing." I paused, thinking of the girl's tendency to blurt. "But I wouldn't mention any of this in front of Rose."

"How come?"

An ancient station wagon pulled into the lot, and I lowered my sunglasses to wave. By the time *Light Within* was revived, I explained, Rose had become quite heavy, and the producers hired someone else to play Krista. "So there are a couple things Rose has never quite forgiven me for. One of them was leaving the show."

"And the other?"

I kept my gaze on the thin, gray-haired man who emerged from the car and ambled toward us. "Rose was the one who got us backstage to meet Elvis," I whispered. "And Elvis picked me."

Chapter 4

Hope

George and I left Weebles in the solarium and returned to my mother's apartment, where I paced from the kitchen to the living room and back. I paused at the window where my mother had stood two days earlier, insisting she needed to see Graceland again. The sun had set and all I could see in the glass was my reflection. I yanked the blinds closed.

George poked around again in the refrigerator, peering into a Thai takeout container that smelled strongly of garlic. That Monday lunch with my mother seemed a lifetime ago.

My calls to Dylan went to voicemail. My daughter never listened to phone messages and hated when I left them. I left two anyway. Finally, I gave in and texted her, convinced they couldn't still be driving. My mother would need to stop and switch to the oxygen concentrator so she wouldn't run out of portable tanks. My message to Dylan was short and to the point: "Please call ASAP."

"What if they're already in trouble?" I moaned to George. I

pictured my mother alone on some deserted road while Dylan trudged for miles to get help. "That car's a piece of crap."

Dylan had bought the bubblegum-pink 1998 VW Beetle three weeks earlier, from a senior at school, spending her entire waitressing savings, $750. The Bug was a steal, she insisted. Completely updated! Bree-Sarah had added cupholders *and* a USB port! All it needed was brakes.

"It doesn't have *brakes*?" I'd shouted, waving both arms. "What else is missing? Tires?"

"Just the extra one."

I'd called Bree-Sarah's mother to explain that a sixteen-year-old couldn't legally buy a car and demand Dylan's money back. She said I needed to talk to her husband and "good luck with that." In the end, I'd grudgingly let Dylan keep the Bug. George fixed the brakes at a massive family discount and insisted we bring it back for a thorough once-over when he was less busy. I should have made Dylan do that. I hadn't. I couldn't afford more repairs.

"I was an idiot to let her keep that car."

George studied his work boots. You can tell a lot about what George thinks by how thoroughly he examines his boots.

I wandered into my mother's bedroom and noticed a handful of pages in the recycle bin beside her desk. Everything was magenta. Her printer must have run out of black ink. I snatched them and flipped through the streaked pages. On top were MapQuest directions to Memphis. What knocked the air out of me, though, were the pages beneath it: an article from the Memphis newspaper, *The Commercial Appeal*. Right there, in the pink headline, his name. Aaron Breckenridge. Speaking this weekend in Memphis.

I lowered myself slowly into the chair.

How long had she known?

And more importantly, what had she told Dylan?

I gathered all the sheets, folded them in quarters, and shoved them into my pocket. It didn't matter. My path was clear.

George was still in the kitchen, his hand in a box of crackers. "Really hungry," he said.

"I'm going after them."

He choked a little. "Say that again?"

I framed it as a safety issue. "I can't let them do this. My daughter can barely drive, my mother can barely breathe."

"How are you gonna stop them, Hope? Drive twice as fast? Catch them on the highway?"

"Maybe," I said, though even I knew crazy when I heard it.

"Sweetie . . ." He circled the counter and rested a hand on my shoulder. "Weebles said they left midmorning. They could've stopped in Manhattan for a six-course dinner at the Plaza and still have an unbeatable head start. Why not fly? Meet them in Memphis."

I pretended to consider this idea. How could I explain to George that I had to find them *before* Memphis? That years ago, I'd signed an agreement saying, among other things, I would never set foot in Memphis again. "If something happens to them along the way, if they break down or my mother needs help, I could get to them faster."

George was squinting past me. "Hand me your phone." He punched in my passcode while muttering, "You need to stop using Dylan's birthday for everything." He swiped through several screens. "Remember when Dylan lost her phone at the Red Sox game, and afterward, I set up that phone-tracking app for you?"

"Vaguely?" My phone was a graveyard of apps I'd down-loaded with the best intentions.

"Well, if we know where her phone is . . ."

I closed my eyes, prayed. *Please God, let this work.*

"Same password for iCloud?" I hung my head. He typed it in, waited, then frowned. "Really?" he asked the phone, then showed it to me. "It says they're in Fairfield, Connecticut. That's only a couple hours from here."

I stared at the phone. "*Fairfield?* What did they do? Walk?"

"I'm zooming in." He flicked the screen. "They're definitely off the highway."

"My mother has friends in Fairfield, but she hasn't seen them in years." Was she so cheap she wouldn't spring for a hotel? Did she plan to crash with friends all the way to Tennessee?

"Well, assuming this is right, I take back what I said about flying. If we act fast, maybe we can catch them."

"We?"

He shrugged. "You can't do this alone, Hope. If you have to chase them all the way to Memphis, that's a lot of driving. Plus, your car is a sack of shit."

"I can't ask you to come." But my protest sounded weak, even to me.

"Come on, we're talking about Dylan," he said. George treated Dylan like she was his daughter. He'd coached her T-ball team and taken her to father-daughter dances. "Besides," George added, "it's been ages since I've been back to Memphis." I must have made a face, because he quickly added, "If we even have to go that far."

I gave him a hug. "If you're sure. I mean, as long as you're willing to drive as far as . . . necessary."

"Absolutely." But from the look in his eye, I could tell there was more. "You don't mind if it's Jordan who drives, right?"

"Of course not," I said. Almost immediately, though, I wondered if that was true.

I'd met Jordan almost eighteen years earlier, after crashing on George's sofa for a few weeks. Still struggling to put my life back together, I'd moved out of his place, begun renting a room from one of his customers, and purchased my first cell. Its buzzing woke me from a deep sleep.

George's voice sounded scratchy and oddly strained. "Hope, I'm in kind of a tough spot and wonder if you could do me a favor."

He'd been driving back from Boston and was pulled over for a missing license plate light. He'd had more than one drink, and the cop cited him for DUI. Could I come pick him up at the Stoneham police station?

On the drive over, I tried to make sense of his final comment: "I don't want to alarm you, but you may not recognize me." Had someone at the bar roughed him up? Had the police?

Once I'd identified myself at the station, I sat on a wooden bench and checked my phone. In my peripheral vision, I noticed a tall blond woman in a black skirt and mauve pumps come through the inner door. A hooker, I assumed, and poked at my messages, not wanting to stare. The woman walked over and stood directly in front of me until I looked up.

"I hope this isn't going to damage our friendship," she said with a soft, southern accent. Under a heavy layer of foundation and lipstick, the woman had George's face.

I took a minute to process this new information. Aware that

whatever I said would set a tone for our future relationship, I chose my words carefully.

"Only if you ask to borrow my sweaters."

I KNEW NOTHING about gender performance or fluidity back then, but on that drive home, Jordan referred to herself as a cross-dresser.

"Don't people these days prefer 'transgender'?"

"Cross-dressing is different from being trans. If I were trans, I'd actually be a woman, born in a man's body." Instead, she explained, the feminine side of her simply demanded an outlet. "Cross-dressing makes me feel whole."

Given the auto-repair business, Jordan said she was content to be George during the week and Jordan on weekends. People could refer to her according to how she presented—George or Jordan—and use "he" or "she" pronouns, respectively.

That was when I learned, too, about the reasons George had left Memphis. My uncle Vern, who'd started his only son tinkering with cars at six years old, had heard rumors about George's cross-dressing. They'd argued, and Uncle Vern ended up in the hospital with angina.

"It was actually my mom who suggested I put some distance between myself and Memphis for a bit," Jordan said. "I picked the Boston area because I knew a drag queen who'd moved there. And yes, Hope, that's a different identity, too."

OVER THE YEARS, because of our work-week schedules, I ended up spending most of my free time with Jordan. We went on walks, took in movies, and worked through the *New York Times* crossword puzzle together. Now, though, as I tried to imagine traveling through the Deep South with six-foot-five Jordan in her poufy wig, heavy makeup, and Italian pumps, my stomach tightened. Even in supposedly liberal Boston, a cross-dressing person brought out the nasty in some people.

"I'm hoping we find Mom and Dylan in Fairfield," I said as I wiped cracker crumbs from my mother's counter. "But if we have to chase them all the way to Tennessee, do you think folks will be okay with Jordan?"

"I'm a southerner, Hope. These are my people."

I raised an eyebrow.

"Yeah, some of them just don't know it yet." He grinned. "Not to worry, I'll be careful."

I wanted to hit the road as soon as possible, but George convinced me we should go home and get a few hours' sleep. He was right. It made no sense to arrive in Fairfield after midnight, when everyone would be asleep. He'd pick me up at four a.m.

We headed home. As we turned out of my mother's parking lot, George was still shaking his head. "I don't get why your mom would do this. What's her deal with Graceland, anyway? How many times does she need to see it?"

"She probably wants to commune with the King's spirit one last time," I said. "Who knows? The woman is a complete cipher. I've never been able to crack her code."

George patted my knee. "In fairness, sweetie, she didn't give you much chance."

He was right. My mother had abandoned my father and me when I was six, jetting off to resume her role in the rebooted *Light Within*, which had moved its filming from New York to LA in the late sixties. My father had always insisted the word "abandoned" was too harsh since Mom returned to Memphis most weekends and holidays, but it felt right to me. For the first year, whenever she packed to leave, I hid under the kitchen table and sobbed. The image of my mother with suitcase in hand weighed on me throughout my childhood, like a heavy wool coat reshaping its wire hanger.

"Your dad was such a sweetheart," George continued. "I was surprised he and your mom stayed married."

"Me, too, but he adored Mom. Tolerated her eccentricities."

"I remember how I'd show up at your house around supper time, and your dad would fix me a Swanson frozen dinner and I'd join the two of you watching *Odd Couple* reruns. He was such a sweet man."

"He was. He didn't deserve to be abandoned like that."

"You didn't deserve it either, Hope."

"Sure." I picked up my phone, checked again for messages. I wasn't going to argue with George, but I knew better. Deserve my mother's abandonment? Far worse than that. I'd caused it.

AFTER GEORGE DROPPED me at home, I wandered through the dark, silent house, searching for God knew what. A note, perhaps? Something that said my daughter had thought about me, had cared that I might worry? I found nothing. No scrawled envelope on the kitchen counter, no memo pad next to my computer, no Post-it stuck to the bathroom mirror.

Dylan and I had argued the night before. No worse than any of our fights, and I'd been more upset than she was. Or so I'd thought.

I'd come home from work to find her in my bedroom, rifling through laundry baskets of unfolded clothes, flinging T-shirts and shorts around the room.

"That's one way to get the laundry out of those baskets." I joked, jimmying off a pump. "I can show you other methods, whereby the clothes are arranged thematically, in piles." When she didn't respond, I added, "You'll need those skills at college."

She didn't lift her head. "Not doing college."

I stood lopsided on the one pump. Dylan had hinted at this before. Never a strong student, her grades over the past year had gone from mediocre to terrible, but she still had senior year to change that. "Dylan, college is important. You don't want to wait tables for the rest of your life."

She held up a camo T-shirt, tossed it in a pile. "I'm going to be an activist."

I kicked off the other shoe, sending it flying. It hit my dresser. "That's not a job."

"Okay, an activist *filmmaker*."

"Then you're better off waiting tables." I wasn't being fair but couldn't stop myself. "You'll make more money."

"That's what's important to you? Money?" Her voice was cold.

"I know what it's like to struggle, Dylan. It's no fun. You need a career, a job that's secure."

"Like yours?" She jerked a finger toward her open mouth.

"Is my job that bad?"

"You can't be serious. Working in little cattle stalls? Sucking up to your boss? Chanting, 'You gotta believe'?" Dylan gathered the pile of clothes she'd been collecting and headed toward the door. "You make fun of Olivia, but at least she's an actress, not a fake." She slammed the door behind her.

I lay down on my bed and closed my eyes. Dylan didn't mean it. She was trying to hurt me. Succeeding, in fact, but that was okay, because, honestly, she was right about my job. Gary and his slogans had sucked all the joy out of it. In recent months, I'd fantasized about finding a new job, doing marketing for a nonprofit like Heifer International or an AIDS foundation. I longed to be part of a team, working toward something I believed in. I'd felt that way once before, when I'd worked for Aaron back in Memphis. Unfortunately, after fifteen years at EduLearn, I worried that my skills wouldn't transfer, or I'd have to take a pay cut. Mostly, though, I worried about my resume. That, too, contained a lie.

I SAT AT my computer desk and opened Outlook. I'd email Gary, let him know I wouldn't be in the office tomorrow. He wouldn't like me disappearing again with little warning, but what choice did I have? Assuming we caught my mother and Dylan in Fairfield, I could work all weekend.

An email popped up from the iTunes account Dylan and I shared, confirming the charge to my Visa for downloading two dozen Elvis songs. Dylan must have chosen some music for the road. I scrolled through the list, pausing briefly at the first song: "That's All Right (Mama)." Somehow I couldn't read it as re-assurance.

In the two hours since I'd found the newspaper article about Aaron in my mother's trash, I'd calmed down a little. My mother might have printed that piece for any number of reasons. Over the next week, both presidential nominees would announce their choice for running mate, and Aaron was strongly favored for the Democratic VP spot. Given that I'd briefly worked for Aaron—which, apparently my mother remembered, though I'd never been sure—that would explain her interest.

I leaned back in the office chair, hands clasped behind my

head, and considered the worst possibility. Even if my mother suspected I'd been involved with Aaron and guessed he was Dylan's father, she wouldn't share her suspicions with my daughter. Not without telling me. This was my mother, for heaven's sake. The woman wasn't evil. She wasn't . . . Andromeda.

It was past eleven and I needed to shower and pack. Instead, I sat looking at my desktop. The background photo was Dylan and me at Nauset Beach, our hair blowing wildly, our arms wrapped around one another. Had that been two summers ago? Three? So much had changed.

I'd sworn I'd be a better mother to Dylan than mine had been to me. Was I? I felt ashamed to admit it, but when Dylan had turned down my offer of a Cape Cod vacation, I'd almost been relieved. Much as I longed to spend time with her, an entire week alone together made me nervous. In a tiny Airbnb, there'd be so little space, so much time for quibbling and probing. Dylan's oblique reference to her father a few days earlier had twisted my stomach like a dishrag. Thank God that for most of her life, Dylan hadn't been all that interested in the man. She'd asked only a handful of questions and seemed satisfied with my answers.

At midnight, when I crawled into bed, I checked my text messages. No response from Dylan. Not then, and not when I woke every half hour until 3:30 a.m.

Chapter 5

Dylan

I've always wondered if Olivia would have chosen to stay at Rose and Rudy's if she'd known about the ferret castle.

Even from the outside, you could tell their house was a mess. The wraparound wooden porch was sinking in one spot, and the screen door had this huge, gaping hole. Rudy held Olivia's arm as they climbed slowly up the steps. I followed, carrying her oxygen tank in its little cart. Despite his ridiculous man bun, Rudy seemed okay. Olivia said he'd danced in Broadway shows like *Hair* and *Grease*, but he was most famous for dancing on sofas in Furniture King commercials.

Rudy held open the screen door and hollered for Rose. A heavyset woman tottered down the hallway. Rose had huge doe eyes, like a Disney princess's, and her white hair was cut chin-length with bangs. "Livvy!" she called out. "So good to see you!" Her voice was all gravelly, like she used to smoke, too. She hugged Olivia then pulled back, gesturing to the tubing around Olivia's face. "What's all this?"

"Air," said Olivia with an exaggerated sigh. "Turns out we need it. Who knew?"

Rose pouted her bottom lip in sympathy, but her expression seemed a little smug. *I may have put on a few pounds*, it said, *but at least I'm breathing on my own.*

Rudy showed Olivia to the guest room and me to a small study with a pullout sofa "courtesy of Furniture King." The room smelled like cat pee, and in one corner, cardboard boxes and tubes were taped together, like kids had made a fort. When something furry slipped past one of the cut-out windows and slid down a tube, I shrieked.

"We'll put the ferrets in the basement," Rudy said, shaking the structure until another one emerged and ran across my feet. Rudy herded it from the room.

I kept my eye on the boxes, not sure if there were more furry things inside. When Rose returned carrying sheets and a pillow, she insisted I go look at the far wall, covered with publicity shots from *The Light Within.*

"That's me," she said, indicating a busty blonde, seated beside a guy in a tux. "And that's your grandma," she nodded toward the dark-haired woman with heavy mascara resting a hand seductively on the man's shoulder. "From Season Two. That's when Andromeda started getting all that attention."

I'd watched some clips of the soap on YouTube. The worst part was the tacky opening music and baritone narrator. "Even when darkness surrounds us, we still have *The Light Within.*" Yeesh.

Rose pointed to another photo. "And this was from Season Four, when Andromeda plotted to steal Krista's husband."

"Did she succeed?"

"Oh, you know soaps. They go back and forth for an entire season. But no, in the end, the bad girl never wins." She patted me on the shoulder. "Not in that world."

RUDY GRILLED SALMON for dinner. Rose lowered herself into a dining room chair, complaining about the heat and her swollen ankles. She opened a bottle of wine and offered glasses to everyone, including me. Olivia raised her eyebrows but didn't stop me from taking it.

The ferrets ran in and out and slithered between everyone's legs. They made my skin crawl. Rose scooped one onto her lap and talked to it like it was a baby. An entire wall was devoted to photos of the ferrets dressed in ski sweaters, cowboy hats, T-shirts, French berets.

Rose kept sneaking glances at Olivia's oxygen concentrator, tucked into a corner beside her chair. When Olivia reached down to adjust the tubing, Rose peppered her with questions. How many hours a day did she need it? ("All of them.") "What would happen if our power went out?" ("I'd switch to the portables.") "What if you run out of portables?" ("You don't want to know.") To each answer, Rose nodded earnestly.

"So why Graceland, Liv?" Rudy asked as he set mismatched plates on the table. "Didn't you get enough of it when you lived in Memphis?"

"I took Hope to Graceland when it first opened and never went back. It was too sad, so soon after we'd lost him."

Rose muttered, "So soon after *you* lost him."

There was an awkward silence, so I jumped in. "Olivia's going to meet with the curator."

Olivia met my eye, and her brows lifted almost impercepti-
bly. A warning?

"Are you?" Rose asked. "Whatever for?"

"Ann and I are just catching up," Olivia explained. "Her
mother was a friend in Memphis." Olivia turned to face Rudy.
"Did you know that Dylan is quite the budding activist? She
helped form her school's Gender-Sexuality Alliance."

Rose looked annoyed at the abrupt shift in topic. Rudy turned
to me. "So nice that kids are coming out early these days. Good
for you, Dylan."

"Actually, I'm not gay," I explained. A ferret leaped onto my
lap, and I shoved it off. "I think I might be pansexual, but I'm
still exploring." "

"*Pan*sexual?" Rose chuckled. "You're attracted to cookware?"

"Rose!" Rudy snapped. "Don't be rude. That's the new term
for bisexual, isn't it, Dylan?"

"No," I said, a bit snippier than I intended, but Jesus, old
people thought they knew everything. "It means I'm attracted
to people regardless of their sex or gender identity."

Rudy said he'd been involved with Broadway Cares/Equity
Fights AIDS and asked a lot of questions about my GSA protests. "What you're doing is important work," he said. "I hope
you continue it in college."

"I'm not sure college makes sense for me." I felt pleased with
that mature turn of phrase. "I might be an activist filmmaker.
Like Michael Moore."

Rudy flicked his eyes to Olivia, who'd taken that moment to
help herself to more asparagus. "Well," he said, "you'll figure
out what's best for you. I wish I'd finished college. Dancing on
sofas was hard at sixty."

"If we'd both stayed in LA—" said Rose.

"But we didn't, Rose," he interrupted, though not unkindly. Still, Rose turned her head with a sniff. "And so now, I'm seventy-eight and work the grill at a breakfast joint to pay the electric bill."

"Enough about you, Rudy," Rose said, pouring herself more wine. This was her fourth glass, by my count. "Teenagers don't want to hear about old people. Let's talk about when we were young and beautiful." She turned to me. "Did your grand-mother tell you how she and I met Elvis?"

Given Olivia's earlier warning, I hesitated. "A little."

"Okay, but has she told you the *whole* story?" She drew out the word "whole" like it was borderline dirty.

"Rose?" Rudy smiled nervously, his eyes on Olivia. "I think Olivia should decide what stories to tell Dylan."

"Oh, not *that*!" Rose said. She was clearly drunk. "Not to worry, Liv, I don't intend to spec-u-late." She made it three separate words.

I didn't know where to look. A ferret circled my feet and I nudged it away.

Olivia reached for the wine and poured herself a tiny bit, replacing the bottle on the side away from Rose.

"I'm sure Dylan would enjoy hearing how we met Elvis." Olivia turned to me. "I only got the opportunity because of Rose. She was a close friend of our soap's producer."

Rose leaned across the table toward me and whispered: "She means I was fucking him."

Taken by surprise, I laughed out loud.

"Rose!" Rudy almost shouted. "That's not appropriate."

Rose sat back, proud of herself. "Dylan is almost seventeen. She knows what it means."

"That's not the point . . ."

"Do tell the rest, Rose," Olivia interrupted. "You're a much better storyteller than I." Olivia winked at me, discrediting anything Rose said.

Rose eyed Olivia, then the wine bottle, now out of her reach. "Oh, there's not much to tell." She slumped back in her chair, defeated. "As I said, I was *dating*"—here she turned toward Rudy to see if the word met his approval—"this producer, and he was a cousin of someone in Elvis's entourage. Red? Sonny? I can't recall. Anyway, he was able to get us backstage after the show." She drained what was left in her glass and plunked it down in front of Rudy, as if he might redeem himself by getting her more. Rudy motioned for me to pass the bottle. "I was quite the looker in those days," Rose continued. "I was hoping Elvis would invite me back to the suite." She watched Rudy pour the rest of the wine into his own glass and sighed. "Elvis did that with pretty girls, you know. Asked them to hang out with his entourage at the hotel where they'd party till dawn."

"Long story short, Rose didn't get what she wanted," Rudy said.

"No, I didn't. Elvis chatted with Livvy and me about the show, and our studio photographer took some pictures. We got barely five minutes before some goon hustled us out so Elvis could change. I was hopping mad. Then, as we're leaving the building, the goon chases us down and asks Livvy . . ." Here she stopped and glared at Olivia, who was studying the ceiling. "He asks *Olivia* if she would like to go to a private party with Elvis."

Olivia chuckled. "Rose actually said to the man, 'Are you sure he didn't mean me?'"

Rose sniffed. "Well, not for nothing, but I was the star. Liv's character was supposed to appear in one season. They kept making her part bigger and bigger."

"I think Elvis actually preferred brunettes," Olivia said. "He dated blondes, but remember, he married a brunette."

"True," Rose said. She seemed relieved to have an explanation and turned back to me. "Beyond that, I know no more. Your grandmother ditched me for her night with Elvis. And she would never tell me—"

Olivia interrupted: "Rose didn't speak to me for weeks."

"I didn't." She snickered. "I was so mad. And right about the time we started talking again, Livvy up and elopes with Harold and moves to Memphis."

"Wow." I'd never heard the story in order before. "Why Memphis?"

"That's where your grandfather lived, dear," said Olivia. "Once he finished his studies at UCLA, his parents needed him home to run the business."

Rose had stolen Rudy's wineglass. "But wouldn't you know it?" she said between sips. "Without that bitch Andromeda, our ratings tanked, and *Light Within* was canceled. My life was ruined. All because your grandmother eloped."

"Now hold on, Rose." Rudy was smiling. "Ruined? If that hadn't happened, you wouldn't have moved back to New York and married me."

"Like I said," she muttered.

Olivia stood and began jimmying her oxygen machine out of

the corner. "Well, it's been lovely, but Dylan and I should get some sleep. Thank you both for a wonderful dinner."

Rose paid no attention. She was speaking to me. "I always wondered if your grandfather would have moved Olivia to Memphis if he'd known about Livvy and the King."

Olivia smiled as she met Rose's eyes. Her tone was matter of fact. "I had no secrets from Harold."

"Really?" Rose smirked. "None?"

Olivia lifted her chin and focused her gaze on the window behind Rose, in that funny way my mother always made fun of. "Not a one," she said.

She swiveled her oxygen concentrator around and headed down the hallway, pulling the machine behind her. "Come along, Dylan. Time for bed."

I followed, nearly tripping over a darting ferret. Behind us, dishes clattered into the sink.

Once Olivia and I were inside the guest room, I closed the door behind us. "What did Rose mean about you and Elvis?"

"Oh, Rose." My grandmother let out a puff of air. "She likes a good story. If she doesn't have one, she'll make one up. You get to bed, Dylan. We have a long drive tomorrow."

I CHECKED UNDER the sofa bed for free-range ferrets. It seemed clear. My phone showed eleven missed calls, seven texts, and four voicemails from my mother. Most said "call me" in different yet increasingly annoying ways.

Olivia's door was still open a crack. I knocked softly and slipped in. Olivia was sitting on the bed, reading a paperback. I thrust the phone at her face. "The gig is up."

"Jig," Olivia corrected. "The *jig* is up." Olivia scanned the messages and handed back the phone. "Goodness. Your mother does have some obsessive-compulsive tendencies, doesn't she?" She shook her head tight and fast, like she was being electrocuted.

"What should I say?"

Olivia lifted her book, *Me Before You.* "Say whatever you want. Hope was bound to notice you were missing at some point."

"I wish she'd mind her own business."

Olivia flipped a page. "Perhaps that's what she's doing, dear. Finally."

Back in my room, I flopped on the squeaky sofa bed. I wanted to call my mother and scream at her, but I knew what would bother her more: silence. How perfect was that? Silence was what my mom had been offering for years.

As far back as I could recall, I'd tied myself in knots to avoid hurting my mother. Anytime I'd ask a question about my father, Mom's eyes would go dull, and her mouth would stiffen. She'd answer in a few words and find any excuse to rush away. I got it. Thinking about my dad was painful. So every time I asked about him, I swore I'd never do it again—never make Mom that sad. Sometimes I'd go a year or more, until I couldn't help it, and some question would burst out of me like an alien exploding from my guts. I'd listen to Mom's brief, pained answer, and be right back where I started. The guilt. The vows to try harder.

From what little Mom said about my dad's protests, I decided he'd been a man of deep conviction. Someone brave and bold, who'd risked his life—even died—in pursuit of his beliefs.

It was all a pack of lies, of course, but I didn't know that. So when Emma and I held our first GSA rally, and I started screaming at this bunch of homophobic bigots, it felt like someone had pulled back a curtain. I understood. I was like my dad. All the things my mother blamed me for—my impulsiveness, my arguing, my risk-taking—I got from my father. Mom wanted me to be cautious, obedient, people-pleasing, like her. Well, fuck that.

I'd heard about this Ancestry.com organization that could help you learn about your family tree, but I wasn't eighteen, so I couldn't do the DNA test. Still, I could search for my father in the company's database. I signed up on the website for a free trial and immediately hit a roadblock. I remembered my father's first name, not his last. Had Mom even told me? This was seriously messed up. My dad was half my identity, and I didn't know his full name.

After a sleepless night, I dragged myself out of bed early and got dressed. In the kitchen, I poured myself some cereal and sat at the counter, kitty-corner from Mom. She was scowling at the cable bill.

When I asked about my father's last name, some muesli tumbled off Mom's spoon. She wiped her mouth with the back of her hand. She was still looking at the bill, but—I could tell—no longer seeing it.

"Smith," she'd said. "James Smith."

I nodded, placed my half-eaten cereal in the sink, and went upstairs to dress for school. In the year since, though, I'd never told anyone that name, not even Olivia. I knew with absolute certainty that my mother had been lying. And it devastated me.

A few days later, on my sixteenth birthday, I dyed my hair.

Not a few streaks of color, but full-on, searing-hot pink. I got turned away from the tattoo parlor for being underage, but went to the mall and had them pierce more holes in my ears.

Before, I had known only half myself. Now I was becoming whole. I was embracing my flip side, the part of me I'd inherited from my father—the bolder, braver, Dylan. The Badass Dylan.

Chapter 6

Hope

The sun hadn't risen when I heard the crunch of Jordan's tires turning into my driveway. Four a.m. Bless her. Grabbing the two travel mugs I'd filled with coffee, I hustled outside with the overnight bag I'd packed. I prayed we wouldn't need it.

Even in the predawn gloom it was hard to miss Jordan's bright orange-and-scarlet dress as she leaped down from her Robinson Repair pickup. She beamed when I complimented her outfit, fanning the skirt to show off the poppies. Given how I was dressed, the two of us seemed like more of an odd couple than usual. Exhausted from lack of sleep, I'd thrown on ripped jeans and an Old Navy T-shirt and had pulled back my hair, still damp from my late-night shower, into a messy ponytail. Jordan, in contrast, looked camera-ready with a heavy application of foundation, eyeliner, mascara, and lipstick. Her wig was a dark blond and flipped back on both sides, Farrah Fawcett-style.

Jordan one-armed my suitcase into the back as I hopped into the cab. The seatbelt stuck and I yanked at it furiously. "Calm down, sweetie," Jordan said as she settled herself in the driver's seat. "We got this." I let the belt retract, took a deep breath, and pulled it out smoothly. Jordan head-bobbed a *told you so* as she threw the truck into reverse.

"Any word from our fugitives?" she asked.

"None." I was optimistic, though. The address I'd dug up online for Rudy Rosenbaum matched where the tracking app placed Dylan's iPhone. If we could surprise them there, I could take my mother aside, talk some sense into her. Right now, she didn't understand the danger.

As we drove, I kept the phone in my lap and lifted it constantly to peek at the blank screen. I knew it wasn't rational. The phone would quack if I had a message, and the odds of Dylan texting me at this hour were nonexistent. Still, every so often, I checked the Find My iPhone app to confirm the red dot was still in Fairfield.

Jordan tuned the radio to a seventies and eighties station and sang along. She had a lovely tenor voice and an odd passion for some of the sappiest pop music of our youth: the Captain & Tennille, Barry Manilow, Starship. I tried not to say anything, but when she began singing harmony to "Muskrat Love," I cringed.

"Don't be a snob," Jordan said.

"That song will be stuck in my head for days."

"Then choose something you like better. Sing along. It'll take your mind off things."

I gave her a sidelong glance. "You know I don't do that." I didn't sing in front of anyone. In fact, I had a horror of any type of public performance—singing, karaoke, line dancing, even reading aloud to school children. I hated having people's eyes on me.

Jordan sipped her coffee and shook her head. "How are you Olivia Grant's daughter?"

"No idea," I admitted. "God knows, my mother tried to change me. She gave up on singing but signed me up for every kind of dance class imaginable—ballet, tap, jazz. I hated them all. Even today, I break out in hives at the sight of a disco ball."

"No offense, Hope, but talk about casting pearls before swine. I'd have killed for tap lessons."

"You would have been great at it, too. It was torture for me, having the teacher and other kids watching." I fiddled with a rip in my jeans. "Before every lesson, I'd hide in the bathroom cabinet, under the sink."

"That's so odd. Olivia must have realized how much you hated it."

"She truly believed she was helping me. She's told me as much."

Jordan replaced her coffee in the cupholder. "Yeah, my father thought he was helping me by kicking me out of the house when he discovered my cross-dressing. He figured if I had to choose between that and my family, I'd choose family. He didn't understand that what he was asking me to give up was me." She adjusted her mirror and changed lanes. "Same with you, Hope. You're not an extrovert, but your mom was deter-mined to make you one."

"Do you remember when I was six, and Mom tried to make me sing 'Happy Birthday' to my father in front of a room full of party guests? She lifted me up on that chair, and I was so terrified, I peed all over it."

"Clearly Olivia didn't get you."

"No. I wasn't her favorite daughter."

Jordan eyed me sideways. "Don't be silly. You're her only daughter."

"Not true," I said. "You know that."

"Yes," Jordan admitted. "I do."

JORDAN WAS OLD enough to remember my sister, Beth. I wasn't.

When I was eight, I discovered the box of photos high on a shelf in my father's closet. Pictures of an elfin toddler, a dark-haired beauty with dazzling blue eyes and long lashes. The photos puzzled me. Who was this girl who'd celebrated a birthday at my dining room table, pirouetted around my living room, wrapped her arms around my beaming mother?

When my father found me on his bedroom floor surrounded by the pictures, he sat next to me and sifted through several, smiling. "This is your sister, Beth," he'd explained. "She died before you were born." He lifted a photo of Beth in a lion costume, roaring at the camera, and handed it to me. Beth was a character, he'd said. A nonstop chatterer. A girl who loved ballet and show tunes. At three, she climbed onto the piano bench at my parents' dinner party to sing "Over the Rainbow."

My father didn't have to tell me I was nothing like Beth. I knew. I was shy and slow to make friends. I adored jigsaw puzzles, pored over books, organized my stuffed animals by natural habitat: jungle, desert, ocean. My hair was straight and the color of Idaho potatoes.

After Beth died, my father said, they'd decided to have another child, right away. I was born less than a year later. When I was older, in college, my father had elaborated on their determination to conceive—how my mother had timed her ovulation, summoned him from work in the middle of the day. In sharing this, my father's heart was in the right place. To him, it proved I was a wanted child. Instead, what I heard was: you were a replacement child.

They named me Hope Elizabeth. What I heard was: they were hoping for Beth.

WE STOPPED AT a rest plaza near Sturbridge to change drivers. I told Jordan I needed to get away from my phone, but really, I was dying to go faster. As I backed out of the parking spot, I handed Jordan my phone, still open to the texts I'd sent Dylan last night. Jordan, nothing if not nosy, scrolled through them. I let her, hoping she wouldn't notice when I picked up speed.

"I hate to nitpick, sweetie, but it's possible sending twenty texts was overkill," she said. "And good grief, were you actually starting a new one just now?"

I checked the side mirror and moved into the fast lane. "Do you think I should send it? We need them to stay put."

"Well, the quickest way to get them back on the road is to send this."

"Okay, erase it, please."

"Done," Jordan said. And then, "Oops."

The text Jordan accidentally sent was gibberish, the letters *hqpun* with a tented accent over the *u*. She had no idea how she'd done it, and I didn't expect Dylan would respond. We'd barely driven a mile, though, before my phone quacked.

"It's Dylan!" Jordan called out. "Do you want me to read it?"

"Yes!" I twisted in my seat, searching for an opening to change lanes. If my daughter was communicating again, I needed to reply.

Jordan typed in my password and scanned the message. "Oh dear."

"What?"

"It's in all caps."

"Read it!"

"It says, 'STOP TEXTING ME IT'S FIVE THIRTY A.M.'"

"Hit reply! Tell her I need to talk to her. I'll pull over."

Jordan glanced nervously at the three lanes of traffic I was crossing, but typed the message, making clicking sounds with her fake nails. A few seconds later, I heard the *bloop* that meant Dylan had responded. Jordan read aloud, "'What part of "stop texting me" don't you understand?'" Jordan shook her head. "I have to say, Hope, I saw that one coming. . . . Oh, wait, here's something more." She squinted.

"What?" I careened into the breakdown lane and hit the brakes hard.

"It says, 'Oh, and by the way, thanks for lying to me all my life.'"

Shit.

I threw the truck into park, snatched the phone from Jordan, and pressed the speed dial for Dylan. It went to voicemail. I texted madly, "Dylan, please pick up. I need to speak to you." I watched, waiting for the message to say "delivered." Cars roared by. Five minutes passed. Why wasn't the message delivered?

"She turned off her phone," Jordan said quietly.

One of my legs was shaking and I pressed on it to make it stop. *She knew. Dylan knew about Aaron.* My mother had stuck her nose into something that was none of her business, and now my daughter understood. I'd been lying to her for years.

WITHOUT A WORD, I unbuckled my seatbelt, slid out of the cab. Jordan didn't ask, just hopped down and circled around the truck. She took my place at the wheel, readjusted the seat, and signaled to merge back onto the highway.

For several minutes, we drove in silence, my thoughts tumbling over one another. I stared at the back window of a passing Volvo decorated with stick figures: father, mother, boy, girl, dog. No doubt the family inside was playing I Spy and snacking on grapes and cashews with healthy fats. I hated them.

"Hope," Jordan asked finally, "what was Dylan talking about?"

I fiddled with the seatbelt strap. "Who knows?" I said. "It's Dylan. What's she ever talking about?"

"Something, usually, is my impression." Jordan frowned at the road ahead.

"Then you tell me!" I snapped, my tone surprising us both. The truth was, Dylan often shared things with Jordan she hadn't told me. Jordan would mention a test Dylan had bombed or a boy she'd kissed, then see from my surprise I knew nothing about it. Jordan always felt horrible. So did I.

"Don't get mad, Hope," she said. She reached into the snack bag between us and took out an apple, then held it against the steering wheel without taking a bite. "Honestly, it's not that hard to figure out. You claim I'm your best friend, but in all these years, there's one thing you won't talk about. What happened to you in Memphis. You cried on my sofa for two weeks after I took you in." She flicked me a look. "That's right. I heard you at night. And then suddenly you're pregnant and won't discuss the father. I decided long ago it wasn't my business, but now I'm gonna ask you, straight-out. Hope, were you assaulted?"

My head jerked back, shocked. "No! Oh God. That isn't it at all."

"Are you sure?" Jordan's tone was gentle. "Because that shit is hard to talk about."

"It is, and no, please don't think that. It's nothing that awful." I paused, taking in everything Jordan had said. She wasn't just my cousin, she was my closest friend, and she was right—I'd told her nothing about my issues with Memphis. I'd abided by the nondisclosure agreement for over seventeen years, too afraid to do otherwise. Now, my world was collapsing, and Jordan had dropped everything and was driving me halfway across the country. The least I could do was tell her the truth.

Or, you know, most of it.

"I'm worried you're going to judge me," I said, sipping my coffee. I'd told Jordan I needed more caffeine before starting my story, so we'd zipped through a McDonald's drive-through in Rockville, Connecticut.

"Seriously?" Jordan said. "You're afraid the person sitting next to you, whose penis is tucked into her brand-new pair of Spanx, is going to judge you?"

"Thank you for that visual, but yes. It's a long and complicated story. The short version is, I fell for a guy who wasn't who I thought he was."

Jordan made a sound like a game-show buzzer. "Sorry, the judges need more information. And it has to be consistent. Not like the two different stories I've gotten before."

"What?" Admittedly, Jordan and George sometimes acted like such different people—Jordan ebullient and opinionated, George more serene and nonjudgmental—I'd occasionally found myself repeating something to Jordan that I'd already told George. But I'd told no one about Dylan's father. "That can't be right."

"Well, one version came from Dylan. She told me her father had lived in a yurt in Alaska and died in a whaling protest."

"Oh, right." I sipped my coffee. "Yeah, that . . . wasn't true."

"It did seem a little convenient. And I can imagine how furious she is if she's discovered it's a lie."

"My mother figured it out. I don't know how." Reflexively, I picked up my phone to check for messages. "What was the version I told you? And why don't I remember?"

"You were drunk. Remember maybe ten years back, when you broke up with that electrician guy? Or was it the firefighter? Which was the one I really liked?"

As far as I knew, Jordan had liked most of the men I'd dated over the years. She couldn't understand why I kept breaking off relationships before they got serious. I had trouble explaining it myself. "Skip past that part," I suggested.

"You invited me over. We put Dylan to bed, and you started making gin and tonics. I stuck with beer."

"Ohhh, this is sounding familiar. Was I really hungover the next day?"

"Horribly. I brought Dylan to the zoo. Anyway, that night

you got hammered and were railing about men being assholes, so I took advantage of the situation and asked about Dylan's father. And you said, drunkenly, 'Do you know him?'"

I rubbed my eyebrows. "So from that you deduced he wasn't dead. Anything else?"

"You said he'd been an ill-advised one-night stand and you hadn't kept his phone number. Not your exact words, but the gist."

I reviewed each of those points. "To be honest, nothing you said isn't true. Just . . . simplified. It *was* a one-night stand. And it *was* ill-advised. And I *didn't* keep his phone number, though I'm pretty sure I could find it if I wanted to." I paused here. This was new territory for me, but if my secret was safe with anyone, it was Jordan. "He's . . . a politician," I said. "So, you know . . . a website, and all that."

"A politician? In Memphis?"

"Well, DC. But he lives in Memphis. At least, his wife and kids are there."

"You're gonna have to help me here. A Memphis politician who works in Washington, DC? You mean, he's in Congress?"

"Yeah, something like that."

"What is *like* Congress?"

"You know. The Senate."

Jordan gave me a long look. Longer than I was comfortable with, given she was driving. "Let me get this straight. Dylan's father is a United States senator? You *slept* with a senator?"

"He wasn't a senator back then. He was just getting started in politics."

Jordan was frowning. "He's not that guy—what's his name? They're talking about him as a possible vice president pick. Breckenridge? Andrew Breckenridge?"

"Aaron," I said, brushing a crumb from my lap. "Aaron Breckenridge."

"Noooo." Jordan drew out the word. "You're screwing with me. The guy who's all about character?"

"Yeah, well, meet the skeleton in his closet."

She turned again to study my face, as if waiting for me to break out laughing. "Jesus, Hope, I'm impressed!"

"It's not something I'm proud of."

"Tell me what happened. No, wait. You said he was married."

"Engaged, back then. Bad enough." Traffic was slowing ahead, taillights popping on and off like warning signs. *Danger, Hope Robinson.* I couldn't focus. "Can we continue this later?" I asked Jordan. "My mind is in too many places. I need to figure out what I'm going to say to my mother when we find her. Not to mention my daughter."

"Of course, sweetie. And don't ever worry about sharing this stuff. I'd never judge you."

I nodded, grateful. Though I suspected she would if she knew everything.

THE ACCIDENT SOMEWHERE ahead of us, right before Hartford, was bad. All three lanes of traffic were stopped dead and a medical helicopter hovered, then landed. Dylan and my mother couldn't be involved—the iPhone still placed them in Fairfield—but that didn't stop my stomach from churning.

Storm clouds had rolled in ahead, dark and threatening. We opened the windows while we still could, listening to the scream of emergency vehicles and the whir of traffic helicopters. Eventually a local radio station reported the breaking story: a six-car pileup with serious injuries. So we sat. The smell of exhaust made my throbbing headache worse. I dumped everything out of my purse, searching for Advil, but no luck. Dylan must have swiped it.

Jordan drummed her fingers on the wheel and kept sneaking looks at me. I'd asked for a break in talking about Aaron, but when it came to gossip, Jordan was the least patient person on earth. I leaned an elbow on the window well and dropped my head into my hand. "Go ahead," I said, finally. "Ask."

"This Breckenridge guy? He knows about Dylan, right?"

I could see the rain starting in front of us, connecting sky and highway. "He found out I was pregnant." The image in my mind, though, wasn't of Aaron. It was of a strange little man in a seersucker suit, sitting on a park bench.

"You didn't answer the question. He knows he has a daughter?"

"Yes," I said. Big drops of rain plopped, one by one, onto the windshield. "He didn't want anything to do with her."

Jordan turned on the wipers. Her jaw was set tight. "Asshole. That's why you didn't want Dylan to know."

I dug my fingers into the tight place between my neck and shoulder. That was one reason.

"It's okay, sweetie. We all love people we wish we hadn't. No regrets. You got Dylan."

Twenty minutes passed before the car in front of us moved, an hour as we crept toward an exit. We no longer had much chance of catching my mother and Dylan in Fairfield. I tortured myself with what-ifs. What if I'd checked on my mother earlier yesterday? What if we'd started driving last night? What if . . . I'd never lied to my daughter?

I pulled out my phone. I knew it might backfire, but I had no choice. I sent Dylan a text message. "On the way to Fairfield. Please stay put. I need to talk to you. It's urgent."

I hit send and the message said "delivered." Ten minutes later, when I checked her location on the Find My iPhone app, the red dot was gone.

Chapter 7

Olivia

Alone on Rose and Rudy's back patio, I sank into a lawn chair, threw back my head, and opened myself like a morning glory to the light. Why shouldn't I enjoy a little early-morning sunshine? Skin cancer wouldn't be what got me.

I've always been drawn to light, rarely bothered by heat. Even on the soundstage of *The Light Within*, under spotlights that made other actors fan themselves with scripts, I didn't perspire. Once, in our early days, Rose brushed against my cool arm and proclaimed, "My God, Livvy, you're a reptile. No warmth, whatsoever!"

Was it a joke or a diss? Hard to tell with Rose. Ours had been such an odd friendship. One part affection to two parts rivalry.

Wind chimes tinkled on the porch, but the house itself was quiet. No one stirring this early. Oh well. I'd hoped for a chance to talk privately with Rose—make peace with her on our way to Graceland. Seemed the right thing to do.

I wouldn't apologize for ruining her life, of course. Not my fault the soap failed after I left. Blame the writers. The new villain meant to replace Andromeda was a churlish buffoon with no cunning, no sex appeal. That's what killed *Light Within*.

In fact, if Rose was honest with herself for ten seconds, she'd recall that she was secretly thrilled when I announced I was leaving the show. When I told her, in her dressing room, a flicker of delight passed over her face before she caught it, and turned it into feigned sadness. Rose was a good actress.

I'm not claiming I never did Rose wrong. I did. It was Rose who'd obtained the backstage passes to meet the King. At the time, she was by far the bigger star. But Rose was lazy, not given to hustle like I was. Hustle had gotten me where I was. I couldn't turn it off.

And so, on the night of the LA Forum concert, when the photographer took a photo of the three of us together—Rose, Elvis, and me—I slipped him a note. Elvis stood between us with a hand over both of our shoulders, and I placed my hand over his, sliding the scrap of paper under his fingers. The King didn't react, didn't flinch. Women slipped him notes all the time. He palmed the note and squeezed my shoulder once to let me know he had it.

As I say, I knew how to hustle. I'd done my research. I'd asked around, talked to people in the industry. I knew where Elvis's heart lay.

My note said: I'm Olivia Grant, your new Ann-Margret.

I'D BEEN HOPING to make amends to Rose during our visit. Tell her that story. Privately. It would please her to know there'd been a reason why Elvis had chosen me. How, once again, I'd played the villain.

But in the end, Rose was still Rose. Never could hold her drink. Even if I'd told her, she wouldn't have remembered it in the morning.

My husband, Harold, used to say that everything happens for a reason. "Bullshit," I'd reply. I had no patience with such nonsense. It wasn't fate that had brought me to Rose's doorstep—it was my will and the damn broken drive shaft. And if God or fate or Tinker Bell or whoever-the-hell-you-believe-in had wanted me to make amends with Rose, they would have stopped her from getting tanked. I was done trying.

No, if there was any lesson in seeing my old costar, it was to remind me of the sad place she'd ended up. Like so many of our friends, Rose had been a white-hot star, gracing the cover of *Soap Opera Digest*, cohosting *The Mike Douglas Show*, swimming in Rock Hudson's pool. One by one those actors had disappeared, sinking silently under the winter ice of oblivion. No one had even seen them struggle.

That wouldn't be me.

A LIGHT CAME on in the kitchen and a flash of pink skirted by the window. Dylan. Surprising to see her up at this hour, but Dylan was nothing if not surprising.

Turned out the girl was decent company. So different from Hope! You could talk to Dylan. She didn't keep her thoughts under lock and key. If you made it past the prelude of teenage angst and unfiltered nonsense, Dylan hit every note in the adolescent aria: exhilaration, despair, longing, fury, confusion, self-doubt. The raw emotion took my breath away.

Oh, Dylan's high spirits would need to be kept in check,

for sure. The child had no self-control. She was a blender with the top off. I'd have to be careful how much I shared with her, especially on the father issue. The last thing I needed was her posting something on Facebook or Twitter.

Dylan threw open the sliding glass door and marched toward me, clearly out of sorts. Her hair was tussled, as if she hadn't bothered consulting a mirror, and her black T-shirt proclaimed, "It's Science, Bitch." She thrust her phone under my nose, demanding, "How'd this happen?"

I guided the girl's hand to where I could read the message. From Hope. She was on her way here, to Fairfield. I released the phone back to Dylan. "No idea."

"How does she know where we are? Did Rose call her?"

"Unlikely." I heaved myself out of the chair. "Given Rose's condition at dinner, I'm not sure she'd have remembered her own name, never mind Hope's." I headed into the house, calling over my shoulder, "Perhaps your mother keeps a tracking device on you."

I was joshing of course, but when I turned back, Dylan glared at her phone. The girl let out a string of curses and followed me inside, poking and swiping, and grumbling about some phone-tracking app, as if I were listening. "It's off," she said. "Now what do we do?"

"Do?" My suitcase was packed and on the bed. I zipped it closed. "Have breakfast, I suppose. Then Rudy will drive us . . ."

"No!" she interrupted. "We have to leave now. We can't let Mom find us here."

"Honestly, Dylan, your mother would have made everything easier if she'd agreed to drive us in the first place."

The girl banged her hand against the door. That got my attention. "You don't understand! Mom will make me go home. She doesn't want me to know about my father."

Were those tears in the girl's eyes? I was speechless. I hadn't realized how much this trip meant to her. The whole let's-find-your-dad angle had been an afterthought, a means to an end.

"She'll talk you out of going," Dylan said.

I had to laugh at that. As if Hope could talk me out of anything, never mind this trip. Still, I moved to the window and craned my neck to check the driveway. The girl had a point: Hope could be unusually stubborn about certain things, and God knows, Memphis was one of them. No, the way to get Hope to Memphis was to stay just out of her reach and lure her there, mile by mile. Hope was the proverbial frog who wouldn't jump out of the pot as long as I raised the temperature a smidgen at a time.

Not that it would kill Hope to return to Memphis. Well, as far as I knew.

I drew the curtains. "Show me the Googley maps again."

Google offered two different routes to Memphis. Both went through Pennsylvania, but the faster route dipped south to Maryland and Virginia, while the other swung west across the state before dropping down through Ohio and Kentucky.

I pointed to the latter. "We'll go this way."

Dylan pushed aside my finger. "No, we don't want to do that. See? It adds forty minutes," she said. "That would be crazy."

I grinned. "Exactly."

FOR A MAN who'd once danced to "Aquarius," Rudy dawdled and dragged his feet beyond belief. I wanted to poke him as he brewed coffee, scribbled a note for the sleeping Rose, and hunted for his car keys. All the while, Dylan eyed the door nervously. She seemed convinced that any second, Hope might pop her head through the hole in the screen, like Jack Nicholson in *The Shining*.

In the car, Rudy gave me the third degree about Graceland. What was the draw? Why now? Well, none of his damned business! I offered perfunctory responses and listened to his completely erroneous account of Elvis's final hours until he accidentally reminded me of something. No one was allowed upstairs at Graceland, where the King's bedroom was. "Only the family," he insisted. "They've left everything exactly as it was when he died. I thought you'd know that, Livvy. You, of all people."

How embarrassing. I'd only been to Graceland that one time and I'd forgotten. Since then, I must have watched a dozen Elvis biopics and could picture every inch of the upstairs. Those TV images had taken the place of memory.

Rudy shot a backward glance at Dylan before adding, with a grin, "Unless you remember his bedroom because the King himself showed you."

"That's what Rose thinks, clearly," I said. "But no, I never laid eyes on Elvis during my years in Memphis." I fiddled with the knot on the red scarf, wrapped twice around my neck and tied sideways. "It's disappointing, though, about his bedroom. I did so want to visit the place he was last."

Rudy smirked. "I believe that was on the commode."

I struggled to tamp down my annoyance. Fine. Before he died, Elvis had gotten up to use the toilet and hadn't made it back. So what? That bathroom was en suite, technically part of the bedroom. I'd see about this arcane rule that barred visitors from that special place. Perhaps the general public wasn't allowed, but surely exceptions were made.

At the repair place, the girl kicked into high gear. While the mechanic charged my card, Dylan dragged my oxygen concentrator around the back of the Bug. When Rudy tried to help by bringing over my extra tanks, Dylan raced around the car and pried them from his hands. She patted Rudy's back and pointed him in my direction. Rudy raised both hands in surrender and ambled back.

A quick hug should have been the end of it. Instead, Rudy took me by both arms and apologized for Rose's behavior.

"Rose has suffered a lot of disappointment," he said. The Bug's horn beeped, and I waved at Dylan. "It's hard to be a star one day and a nobody the next."

"Never occurred to me," I deadpanned. Another, longer beep from Dylan. I raised a finger. One minute.

Rudy, though, didn't take the hint. He launched into a story about some fan who'd asked for Rose's autograph, then realized she wasn't Debbie Reynolds and tore it up, right in Rose's face.

Enough. I had to put an end to this. I promised to call Rose, even though I had no intention of doing so. Quite frankly, what had happened to Rose was my worst nightmare, and I couldn't get away fast enough. I was still detangling myself from Rudy's grip when Dylan laid on the horn and threw the car into reverse.

I heard the crunch immediately. Everyone did.

Chapter 8

Hope

Rose and Rudy frowned at me through the screen door. They had no idea who I was. I'd met them once when I was twelve, on a rare family trip to New York, but back then I'd had wire-framed glasses, braces, and legs like a newborn giraffe. My story about a last-minute decision to follow and surprise my mother and daughter probably sounded as loony to them as it did to me.

Rose said they'd left an hour ago. She cradled something in her arms that looked like a weasel wearing a sunbonnet.

"Car's all fixed," Rudy added. "Brand new drive shaft." He must have seen me blanch. "They didn't tell you it broke?"

"We haven't been in touch in the last . . . day or so." *Holy shit, a drive shaft?* That sounded important.

"Too bad about your mom's oxygen machine, though."

"Sorry?"

Rudy explained how Dylan had backed over my mother's oxygen concentrator. I put a hand to the door frame to steady myself. Without the concentrator, could my mother even make it to Memphis? She often seemed way too dismissive of her need for oxygen. Like she could go cold turkey anytime she put her mind to it.

"They were gonna have a new machine sent to their next stop," Rudy said.

"*Where?* Did they say?"

Rudy squinted into the distance. I wanted to reach through the screen and shake the man. He looked to Rose, who shrugged. "Can't recall that they did. You might want to phone them. If it won't ruin the surprise."

As I climbed back into the truck, the Rosenbaums ventured onto the porch, still cradling the furry rodent. Rudy shaded his eyes, studying the pickup, no doubt curious why my daughter's car was a piece of crap while I rode in a truck with "Robinson Repair" decals on the doors. Fair question.

When I told Jordan about the drive shaft, she lowered her forehead to the steering wheel.

"Hope, I'm so sorry. I told Dylan to bring it back to the shop."

"It was my fault. I was waiting until I could pay you." Stupid, stupid, Hope. How had I let money take center stage in the worst decisions of my life?

I pulled out my phone and typed: "Dylan, that car is a menace. Tell me where you are *now*. We'll meet and make a new plan." I hit send, reread the message, and added: "Your grandmother's health is in danger. Call me."

I dropped my head back and closed my eyes. "Ferret," I whispered. "That's what it was."

"Onward?" Jordan asked quietly. "To Memphis?" When I nodded, she tapped at her GPS. "Which way?"

Shit.

I sat upright and examined the two routes Jordan showed me. Of course there were options—why hadn't I thought of that? I chose the shorter, praying it mapped the same way from the repair place.

Jordan backed down the driveway and turned on the radio. As she followed the directions to the highway, she hummed along with the piña colada song. I hugged my arms across my chest and tried to calm the cyclone stirring in my gut.

I was headed to Graceland.

I'D BEEN TO Graceland once, when I was six.

My mother took me when the mansion opened to the public, in 1982. I have a vague memory of the Jungle Room, with its green shag carpet on the floor and ceiling. What fixed the visit in my mind, though, was what happened after. On the drive home, my mother made me promise not to tell my father where we'd been.

"Why?"

"Your father's not a fan of Elvis."

This rang true. My mother only played Elvis records when my dad was at work. I agreed not to tell. I liked sharing a secret with my mother. Having recently peed on her chair in front of party guests, I wanted desperately to please her.

Unfortunately, my dance school was having a recital that night, and even though I'd sworn I'd perform, as the day wore on, I dreaded the sea of eyes, the flashing cameras, the teacher hissing at me. After my mother dragged me, shrieking, from the closet where I'd been hiding, my father intervened, squatting down to my level and encouraging me to take deep breaths.

He smoothed back my hair and asked me what was wrong. "I can't go," I cried. "I'm too tired!"

"Too tired to dance?" he teased. "That's silly."

"I am!" I insisted. "Mom made me walk all over Elvis's house and I feel sick."

There was silence, then, except for my sniffling. My father's eyes were on my face, but his mouth grew tight.

My mother said, casually, "We did the Graceland tour. Everyone is talking about it. You can't live in Memphis and not go."

My father rose without looking at either of us. He grabbed his wallet and keys and left the house. I heard his car turn over in the driveway.

My mother sat down in her chair, lit a cigarette. "Well, now you've done it," she said. "I'll have to call us a cab."

"Daddy says we shouldn't lie," I said, ignoring that I'd just lied about being tired.

My mother blew a smoke ring and sighed. "Sometimes a lie is a kindness, Hope. It can protect someone's feelings."

I performed in the recital that night, in my little French can-can outfit with the jaunty beret. My mother was right—apart from the flashing cameras, it wasn't that bad. I missed only one sashay, when I noticed the empty seat beside my mother. My father stood in the back of the room.

In my memory, it was the very next day that my mother received the phone call asking her to return to LA, to star in the resurrected *Light Within*, but that timing seems unlikely. It's equally unlikely that she hung up the phone and immediately rushed upstairs to pack. And yet, that's how it plays out in my mind.

What I remember clearly is sitting on the floor, under the

kitchen table, sobbing, while my mother waited outside for the taxi that would take her to the airport.

"This is a great thing for your mom," my father said, crawling under the table to sit with me. "Acting makes her happy."

But even at six, I knew what lay behind his words. That I didn't.

I scanned the road constantly for Dylan's Volkswagen, certain its Pepto-Bismol color would stand out against the gray, overcast day. Given Jordan's slavish devotion to speed limits, any chance of catching up to them was slim. Still, I couldn't stop searching. Around Parsippany-Troy Hills, New Jersey, I glimpsed something pink on the horizon and pitched forward in my seat. It turned out to be a tattered billboard of a couple frolicking in a Poconos hot tub. Part of the heart-shaped tub had torn off and was flapping below the sign.

What was I going to say to my daughter when—if—I caught up with her? She was already furious at how I'd lied to her. My one consolation was that she didn't know about my agreement with Aaron. By signing that, I hadn't just promised to lie to Dylan for her entire life, I'd done something much more shameful. I'd taken money for it. Dylan would never forgive me. So if somehow she made her way to Aaron and found out . . . I couldn't bear to think about it.

Reminders of the coming election were everywhere: on the bumper stickers of passing cars, the competing lawn signs at every exit. For the first time in history, a woman was about to become a presidential nominee, and in the next few days, she was expected to announce her VP pick. Some commentators named Aaron the favorite, others leaned toward the labor secretary or the guy in Virginia. I didn't know what to hope for.

Aaron had broken my heart, chosen someone else over me, then paid me to keep silent about his daughter. I had every reason to hate the man, but my feelings about him had always been a confused jumble of regret and longing, anger and hurt, admiration and disdain. Aaron had made me promise never to return to Memphis, and if somehow he learned I was there, it would spell disaster. It would mean I'd broken our contract, and I'd have to pay back money I no longer had. And yet, in utter defiance of logic, I actively indulged in a fantasy of bumping into him, perhaps as he jogged along the river path. He'd tell me he regretted the agreement and would ask to see a photo of our daughter. He couldn't acknowledge her right now, but he'd stare at the picture and grasp my hand for a long second before parting.

Jordan had tuned the radio to a twenty-four-hour ABBA-thon, and I jumped as she began belting out the chorus of "Dancing Queen." After the second time the station played "Mamma Mia," though, I begged for something new. Jordan told me to open the glove compartment. An Elvis CD in a cracked jewel case dropped onto my lap.

"Excuse me?" I eyed her sideways.

She grinned. "All great road trips need a soundtrack."

"No thanks." I tossed the CD back into the glove compart-ment. I knew my aversion to Elvis was irrational and directly related to how much my mother loved him, but I wasn't in the mood.

When my phone rang, I grabbed for it, praying it was my daughter. I was disappointed to see Gary's number, though not surprised. In the email I'd sent him, I'd said to call if he needed anything.

"Is this the Great Vanishing Hope?" Gary asked, a clear edge in his voice. "One minute she's here—"

"It's a family emergency, Gary," I jumped in. "Unexpected. I'm trying to deal with it quickly."

"Hope, I'm not going to mince words. This disappearing act—"

"I've been meaning to talk to you," I interrupted again. "You asked for ideas to combat the used-book problem and I want to volunteer."

There was a long pause. "Say that again?"

I explained how I wanted to help him out on this issue. I could suggest some ideas, write up a proposal. Exactly *what* I'd propose was a problem for another day.

Gary's silence may have been surprise, or possibly surprise mixed with horror, but after some throat-clearing, he warmed to the idea. Yes, now that I mentioned it, he'd love something to present to the Editorial Board. They were meeting on Monday. Was that possible?

I swallowed hard and choked out, "Sure!" I'd brought my laptop. Once we stopped for the night, I could put in some time.

"That's what I like to hear!"

"Okay, great—" I tried to end the call, but Gary wasn't finished.

"Hope?"

"Yes . . . Gary?"

"What is it you have to do?"

I looked skyward for help. "Write the proposal?"

"No! You've gotta . . ."

"Oh!" I cringed. "Believe."

"That's it, Hope! That's how you get to be a star."

"Yessiree," I said, chuckling in a way that made me hate myself. Perhaps I'd inherited more of my mother's acting skills than I'd realized.

I shot Jordan a puzzled look as she steered the pickup into a deserted pull-off somewhere in the middle of God-Knows-Where, Pennsylvania.

"Bio break," she explained. "Too much coffee."

There were no porta-potties in sight, only a drooping plastic fence separating pavement from woods with two no-trespassing signs. I couldn't tell if the place had once been a weigh station or was private property. "You don't want to wait for a rest area?"

She rolled down the windows and turned off the ignition. "No, this is easier."

I understood. At rest stops, Jordan often got in trouble no matter which bathroom she used.

As Jordan stepped over the downed fence and entered the woods, I cringed for her beige espadrilles. Jordan spent a lot of time at Nordstrom Rack clearance sales, searching for size 14 shoes that weren't hideous. It took a while for her to disappear from sight, as her dress, with its explosion of scarlet and orange poppies, wasn't exactly designed for camouflage. Not unless one were hiding in a Marimekko outlet.

I thought again about the rural areas we'd be driving through. With the frame of an NFL linebacker, Jordan didn't pass easily as a woman. Even in supposedly liberal Massachusetts, people stared. Once they got it, most folks shifted their gaze, but not everyone. Jordan herself was admirably patient. "I'm tall. Their brains need a little processing time." As grateful as I was for Jordan's company on the trip, I worried folks in backwoods Virginia might need more than a little processing time. Then I chastised myself. *Don't make assumptions. Don't be a snooty northerner.*

A cool breeze blew through the truck's open windows, raising the hair on my arms. I scrolled through my phone, ignoring the gravelly crunch of a car pulling into the drive behind me. I had a text message from the sandy-haired firefighter I'd dated last fall. Could we have coffee sometime? He'd enjoyed our time together, still didn't understand why I'd broken things off. I closed my messages without responding. How could I explain what I didn't understand myself?

I was checking my work email when a hand slapped the driver's-side door. My shriek reminded me of the sound Dylan's guinea pigs made when I used to clip their nails.

"Sorry to frighten you, ma'am." The state trooper looked the part, right down to the aviator sunglasses and Dudley Do-Right hat. I kept my hand on my heart. He pointed to the empty driver's seat.

"Oh. My friend took a stroll in the woods to, uh . . ." I couldn't hit on the appropriate word for this context. "Urinate," I finished, not quite satisfied with the choice.

"Didn't see the signs, I guess." It was sarcasm. He flicked his head toward the woods. "We see a lot of drug activity in the woods here. You don't have to walk far to step on a needle."

"Oh, we didn't know. We're not from around here."

"It's also got a reputation as a hookup spot. For men."

"Huh," I said. "Wouldn't have guessed that, either."

The officer squinted at something over the hood of the truck: Jordan's orange shape emerging from between two oak trees. The trooper clearly struggled to reconcile the skirt with the six-five frame.

"Your driver?"

I nodded.

"License and registration please."

"NATURE CALL" WAS how Jordan explained her trip into the woods. I filed that phrase for future use and passed Jordan her wallet and registration. The trouble would start now.

"And you'd be George Robinson?" The trooper shifted his eyes between the picture and her face.

"Yes," Jordan replied.

"And where are you headed, Mr. . . . ." He caught himself, stopped, and didn't try to correct it.

Jordan said, "Memphis."

"Love Memphis," the cop said. "I'm a huge Elvis fan."

"Me, too!" I called out, opening the glove box to hand him the Elvis CD with the cracked jewel case, as if this corroborated my story.

"Love the King!" he said. "Been to Graceland twice."

"Oh, yeah," I agreed. "Can't get enough of that . . . Jungle Room."

He examined both sides of the CD, no doubt wondering why it had been stepped on more than once. "What's your favorite Elvis song?"

My mind went blank. "Ohhh, that's tough," I said, squeezing my eyes tight, as if struggling to choose just one. Finally, a title popped into my head. "Jailhouse Rock!"

"Huh." The trooper looked surprised. "I like 'Unchained Melody' myself." He handed Jordan back her license and registration. "You'd think it'd be vice versa."

Jordan nodded. "Funny world we live in."

THE TROOPER LET us off with a warning about trespassing and suggested we use a Dunkin' restroom in the future, as they were cleanest. After a five-minute discourse on who wrote the best Elvis tell-all, he made me type the author of a two-volume Elvis biography into my phone.

"Why in God's name did I claim to be an Elvis fan?" I said as I deleted it.

Jordan merged back onto the highway. "No clue. Puzzles me when you do things like that."

Her tone was light, but I bristled. "Like *what*?"

"We've discussed this before, Hope," she said. "You have a tendency to—how shall I put this—make shit up."

Jordan had mentioned that before, and I'd brushed it off. Now I was annoyed. "For instance?"

"I don't know." She tapped her thumbs on the steering wheel. "If someone gives you a purple scarf, you'll say 'I love it! It'll look perfect with my new sweater,' when I know you hate purple and don't have a new sweater."

I blew out a puff of air. "Everyone does that."

"Do they? Do you really like my outfit today, or were you just being nice?"

"I love it!" I insisted. What I thought was: *Shit. She's right. I do that.*

"I'm not criticizing, Hope, just observing. Not ten minutes ago, you were hating on Elvis. Next thing I know, you whip out his CD and claim to be his biggest fan. It's like a reflex with you. Like throwing people off track is what's important."

I changed the subject, pointing to a sign for Philadelphia and asking Jordan if she'd ever been there. No point continuing that conversation; I wasn't going to make Jordan understand. That's what lies do. They protect us and those we love. My mother had taught me that.

Chapter 9

Dylan

I wondered if Olivia might be having an aneurysm. Her eyes were closed, and she held her phone in one hand while pinching the bridge of her nose with the other. She'd been arguing with her oxygen company forever.

Seriously. For. Ever.

"Wait, wait, wait," Olivia shouted, making me leap about a foot in the air and grip the steering wheel harder. "You're charging me *what* for delivery to Roanoke?" She threw back her head and muttered, "Will no one rid me of these scam artists?"

I was glad Olivia didn't yell at me for driving over her oxygen machine, but she hadn't been real chatty since then, either. We'd had to remap our route. Without her oxygen concentrator, we couldn't risk taking the slower route through Pennsylvania, even if it might lose Mom. Olivia plotted how far we could drive with the tanks she had left, added some wiggle room, and confirmed our room at the Hampton Inn in Roanoke, Virginia. I looked at her calculations and grumbled a bit, convinced we could make it farther.

Thank God Olivia didn't listen to me.

As soon as Olivia hung up, she speed-dialed her fan-club president, Frances, who did all her social media. Olivia said there used to be an Elvis-themed diner outside Pittsburgh. Could Frances Google it and post a photo? Mention Andromeda might visit?

I shook my head and whispered, "We're not going by Pittsburgh anymore. We're going the other way."

Olivia asked Frances to hold and lowered the phone to her chest. "Yes, but your mother doesn't know that."

I had to laugh. "Olivia, you're kind of diabolical."

"Well, you don't play an evil character for almost forty-five years without some of it rubbing off."

After Olivia finished with Frances, she dropped her phone into her bag, leaned back, and closed her eyes. Olivia had been more tired on this trip than I'd expected. I'd been saving a bunch of questions for when she was in a better mood—like once we'd gone a few miles without breaking something—but now my grandmother looked like she could nod off, and I needed to talk. The endless trees, highway, and gray sky were starting to hypnotize me. I had no idea driving cross-country would be so boring.

"Olivia." I poked her arm. "Can I ask you a question about my father?"

Olivia clapped a hand to her forehead. "Dylan, we've been over this."

"No, listen," I cut in. "I'm not asking who he is. I'm just wondering . . . do you think he knows about me? I mean, that I exist?"

Olivia exhaled loudly. Her head was thrown back, like she

was searching the car ceiling for an answer. "Honestly, I have no idea. If he does know and he's never acted on it . . ."

"Then he's a douchebag."

"That *is* a possibility," she acknowledged.

"But if he doesn't know—I mean, if Mom never told him . . ." I waited to see if Olivia would finish the sentence. When she didn't, I did. "Then Mom's kind of the douchebag."

Olivia leaned forward and checked the gauge on her portable tank. "Don't be too hard on your mother, Dylan."

"Why not? She's a liar."

"Hope has a long history of getting in her own way." Olivia lifted her seatbelt to brush something off her shirt. "People like that, sometimes they just need a little push."

After I turned off the ignition at the 7–11 in Allentown, Pennsylvania, Olivia was still asleep, so I poked her shoulder until she opened her eyes, sputtering and complaining. Well, too bad. If she didn't want us to drive off the road into a ditch, she needed to stay awake and talk. Olivia asked for a hot tea. When she noticed my hand out, waiting for money, she grumbled some more, but gave it to me. You just can't please some people.

Once we were back on the highway, I realized there was one way to keep Olivia talking to me. "What's so great about Graceland?" I asked. "I mean, it's just a house, right?"

"Yes, a house." Olivia sighed, tossing her phone at her purse. "And not an especially big one, by today's standards."

"So . . ."

"Good grief, Dylan, give me a minute! I'm thinking how to explain." Olivia churned the tea bag up and down through the hole in the lid. "How about this. Have you ever felt like someone saved your life? Metaphorically, I mean. Gave you the strength to keep going in hard times."

I considered the people who'd been there for me in a pinch. George, maybe, after I was arrested for slashing that asshole's tires. Mom had gone apeshit, but George had rubbed my head and whispered that next time I wanted to trash a car, he'd show me better ways.

Olivia, though, didn't wait for me to answer. "Elvis had his first hit when I was seventeen, and I fell hard for him. Those ice-blue eyes. Sometimes they were twinkly and sometimes haunted, but they were like a window into his soul. I could tell he struggled, like me." Olivia sipped her tea and made an ugly face. The apple-cinnamon organic must have been a bad choice. "I bought Elvis's records with my allowance. I had to sneak them into the house and play them on an old record player in the basement when my mother wasn't home."

"Why?"

"Mother thought Elvis was the devil, the way he gyrated his hips. This was the 1950s, remember. My mother was a religious nut, but she wasn't alone in her opinion. Not in Hackensack, New Jersey. Plenty of preachers gave sermons on the immoral way Elvis moved his body. Frank Sinatra called him a sex maniac."

I almost choked on that one. Had my grandmother seen Miley Cyrus? Nicki Minaj?

"I read all his fan magazines, too, and learned that Elvis had bought a mansion, with tall white columns and a sparkling blue pool. To me, Graceland seemed like heaven. I planned to marry Elvis someday and live in that mansion. That dream kept me going when living with my mother was hell.

"When I was nineteen, just after the release of 'All Shook Up,' I came home from the secretarial school I was attending and saw a fire burning in the backyard. My mother was throwing my magazines and records in it. I caught her arm midair and begged her to stop. She pushed me to the ground. Said she was doing it for my own good, and I'd thank her someday."

"Jesus."

"Yes, I believe she mentioned him, too." Olivia sipped her tea and grimaced again. "I barely spoke to my mother after that. The following year, I took a secretarial job in New York and started auditioning. At twenty-five, they cast me on *Light Within*."

I had to admit, Olivia's mom sounded worse than mine. "What did she say about your date with Elvis?"

"Mother was gone by then."

"Sorry. When did she die?"

"Oh, she didn't die. Well, she did eventually, of course, but starting in my early twenties, she was in and out of institutions. They'd have some name for it these days. Borderline personality disorder, or similar. Back then, people just said she was crazy."

"You had a kind of messed-up childhood." Mom had never told me any of this.

"It was a long time ago. My father did what he could. He was my rock." Olivia dropped the apple-cinnamon tea in the cupholder, done trying. "In my experience, mother-daughter relationships are always a bit fraught," she said. "A girl needs a father."

AROUND HARRISBURG, OLIVIA suggested we grab Panera sandwiches and top up the caffeine. I don't know how they brew their iced coffee in Pennsylvania, but man, did it improve my mood. While I fiddled with the Elvis playlist, Olivia switched her portable oxygen tank, then studied her watch.

"Everything okay?"

She said it was, so I pulled out of the rest stop and turned up the volume on the King. I had to give the guy credit—his stuff was catchy. I learned the words to "All Shook Up" and "Memphis, Tennessee." Olivia said that when Elvis first started performing, he was just a nervous kid who couldn't control his knees, but the girls shrieked and clapped, so he kept doing it. Olivia and I sang along and jiggled our legs and laughed until I almost peed myself.

After we'd driven for an hour, Olivia leaned back against the headrest and closed her eyes. I switched off the music and kicked up my speed. Around Boston, 80 miles per hour is nothing. Cars zip by you on both sides.

When blue lights flashed in the rearview mirror, I lifted my foot off the gas and moved right, hoping he'd pass. The cop moved right, too. My pulse fluttered, but the cop didn't put on his siren. Maybe he was getting off at the exit. I returned to the middle lane. He followed, turning on his siren and jamming his cruiser up my car's butt.

"Jerk!" I signaled to pull over.

Olivia woke up and looked back over her shoulder. "Were you speeding?"

"A little."

"Good."

Olivia never said what I expected. After I turned off the car, though, I got what she was thinking. "Shit. Do you think Mom reported us?"

"Unlikely," she said. "You were speeding. Apologize and take the ticket. We don't have time to spare."

The cop sat in his cruiser, doing God knew what. Olivia opened the glove compartment. Out tumbled a tire gauge, a metallic blanket, a tube of wet wipes—every safety device Mom had shoved in there. "Where's the registration?"

The cop knocked on the window. I rolled it down. From TV, I knew just what to say. "Can I help you, officer?"

"You can help me," he shouted, in a major rush of bad breath, "and yourself in the future, by pulling over when an officer has his lights flashing." Spit flew out of his mouth and landed on my hand.

"Jesus!" I wiped his gross spit on the car seat. "You don't need to be a dick about it."

Hard to say who yelled first: my grandmother, shouting, "Dylan!" or the cop, screaming, "Out of the car!" It was pretty much a tie.

Roanoke, VA

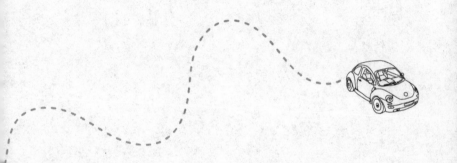

Chapter 10

Hope

As we drove through the green hills of the Shenandoah Valley, Jordan sang along to the Elvis CD, and I felt cracks developing in my aversion to Elvis. His soulful rendition of "Can't Help Falling in Love" got to me. I'd heard the song before, hundreds of times, but context changes everything. Now it collided with memories of Aaron.

I'd fallen so hard for him. In all the years since, I hadn't experienced those feelings with anyone else. It made no sense—I knew how the Aaron story ended, and it wasn't good. He hadn't been the person I'd imagined he was. Yet thoughts of him still crept in when I watched an old Cary Grant movie or indulged myself in a romantic novel. I've learned that you can love somebody truly, deeply, regardless of whether he deserves it.

As I quietly searched my bag for a tissue, my phone quacked, and my heart leaped from my chest. I snatched my phone from the console and stabbed frantically at my messages.

"What is it?" Jordan asked.

"Damn. CVS. I can get forty percent off one item."

"Honey, next time we stop, let me show you how to turn that shit off."

With my phone in hand, though, I did another check of email and social media. Dylan rarely used Facebook anymore. "It's been taken over by people *your* age," she complained. She preferred Instagram, though even there, she rarely posted.

My mother, in contrast, had thousands of Facebook followers, not to mention a deranged sycophant who ran her fan page. Olivia Grant's posts fell into three categories: Elvis news (amazingly, the man still generated it, decades after his death), soap opera gossip, and photos of kittens, because apparently kitten posts got the most likes. Mom also had a Twitter account, @WhatWouldAndromedaDo? Her followers tweeted their problems and Andromeda solved them. Trouble with an unruly teenager? Military school. Neighbors with a barking dog? Poison its kibble. Cheating husband? Rub his boxers in poison ivy.

I read a few of her old posts to Jordan. "They're meant to be funny, but still. The idea of my mother giving advice is scary."

Jordan was munching on roasted almonds. After a few minutes, she said, "Know what I find odd?" I waited as she finished chewing. "You're a good judge of character."

"You find that odd," I said. "Thank you."

"Hear me out. Remember when your colleagues at Edu-Learn were so excited about the new boss? The minute you met Gary, you knew he was a tool."

"Please let's not talk about Gary."

"Okay, okay. So think about the men you've dated over the years. The electrician . . . was that one Jim? Or was Jim the banker?"

"Both were Jim." I didn't want to talk about old boyfriends, either. Jordan claimed I went through men so quickly that she didn't bother to learn their names, only their professions: electrician, firefighter, merchant marine. "Get them together in a room, and they could sing 'YMCA,'" she'd once joked. I wasn't in the mood for that.

"My point," Jordan persisted, "is they were all decent, well-meaning types. The kind of guy who returns his shopping cart to the corral." She tapped her thumbs on the steering wheel. "So how did you not see that this Breckenridge guy was trouble?"

It was a question I'd often asked myself. "No idea. I worked closely with him for five months. I thought I knew him."

Jordan crunched her almonds. "I'm just surprised he turned out to be such a jerk."

"Me too."

UNFORTUNATELY, NOT TALKING about Gary didn't make him disappear. Our earlier phone call had excited his interest.

"Hope," he bellowed when I grudgingly picked up his next call. "Do you have a minute?" He didn't wait for an answer. "I've come up with an idea."

"For . . . ?"

"The used-book problem! I don't mean to steal your thunder. I'm just an innovator by nature."

I squeezed my eyes tight. "Great. Fire away."

"Coupons!"

"Sorry. What?"

"Sprinkled throughout the books. Students will tear out the coupons and voila! No resale."

"That's certainly . . . creative." I crossed my eyes comically at Jordan, who stifled a laugh. "I worry instructors won't like it much."

"They'll warm to it. They like free stuff, too. I'm giving this idea to you at no charge, Hope. You figure out how to execute. Send me a proposal tomorrow."

"I'll try, Gary. I'm on my way to Memphis."

"Memphis?" I couldn't blame him for his confusion. I never spoke of my hometown and didn't sound like a southerner. "You'll be back tomorrow, though."

Did he not understand where Memphis was? "I'll be gone the rest of the week." My email to him had mentioned only Thursday, but I was slowly adjusting to a new reality.

"Hope, the board meeting is Monday."

"I'll work this weekend," I added quickly. "You can call me anytime."

"I will. Remember, I took a chance on you." Gary loved nothing better than a good underdog story—an employee pulling something out of his or her butt to win the day. He believed his management style inspired this. "I know you won't let me down."

I hung up, thinking, *If I don't, Gary, you'll be the only one.*

WE'D PASSED SIGNS for Lexington, Virginia, when Jordan switched the radio to an NPR station covering the upcoming national conventions. "Noooo," I moaned. "Find another station. Whatever you want! Ricky Martin, Wham!, the Partridge Family. . . ."

Jordan clicked the radio off. "At least now I understand why you hate politicians," she said. "Though I do need to point out,

Hope, that it's a privilege to be able to ignore politics. Not all of us can afford to—"

"I know," I cut in. "Dylan lectures me all the time on my white, heterosexual, cisgender privilege. And it's not that I don't care or want to support the right causes—it's just easier not to hear Aaron's voice or see him on TV."

Jordan threw me a look. "It does beg the question: How in the world did you get involved with that man in the first place?"

I took off my sunglasses and wiped them on my T-shirt. This part of the story was innocent enough. "By accident. I needed a job."

"Wait—you were on his staff? How did I not know about this?"

"I wasn't paid at first, just a volunteer. It was soon after . . ." The words stuck in my throat, and I felt foolish. How many years had it been?

"After your dad died?"

I nodded. My father and George had remained close, even when George's relationship with his own father was strained and he'd moved to Boston. Dad and George exchanged letters, photos, Christmas gifts. When my father passed away during my last semester of college, George had returned to Memphis for the funeral. He'd seen firsthand what a wreck I was. For weeks, I could barely drag myself out of bed. I cut classes, skipped exams, didn't turn in papers. What George didn't know—what no one knew—was that I'd never graduated from the University of Memphis.

"I had a horrible time finding a job" was all I said. "I was so desperate, I applied at Kroger, and even they rejected me."

"Seriously? You'd have bagged groceries?"

"I needed to pay rent."

Jordan frowned. "Hope, I'm sorry. Your mother may be tight with a penny, but she wouldn't have let you starve."

"I refused to take money from my mother. We weren't on good terms back then."

Jordan nodded. "Oh, right. I forgot. You blamed her for what happened to your father."

"Well, not blamed her exactly . . ." I stopped to consider. "No, you're right, I blamed her." I lifted my phone for a quick check. "Let's not go there. I'm mad enough at her right now."

"Okay, but you still didn't explain how you ended up in politics."

"Oh, right. I started as a volunteer on Aaron's campaign . . ." I trailed off, still looking at my phone. Something new on my mother's Facebook page had caught my eye. "Shit."

"What?"

The photo she'd posted was of an Elvis-themed diner in western Pennsylvania—a place advertising Heartbreak Hamburgers and Hound Dogs. The caption said "Andromeda" might stop there. I switched to Google Maps and reviewed the options from Fairfield to Memphis. "I can't believe it," I shouted. "They took the longer route? Why?" I tugged at my hair. Had she done it on purpose? To lose me?

Jordan said nothing. I knew she wouldn't want to change course to follow them. I did and said so.

"Hope, that's crazy talk. Even if we made up the time we've lost and drove the exact same roads, the odds of catching sight of them are one in a million."

Jordan was right, but I couldn't let go. If there was any chance of stopping them before Memphis, I needed to try. "What are our options?"

"There are no options! You're just going to have to meet up with them in Memphis."

"I can't!" I was slapping my sunglasses against my leg in a way that probably wasn't good for them.

Jordan glared. "Don't be ridiculous."

"I can't go to Memphis!" I repeated. "I . . . signed an agreement."

She squinted so hard her eyes were slits. "I'm sorry. What?"

"I signed an agreement with Aaron. I promised to never return to Memphis."

"You're kidding, right?" She kept jerking her head to look at me. "A contract that says you can't go back to your hometown? Hope, that's not a thing."

"It's complicated. It's a long story."

"Well then," she said, signaling and swerving into the exit lane, "I need to hear it. We'll get dinner, and you'll start from the beginning and tell me everything. I mean it, Hope. Everything."

Chapter 11

Olivia

The girl was right: that cop was a dick. Still, I planned to have a stern talk with Dylan about the difference between being right and being stupid.

By the time I pried myself out of that clown car, the officer had cuffed Dylan and dragged her to his cruiser.

"Officer," I cried, all weak and warbly. Andromeda had used that shaky voice in Season 37, when the Libyan pirate tied her to the captain's chair before she broke free and clocked him with a whale bone. Yes, *The Light Within* had jumped the shark that season.

"Ma'am," yelled the cop. He had one hand on Dylan's head, ready to shove her inside his car. "I told you to stay put."

"I need . . . help." I dropped to my knees. My slacks would be filthy.

"She's out of oxygen!" Dylan shouted. I gave the girl credit. She was quick on the uptake.

A door slammed. No doubt Dylan was in the squad car now.

What was taking the man so bloody long? If I hadn't been faking, I'd have been dead.

As I clung to the open door, something under the passenger seat caught my eye. A jumble of papers. I slid them out. Several homework assignments, tests marked with a C or D, and—hallelujah—the registration. I placed it on the seat as footsteps approached.

Lights, camera . . .

I could have played the scene in my sleep. The coughing, the sucking for air. In Season 12, Andromeda had been trapped in a smoky elevator in a burning skyscraper, and in Season 23 (or was it 24?) she'd caught double pneumonia after her mobster boyfriend capsized his cigar boat in a frigid lake.

"Ma'am, do you need an ambulance?" The cop still sounded angry, like I was doing this for my amusement. Well, I was . . . but he didn't know that.

"My tank." I coughed. With a shaky hand, I pointed to the back seat.

The officer peered into the car suspiciously. Pushing the front seat forward, he lowered my portable tank to the ground, so I could switch the tubing. The old tank hadn't run out, but, again, the cop wouldn't know that.

"Thank you." I sucked in air with grateful gasps. "That's why . . . my granddaughter . . . was speeding. Had to . . . switch tanks."

The man responded, as expected, with a lot of blathering, his tone registering somewhere between grumble and shout. The girl shouldn't have done this, that, and the other thing. I made a big show of agreeing. Eventually, he got to the part I'd been waiting for. He'd let the girl off with a warning, this time, but she needed to obey speed limits and show proper respect. In other words, he didn't want to deal further with my medical issues.

After the officer helped me to my feet and returned to his car, I arranged myself in the Bug and waited. No doubt Dylan, when she returned, would be fuming. Or traumatized. Or both. That was okay. I'd happy her up.

I'd decided to give the girl a gift.

DINERS ARE MEANT to be fast, but nobody had told the staff at this one. The lone waitress was regaling truckers in the back with some long-winded story.

Dylan and I slid into the red Naugahyde booth. Keeping one eye on the blathering waitress, I removed the file folder from my bag and placed it on the table, keeping one hand on it, as if training a dog. Dylan needed to demonstrate patience and control. The girl started to reach out, then caught herself. That was okay. Self-control was a muscle. It could be strengthened.

The waitress was jabbering before she even arrived at our booth. When she came up for air, she leaned in to stare at me. "Your eyes are amazing. Are you . . . "

"Yes, I am," I said. "And I'll have iced tea, thank you."

"You didn't let me finish."

"You were going to ask if I was Andromeda."

She looked puzzled. "No, I wanted to know if you're wearing tinted contacts."

"In that case, the answer is no, and I'd still like the iced tea."

The waitress stepped back. "Hold on! Were you in—what was that soap?"

I forced a tight-lipped smile, nodded, and handed back the menu.

"I'm sorry," she gushed. "I didn't recognize you because of the . . ." She gestured across her face to indicate the cannula.

I'd had it. "Yes, and I didn't recognize you as a waitress because you're not actually waiting on anyone. Could you try to be more convincing in that role?"

The woman jerked her head back, as if slapped. She took Dylan's drink order and turned on her heel.

I tapped a finger on the folder. "Here's why I've been secretive about your father's identity, Dylan. I'm only making a guess. If I'm right, he's a public figure, a person of some importance. You cannot share this information with anyone." I slid out a copy of the Memphis *Commercial Appeal* article and pushed it toward Dylan. The headline read: "Breckenridge to Head Fundraiser. Senator a Likely VP Pick."

I'd seen the article last Sunday—a piece of luck, for sure. It reported that Memphis's favorite son, Senator Aaron Breckenridge, would headline two local events in the coming week: a fundraiser for city- and state-wide candidates Friday evening, and a speech at the University of Memphis on Saturday. Then all the stuff about him being a possible choice for vice president, a decision that could be announced any day.

I waited patiently as Dylan scanned the article, her brows knit. You couldn't predict Dylan. Sometimes quick, sometimes dreadfully slow. I pointed to his name: Aaron.

"No, I get it. But are you showing me this just because the guy's name is Aaron, and he's from Memphis?"

I closed my eyes and mentally counted to three. "I'm showing you this because your mother worked on his campaign for state legislature."

"Are you sure? Mom hates politics."

"Yes, I'm sure. That part isn't in question."

"Mom never mentioned it."

"Well, how surprising!"

Dylan bit off whatever she was about to say as the waitress returned. The woman placed our drinks on the table and took our order making no eye contact.

I inhaled deeply and adjusted my tone. "Your mom worked for this Breckenridge fellow after college. Hope didn't call me often in those days, but when she did, she sounded quite taken with him. I can't recall the specifics. To be honest, it wasn't so much what she said as how she said it. Your mother doesn't hide her feelings well."

"That doesn't prove . . ."

"What would you like, Dylan? TMZ footage? I told you it's an educated guess."

"And that's all it's based on?"

"That, and the fact that your mother quit her job with Breckenridge and left Memphis exactly eight months before you were born."

Dylan raised her eyebrows. Finally, the girl was interested.

"After she left the campaign, Hope phoned me from a friend's place in Nashville and insisted I play dumb if anyone wanted to locate her. I asked what any parent would: 'How much did you embezzle?' Got a rare laugh at that one." I closed the folder, jimmying it back in my bag. "All she'd say was that she'd had a falling out of sorts. Didn't want to talk about it."

"Well, that sounds like Mom. The not talking about it part."

"Yes, and here's the kicker. Shortly after Hope called, my agent received a phone message from Mr. Breckenridge asking to speak with me. He wanted to know how to get in touch with your mother. She'd left no phone number or forwarding address."

"Did you give it to him?"

"No. I respected your mother's wishes. I mean, who knew? Perhaps she *had* embezzled!" Dylan's jaw dropped. "I'm joking, Dylan."

"So you never talked to him? Breckenridge?"

"No. Sylvia played me his message, and I had her call back saying we had no information."

Dylan sipped her water. "The timing fits. And his name. But how can we know for sure if he's my father?"

"A reasonable question," I said. "I propose the most direct method."

"Which is?"

"You ask him."

Dylan collapsed back against the padded booth. "You want me to walk up to a US senator and ask if he's my father?"

"Not exactly. We'll work out the details later. But politicians are slippery, so it has to be done in person. We want to catch him off-balance."

Dylan fought to suppress a smile, but I could imagine the neurons firing, lighting her up from inside. Her father wasn't just alive. He was *somebody*.

The waitress brought our lunch and Dylan picked quietly

at her salad for a while before asking, "So why are we driving all the way to Memphis? We could have ambushed this guy in DC."

I offered my best pouty face. "Then I wouldn't have been able to visit Graceland."

The girl's laugh was full-throated. She was turning out to be a decent companion. For the briefest of seconds, I wondered if I could explain my plan for Graceland in a way Dylan could understand. Not yet. Maybe later.

I PULLED MY oxygen cart from under the diner's awning, lifting my face to the warm afternoon sun as Dylan retrieved the car. I could just devour bright, warm days like this. No telling how many more I'd have. I closed my eyes, tested my resolve. Yes, I could still carry out my plan for Graceland. Olivia Grant was no sentimentalist. I'd do what was best, even if in rare moments like this it made me a teeny bit sad.

As I settled myself in the Bug, Dylan flicked her head toward our waitress, smoking around the side of the diner. "I can't believe that woman recognized you. How long has that soap been off the air? Ten years?"

It's possible I clicked my seatbelt with more force than necessary. "Four. But it aired for nearly forty-five. So, really? Not so surprising." Pulling down the visor, I rubbed lipstick off my front teeth. "I'll have you know, Dylan, that at one time, everyone knew my face. I could barely eat in a restaurant. So many fans would stop by my table, my dinner would get stone cold."

"Wow. That sounds horrible."

I ceased rubbing, considered this odd comment. *Had* it been horrible? Annoying, perhaps. Especially those nights when I'd stayed home because it wasn't worth the trouble to go out. "It was also quite flattering, of course," I hurried to explain. "I couldn't shop for groceries without seeing my face on one tabloid or another."

"You and Mom are so different. She hates having her picture taken. She said just knowing her photo would be on a magazine cover would make her sick to her stomach."

"Well, lucky for Hope she's in no danger of that happening."

"So, how are we going to approach my father?" Dylan asked, in an apparent non sequitur that made my head spin. "He's kind of famous, right? We can't walk up to him on the street."

"No, of course not. Let me handle that. You concentrate on getting us there on time."

That seemed to satisfy Dylan, who shifted into the fast lane and sang along to "Heartbreak Hotel." A few dark clouds had rolled in and a smattering of raindrops hit the windshield. Dylan flipped on the wipers. I checked the gauge on my oxygen tank. I'd feel better once we got to the hotel, where the new tanks and concentrator would be waiting. And though it felt a tad obsessive, I twisted around to check the gauge on the tank behind Dylan's seat—the one the cop had helped me change. My memory was that it was half full.

Only it wasn't. My heart hammered as I checked the meter again. In the commotion with the cop, I must not have closed it all the way.

It wouldn't be enough.

Chapter 12

Hope

I pushed the combination plate closer to Jordan, who wasn't pulling her weight with the nachos. The Roanoke Mexican restaurant was quiet at this early dinner hour, the smell of chili powder and cumin wafting from the kitchen. Over the sound system, Waylon Jennings lamented his "Burning Memories." Jordan nudged the chips back toward me and leaned forward, her elbows on the table. No one was leaving until I coughed up the story I'd promised.

I started at the beginning.

AFTER MY FINAL, horrible semester at college, I'd been a mess, unable to find work. A local bakery had advertised for counter help, and when I headed in to apply, I ran into a former sorority sister gripping a large coffee in each hand. Veronica could talk a blue streak, and I pitied her coworkers if she planned to drink both. She'd graduated two years earlier, so she knew nothing about my father's death and its aftermath. When I told her about my frustrating job search, she said she was helping a guy running for Congress from Tennessee's 9th district and insisted volunteer work would beef up my resume. Before I could protest that I knew nothing about politics, she was leading me to campaign headquarters to give it a try.

As I trailed Veronica up the stairs to the third-floor walk-up, I was surprised by the graffiti, broken railings, and battered floorboards. At school, Veronica had bragged constantly about her brushes with the rich and famous, and I was certain she'd befriended me because of my mother, Memphis's Soap Queen. When she opened the door to the office, I couldn't picture Veronica working there. The place had once been an apartment, with kitchen cabinets painted an electric blue. Folding tables were piled high with computer printouts and a jumble of phones. Behind a Formica counter serving as a desk stood a sturdily built woman with a short blond afro. She was on the phone, breaking someone's balls over missing lawn signs.

Veronica waited for the drill sergeant to finish. "Our candidate, Aaron, is the underdog," Veronica whispered. "The incumbent is a jerk, but it'll take a minor miracle to unseat him."

"And Aaron is . . . a Republican?"

She looked at me aghast. "No, a Democrat. Aren't you?"

"Kind of apolitical. Will that be a problem?"

She shrugged. "Probably not. We're desperate. Just don't advertise it."

The sturdy woman hung up and sauntered over, sizing me up. "Who've we got here?"

Veronica said, "Shelley, this is Hope. She needs some office experience. Her resume is a disaster."

I shot Veronica a horrified look and thrust out my hand. "I'm a good writer."

Shelley squeezed it so tight I winced. "How are you at licking stamps?"

"Fabulous."

"I like your friend," she said to Veronica, then turned back to me. "When can you start?"

I glanced at my watch for no reason. "Now?"

"I take that back," Shelley said. "I adore your friend."

I stayed all day: stamping envelopes, folding fliers, proofing a mailing piece. The mindless work was soothing ointment for a soul scraped raw. I looked forward to meeting our candidate, this guy I was blindly helping. Veronica was reassuring. "You're going to just love Aaron."

I paused my narration, staring at the guacamole on my chip.

"And so you did," Jordan said.

"And so I did." I set down the chip. "Damn those Jedi mind tricks."

"I'm sorry, sweetie," she said. "Sorry you got hurt."

"No one to blame but me. I walked into it."

"Stop being so hard on yourself, Hope. You couldn't have known."

No, I explained to Jordan, there was definitely a moment on that first day, before I met Aaron, when I should have walked. Because Veronica, for all her nonstop chatter, had managed to bury the lede. As we descended the crooked stairs at the end of the day, I asked how she became involved in the campaign. She gave me a puzzled look, then mentioned a name I'd hoped never to hear again.

"Carly, of course. Didn't I say that? Aaron is engaged to Carly Boyd!"

"Great!" I beamed. But all I could think was *Shit, shit, shit.*

"So who is this Carly ho?" Jordan asked.

I struggled with how to describe Carly Boyd. She'd been a sorority sister at the U of M—my year, not Veronica's. Strawberry-blond and stunning, Carly was outgoing, hysterically funny, and hated me for no reason I could figure out. As best I could explain it to Jordan, Carly was a carnivore, and I was a leaf-eater. She saw me as prey.

Carly had an infectious laugh and was a wicked mimic. Her friends stayed close out of fear she'd turn on them. I knew Carly had money, though not the extent of it. The Aston Martin she drove should have been a clue. She'd lost her mother to cancer when she was only five—a pain I could empathize with, even though I'd lost my mother somewhat differently. Rumor was her father gave her anything she wanted except the time of day.

In fairness, Carly had a generous, giving side. She volunteered with disabled students at a local high school. Ever since she was sixteen, she'd taken two of those teens to the prom, helping the girl choose a beaded gown, the boy rent a tux, and the couple pose together for photos against glittery streamers. Her picture appeared in the paper with the new couple each spring.

I never should have joined that sorority. Veronica had talked me into pledging, certain the girls would be as enamored of my Soap Queen mother as she was. The pledges were invited to a huge party, and I decided that for once, I'd be the life of it. I drank and was loud, throwing my arms around my new friends to sing "American Pie," falling and laughing during the Electric Slide. The sorority sisters loved *that* Hope; unfortunately, she wasn't the same Hope who moved in sophomore year and reverted to her bookworm, quiet self. After leaving the dining room one night, I heard one girl whisper, "Wasn't she the one who was so much fun at the party?"

In the spring of that year, I came out of my room late one night and heard some girls laughing in the kitchen. As I descended the stairs, I realized they were poking fun at my Eeyore pajamas. The pj's were a gift from my father that apparently nobody but me found cute. "I feel so out of it," Carly was saying. "No one told me that Eeyore is the new Pooh!" She made another crack about my baggy sweatpants and Gap sweatshirts. Everyone laughed. I slunk back to my room.

That might have been the extent of it if I hadn't started dating one of Carly's old boyfriends in the fall of my senior year. I had no inkling it might be a problem until a sorority sister hinted, "I'd be careful about that if I were you." Another asked if I'd gotten Carly's "permission." I thought she was joking. Carly had been the one to dump him, after all.

One night I came home from the library and found Carly and a handful of her friends in the living room, leaning over a coffee table, listening to something on a tape recorder, and howling with laughter. Halloween was the next week, and the recording sounded frightening: whispers, moans, and screams like a woman being stabbed repeatedly. Finally, I understood: the recording was of a couple having sex. One of the girls looked up and noticed me. She whispered to the others. Carly looked away. The post-coital giggling and conversation continued. I realized the couple on the tape was Ben and me.

Someone apparently had placed a tape recorder under my bed, and though no one would identify the person responsible, I thought I knew. An anonymous Good Samaritan left the cassette on my desk, and I destroyed it, but the damage was done. The story had gotten around the school. I quit the sorority and searched for a room off campus. I could have moved home with my father—in retrospect, I'd have given anything if I had—but at the time, it seemed childish. I rented a room from a hair stylist named Ashlee who had three rotating boyfriends and asked if that would be a problem. I said nothing was a problem. I believed that. Until three months later, when my father died.

AFTER LEARNING WHO Aaron was engaged to, I probably shouldn't have returned to his office. I almost didn't. But I woke the next morning depressed about my job prospects and frustrated from having to tiptoe around one of Ashlee's boyfriends snoring on the sofa. I'd keep my promise to Shelley and work one more day. I liked Shelley. She'd gushed over a press release I'd rewritten and shared photos of her little boy, Owen, and her partner, Sandy. "Shelley and Sandy," she'd joked. "Why we don't live in Aruba is beyond me."

Aaron, on the other hand, I was prepared to dislike. What kind of person would marry Carly Boyd? I worried Carly might drop by and asked Shelley that morning about Carly's involvement with the campaign. She said Carly had never set foot in "this pit," and wanted nothing to do with politics. That said, Carly's father was Aaron's biggest backer, a real player in the party and the person who'd recruited Aaron to run. "Richest man in Tennessee," Shelley whispered. "You didn't hear that from me."

Shelley and I were alone in the office late that afternoon when I finally met Aaron. He barreled in and waved distractedly in my direction while calling out to Shelley that he'd located the missing lawn signs. His opponent's volunteers had been caught stealing them, he said, pounding the counter with glee. I didn't think Aaron was as good looking as Veronica had implied, but with his lanky frame and wavy dark hair the word "wholesome" came to mind. He reminded me of Tom Hanks in *Splash*. My father and I had loved that movie.

"Have you met our new volunteer?" Shelley asked as Aaron headed for the inner office.

He pivoted to look at me, then Shelley, then back at me. "You're not Kendall?"

I'd met Kendall earlier that morning. I wasn't thrilled to be mistaken for her.

Aaron rushed over, holding out his hand. "I'm so sorry. I thought we'd met. I'm Aaron."

"Hope," I said, shaking his hand.

"Perfect!" He grinned. "You don't happen to have a sister named Prayer, do you?"

I shook my head. "I once had a friend named Destiny, but she moved."

"No worries," he laughed. "Hope is just what we need."

I STOPPED THE story there, as Jordan and I needed to get back on the road. While Jordan signaled the waiter for our check, I had to smile at the irony.

As it turned out, I was the last thing Aaron Breckenridge needed.

Chapter 13

Dylan

Just as we passed a "Roanoke, 1 mile" sign, Olivia gasped and pitched forward in her seat.

"What's wrong?" I yelled. "Are you okay?"

Olivia waved at me to keep driving, so I did, but she kept taking in sharp little breaths followed by endless exhales. Like she had bad air in her lungs and couldn't get it out.

By the time I saw the sign for the Hampton Inn, I'd nearly missed the turn, and the Bug jumped the curb. At the hotel entrance, I drove onto the sidewalk and leaped from the car.

"Wait here," I shouted.

Stupid thing to say.

I sprinted to the check-in desk, pushing aside an elderly couple in matching golf outfits.

"I need help!" A young, bearded man was on the phone and held up one finger. "It's an *emergency*!" I shouted. "You have a package for Olivia Grant. Oxygen tanks. She can't breathe."

The man put down the phone. "Should I call an ambulance?"

"Just get the package! Now!"

He ran an eye over the reception area and checked under the counter before running his fingers across a keyboard. "I have a reservation for Olivia Grant. Nothing about a delivery."

"She had them sent here. Where are your packages delivered?"

"Right there." He pointed to a small FedEx box in the corner, clearly not big enough, and returned to the computer. "There's no note with the reservation." His head shifted between me and the screen like a Boomerang video. "I don't know what to tell you."

"*Shit!*" I slapped a hand on the counter and raced back outside, throwing open Olivia's door. Olivia was pulsing up and down in a horrible way. Her lips were blue.

"They don't have the tanks."

She closed her eyes and heaved forward in a hideous gasp for air.

"The hospital's five minutes away," shouted a voice behind us. The clerk had followed me. "Quicker than an ambulance." He pointed down the street. "Turn right, then go straight for about a mile, then left. You'll see it."

I jumped into the driver's seat and bounced the Bug off the curb. At the corner, the car in front of us stopped for a yellow light, and I laid on the horn. Snatching Olivia's phone from the console, I yelled, "I'm calling your oxygen company." I took Olivia's thumb and held it against the home screen to open it. I found Air Systems in Olivia's recent calls and pushed redial just as the light changed. "We are experiencing unusual call volume," the recording said. I pressed zero, and it went to voicemail. As we careened around the corner, I waited for the beep and screamed: "You idiot, douchebag, incompetent assholes. Can't you do a single fucking thing right?"

Rocking forward in her struggle for air, Olivia gave me a thumbs-up.

I THOUGHT OLIVIA would be fine once she was hooked up to oxygen. Even in the ER, though, her breathing was ragged, like she'd just run a 10K. Three doctors examined her. No one seemed real keen on talking to me, but from what I overheard, they were worried Olivia's "air hunger" episode had created other issues with her heart. An orderly wheeled Olivia out for tests.

When they returned, Olivia waved me close and whispered, "Take some money from my bag and get something to eat." Her voice was still raspy. "Circle back in half an hour. I'll see how fast I can get out of here."

"What about the tests? What if the doctors want you to stay?"

"Grifters, all of them," Olivia huffed. "They need to fill beds. If they can't find something wrong, they make it up."

I plucked a twenty from Olivia's purse and wandered the halls, pretending to study the black-and-white photos of old Roanoke while I tried to piece things together. How could Olivia leave the hospital? She needed her oxygen tanks. And now that it was after business hours, the freaking Airhead company wouldn't call back—especially since I'd been so busy cursing them out that I hadn't left a name and number.

Other questions worried me even more. What should I do if Olivia insisted she was fine, and the doctors said she wasn't? Mom claimed Olivia inhabited her own reality. Was that true? What if—here was a truly scary thought—*I* was actually the more responsible party on this trip?

Eventually I found the hospital cafeteria and bought a Greek salad, no feta. I snagged a table in the back next to a bulletin board full of boring shit about patients' rights. Searching through my bag, I picked out a pink-and-blue bumper sticker that said, "Trans Rights Are Human Rights," pulled off the backing, and stuck it across the bottom of the bulletin board. When I turned around, a young woman in scrubs was eating pizza at the next table and watching me. Shit. Was I in trouble? The woman smiled and lifted her chin in approval.

I grinned back. Before I became an activist, I'd been a nobody. Then I'd slashed that jizzbag's tires at school, and kids clapped me on the back, said I was ballsy. I felt like a woman of action, someone my father would've been proud of. Now I was going to meet him. I imagined his strong grip as we shook hands, the way his forehead would crease as we discussed important issues. I had lots of ideas, and as a senator—hell, maybe vice president—my father had the power to make those things happen. Most importantly, though, he'd love my spirit. Appreciate me for who I was, not the boring person Mom wanted me to be.

I picked up my phone, ready to give that oxygen company another piece of my mind—plus, a callback number—but my phone was already vibrating. The manager at the Hampton Inn had our packages. They'd been sent to the other Hampton Inn, out by the airport, by mistake. Did I want to come get them? Well, hell yeah!

When I got there, the hotel manager was so apologetic, she paid for our room and upgraded us to one with a balcony. Olivia was going to lose her mind. I drove back to the hospital blasting "That's All Right (Mama)" at full volume and brought a fresh oxygen tank to the ER in Olivia' cart. I'd help her get dressed and we'd leave. Maybe check out the minibar.

But the ER room where Olivia had been was empty. I asked at the desk for Olivia Grant, and the guy typed in her name, then excused himself. A woman accompanied him back and hovered behind him, scanning the screen. She moved around the counter to speak to me.

"I'm sorry, honey. There was a problem with your grand-mother."

Chapter 14

Hope

From the outside, the Tater Tot Motel and Grille in rural Virginia made me worry we'd been wrong to pass up the Super 8 twenty minutes earlier. Although the billboard-sized sign looked freshly painted and proudly offered free ice, the tater tots logo resembled nothing so much as a pile of dog droppings.

The office smelled like ketchup, apparently from the dark red scented candle on the counter. An old man hobbled in from a back room. A few tufts of white hair sprouted from the top of his head and his eyebrows turned up at the end like a Klingon's.

Before I could open my mouth, he said: "Only got one room left and it's got two twins." He gestured vaguely at our truck. "Feel free to push 'em together, if you and the mister prefer."

I glanced back at the truck, wondering how Jordan would feel about sharing a room with me, and also what the motel owner would say if he saw my mister. Right on cue, the truck door opened, and Jordan emerged, her arms clasped behind her, stretching forward and back. "Let me check with my friend," I said.

I told Jordan I was fine to keep driving, but she yawned. "I'm okay sharing a room if you are, Hope. It's after nine and I'm pooped. I could sleep on a sidewalk." We'd lost almost an hour when, twenty minutes outside Roanoke, I realized I'd left my wallet in the restaurant. We'd had no choice but to retrace our steps.

Back inside, I handed the man my credit card and waited for him to say he'd been wrong, that room was taken. He didn't. As he ran my card, though, he watched out the window as Jordan did tai chi. With a sly grin, he handed me the receipt to sign.

"Your friend—she wouldn't happen to be a performer, would she?"

I almost said no, she was an auto mechanic—maybe like the one who fixes your car, because, really, do you know what your mechanic wears on weekends? But I was tired. My tight-lipped smile was a nonanswer.

"I know'd it," he said with pride. "I seen a great show over in Louisville with a big gal like that."

I had no idea what kind of show he'd seen and wasn't going to ask. I slid my receipt from the counter and left.

THE PANELED ROOM was unremarkable if you didn't count the bright orange bedspreads and Mr. Potato Head wall clock. Exhausted from worry and lack of sleep, I longed to pull the blanket over my head and melt into oblivion. Unfortunately, I needed to get started on that presentation for Gary. As Jordan unloaded her toiletries, I tossed my laptop into my bag and slung it over my shoulder.

"I'm going to check out the Tater Tot Grille. See if they serve anything that isn't alliterative."

"Oh, don't be so damn picky, Hope," Jordan called after me. "Just go with the tuna tartare."

Outside, the sun had set behind the huge motel sign, and a pink haze rested on the distant hills. Procrastinating, I unlatched the gate on the chain-link fence to take a closer look at the pool and sat on the end of a chaise lounge. Discarded towels were draped over plastic chairs and a solitary pool noodle floated in the deep end. The water, illuminated by pool lights, was turquoise yet oddly opaque. A few years back, when a Boston woman had lain dead in the deep end of a public swimming pool for two days before anyone noticed, I'd wondered how that was possible. Now I knew.

After that tragedy, the media had been full of articles about drowning, reminding people that a swimmer's distress is harder to recognize than one would think. A drowning person doesn't shout or flail their arms. Instinct takes over, prioritizing breathing so the person can't call for help, and forcing their arms to the side to keep their head above water.

This wasn't news to me. Years earlier, in the wake of my father's death, I hadn't thrashed about or called for help, but quietly slipped under. It was Aaron who'd thrown me a rope. Working for him had given me purpose, a reason to get out of bed each day. Something—someone—I believed in.

By midsummer, my responsibilities on Aaron's campaign had snowballed. It had nothing to do with skill—I was simply putting in more time than anyone else. I drafted personal letters to supporters and likely voters. I clipped newspaper articles about high-school scholars and athletes, laminated them, and mailed them to parents with our congratulations. Impressed by my initiative, Shelley gave me a key to the office and had me supervise the phone volunteers while she canvassed with Aaron. Veronica made a snide remark about my promotion, but she put in half the time I did and gossiped more than worked.

I returned to the office in the evenings, eager to hear Shelley's and Aaron's canvassing stories. We pulled beers from the minifridge and opened bags of Tostitos. The energy of the campaign lifted me up, and I offered my own ideas. What about meet-the-candidate backyard barbecues? Wasn't a new park being dedicated in East Memphis? Should we go to that? What could we do to make a splash at the Fall Festival? Shelley and Aaron praised and encouraged my suggestions. Walking home after our meetings, I wanted to skip down the sidewalk.

Through Aaron, for the first time, I became interested in political issues. Aaron believed deeply in bipartisanship and thought people of integrity from both parties should work hard to compromise and find common ground. He worried that the politics of hate was taking us down a bad road and recalled the unlikely friendships of Tip O'Neill and Ronald Reagan, or Ted Kennedy and Orrin Hatch. Coming from a family of hunters, he supported people's right to own handguns and rifles, but was determined to get automatic weapons off the street. And probably because of his graduate degree in geology, Aaron was already, in 1998, concerned about global warming, and promoting sources of clean energy. In his carefully researched positions, I found something I could believe in.

My feelings about the man himself were more complicated. Aaron was good with people—funny, charismatic, charming—but he also knew it. He was a little too sure of himself for my taste. I watched him lose his temper more than once over the tactics of his opponent, and although Shelley stopped him from doing anything rash, her furrowed expression told me she worried. Sadly, none of that got in the way of the little crush on him I was nursing. Aaron was a good listener and I delighted in making him laugh. He always asked what I was reading, or what movies I'd seen, and begged for stories about my crazy roommate and her rotating boyfriends. Once, as I pointed to a problem in the database and he leaned in, putting his hand over mine to control the mouse, sweat broke out along my hairline.

Still, I told myself my little crush on Aaron was harmless. The man was engaged, after all. To a woman who hated me.

One Friday, Shelley and Aaron took the night off, and I was alone in the office, updating the database and feeling a little blue. I wandered into the tiny inner room and opened Aaron's desk drawers. Bins of pens, Post-its, and paper clips were meticulously organized. Below them was a drawer with a boxed dressed shirt and three rolled ties. On a bookshelf I found a boombox and small stack of CDs. Two were Bob Dylan albums. My father had loved Dylan, and I'd grown up with his music.

I shouldn't have brought the CDs and boombox back to where I was working. When Dylan began singing "Time Passes Slowly," one of my dad's favorite songs, my eyes filled, and I lowered my head onto my folded arms.

The CD had been finished for several minutes when I heard a key turn in the lock. I was upright and blowing my nose when Aaron appeared. He started to say something, then stopped.

"It's not the work," I said quickly, wiping under my eyes.

"Good," he said. "Because if my campaign has this effect on people, I may need to rethink things."

"It was the song." I stopped, afraid my voice would break.

He squinted, confused.

"Sorry." I lifted the boombox from the floor to the table. "I borrowed your Bob Dylan CD."

"Dylan did this to you?"

His face was so serious, I couldn't help smiling. "My father was a huge fan. He died earlier this year and I've had some trouble getting past it." I pressed my mouth tight to regain control. "Probably more than is healthy." I made it through the sentence, barely.

"Losing a parent is hard." I'd heard Aaron mention his dad in speeches but had no idea if his parents were still alive. "Maybe you could use a break," he said. "Why don't we go get coffee next door? We can talk about Dylan." He added hastily, "Or not, if that makes it worse."

"You must have tons to do."

"Not till eight thirty. I'm taking my fiancée to a movie. She won't mind if we have coffee first."

I was pretty sure she would, but I grabbed my sweater and followed.

TURNS OUT IT's hard to have coffee with a guy running for Congress. Two firefighters, a young couple, and an elderly woman using a walker stopped by our little table to shake his hand. I nearly spat my coffee when the woman asked if I was Aaron's fiancée. He joked I was a campaign volunteer who only got paid in caffeine. After she left, he said, "We're not going to be able to talk here. Let's take the coffee back to the office."

Outside, though, the sweet smell of barbecue filled the air and a gentle breeze cut through the day's humidity. I didn't want to return to the office. I suggested we walk a couple blocks to a small park overlooking the Mississippi.

I often brought my lunch to this park, with its gorgeous oak trees and benches tucked randomly into curves of the paths. Scattered throughout were some historical markers, cannons, a large statue. We found an empty bench and sipped our coffee. Aaron asked about my father.

How could I describe my dad? A man who read me the entire Lord of the Rings series, beat me at Scrabble, and helped me with thousand-piece jigsaw puzzles. After my mother returned to her soap opera, my dad and I ate dinner most nights on TV trays, watching *The Light Within*, which our housekeeper videotaped daily, and then some seventies rerun, like *The Odd Couple* or *M*A*S*H*. The sound of my father's nasal, honking laugh made everything funnier.

Aaron said his dad was an ex-Marine who later trained as a Presbyterian minister and died in a hunting accident when Aaron was thirteen. His father had been soft-spoken but firm and highly principled—a role model to his son, whom he took on long hikes and camping trips. "I still talk to him, ask his advice on things. Do you think that's crazy?"

"Depends," I said. "Does he respond?"

He grinned. "You sound like my fiancée. She's a skeptic, too." A breeze on the back of my neck made me shiver. Had Aaron mentioned my name to Carly? I knew I had to say something soon before it was too late.

"The day my father died, he sent me a sign." He tilted his head to watch my reaction, then continued. "The afternoon of his hunting accident, I went completely numb. I didn't know what to do. I wandered deep into the forest behind our house, and standing there, right in the middle of the path, was this amazing buck with, I swear, antlers this big." Aaron held out both arms. I widened my eyes, impressed. "The sun was shining through the leaves, and the buck's head and neck were shimmering. I stood there and it looked right at me. I knew it was my father telling me that he was okay."

"Amazing." Although I didn't believe in signs, it was clear Aaron did, and I respected that. "I wonder what sign my father would have sent me, since we didn't hike." I laughed. "Maybe an *Odd Couple* rerun."

Aaron shrugged. "Or a Bob Dylan song."

That sent a shiver up my spine. I picked off a leaf that had blown onto my skirt. "My father's favorite song was 'Time Passes Slowly,' about the unhurried pace of life in the mountains. It reminded him of his childhood around Gatlinburg. Do you know it?"

"Well, that *was* my CD," he said, rolling his eyes. "I won't sing it for you, though. For that, you should be thankful."

"I'm not sure it's Dylan's singing that makes the song."

"Hey, hey, hey," he warned. "Watch that."

"Oh, I love Dylan's lyrics. Very poetic. My father wanted to name me after him, but my mother didn't like Dylan for a girl."

"I love the name Dylan, girl or boy," Aaron said, sipping his coffee. "And that song is one of my favorites, too. There's a line at the end, something about staring straight ahead and trying hard to stay on the right path. Sounds like something my father would say. Keep moving toward what's right." He wiped a drip off the side of his cup. "It can be hard to do in politics. More complicated than it seems."

"Hard to do in life," I agreed. "More complicated than it seems."

We were both silent. I thought about the disagreement Aaron had with Shelley two nights earlier. Someone had given Aaron dirt on his opponent, a man whose business dealings were underhanded and arguably illegal. Aaron wanted to make the information public, even though leaking it might compromise our source. He argued that the incumbent was scum, with ties to every unsavory element in Memphis. Taking him down was for the greater good—the end would justify the means. Shelley disagreed, insisting they keep their campaign positive and above reproach. "We won't sell our souls," she said. Aaron deferred to her, but I had the sense that he wasn't happy. The next day, when I mentioned the argument, Shelley shook her head. "Aaron is more ambitious than he seems," she said. "We need to watch that."

Aaron tipped his head back for the last swig of coffee, then crumpled the cup. "I'd better go. I'm meeting Carly in fifteen minutes. Can I walk you back to the office?"

It was now or never. I had to come clean. I screwed up my face, as if having trouble with my memory. "Did I mention that Carly and I were in the same sorority at the U?"

"Really? You know Carly? No, you never told me that."

"I doubt she'd remember me." I was downplaying it, hoping he might not say anything to Carly. "I was the quiet type."

"Yeah." He laughed. "Carly's definitely not the quiet type."

As we walked back toward the office, silently, enjoying the beautiful evening, I made excuses for why Aaron had fallen for Carly. She blinded people with her charm and drew them closer to her with confidences and quick-witted barbs. Aaron was thirty-two, a decade older than me, but he'd done his graduate work in geology in the Yukon and served five years in the Marines. I wondered if he might be a little naive about women. He shrugged off Carly's shopping sprees and lack of interest in his campaign as if most women were like that. Something very old school there.

I asked what movie he and Carly were going to see.

"No idea." He grinned. "She'll tell me when I get there."

THE SOUND OF giggles woke me from that memory. The moon had risen above the Tater Tot Motel and in the dusky light, a young couple unlatched the pool gate. The man carried a bottle of wine and plastic cups; the bikini-clad woman held towels. They were headed for the hot tub, and the woman shrieked when I moved from the shadows. I assured them I was leaving and scooted out the gate.

A phone was ringing nonstop in the dark motel office and reminded me I should check my own landline at home. Almost no one used that number, including me, and it took three tries to access my voicemail. When I finally succeeded, though, I had a message. A woman named Brenda from someplace in Roanoke, Virginia. Her soft voice was hard to hear, and my first thought was Crap, what else did we leave at that Mexican place? But no. Something about my mother.

Shit, shit, shit.

I raced back to the room and dumped out my purse on the bed to find a pen. I managed to play the message again without deleting it and took down the number.

Jordan emerged brushing her teeth. I was surprised she was still awake. "Wha'a matter, sweetie?" she asked as my shaky fingers hit the wrong button and I swore. "Wha' wrong?"

"Some hospital in Roanoke has my mother. Shit! I hate these menus." Finally, a human being picked up. When I repeated the message I'd received, he put me on hold and then transferred me. Jordan spit out the toothpaste and brought me a glass of water. "I can't believe this." I moaned. "We were just in Roanoke! I thought my mother and Dylan went the other way."

After two more transfers, a woman with a heavy Scandinavian accent answered. "I'm so sorry you've been passed around," she said. "Unfortunately, the situation has changed."

"Changed how?"

"We've lost your mother."

Chapter 15

Dylan

I was gasping by the time I skidded around the corner into the hospital room where the nurse said they'd put Olivia. I nearly collided with a technician wheeling out some monitor. "Be careful!" the woman snapped.

Olivia was propped up in bed. Her eyelids fluttered, as if she could barely hold them open. "They drugged me." Her words slurred together, like she was drunk.

"They said you had a panic attack."

She lifted a hand in a half-hearted *whatever!* It flopped back down. "Told them I couldn't stay. Wouldn't take no for an answer." She reached for her phone on the side table and knocked it off. "Hampton Inn called."

"I know! I have your oxygen tanks and the new concentrator." I picked up her phone and sat in the chair beside her. "What happened? Why did you freak out?"

"Can't stay in hospitals."

"Your insurance won't pay for it?"

"Not that." Olivia shook her head wearily. "Long story." She closed her eyes again, and I assumed that was the end of it until I heard her murmur, "Last time I woke up in a hospital, my daughter was dead."

OLIVIA MADE A popping sound when she slept, like spaghetti sauce starting to boil. I slunk down farther in the chair. At first, Olivia's words had scared the living crap out of me. What did she mean, her daughter was dead? What a creepy-ass thing to say. Then I realized it was the drugs talking. The doctors must have given her some good shit. As soon as Olivia dropped that bombshell, she'd conked out, and I'd checked my phone. Nothing was wrong with my mother. In fact, Mom was texting me nonstop. Verifiably not dead.

I wanted to get to the hotel, but when I jiggled Olivia's arm and said her name, her eyes opened to little slits, then closed again.

"The sedative should wear off soon. They didn't give her much." The shadowy figure in the doorway stepped inside. It was the same nurse I'd seen in the cafeteria. "When your grandmother panicked, she tried to rip out her IV. The orderlies had to tackle her."

"Can't we do something to wake her up? We need to get going."

"I don't think so, but the doctor will come through soon. You're welcome to wait."

Like I had a choice.

I slumped back in the chair and picked up my phone. For the first time all day, I had time to kill, so I Googled Aaron Breckenridge. Since the diner, I'd managed only a quick glance at his photo. He had wavy dark hair like me—well, when mine wasn't pink—and a single dimple. Now I went to his Senate website and pored over his bio. The man was an ex-Marine who'd done geology graduate work in the Yukon, which wasn't exactly living in a yurt, but closer than I'd expected. In terms of his politics, though, I found little about the issues that interested me, like #MeToo or LGBTQ rights. On Twitter, Breckenridge posted stuff about tax breaks for small business owners and improving veterans' hospitals. Blah, blah, blah, shoot me now.

Switching to Google Images, I discovered a photo of him and his wife. So he *was* married. His wife was pretty good-looking for someone my mother's age. I clicked on a photo of Breckenridge with a boy at a Little League tournament. The caption said the kid's name was A.J. Aaron junior, no doubt. Ick. A different shot showed him with two boys. The other one was probably Chase, or Blaine, or, God help me, Zander. But no, when I clicked on the photo, it said his younger son's name was Dylan.

I WAITED AN hour while Olivia slept. When I couldn't stand it any longer, I tried gently shaking her arm and whispering her name. I nearly lost my shit when suddenly, with a loud scraping of metal rings, the curtain was yanked aside by a hugely pregnant doctor. The woman started talking to Olivia before she was fully awake, pumping a pedal to raise the top of the bed. She introduced herself as Dr. Chu and ordered me to leave. Olivia, her voice still hoarse, insisted I stay.

Being that pregnant must be a bitch because Dr. Chu was cranky as hell. The woman's navel looked like a cork about to pop through her tight scrubs As she checked Olivia's heartbeat, sliding the stethoscope down the back and front of her gown, I explained that we had Olivia's oxygen tanks now, so we should be all set. Doctor Downer didn't even respond.

"Your blood work showed dehydration," she told Olivia. "Probably from when you were breathing so hard, though maybe just from traveling. Did you bring water in the car?"

"I certainly can do that going forward." Olivia's voice was steadier now, and her tone was polite. "Air and water are two things I should be able to control."

"And yet," the doctor said crisply, "here you are." Perched on a stool, her belly pressed against a portable desk, Dr. Chu typed into her laptop. "I want you to stay the night, so I can keep an eye on you."

I started to interrupt, and Olivia shook her head quickly. "I can't do that," Olivia said. "We're on a schedule."

"You can change your schedule. Your EKG was abnormal when you came in. I'm going to order more blood work so we can rule out an MI."

"MI?" Olivia huffed. "I already have COPD. Aren't those enough letters?"

"Funny," the doctor said, though she didn't smile. "Myocardial infarction. Your low oxygen might have caused a heart incident. I need to make sure before I let you go—especially since, apparently, I'm releasing you into the care of a teenager."

I noticed a slight pause before Olivia replied, "Of course," in a voice that was hard to decipher. Annoyed? Resigned?

The doctor was reading something on her laptop. "When you were incapacitated, we phoned your emergency contact. Hope Robinson?" Olivia wouldn't meet my panicked stare. "I'd feel better releasing you to her care. Let's see what tomorrow brings."

As soon as the doctor left, I let loose the string of f-bombs I'd been holding in.

"Dylan, calm down. We're going to be fine." Olivia shot a glance over her shoulder. "I've busted out of tougher joints than this."

Chapter 16

Hope

You *lost* her?" I yelled into the phone. "What does that mean? My mother . . . died?"

"No, no!" the hospital administrator replied. "Sorry! I mean, literally, lost her. We can't find her."

I lowered myself onto the bed. Jordan had spit out her toothpaste and stood behind me, her hand on my back. "I don't understand," I said.

"Her granddaughter wheeled her to the cafeteria, and they must have left the hospital together. Security is checking the video. We believe your mother left willingly, though, of course, we can't be sure."

Of course she did. Massaging one temple, I tried to refocus. "Why was she in the hospital?"

The woman read through the doctor's notes. Apparently, my mother's portable oxygen supply had run out, and they'd resolved that issue, but wanted to keep her for observation. Unfortunately, the doctor treating her had gone into labor two hours earlier. Maybe one of the ER doctors could call me? The woman didn't sound terribly confident.

I squeezed my eyes shut and said that wouldn't be necessary. "I think I have a pretty clear picture."

The woman heard this as criticism. "Well," she scolded, "your mother should not have taken off like that. There are procedures. She could have signed herself out against physician's orders."

Just what I needed—to be yelled at for my mother's misbehavior. I hung up.

JORDAN WENT TO bed, but I was too rattled to sleep and headed off again to the Tater Tot Grille. I nabbed a booth in the back and asked for coffee. And then, screw it, a side of tater tots.

Roanoke? *Roanoke?* We'd had *dinner* there. How the hell could my mother be in Virginia, when according to her Facebook post, she'd stopped at some Elvis-themed diner near Pittsburgh? I opened Facebook and reread her post. It was vaguer than I'd remembered, saying only that Olivia Grant *might* drop by. I Googled the diner. The photo she'd posted was a screenshot from their website. I slammed the laptop shut. My mother was deliberately throwing me off their trail.

I ran through our options, but nothing had changed. They'd probably left Roanoke already. All Jordan and I could do was stay the course and try to beat them to Memphis. I had to keep them from going anywhere near Aaron.

The tater tots arrived, hot, golden, salty, and crisp. I inhaled them, then opened my notes on Gary's project. "Coupons" was all I'd written. Ugh. How could I make coupons in a textbook less tacky? Perhaps something from Staples or OfficeMax, to help students buy school supplies? Special offers from Dell and Apple? Maybe we could work with Barnes & Noble, to get discounts at their campus bookstores. I listed a few more ideas, suggested how we might partner with those organizations, drafted an email to Gary, and hit send. I prayed it would be enough to appease him. Show him I was on the job.

I ordered one more cup of decaf and gave myself permission to type Aaron's name into my browser. It had been several months since I'd done this, and not surprisingly, the search linked me to a dozen op-eds on possible vice presidential candidates. Aaron was the most moderate choice, which could be a plus or minus. Several commentators claimed his popularity was all about character. Aaron was principled, for sure, but Shelley had often reined him in—fought his impulse to go after his opponent with guns blazing, using every tool at his disposal. She'd argued against leaking that dirt even as he argued the end result would justify the means. No denying Aaron was ambitious. I'd learned that the hard way.

I clicked on a few more links. A *New York Times* op-ed said Aaron's record was "so clean it squeaks." An NPR interview hit on the same point, with the interviewer asking, "Are there no skeletons in your closet, Senator? None?"

"My life is an open book," Aaron had replied.

I closed the laptop with more of a snap than I'd intended.

If that's so, Aaron, it's only because you've ripped out some pages.

I SLEPT TERRIBLY and hauled myself out of bed just before seven, throwing on cutoffs and a clean T-shirt. My stomach sloshed around like a washing machine. If lack of sleep and nonstop worry weren't the culprits, the four cups of coffee—two regular, two decaf—I'd downed at the Tater Tot had pushed it over the edge. And yet, somehow, my solution was more coffee.

I was determined to leave the motel as quickly as possible, and had my bag packed, but was torn about waking Jordan. The shadow of a wig on top of the dresser encouraged me to give her space. Hand on the doorknob, I called out: "I'm getting some coffee at that convenience store down the road. Can I bring you anything?" Subtext: we'd be eating on the fly again.

I expected a groggy reply, but Jordan was awake. "Big and black, please. And the largest muffin they have."

"Will do. I'd like to get on the road as soon as possible."

"Roger that. Ready in a flash."

I appreciated her enthusiasm, even if I didn't quite believe the time estimate. She'd told me once how long it took her to shower, shave everything, fix her hair, and apply makeup. I was prepared to be grateful if she was ready in under an hour.

The Food 'N Fuel convenience store offered pump-your-own coffee and a unique assortment of muffins including pistachio and apple chai. The girl behind the counter had hair streaked with periwinkle blue and a lower lip pierced by an arsenal of metal. Two studs hanging from her nose looked to me like dripping snot. I trained my eyes on the muffins.

"Any you'd recommend?"

She cupped a hand to her mouth, as if someone in the empty store might hear us. "Stick with the blueberry."

"Okay, two blueberries," I whispered back. I added, "I like your hair," even though I didn't, at least no more than I liked Dylan's. This was exactly what Jordan accused me of—saying stuff to please people. But I'd felt the need to say something, and her hair was more attractive than the artillery.

Outside the store, I rested the coffees and muffins on a picnic table. Jordan wouldn't be ready yet, so I took a seat, punched open my coffee lid, and sipped. No aroma. It tasted like coffee-flavored water. I considered asking for my money back but decided not to. The girl had reminded me of Dylan.

I stared down the road at a line of billboards promoting a law firm, two local candidates, and a new breast cancer facility. I paused on the last one. It made me think again of Shelley. Had she been one of the lucky ones?

AARON'S CAMPAIGN HAD taken a sucker punch to the gut in late August when Shelley was diagnosed with a malignant breast tumor and needed a radical mastectomy. She told us this early one morning as she and Aaron were leaving to canvass for the day. Even Veronica was too shocked for words, and Aaron hugged Shelley and told her to go home, take some time off. Wiping at an eye, she insisted that was the last thing she needed. She grabbed her bag of brochures, headed for the door, and called back to Aaron, "Get a move on, lard ass."

Shelley interviewed three candidates to replace her, but none were even remotely a good fit. Aaron decided we would make do until Shelley recovered and split her job between Veronica and me. I was shocked when Aaron added us to the payroll. I asked Shelley how this would work with our stretched-to-the-limit budget, and she assured me it would be fine, though she didn't elaborate.

Veronica's nonstop talking made her a nightmare at door-to-door canvassing, so Aaron and I took to the streets together, every day from ten to four. We chatted up old men in bed-room slippers, women in gardening gloves, and beer-bellied guys pushing lawn mowers. Most folks were cordial, though a few griped about roads or taxes or too much government. One geezer who interrupted Aaron every time he started to speak said, "Well, I still ain't voting for you, but I'll shake your hand." Another woman screamed at him and threatened to write a letter to the newspaper. After she slammed the door in our faces, Aaron deadpanned, "That went well."

I wasn't the relaxed schmoozer Aaron and Shelley were, so I took notes while Aaron did the talking. At the end of the day, Shelley would call me from her hospital bed or living-room recliner to go over the numbers. The work was both exhausting and oddly exhilarating.

The fact that my feelings for Aaron were straying danger-ously toward the romantic was neither here nor there. He was engaged. I tried not to twist everything he said about Carly into a fantasy that he was growing frustrated with her and checked my elation when I learned that he and Carly didn't live together. Apparently, Carly had a part-time job coaching gymnastics an hour from Downtown Memphis and preferred to hang by her dad's pool while Aaron worked day and night on the campaign. "Plus," he added, "she thinks my apartment is a dump."

As Aaron drove us to canvass in Millington one morning, he said, "Oh, by the way, Carly does remember you."

My heart sank. "She didn't like me much," I blurted.

He puckered his mouth into a that's-absurd face. "You're imagining things. Carly can come off as judgmental some-times. I don't think she means to. It all depends on her mood. She and I have definitely disagreed on people."

I felt certain I was one of them.

I gripped the armrest and asked if Carly minded that he drove around all day with another woman.

Aaron fiddled with the radio, trying to get a weather forecast. "I don't think so. She never minded that Shelley came everywhere with me."

Shelley was pushing fifty and in a committed relationship with another woman. I didn't think the situation was comparable. Part of me was devastated that he did.

The other part of me heard, with interest, that he hadn't specifically told her.

Not long after that conversation, Aaron took off a Sunday afternoon to spend with Carly. "So she doesn't dump me." The next day, he looked like shit. When he couldn't focus on my copy for a mailing piece, he apologized. "Carly and I had a little blowup last night. Still trying to find my equilibrium."

"I'm sorry," I said, though I wasn't.

"The campaign hasn't been easy for her. She hardly sees me."

"Should we . . . get her involved?" I asked, planning to kill myself if he said yes.

"Oh, God, no." He laughed. "She'd be a horrible distraction. She demands my full attention."

I WAS STILL clutching my coffee on the picnic table—though not drinking it—when a shuffling behind me made me sit up straight. The blue-haired girl from the convenience store was striding toward me, a large cup in each hand.

"I'm so happy I caught you," she said. "That coffee was horrible. I made you two new ones."

I thanked her, and she trotted back to the Food 'N Fuel. I stood and headed back toward the motel. Even from a distance, I could make out a tall figure in a mint-green skirt hoisting our suitcases into the truck. I checked my watch. I'd been gone less than twenty minutes.

"Bless you, Jordan," I whispered.

THE BLUEBERRIES THEMSELVES were fresh and tart, but the muffin crumbled into a million pieces. We were headed toward Knoxville, driving through some gorgeous green hills and valleys. I must have passed through here when I'd left Memphis almost eighteen years earlier, but I had almost no memory of that trip. A flat tire somewhere in Maryland. A new box of tissues purchased at each stop.

As we passed another hospital sign, Jordan asked, "Do you think your mom's really okay?" For all her joking about Diva Olivia, Jordan was fond of my mother. In May, they'd had a ball watching the Daytime Emmys together. They'd rated all the gowns on a scale of exquisite to wouldn't-wear-it-on-a-bet.

Jordan's question was fair. When I'd checked my landline messages again, I'd discovered an earlier message from the hospital saying my mother had suffered a panic attack, asking me to call. "No idea if she's okay."

My answer must have sounded short, because she added, "I realize you're pretty upset with Olivia right now."

I sighed. "That's how Mom and I work. We take turns upsetting each other." I crumpled my muffin paper. "Or maybe 'disappointing' is a better word."

"Hope . . ."

"What? It's true."

Jordan sighed. "I'm sorry that having Olivia as a mother made you feel somehow not worthy."

I let out a long exhale. "It's not that I feel unworthy, exactly. Just not . . . enough." When I glanced over, Jordan was frowning. "That's the best I can explain it. I've never felt that I was enough for her." I hadn't been enough for Aaron, either.

Jordan reached over and patted my hand. "You're plenty for me, Hope."

"Thanks." I mustered a weak smile.

Probably sorry she'd taken the conversation down this road, Jordan switched on the radio. As we listened to Hall and Oates beg Sara to smile, I thought about something I'd overheard when I was maybe seven or eight. My dad and I had picked up my mother at the airport, late. I'd been dozing on and off in the back seat until I heard my mother, all excited, say she'd shown my photo to an agent who thought I could be the next Punky Brewster.

My father shot a look to the back seat to confirm I was sleeping. "Livvy, that's nuts. Hope can't even bear to sit for school photos. I had them retaken twice, and she still has this pained look on her face, like she desperately needs to pee."

"She'll learn."

"No, she won't." His voice was warm but firm. "You have to let Hope be Hope. Otherwise, we shouldn't have had her."

My beloved father would have been devastated to know that whenever I replayed that conversation in my mind, it was in his voice that I heard, "We shouldn't have had her."

Chapter 17

Olivia

What a world! Who thought I'd see the day I'd be delighted to wake up in a Hampton Inn?

Hoisting myself out of bed with an unbecoming grunt, I steadied my feet on the dizzying striped carpet and scanned the queen bed next to me for signs of life. Dylan had to be somewhere under the mountain of blankets and comforter. God help us if the girl had stayed up all night watching an *Erin Brockovich* marathon.

I detached my cannula from the oxygen concentrator and hooked it to one of the new portables, still chuckling over the bossy, prego-saurus doctor who'd wanted to impound me in that hospital. I'd shown her. After she'd waddled off, I asked permission for Dylan to take me to the cafeteria in a wheelchair. Once there, I'd changed into my own clothes in the restroom, and Dylan and I had strolled out the front door.

Well . . . Dylan had strolled. I shuffled. The whole hospital experience had knocked the wind out of me. I could admit to that.

Hospitals gave me the heebie-jeebies. Nursing homes, too. I refused to pass from this life into the next smelling of disinfectant and pee, my last act on earth drinking apple juice through a straw. That was how people ended in such places—not with a bang, but with a diaper.

I'd seen that kind of death before. My beloved father had wasted away from Lou Gehrig's disease, and I had no intention of following in his footsteps. I'd direct my own final act, thank you very much. That hospital experience had taught me a valuable lesson. I'd been too cavalier about my oxygen. I wouldn't repeat that mistake.

Once I'd showered and dressed, I turned my attention to Dylan. We needed to get moving. I grabbed what felt like a leg under the comforter and shook it. The girl sputtered, then threw off the covers and glared at me. I began folding my clothes and noticed her watching me as I stowed my pill bottles. When I reached down to hoist my suitcase onto the bed, Dylan leaped up, shouting she'd get it.

"For heaven's sake, Dylan! I'm not an invalid."

Dylan stepped back. "Sorry! You seemed a little shaky last night."

"Shaking with relief! I'm just delighted to be free of that place."

Dylan moved to the window and twisted open the blinds. "You sure said some crazy shit after they drugged you."

I stiffened. Had I let slip something about Graceland? "For example?"

"You said last time you were in a hospital, your daughter died."

Ah. That was a different issue altogether. Was it possible

Dylan knew nothing about Beth? Of course it was. Hope was good at secrets, even those not her own.

Well, if I was going to chastise Hope for hiding things, I needed to be more forthcoming myself. I'd enlighten the girl. Do some sharing, as the touchy-feely types like to say.

I'd practiced talking about Beth. Over the years, through trial and error, I'd learned to keep my hands occupied. People were more comfortable if we didn't make eye contact. So as I told Dylan about my first child, I fiddled with the clothes in my bag, refolding things several times that had been folded adequately to begin with. I spoke about the small girl who'd been Hope's sister, and about the accident. How my four-year-old had been in the back seat when a truck had T-boned our car. How I'd woken in the hospital to learn my daughter was gone. "Ever since," I concluded, "I've suffered from a bit of PTSD about hospital stays."

When I looked up, Dylan was sitting on her bed, a hand over her mouth. "I had no idea about any of this," she said. "I'm so sorry. How bad were you hurt in the crash?"

"Pretty badly." I tucked my meds into a corner of the suitcase. "This was before airbags, remember. I was in a coma for nineteen hours. Broke my arm, two ribs."

"Your husband, too?" The girl had never met her grandfather. She slid off the bed and reached under it for her duffel.

"Harold wasn't with us. I was bringing Beth to preschool."

"Wait." Dylan jerked upright. "You know how to drive?"

"Technically."

"But Mom said you never learned."

"Hope has never seen me drive. I haven't since the accident." Dylan flung her duffel onto the bed with some force. I understood. Here was yet another untrue thing Hope had told her.

I hadn't meant to fuel that flame. "You need to cut your mother some slack on this one," I said. "The accident was a painful subject in our family. I never spoke to Hope about it. Not once."

The truth was, I had no memory of the accident. A blessing, surely, though I'd always wondered if my horror of screaming children was a remnant of that terrible day, some repressed memory of the moment before impact. I shivered. The air-conditioning.

"Well, thank you for telling me," Dylan grumbled. "At least someone isn't keeping secrets."

I leaned over my suitcase to pull the zipper around. In all honesty, I'd liked talking about Beth, saying her name. Now that we were headed back to Memphis, it felt right to remember my daughter.

As I straightened, Dylan was suddenly beside me. I started to protest that I didn't need help, when the girl lurched forward and hugged me. A long embrace. Tight. It took my breath away.

THE BUFFET BREAKFAST offered chafing dishes of rubbery scrambled eggs, undercooked sausage, and biscuits and gravy. Free, though—there was that. And fast. I made myself tea and snagged a table at the far end of the room while Dylan loaded a bowl with granola and a mountain of fruit.

I couldn't stop thinking about that hug. I hoped the girl wasn't getting attached. Something I hadn't considered, though God knows why not. People adored me, often regardless of how I treated them. It was a gift. I'd pay better attention going forward. Hard as it might be, I'd have to make myself less lovable.

I felt bad, too, that Dylan believed I wasn't keeping secrets. The fact was, I had a big one I couldn't share with her. No telling how Dylan might react to my plan for Graceland. She'd done well enough with the news about her father. I might tell her eventually, just not yet. I needed to get my own house in order.

While Dylan helped herself to toast, I unzipped the little compartment inside my handbag and pulled out the bottle of pills. I opened it and counted them, then replaced the lid, locking it with a twist. The recent experience with air hunger had unnerved me. Suffocation and panic were not what I wanted to feel as I took leave of this world. Counting the pills was reassuring. I had more than enough to transport me to la-la land, to avoid any discomfort. Enough, even, to do the job, though removing my cannula at the last moment would seal the deal.

Dylan dropped her heaping plate on the table. "Mom won't stop texting me. I'm thinking of blocking her."

"Don't. We need to keep tabs on her. What was this morning's missive?"

"Same old crap. I'm endangering your health. Please meet up with her somewhere. Yada yada yada." Dylan shoved a spoonful of granola into her mouth and didn't stop talking, a habit I needed to speak to her about. "What's wrong with Mom, anyway? Why doesn't she want me to meet my father?"

I sipped my tea. "Not sure. Perhaps the man doesn't know about you, or perhaps she's trying to protect his career, but she's making too much of this. We're going to approach him quietly, in private, not schedule an interview with Fox News. Whatever happened between Hope and that man, she needs to acknowledge it, get over it, and move on." I reached over and snatched a piece of toast from Dylan's plate. We had to get going.

"I've been wondering," Dylan said. "When did you figure out Aaron Breckenridge was my father? When he called you all those years ago, looking for Mom?"

"Of course not. I didn't even know your mother was pregnant then. No, it was not that long ago, actually. The last time I visited Boston. Three years ago? Four?"

"Five. I was eleven."

"Whatever. I'd turned on the TV and there he was on *Meet the Press* or one of those political shows. I said to Hope, 'Isn't that the man you worked for?' Do you know what she said?" I leaned forward, opened my eyes wide for effect. "'No!'"

Dylan's fork halted midair. "It *was* him she worked for, right? You're sure?"

"Of course I'm sure! The question was rhetorical, for God's sake. Did Hope think I was stupid?"

"Phew." Dylan opened a small tub of maple syrup and poured it on her granola.

"Even if I hadn't known better, your mother wouldn't have fooled me. Hope is a horrible actress. When she lies, her voice goes up an entire octave."

Dylan nearly choked with laughter. "And she talks way too fast."

"Exactly. Like Kristen Chenoweth on crack. You should have seen the way she lunged in front of me to switch off that TV! That's when I put things together. Later that morning, I asked you to remind me of your birthday and sure enough, when I counted back nine months, Hope had been in Memphis, working on his campaign."

I steeled myself for Dylan's next question. Why hadn't I told her any of this before? If I'd known who her father was years ago, why wait till now? And really, what could I say? It had never occurred to me. Dylan had been a child, not a real person. I'd filed away the information until I had a use for it.

Dylan's mind was elsewhere, though. She rotated the cube of cantaloupe on her fork, examining it from all angles. "You didn't remember it, though."

"What?" The girl could be confounding.

"My birthday. You've never remembered it. No card, nothing."

True. Over the years, I'd chosen to ignore birthdays, especially my own. "When is it again?"

"Next week. July twenty-first. Maybe this year, we can celebrate together. Get a cake."

"Yes." The toast had lost it appeal. I put it down, half-eaten. "That would be fun." I pointed to Dylan's plate. "Two more bites and we need to leave."

Dylan scowled, but I dropped my napkin on the table and stood, pleased. Already I was making myself less lovable.

IN A VEHICLE the size of a postage stamp, pretending to sleep was a practical matter. I could take only so much of Dylan's blathering about #MeToo or banning six-packs to save turtles. I needed time to think, to plan.

I was also spending an inordinate amount of time arguing with Harold.

I bickered with my husband silently, of course. Only idiots speak out loud to the dead, as if they can't hear you otherwise.

When I pictured Harold up there in the ether, he was wearing his favorite argyle sweater, relaxing in his favorite armchair, his reading glasses still a tad crooked on his nose. (In heaven, they'd managed to fix the bald spot on the crown of his head, though. That was nice of them.)

On most issues, Harold was easygoing. About Hope, though, the man could be downright opinionated. Harold didn't agree with my plan to force Hope back to Memphis. I knew he wouldn't. Over the years, whenever I'd given Hope a little push for her own good, Harold had fought me tooth and nail.

"Liv," Harold said this time, "you've got to let Hope handle her problems in her own way."

"Handle? Hope can't even see that she *has* a problem."

I couldn't fault Harold for being blind to Hope's issues. I hadn't recognized them myself until earlier that spring. Alone at home, tethered to the bloody oxygen tank, I actually listened to what my daughter said on the phone. (Funny when you thought about it. The oxygen was meant to help my breathing, but it'd done amazing things for my hearing.)

And that was the trick, wasn't it? You have to listen closely to Hope because she rarely shares what matters most. Back then, when I asked what was new, she'd insist breezily that everything was fine. "Oh, Dylan and I are great! Nothing to report!"

Once I was paying attention, though, I called out Hope on her faux-breezy bullshit. It took time, of course, but over the course of a few weeks, Hope gradually offered more. Turned out, she was going through a tough patch with the teenager. Dylan had become a stranger, grunting at her mother, not meeting her eyes, dressing like Bradley Cooper in *American Sniper*. Hope was terrified she was losing her daughter.

I knew how Harold would react to this news. "Dylan needs a father."

That was Harold's answer for everything, and maybe it would help, but I didn't see any prospects on the horizon. Hope went through men like chewing gum.

Then, suddenly, that Breckenridge man was all over the news, and I'd all but kicked myself at my own stupidity. That secret I'd figured out years ago. Was *that* where Hope's issues had started? With that man? That one big secret, and the boat-load of lies needed to cover it up?

"Don't you see, Harold?" I persisted. "Dylan was getting older, asking questions. To keep everything hidden, Hope was pushing her away."

I knew Harold would understand, eventually. A problem like Hope's had to be confronted head-on, and this trip to Memphis was the way to do it. The experience would be painful, for sure, but there was no getting around it. Hope needed to rip off the Band-Aid, give her wound some air, some sunlight. What we keep hidden doesn't heal. It festers.

Knoxville, TN, to Nashville, TN

Chapter 18

Hope

"This is it!" Jordan sang out. I had to grip the armrest as she veered hard into the parking lot of the Lookie Here Bar & Grill.

"You can't be serious," I said. The sign featured a giant illuminated winking eye.

"Hope, you have no sense of adventure."

Jordan loved nothing better than a good dive and had been craving barbecue since we left New England. Something about these run-down joints said home to her. Something about them said *Deliverance* to me.

We entered through the saloon-style doors and grabbed a booth. A sheet of white paper was spread over the red-checkered tablecloth. This was gonna be messy. Jordan ran her hand across the table lovingly. "My daddy used to take us to a great barbecue place over the bridge in Arkansas," she said. "I was eating their pulled pork and white bread before I was weaned."

I pictured a chubby baby George and his four older sisters, their faces covered in barbecue sauce. "Sounds blissful."

"It was." Jordan's smile was thoughtful. "I miss those times with my dad."

George and his father had reconciled, if imperfectly, before Uncle Vern died. Vern had told his son, "I don't care what you do as long as I don't have to see it."

"It wasn't ideal, but I understand how much it took for my father to meet me there," George had told me, philosophically. "Thank goodness love wins in the end."

A server arrived with large, dripping glasses of ice water. While Jordan quizzed her about specials, I glanced at my phone. Nothing new. As I waited for Jordan to finish, I noticed a tattooed guy at the bar to our left squinting at her. The man caught my eye before slowly twisting back.

A PILE OF crumpled, orange-stained napkins surrounded our plates by the time I thought about the squinty-eyed man again. He'd been joined by two companions and flicked his head in our direction while they craned their necks to see. My last bite of coleslaw tasted sour.

I'd been with Jordan before when someone had lobbed a slur in her direction. Earlier this spring, with my car in the shop for a new transmission, Jordan had driven Dylan and me to Stop & Shop for groceries. We were carrying our bags from the store when, across from us, three middle-aged women in church clothes stuffed themselves into a Ford Focus. As they backed out, the woman in the back, whose fake eyelashes would have put Tammy Faye Bakker to shame, rolled down the window and called to Jordan, "I hope you know you're going to hell."

Dylan charged at the car. "You'll get there first, you ugly, bigoted bitch," she screamed before the car peeled away.

Jordan shook her head and grinned. "Now, Dylan. That's not very Christian of you."

As they stowed the groceries, Jordan and Dylan laughed about the lady's terrified face and how she'd probably peed her Depends. I hung back, stunned, wishing I'd had the presence of mind to do what Dylan had.

Now, as I shifted in my seat at Lookie Here to keep an eye on the men, I knew we should hightail it out of there. I beckoned our server to ask for the check.

As the waitress started to leave, Jordan touched her sleeve. "Quick question? I need to use the powder room, and don't want to cause a ruckus. Which room would you prefer I use: the one that I'm dressed for, or the one I have the plumbing for?"

My stomach twisted. The restrooms were down a hallway behind the bar.

Our server frowned like she didn't understand, then took in a quick breath and mouthed, "Oh!" Given Jordan's size and heavy makeup, most people understood she was cross-dressing, but apparently our waitress had seen only a very tall woman.

"Gosh," she said, smiling and shaking her head in a pleasant way that instantly doubled her tip. "I don't know. Let me ask my manager."

"Hold on," I interrupted, fumbling with my wallet. I was covering our meals, gas, and hotels for the trip, though Jordan had tried a couple times to snatch the check out of my hand. "Let me give you my credit card, because we need to run." After the waitress left, I whispered, "Those guys at the bar have been giving us the stink eye."

Jordan glanced over. The men were watching TV. Shit. Had I been imagining things? "I'll pee quickly, and we'll zip," she said.

The waitress returned with the credit card receipts. "On the restrooms?" She leaned toward Jordan, sharing a secret. "Here's what the manager suggests. I'm gonna check and be sure that no one is in the ladies'? And then, if you wouldn't mind," she said turning to me, "while she's in there, why don't you wait outside and tell people it's occupied? Is that good? That way, we won't surprise anyone or ruffle any feathers."

I could have kissed the girl. Even when people meant well, they sometimes screwed up Jordan's pronouns. I exhaled deeply and thanked her.

As soon as the waitress gave the all-clear signal, we picked up our stuff and headed to the narrow corridor with "Ladies" and "Gents" signs sticking out of the wall. The hallway was only steps from the end of the bar. Once Jordan had gone inside, I rested my back against the wall, pretending to be absorbed with my phone. In my peripheral vision, though, I could see the three men whispering and jerking their heads in my direction. A drop of sweat ran down the side of my face.

The guy next to Squinty, with a shaved head and bushy walrus mustache, slid off his stool and moved toward me. His buddy, a skinny fellow whose jeans hung off his hips, followed. If things got ugly, I decided to take the skinny one and let Jordan handle the Walrus. Behind them, though, was Squinty, with a giant eye tattooed on his neck. Who'd handle him?

"Howdy," I said, then wanted to slap myself. *Howdy?*

The Walrus jerked his chin toward the restroom. "Your friend ain't no lady."

"Don't see many folks like that around here," added Skinny. "He got a problem?"

My heart was thumping so hard I was sure they could hear it, but something in Skinny's "folks like that" comment called to mind the Tater Tot motel owner. The one who'd been excited to see a "performer" like Jordan.

"As a matter of fact"—I smiled, forcing myself to switch pronouns—"he does." I stepped in closer to them, which seemed to catch them off balance. "He wasn't supposed to leave the movie set dressed like this," I whispered. "Ron Howard is going to kill us! But we were just dying for some good barbecue, you know? The caterer on set is horrible."

Skinny backed up to look me over. "You're in a movie?"

"Well, *I'm* not. I'm . . . a makeup artist." I flushed as I realized I wasn't wearing a speck of makeup. "But my friend . . . well, if people realize who she—I mean he—is, we're gonna be in huge trouble. Someone takes photo, it goes viral, and suddenly our secret filming location isn't secret."

"What secret location?" asked Skinny, his eyes wide. "Around here?"

Sweat slithered down my back. I didn't even know what town we were in. The Walrus gave Skinny a look like he couldn't believe what an idiot this guy was. "If she says it's secret, do you really think she's going to tell you?"

"Dang. You can't say?"

"No." I resumed breathing. "So please don't create a scene, okay? We're already late getting back to the set, and you know what a bitch Angelina Jolie can be."

"Angelina *Jolie* is in the movie?" Skinny did a little jig.

I slapped both hands over my mouth. "I didn't say that. You did not hear that from me."

The Walrus gestured at the restroom door. "Who is he?"

I locked my lips with an invisible key.

At the bar, Squinty slid off his stool and sauntered over. Skinny pulled him aside and whispered.

As if on cue, Jordan opened the ladies' room door. She took in the whispering duo and turned to me, trying to decode the situation. I gripped her arm and gestured to the men to let us pass. Nobody was more surprised than I when they did.

I turned back to them. "Remember, not a word." Their eyes were fixed on Jordan's face.

Jordan waited until we were in the parking lot before she said, "Hope, what the . . . " I pointed vigorously at the truck doors, and she clicked the remote to unlock them. Before we could get in, though, the three guys pushed through the restaurant's doors and barreled toward us, Skinny waved a knife.

Or not a knife. An iPhone.

"Just one photo," Skinny called out. "We won't show it to anyone."

I feigned impatience and took the phone, telling Jordan to go pose with the nice men. Jordan shot me an appalled look. "Quick!" I repeated through gritted teeth.

Jordan was a head taller than all three, and Squinty yanked Skinny out of the way to stand next to her. Jordan cautiously lifted her arms around the shoulders of the two closest men and gave a lopsided smile.

"There." I thrust the phone back at Skinny. "I took a bunch in case someone was blinking." The Walrus tried to hand another phone to me. I waved him off. "You'll have to share. And please keep your promise. If those photos get around, my ass will be in a sling."

Jordan and I climbed into the truck as the three men huddled to check the photos. "Go!" I whispered. "But don't gun it. I don't want to seem scared." I was, though, and my heart raced as I glanced in the side mirror and saw the Walrus striding toward us. Jordan reversed out of the space, but the Walrus knocked at my window. I rolled it down a crack.

"Vince Vaughn, right? He's just got to be Vince Vaughn!"

I shrugged and gave my best *sorry!* smile. As we pulled away, I told Jordan, "Don't stop moving."

Behind us, I heard Skinny yell, "We love you, Vince!"

As we drove down the dusty frontage road, I stayed turned in my seat, watching for anyone following us. I gave Jordan a running commentary on everything she'd missed. It wasn't until we merged onto the highway, and I faced forward again, that I noticed the stiff way Jordan was holding her jaw. She was angry.

"What?" I asked.

"*What?*" Her tone was incredulous. "Hope, what the hell were you doing back there?"

"Saving you from getting the shit kicked out of you?"

Her laugh had an edge. "Seriously? You thought those people were dangerous?"

I huffed but said nothing. I *had* thought that.

"Those guys were weenies. Maybe they wanted to bully someone, push them around a bit. But they weren't interested in a fight."

I fiddled with the broken edge on my phone case. "You don't know that."

"Trust me, I've gotten the shit kicked out of me enough to tell the difference."

"Fine. We perceived the situation differently. No big deal."

"No big deal to you. Very big deal to me. How are people like that ever going to understand people like me if you go pretending I'm not real?"

I squirmed in my seat. "Those guys weren't going to understand you no matter what either of us said."

"Maybe not, but it sure would have felt good to try. Even if I had to get punched a few times, I would have been proud to tell them who I really am, knowing that my friend Hope was standing with me." Clouds had drifted in to cover the sun and Jordan pulled off her sunglasses and dropped them on the console between us. "Lie about yourself if you want, Hope. But going forward, please don't lie for me."

We didn't speak for a long time. I stared at nothing—trees, highway, horizon. Jordan was right, of course. I could see that now. Instead of standing up for her, as Dylan had done in the supermarket parking lot, I'd pretended she didn't exist.

I leaned my head against the window. What was wrong with me? How long had I been "making shit up," as Jordan had put it? Had I always?

Maybe. Even Aaron had called me out on it once. I closed my eyes and remembered that night. It was the same evening, toward the end of the campaign, when my world tilted on its axis.

ONE THURSDAY NIGHT in late October, Aaron and I were working alone, shoving cold pizza into our mouths with one hand while going over spreadsheets. Around seven thirty, he glanced at his watch and rose from the table, saying he was meeting an old Marine buddy for a beer. He'd been moody over the past week, even a bit sullen, so I was glad he was taking a break. I stayed in the office to revise a mailing piece. Veronica stuck her head in and rummaged around but seemed tired and didn't say much. She took some paperwork home.

It was after nine p.m. when Aaron reappeared and dropped into the chair across the table. I guessed he'd had more than one beer.

"Shelley called," I told him. "She's planning to be back Saturday and cover the festival with you." When I looked up, his head was on the table. "You okay?"

"Fine. It was good to talk with my buddy."

"I hope you discussed something besides the campaign," I said as I closed the program.

He lifted his head, studying me. "Dave was helping me with some personal issues."

"Oh." Unsure if I should ask more, I said, "Well, that's what buddies are for."

"Buddies tell you the truth."

Yep, definitely more than one beer. Maybe three or four.

"Are you my buddy?" he asked.

I didn't know if I should be flattered or devastated by Aaron considering me a buddy, but I nodded cautiously. "Of course."

"Then why haven't you told me the truth?"

Adrenaline rushed through my body. I had no idea where this was going. "About?"

He picked up a pen and twirled it. "About Carly."

My throat tightened. Shit. I shook my head, feigning confusion.

"You knew her better than you let on."

I struggled to keep my tone neutral. "I knew her, Aaron, but not well. I wasn't somebody Carly had much interest in."

"Explain," he said. "And stop using that kind of language."

"I don't understand . . ."

"Somebody she didn't have much interest in." There was a mocking tone in his voice I didn't like. "Tell me the truth, Hope, or you're not doing me any favors."

"Fine," I said, exasperated. "Your fiancée hated me. She was an incredible jerk to me."

"Thank you!" He tossed the pen and let it drop. "Now you're being honest."

Immediately, though, I regretted it. "Look, I really didn't know Carly."

"No, no, no. Stop changing your answer. This is helping. I mean, it's not fun, but . . . helpful."

I couldn't stop. "Most people at school thought Carly was hilarious. It's just—she could be hard on people. You said so yourself. Can you please not repeat that to her? She hates me enough as it is. I'm going to lose my job over this."

"You're not losing your job. Don't be stupid."

"You wait."

"Anyway, what you say is true. Carly is funny. And smart. There are dozens of things I adore about her. But lately I've been noticing that she and I have real differences in the way we deal with people."

"For instance?"

"You said it. She can be pretty rough on people. The other night, she referred to some woman as a slut." I tried to catch Aaron's eye, convinced that woman was me, but he was talking to the table. "To be honest, it's been eating at me for a while. That's why I wanted to talk to Dave."

I couldn't stop myself. "What did Dave say?"

He blew out some air and gazed up at the ceiling. "'Cut and run. She's not the one for you.'"

"Yikes." I hadn't expected that.

Aaron hadn't either, apparently. "I know. Hard to think about. My father taught me to honor my commitments. It's never led me wrong."

I struggled to keep my words neutral. "Yes, that's a tough one."

"Tough isn't the issue. The question is, what's right? Is it right to keep a promise, even if I'm worried it might be a mistake? Maybe I'm not trying hard enough. Relationships take work." His eyes met mine, held them. I could feel the heat rising in my face.

"Aaron, I don't know what to say."

"No advice?"

"I can't offer an opinion on this. I'm too . . ." I stopped, having no idea where I was going.

"Close?"

I opened my mouth, but no words came out. My ears were on fire.

"Because that's the other part of the equation. That's where it gets complicated." He stood, taking his jacket from the back of the chair. "If Carly is the woman I truly want to marry . . ." He paused, one hand still on the chair. "Then why do I want to spend every waking moment with someone else?" He shook his head as he put on his jacket. "Don't answer that. It's better if you don't." He moved toward the door.

"Did you drive?" I whispered hoarsely. His apartment was a few blocks from the office. Usually he walked.

"No." He was holding the door open. "But just so we're clear? I'm not as drunk as you think I am." Without a glance in my direction, he closed the door behind him.

THE NEXT DAY we'd canvassed as usual, taking notes on the people we met, rating their likeliness to vote for Aaron, and discussing the Fall Festival. We didn't mention our conversation from the night before, but if eye circles were any indication, neither of us had slept well. We'd taken my car, and when we quit around six p.m., I drove to Aaron's apartment and parallel parked. He sat there as if struggling to remember how a car door worked.

"I'm going to talk to Carly tonight," he said, finally. "I need to be honest with her. About my doubts."

"I hope that goes okay," I said. I couldn't imagine how it would. "Her father's put so much money into your campaign."

"Thank you, Hope," he said crisply, his eyes downcast. "I hadn't considered that."

"Sorry, that was stupid." Everything told me to shut up, but I plowed ahead. "Would it be better to wait until after the election?"

"Dump her once I've gotten what I want? Assuming I win, of course, which isn't looking likely." He linked his hands behind his head and squeezed. "Forgive me. I'm on edge." His voice was thin and raspy. "I'm hoping Carly's father backed me because I was a good candidate, not because I was dating his daughter."

I went back to the office. I was still there, around eight p.m., when the phone rang. Veronica answered and launched into a long story about the afternoon's phone-banking. Aaron must have interrupted her because she handed me the phone looking hurt. He asked if I could meet him in twenty minutes at the park, by our tree. I agreed, trying not to sound giddy in front of Veronica. I'd been struggling all day to keep my expectations low. Carly represented everything I longed to be—gorgeous, outgoing, the life of any party. How could I possibly win against her?

When I packed up to leave, though, Veronica said she'd walk with me. After we'd gone a block together, I stopped, smacked my forehead in mock frustration, and said I'd forgotten something at the office. Her eyes fell to the ground. Given Veronica's tendency to talk nonstop, she probably sensed when someone was ditching her.

By the time I circled the block and made it to the park, I was out of breath. Aaron was there, illuminated by the path lights. He guided me into the shadows under the tree, leaves crunching beneath our feet. I thought his hand lingered on my back a moment longer than necessary.

Carly had taken the news surprisingly well, he said. She'd teared up and suggested Aaron take some time to think about it. They'd made a date to talk on Sunday.

"And you?" I was scared to ask. "How do you feel?"

"It was hard. Maybe even harder because she took it so well. Carly is a wonderful person, and it's not that I don't love her. I'm just not sure we're a good fit. It kills me to break a promise, but I can't move forward with these doubts." He took both my hands in his and heat flashed through my body. "I might feel differently if it weren't for you, Hope. I get up each day excited to be with you. Given that, it doesn't feel right being engaged to someone else."

The wind had picked up off the river and he brushed my hair from my face. I could have died, right there, and been happy. He'd chosen me. He could have had Carly, the most jaw-dropping and room-silencing person I'd ever met, and he'd picked me. Hope Robinson.

We talked for a while about what came next. We agreed, more than once, to wait before exploring any kind of relationship. Finish the campaign. Let Aaron free himself from obligations. And then, I reached behind his neck and was kissing him, thinking all the while that it was a mistake, but the greatest, most wonderful mistake I'd ever make.

Instead of a key, Aaron's apartment had a keypad where you punch in a code. The lock clicked and he pushed open the door, holding it for me, then closed it behind me. He didn't turn on a light, but the shades were open, and the city lights illuminated the room as he brushed back my hair, gripping it without letting go. He leaned in and pressed his lips softly against mine, and gently moved forward until his body melted into mine and his mouth was moving all over my mouth, and I drew him in closer. I was sinking into something way too deep and didn't care.

WHEN I WOKE, Aaron was sitting in an upholstered chair, his head bowed. He wore boxers and a T-shirt and rested his elbows on his knees.

"You're thinking this was a mistake, aren't you?"

"No." He raised his head. "No, not for a second. I do need

to put my house in order, though. I need to officially break off my engagement."

"Maybe you should wait."

"Excuse me?"

"I know, I know." I waved off his puzzled expression. "I did a lot of thinking after you were asleep. Amazing what occurs to you between one and two a.m. There are only ten days before the election. I'm worried breaking your engagement will suck attention from your message."

"Really?" he murmured. He was staring at the floor again. "It's only an engagement. Why would anyone care?"

"You know what Shelley says. You can't predict what voters will latch onto. The race is a nail-biter. The last thing you need is to look flighty or commitment-phobic." I rose from the bed, wrapping the sheet around me.

He half smiled, his mind clearly elsewhere.

I took a few steps toward him. "And here's what else. With Shelley returning, I'll step back and be less visible."

"I don't like you less visible," he said, picking at the sheet.

"Aaron, if word gets out that your engagement is on the rocks, people are going to look for anything salacious, especially another woman."

"Okay, okay," he said. "So we won't do *this* anymore." He grabbed both my arms. "But I need you, Hope." He kissed me. "Being with you keeps me centered. You make me laugh."

"Shelley is worth three of me. What you need is to stay focused, finish the campaign. After that, we won't need to hide." He started to argue, and I took his face in my hands.

"Aaron, even before I fell for you, I believed in you. I refuse to be the person who gets in your way."

He started to say something, and I kissed him to shut him up. I didn't know it would be the last time.

JORDAN HADN'T SAID a word since our disagreement after the barbecue joint. I offered her some trail mix, and she said no. I asked if she wanted me to put on the Elvis CD, and she bobbed her head once. Clearly, she wasn't over my blunder.

I apologized. Told her I wanted to do better. "I respond well to a little kick now and then."

She gave me a half smile and one of those puffs through the nose that's not really a laugh. I thought I'd really blown it. Then Jordan started to talk. What she said wasn't new, but I heard it in a new way. How hard it is for cross-dressers to feel accepted when for years, they've been the punch line of jokes. How hidden they can feel, how different, even within the LGBTQ community. Why so many remain closeted to their families— the pain they experience, knowing they're not being loved for who they are.

As a teenager, George had come out to his mom long before his father learned about his cross-dressing. George begged his mother to please see him as Jordan. Aunt Joan had finally agreed and stood in the doorway to her bedroom, staring at Jordan in her thrift-store dress, pearls, high heels. She'd slowly walked over and held Jordan's face in both her hands. She'd said, "Not the blue eye shadow, sweetheart. Not with your complexion. Try brown."

Jordan grinned. She loved that story. "I know it was hard for my mom. This was Tennessee, in the eighties. It meant the world to me that she saw me. But that's as far as she took it. She couldn't tell my father. She couldn't be a true ally."

Jordan glanced at me. "I know you love me, Hope, and I understand if you can't be an ally, but you have to understand that it hurts."

I told Jordan that I wanted to be an ally, that I would try harder. I said, "If it's any consolation, when I thought there might be a fight back at the restaurant, I was planning to take the skinny one."

She turned her head to regard me for a moment. "The fella with the bad leg?"

"Yeah."

Her nods were slow, deliberate. "Well, that was real brave of you, Hope. Damn brave."

I reached my hand across the seat, and she put hers in mine and squeezed. I promised myself that going forward, I would be the friend, cousin, and ally Jordan deserved. Speak only the truth.

Just as soon as this mess was over.

Chapter 19

Dylan

Was there a difference between acting and lying? I wasn't sure, but I was laughing my ass off at Olivia. She was on the phone, bullshitting someone in Aaron Breckenridge's office with a dead-on southern accent. Who would have guessed Olivia had grown up in Hackensack? I hadn't known myself until we'd passed through New Jersey, and she'd riffed on *The Real Housewives*.

Olivia was pretending to be a faculty adviser for the University of Memphis newspaper. "You may recall," she was telling Breckenridge's office manager, "how the *Daily Helmsman* did a lovely piece on the senator a couple years ago? Oh, you *do* recall?" Olivia turned to me with comical wide eyes. "Wonderful! We have a young reporter keen to interview him before his speech Saturday." There was a long pause. Olivia scowled. "She needs only fifteen minutes. I'm sure you can squeeze her in." Pause. "Tons of young voters on campus, you know."

Olivia made a hand puppet to show the woman was blathering on. "Tomorrow, five p.m.? Perfect. The reporter's name?

Dylan . . . Grant. You'll love her. She's a real peach." Olivia hung up and tucked away her phone.

Pinpricks of excitement danced down my spine. "What will I say? I mean, how do you ask someone if he's your father?"

"I might not start with that question out of the gate," Olivia said. "Warm him up. Say you're interested in his Memphis roots, his first campaign for Congress. Then ask if he remembers a volunteer named Hope Robinson."

"What if he says no?"

"Then he's lying, and you'll want nothing to do with him. I don't think that will happen, though."

I didn't either. "Do you think he really cared for Mom? I mean, they didn't just . . . hook up?" I wasn't sure Olivia would understand that phrase, but she seemed to.

"I'm a pretty good reader of voices," Olivia said. "And trust me—the man who left me that phone message almost eighteen years ago? He wanted to find your mother. Badly."

OLIVIA LIFTED A spoonful of her chicken noodle soup and let it dribble back into the cardboard bowl. She was pissed that I'd insisted on Subway for lunch. Well, excuse me! I thought we were in a hurry.

I'd nearly finished my Veggie Delite sub when an ancient woman in a wheelchair burst through the door, pushed by a round-faced priest. The old woman had huge eyes and a pencil-thin body, like a gecko's. She stared at Olivia, then whispered to the priest, who bent to listen.

The priest pushed the wheelchair close to our table. "Sorry to bother you," he said to Olivia. "By any chance, were you on TV?" When Olivia nodded, the man clapped his hands together.

"You were right, Mom," he shouted into the gecko's ear. "That's Andromeda!" He turned back to Olivia and me. "My mother watched *The Light Within* every day at three o'clock."

The old woman raised a knobby finger that shook as it hovered. "Very bad woman!"

"No, Mom! That was her *character*." The man giggled, his cheeks rosy. "She's a little confused."

"Very bad!" spat the woman.

I flashed Olivia a look that said, *Time to get out of here*, and crumpled my sandwich paper.

"I'm so sorry," the priest stage-whispered to Olivia. "It's a tribute to your acting. She believes you really are Andromeda."

"No worries." Olivia smiled as she stood to collect her trash. "At times, I was confused myself."

The priest pushed the chair toward the counter, but the gecko twisted to keep a wary eye on Olivia, who stuck out her tongue and wiggled it devilishly. The woman clutched at the priest's jacket.

I held the door for Olivia. Once we were outside, I laughed. "You shouldn't be so mean to your fans."

"They expect it," she said. "They love Andromeda because she was evil, not in spite of it."

I wanted to ask Olivia more about that once we got going. When I climbed into the Bug, though, she was reading something on her phone and grimacing, like she was in pain.

Olivia said, "Not possible. She can't do this to me."

Chapter 20

Olivia

The selfish, irresponsible woman! How dare Ann Abernathy cancel on me! Although not surprising when you consider that family. The father was a vodka-swilling lech; the mother, a tennis-skirted, bleached blonde with a precancerous tan. The Abernathys always had more money than class.

My hand shook as I hit redial and got Ann's assistant, a young woman with one of those annoying baby voices. She sounded twelve.

I laid into the babysitter. "Does Ann Abernathy care nothing about her commitments? If she wants to skip town, she can leave after she fulfills her obligation to me. Why does it have to be Sunday?"

"Her father died."

"He'll still be dead on Monday!"

No response to that, only a keyboard clicking. Finally the child reported that Ann wasn't in, and unfortunately, her schedule before Sunday was fully booked.

"Will Ann be at her office on Saturday?"

"Yes, but . . ."

I hung up. I'd go to Graceland early Saturday and talk to Ann. The only way to get things done was in person. That's how I'd handle Ann Abernathy, and that's how Dylan would confront Aaron Breckenridge. The personal approach had become something of a lost art. A shame, really. It got results.

I'LL ADMIT I was cranky after that phone call. I'd grown tired of listening to Dylan complain about her mother, how Hope didn't understand her adventurous nature, didn't want her to be an activist. Not true, I protested. Hope simply didn't want her to be a *stupid* activist. That got her bent all out of shape.

"Why do you keep defending her?"

"Dylan, your mother isn't perfect. That said, you're not the first person whose parent didn't support her life choices."

"Oh, because your crazy mother didn't want you marrying Elvis? Like that was going to happen."

"Mother also wasn't keen on my becoming an actress. She said it was a harlot's profession."

"What's that?"

I searched for the politically correct term. "Sex worker."

Dylan raised her eyebrows. "Harsh. Did your dad think that, too?"

"No. Dad tried to broker the peace between us. It didn't work. In the end, my acting drove Mother over the edge."

While I rummaged in my bag for hand lotion, I told Dylan about my starring role as Amanda in my secretarial school's production of *The Glass Menagerie*. How my mother had railed, for weeks, because the play was written by "an immoral homosexual." Mother had lost her grip at that point. She'd shower daily for over an hour to "cleanse" herself. Twice she'd walked out our front door with no clothes on.

"My father went to see the play alone. During my soliloquy in scene one, when Amanda prattles on about her gentleman callers, I saw this ghostly figure enter the theater from the back. My mother's hair was dripping wet, and she was holding a shower brush out in front of her. The white bathrobe didn't do a good job of concealing that she was naked underneath. On the plus side, she'd remembered the bathrobe."

Dylan's mouth hung open. "What did you do?"

"What I had to—I stayed in character. My father and another man leaped up and dragged my mother from the theater. I just stood there, staring into the near distance, until everything died down. Then I finished my speech. Got a standing ovation."

Dylan had forgotten her earlier annoyance with me. "You deserved it. That must have been hard."

I squeezed the hand lotion on my fingers and rubbed it in. "It was a lesson. I learned staying in character could get me through the tough times."

The girl squinted at the road ahead. "I didn't know what you meant, earlier, when you said sometimes you believed you were Andromeda. Maybe I get it now. You had to stay in character."

I considered. "Sure," I said agreeably. "Close enough."

In truth, that wasn't it at all, but how could I possibly explain in a way the girl could understand? Stay in character, yes, that got you through. But at what cost?

Dylan wouldn't know about the physicality of acting. One couldn't slip into an evil woman's skin every day for decades, as I had, without it having an effect. The emotion might be faked, but what it did to your body, your mind, was real. The character takes up residence inside you. After a time, you lose sight of where you end, and the character begins.

When Harold was alive, and I'd slip into Andromeda behavior, he'd call me on it. Tell me to snap out of it. After Harold was gone, I had no one. Then *Light Within* was canceled, and it had taken me years to separate from my dark side. To figure out what I'd lost. And more importantly, what might remain.

Chapter 21

Hope

After the experience with Squinty and the Rednecks, I wanted to make amends to Jordan. So as we drove from Cookeville to Nashville, I shared more of my Aaron story. I left out only the most shameful part—what happened later, after my move to Boston.

THE DAY AFTER I slept with Aaron was the start of the Fall Festival. It was to be Shelley's first day back, and she would accompany Aaron, working the crowd as needed. I'd planned a day full of the errands I desperately needed to do, like laundry and grocery shopping.

That morning was sunny with a soft breeze that smelled of burning leaves. I stopped by the office to drop off some envelopes I'd stuffed. Veronica had on headphones and didn't look up, so I left the materials and made a quick exit. I grabbed coffee at the shop next door and strolled to the park, sitting on the bench near the gorgeous shingle oak where I'd kissed Aaron. I'd brought a paperback and opened it without reading.

My mind was full of Aaron—his mouth on my mouth, the way he'd run his thumb along my cheek and neck, then let his hand wander down my back. After we'd made love, we'd raided his freezer and eaten bowls of Ben and Jerry's before starting in again.

A shadow fell across my lap. When I looked up, my face went numb.

Even crying, Carly was stunning. Her long, wet lashes clumped together, making her eyes look greener than I'd remembered. She wore a sundress and cardigan while I had on a stained sweatshirt and baggy sweatpants. She was Marcia Brady to my Jan. No—not even Jan. Peter.

"I'll keep this short," she said. "Aaron didn't mention names, but I know it's you. He talks about you in such glowing terms."

I didn't speak. I had no script for this situation.

"I'm not going to pretend we're friends," she continued. "You blame me for what happened at school, even though I wasn't responsible. Some of those girls would do anything to please me."

That put me back on firmer ground. "And did it, Carly?" I coughed, finding my voice. "Did it please you?"

"Let's just say I've learned a lot about karma over the past two months as I watched Aaron drift away." She pulled a tissue from her pocket and dabbed at her eyes, somehow without smudging her mascara. She sat on the bench beside me. Shit.

I shifted instinctively and tried to cover it by dropping my paperback into my bag. "What is it you want from me?"

"I'd like you to do the right thing and give Aaron and me a chance to work it out. Stay out of our way for a couple weeks. Take a . . . vacation or something."

"I can't do that. We're in the last days of the campaign."

Carly brushed at a spot on her Coach handbag. "Why am I not surprised?" she said quietly, then turned to face me. "Then consider what's best for Aaron. My father is furious. If Aaron breaks our engagement, Daddy will crush him. You know how close this race is. If my father trashes Aaron in the press, he'll lose. Not only that, he'll demand Aaron return the twenty thousand dollars."

"He can't take back a campaign contribution," I said. Was that even true? I didn't know.

"It wasn't a contribution. It was a personal loan to pay you and Veronica."

I closed my eyes. *Oh my God, Aaron. How could you be so stupid?*

"So," she said, "since you've always had trouble doing what's right—"

I interrupted. "Why do you keep saying that?"

"Come on, Hope. Let's be honest. Cheating isn't new to you."

Was she talking about her old boyfriend I'd dated? I frowned in confusion, lifting my palms, the picture of someone falsely accused—until instantly, I understood. I lowered my hands.

During my final, horrible, semester at the University of Memphis, I'd tried at the last minute to save myself. Even though I'd attended few classes, hadn't studied for tests, and submitted laughably stream-of-consciousness papers, I was still passing most of my classes with a D, and in one case, a C-minus. The exception was Communications Ethics, a course I needed for my major. The instructor was new and kind. In recent weeks, I'd confided in him about my depression after my father's death and showed some effort by turning in a couple assignments. The problem was the twenty-five-page research paper that composed half our grade. I simply couldn't pull it off.

My friend Josephine had taken the course the previous year, with a different instructor. I asked if I could borrow her paper and alter it slightly. I convinced myself that it wasn't truly plagiarism and was harmless. A victimless crime.

What I didn't know was that Josephine's instructor had saved several model papers for his successor, and Josephine's was one of them. My professor called me into his office two days before graduation. Josephine was there, sobbing. "Tell him I didn't know about this!" she cried.

Of course I took full blame. It wasn't Josephine's fault. And so, I was expelled from the University of Memphis.

Carly's smile grew wider. "That's right. I've been doing a little detective work. I always wondered why you didn't walk at graduation."

The corner of my mouth was twitching, like it had when I was a child, sitting for school photos. I pressed my lips together to make it stop. I needed to talk to Aaron, to tell him. But what if this changed things? What if this stupid, horrible mistake turned his stomach, as it was doing to mine just then? He and I had barely started anything. He might decide it was best to walk away.

Carly continued. "You're familiar with daytime TV, Hope. So let's make a deal. You disappear, and I won't tell Aaron about what an unbelievable slimeball you are."

"Disappear? What does that mean? For how long?"

She shrugged. "A couple weeks. Doesn't matter where, just no contact with Aaron."

"That's impossible. I need to tell Aaron something. I can make up an excuse."

She was shaking her head. "No seeing him, no calling him. Starting now."

"You know, Carly, this isn't just your decision. Aaron gets a say . . ."

"Hope, you may be a colossal fuckup, but you're not stupid. We both know Aaron. When he wants something, he's blind to the pitfalls. You may be who he wants in the moment, but he'll wise up when he considers the optics. You're not who he needs. You don't have the skill set. You'll drag him down."

I closed my eyes. I felt like Carly had sliced me open and I was bleeding out. I wanted desperately to protest. The problem was, I knew in my heart she was right. I was a fuckup. I was not what Aaron Breckenridge needed.

"How do I know I can trust you?" I whispered. "I could return in two weeks, and you might still tell him."

"Unlike you, Hope, I'm honest. I'm tough, but I'm real. I'm one hundred percent me." She stood up and looked out toward the river. "You're not real, Hope. I don't know what the fuck you are."

I helped her out. "A disappointment."

I LEFT A note in the office for Aaron, Shelley, and Veronica. I had to leave town for a family emergency and wouldn't be in touch until after the election. I didn't say where I was going. I apologized, said I was resigning from the rest of the campaign, and would root for them from afar. Then I went to Aaron's apartment and used his keypad to open the door. He'd apologized the night before for his password, CARLY. The note I left him was in a sealed envelope and didn't mention her. I couldn't risk Carly going back on our deal. Instead, I repeated the lie about the family emergency, and insisted the timing was fortunate—he could focus on the campaign without me as a distraction. I told him how much I'd enjoyed our night together and cared about him. I implored him to focus on what was important. Win the election so he could be who he was meant to be.

I didn't own a cell phone back then. Aaron did, but I'd uphold my end of the bargain and not call. In my heart, I didn't believe Aaron would go back to Carly, though that didn't mean he'd choose me. Not if he understood the baggage I came with.

Josephine had been begging me to visit her in Nashville. She was thrilled when I asked to stay with her for a couple weeks. I threw what I needed into two duffel bags and left before Aaron and Shelley were done at the Fall Festival.

In my rush to leave, I left my toiletry bag on the sink at Ashlee's apartment. The bag had my birth control pills. It was Saturday night when I discovered it was missing, and Ashlee's boyfriend Lamar, who worked for FedEx, promised to overnight it to me. By Tuesday morning, though, the package still hadn't arrived, so I went to Planned Parenthood. They gave me new pills, told me to take two, and said I'd probably be fine.

I tried to enjoy my time with Josephine, appreciate the Nashville sights she took me to, but my mind was two hundred miles away. Should I call Aaron? At least twice, I repacked my duffels, then convinced myself to wait, to be patient. All would be well.

Three days before the election, the Memphis paper broke a damning story about Aaron's opponent. An anonymous source accused the guy of accepting illegal campaign contributions and conducting shady business deals. I couldn't believe Aaron was involved in the leak—Shelley wouldn't have allowed it—but Josephine just shook her head. "That's politics," she said. "It's a dirty business."

Aaron won the election by three hundred votes. I was packing to return to Memphis the next day, when Josephine handed me a letter that had appeared in her mailbox. It was addressed to me but bore no return address. Inside was a newspaper clipping with an engagement photo of Aaron and Carly, listing a wedding date in two weeks. I called the church to confirm, then the venue, a private club. They'd all been booked in the last week.

So Carly had told him. And he'd chosen her—the one who would help him succeed, not the one who would drag him down.

I had no idea who'd sent me that clipping or how they'd found me. It didn't matter. I drove back to Memphis and dragged everything out of my room that could fit in my Corolla. I owned no furniture except my father's old comfy chair, and I sobbed as I dragged it out to the street. I taped a note to it that said, "Free to a good home."

When I left that afternoon, I couldn't see out of the back of my car. I drove north with no clue where I was heading.

WHEN I TOLD the story to Jordan, I didn't mention being expelled, and she didn't notice anything missing. She directed her fury at Carly.

"Well, that explains it," Jordan said. "Breckenridge married that woman for her money. Who cares if she's evil, as long as she's rich?"

I wasn't going to argue with Jordan, though my take was different. Carly had convinced Aaron that she was an asset, and I was a liability. He'd wanted to win that election—to have a career in politics—more than he wanted me. Shelley had said that Aaron was more ambitious than he seemed. She'd been a good judge of character.

We were approaching Nashville, and a billboard showed the iconic image of young Elvis strolling down the driveway outside his mansion and read "Graceland, 4 Hours." The temperature outside had hit ninety and Jordan fiddled with the air-conditioning. "At least Breckenridge had the sense to divorce her."

I was checking my messages and put down my phone. "I'm sorry. What?"

Jordan turned, her eyebrows raised almost to her hairline. "You didn't know they're divorced?"

"How would I know that? It's not like he sends me Christmas cards."

"Normal people Google their exes."

I had, of course, done exactly that at the Tater Tot the previous night, though nothing I'd read had mentioned that detail. Now I searched on my phone. The dates given for Aaron's marriage on Wikipedia showed he and Carly had divorced late last year. I was still processing this information when Jordan said, "You never told me how Breckenridge found out you were pregnant."

"Oh," I said, pretending to search for something in my purse to buy myself time. "A mutual friend." I found a pack of gum and offered a piece to Jordan, who frowned and declined. We'd reached the part of the story I wasn't going to share, not even with Jordan.

"So . . . Aaron got in touch with you? "

"His representative did," I said, stuffing the gum in my mouth.

Sensing from my staccato answers that I wasn't going to talk about it, Jordan whispered an almost inaudible "okay, then." She clicked on the radio, and I fiddled with the gum wrapper, reorganized my purse, stared out the window. I wished I could crawl into the glove compartment and disappear.

I'd always had a talent for making myself invisible. Only once had it failed me.

SEVENTEEN YEARS AGO, hugely pregnant, I sat on a park bench in Stoneham. I kept my eye on a six-year-old girl who shrieked and chased other kids around a climbing structure. Eight months earlier, I'd made a deal with the girl's mother to babysit her daughter after school and on breaks if I could live rent-free in the extra bedroom in her house. The mother's name was Tiffany. Another hair stylist. Go figure.

I smiled at the thin man who sat down next to me on the park bench. He was oddly dressed in a blue seersucker suit and straw fedora. With his slight build and huge glasses, he reminded me of the actor Wally Cox. He opened a box of Thin Mint Girl Scout Cookies and held out the open sleeve. I wasn't in the habit of taking food from strangers, but he tore open the wrapper right in front of me, and I was so hungry.

The baby inside me shifted and I felt something—a foot? An elbow?—protruding below my ribs. I should have eaten more than the single slice of bread and peanut butter I'd shoved in my mouth at lunchtime, but I hated to take Tiffany's food. She was a struggling single mom, too.

"When's your baby due?" The man had a southern accent. I'd become used to such questions from strangers.

"Four weeks." I smiled. "Too soon." I wasn't joking. I had no idea how I'd pay for the hospital. Little money, no insurance. I'd been to the obstetrician three times. During the last visit, the nurse had lectured me for canceling appointments.

"Planning to stay here?" the man asked.

"Sorry?" My eyes were searching for my little charge, Miriam. She was on the swings.

"I was asking if you intend to live here. In this area."

"I . . . guess so."

The man folded over the cookies' plastic sleeve and closed the box. "Let me be more direct, Ms. Robinson. Do you plan to make Boston your home or return to Memphis?"

Cold pinpricks raced down my spine. My head said run, but I could barely waddle and couldn't leave without Miriam. I scanned the park. The picnic area was full of young mothers who would rush to my aid if I screamed. The danger wasn't physical. I simply didn't know what it was.

I used my iciest voice. "How do you know me?"

"I've been looking for you for quite a while, Ms. Robinson. May I call you Hope?"

"No."

"Very well. No need for animus. I'm here to offer you help." He reached inside his suit jacket and handed me a business card. Marlin A. Fish, Private Detective.

"Your parents were funny people," I said, instantly regretting my cruelty.

He sighed. "They were anglers all right."

I checked on Miriam again. "I need to get a child home soon. What is it that you want, Mr. Fish?"

"You usually stay longer. Tiffany works late on Tuesdays."

I pushed myself off the bench and turned to face him. "So let's review what we've established: you're a creep who's been stalking me and my friend. What else do I need to know before calling the police?"

"Ms. Robinson, please sit. Again, I'm here to help. I think my offer will interest you. It comes from someone who wishes the best for you and your child. My client was . . . concerned . . . to learn of your current situation."

Aaron. In spite of everything I'd told myself about him over the last eight months, I felt a surge of elation. Aaron had been looking for me. I swallowed my pride and choked out: "Aaron sent you?" I hadn't tried to contact Aaron to tell him about the pregnancy. Even if I could have faced that humiliation, I wanted to keep the baby and feared he wouldn't. Better he didn't know.

He sighed. "I'm sorry, Ms. Robinson. As a private detective, I'm not at liberty to divulge my client's identity."

What was this game? I clutched my tote bag.

"And in this case, protecting the name is not simply policy, it's also the point. The reason I was hired."

"I'm sorry. To protect . . ."

"The father's name."

I sat then, slowly, lowering myself onto the bench with one hand pressed against my belly. Had I understood that correctly? The man was here to keep Aaron's name from being sullied—by me, by my baby? Not possible. Not Aaron. Yes, the man had hurt me. He'd chosen someone else over me. But this was a whole new level of ugly.

"I don't believe you," I said. "I don't believe your goofy business card or—"

He interrupted. "I can't give you a name, Ms. Robinson, but let me offer some details that might help: the evening of October twenty-third, 1998. A park, overlooking the Mississippi. Two people in the shadow of a shingle oak tree. Need I go on? Or does that assure you we have the correct parties?"

Of course it did. Only Aaron could have described that scene, would have mentioned our shingle oak tree. It felt like a sucker punch to the gut.

Fish continued. "My client is prepared to offer you a deal—a significant sum of money if you sign an agreement to never reveal the identity of your child's father and never return to Memphis."

"I'm not planning on doing either of those things," I said. "I don't need his money."

The man chuckled. "Ms. Robinson, with all due respect, you do. Or if not, your child does. My client is prepared to offer you an initial payment of a hundred thousand dollars, with follow-up payments of ten thousand a year until the child reaches maturity. The initial sum should be enough to pay your medical bills and provide for a maternity leave until you can get settled and find work. The rest? Well, consider it . . . child support."

I lowered myself back to the bench. I couldn't believe the amount, but then, $100,000 would be nothing to Aaron now that he was married to Carly. He could afford that kind of insurance.

Fish continued speaking and I caught random phrases. ". . . generous offer . . . enough to get you past this unfortunate accident . . . well, if it was an accident . . ."

I stood again, leaned down, and put my face close to his. *"How dare you?"*

"Ms. Robinson, forgive me. That was uncalled for." He rose and removed his hat, brushing off a dead leaf that had lodged in the brim. "Please take some time to consider this offer. It will be the only one you receive." He raised a hand. "No, don't answer now. I'll meet you here tomorrow. Let me know then." He replaced his hat, tipped his head, then ambled toward the parking lot with a bowlegged gait.

Once Marlin Fish was out of sight, I glanced over at Miriam, happily digging by the pond, then I sat and crumpled forward, my face hidden in my hands so the mothers in the picnic area wouldn't see my tears.

That night, I lifted Tiffany's cordless phone from its stand and replaced it several times. I hadn't spoken to my mother in months, not since I'd told her about the pregnancy. She'd offered to help, and I'd said no. Since my father's death, I'd been barely able to listen to my mother's voice. I hated the thought of taking money from her, but the encounter with Marlin Fish had been a wake-up call. My situation was desperate.

When I finally dialed my mother, though, a man answered.

"I'm trying to reach Olivia Grant," I said, confused.

"This is Remy." The man had a French accent. "Olivia is out right now. May I help you?"

"I'm Olivia's daughter?"

"Ah, you are Hope!"

"Yes, Hope. And I'm sorry, Remy . . . who, exactly, are *you*?"

He laughed. "Why, the love of your mother's life, of course!"

I hung up, appalled. That was how long it had taken my mother to replace my father? I wanted nothing to do with her.

The next day in the park, I accepted Marlin A. Fish's offer. I felt ashamed, but the money would provide security for my baby. It would pay for the hospital, an apartment, and a little time before starting a job search. It would be Aaron's only contribution to our child's life. On that, at least, we seemed to agree.

I signed the single sheet of paper that Fish had handed me: for a one-time payment of $100,000, with annual payments of $10,000 a year over eighteen years, I agreed to never reveal my baby's father to anyone, and never return to Memphis. The last part wasn't a sacrifice. For me, Memphis was an endless museum of hurt.

Fish wrote the check as I sat there. I realized he'd probably expected me to negotiate. No matter. It was more than enough.

The detective rose and again tipped his hat. "You've made a good choice, Ms. Robinson," he said. "You did the right thing."

AFTER SHAKING OFF that unpleasant memory, I felt grumpy. I asked Jordan to please stop humming "Walking in Memphis." It was making me crazy. She switched the radio back on, and we listened to Elvis croon the opening of "Kentucky Rain." Jordan shot me a helpless look. The number of Elvis songs had doubled since Knoxville.

"Leave it," I said. Elvis's achy, soulful rendition suited my mood. Damn him.

As we left Nashville, signs warned of construction ahead.

All lanes merged into one and we crept along, bumper to bumper. I clutched at my hair in frustration. Aaron's fundraiser that night was being held at the ritzy Peabody Hotel, diagonally across the street from the Doubletree, where I'd booked rooms for Jordan and me. I'd hoped to arrive an hour before the event started and wait outside the ballroom, watching for my mother and Dylan. I doubted they'd attend—the tickets were outrageous—but my mother was nothing if not unpredictable.

Earlier, Jordan had begged to come people watch with me. I explained that as much as I loved her company, I needed to be invisible, and she was not helpful in that respect.

"I do turn heads in my lavender dress," she'd acknowledged.

We made it through the construction in twenty grueling minutes. For some reason, though, traffic still crawled. A breeze carried the smell of something burning.

"Look." Jordan pointed to a plume of smoke that blackened the road ahead. "There's the slowdown." She glanced over at me. "Honey, if you keep yanking on your hair like that, you'll go bald."

I released the fistful I'd been holding in a death grip. "I won't make it to the fundraiser now. Not before it starts."

"Maybe you could sneak in late, once the lights are down."

It wasn't a bad idea. I certainly didn't want to pay the $250 per plate ticket, and this would give me more time to get ready. "I might even have time to shower and wash my hair," I said.

"Yes, you want to look your best."

"That isn't it," I snapped. "It just needs it."

"Right," Jordan said. "That's what I meant."

We crept slowly past the long line of flashing fire trucks and police vehicles until, finally, we saw the smoldering remains of a Ford Taurus. I let out a breath I hadn't been aware I was holding. It wasn't a VW.

"We should be good now," Jordan said as the traffic thinned, and she picked up speed. "Clear sailing."

"Thank God," I said. Finally my luck was changing.

Memphis, TN

Chapter 22

Olivia

Impossible. The child had never heard of the Peabody ducks? I was dumbstruck. Had Hope been raising her daughter under a rock?

The girl didn't even notice the ducks at first, she was so busy gaping at the Peabody's two-story lobby, marble staircase, and wood-and-stained-glass ceilings. When I directed Dylan's attention to the five mallards swimming in the grand fountain, she seemed perplexed. I explained that these ducks lived in a special duck palace—that's right, a palace—on the hotel roof. A uniformed Duckmaster—yes, that was his title—brought them down each morning on the elevator. He guided them as they waddled along a red carpet and hopped into the fountain. There they swam until the Duckmaster marched them back to the elevator at five p.m.

"You're shitting me," Dylan said.

"I never shit anybody," I said. "The tourists love it."

To be honest, I'd forgotten how lovely the Peabody was. Harold and I had known the family who renovated the hotel in the early eighties. Thank goodness I asked at the front desk for their son Jon-David because I wouldn't have recognized the stout, bearded man who waddled toward us, as if in kinship with his ducks. He kissed me above the cannula on both cheeks.

"I'm delighted you called ahead, Olivia! I've put you and your granddaughter in a Celebrity Suite. On me."

"Oh, Jon-David, I never expected that. I can't let you." In fact, I had, and could.

"I do have a favor to ask." He lowered his head and regarded me coyly.

"Listening."

"My daughter-in-law produces one of the Memphis morning shows. She'd love to have you as a guest."

I sighed. "J.D., look at me. I'm a mess. I have to wear this cannelloni." I screwed up my face in comical frustration. "Nobody wants to see me like this."

"Olivia, stop. You look stunning, as always," he said. "Come now, what will it take?"

"Well . . . perhaps there's one small thing."

What I asked wasn't much. I wanted the hotel to keep news of my stay quiet, perhaps use a pseudonym at the front desk. I hated to sound paranoid. Toward the end of my time in Memphis, I'd experienced a problem with a stalker: a very tall blond woman. As unlikely as it seemed, I could have sworn I'd seen that woman earlier that day.

I wasn't making that up. Well, not all of it. As Dylan and I'd driven into town, Dylan had noticed an unusually tall woman on the block ahead and slammed on the brakes. From the back, the woman had looked exactly like Jordan. Was Hope already here, in Memphis? Had she brought Jordan? And who else?

An entire SWAT team? Out of an abundance of caution, I'd directed Dylan around the block, and we approached the Peabody from the other direction.

Now, as the bellhop loaded our bags onto a cart, Jon-David assured me I'd have privacy. I was to alert him immediately if the tall woman appeared at the hotel. Downtown had become safer since I'd lived here, but one couldn't be too careful.

THE TEAL WALLS of our Celebrity Suite were hung with landscapes in gilded frames, and arrangements of lilies and hydrangeas graced every nook. Lovely! The girl's jaw dropped as she explored the kitchenette, bedroom, and formal dining room. In the parlor, she flopped backward onto the sofa, picked up the TV remote, and clicked excitedly.

"Olivia, you won't believe this!" she called after me. "Netflix *and* Hulu!"

"Oh, brave new world that has such streaming options," I murmured.

Much as I enjoyed Dylan's enthusiasm, I was tired. I rolled my oxygen cart to the bedroom and opened the blinds. I had to lean forward on the sill to catch my breath. The emphysema was getting worse. No denying it.

Below my window, out on B.B. King Boulevard, young people chattered and laughed. I moved closer, brushing back the curtain. Such a gift to be young! How many times had I strolled down that sidewalk in the dusty light of summer, a warm breeze on my face, Harold on my arm? Did these millennials appreciate what they'd been given? I hadn't. Over the years, I'd imagined myself into dozens of characters, acted out a hundred adventures, but I'd never imagined myself old.

Still, I was handling the descent with dignity if I did say so myself. And I had my plan for Graceland in place. I'd never deluded myself it would be easy. What I knew in my bones was this: the danger was in waiting.

My beloved father had done that. Waited too long.

It was during my third year on the rebooted *Light Within* that I'd moved my father to LA, to be closer to me. Bedridden, he was sinking deeper into ALS. I hired caretakers and visited him daily unless our shooting schedule went to hell, which it often did.

One day, I raced over at lunch and found him crying. He'd sent his caregiver away. He pointed to his lower nightstand drawer, indicating I should open it. Inside was a pistol.

"Can't . . . lift," he said. His words, by then, were a soupy burble.

"I don't understand, Dad." I did, but I couldn't accept.

"Prop . . . it . . . up."

"I can't."

I sat on my father's bed and covered his hand with my own. Sobbing, he finally made me understand. He'd come up with this plan a year earlier but had procrastinated. Kept putting it off. He'd waited too long.

I believed in my father's right to die—to choose his own time—but I couldn't help him. I'd go to jail. My beautiful career . . . ruined.

I put the gun in my purse and called his backup caretaker. I had to return to the set.

In the end, it took my father two years to die, paralyzed, unable to see, hear, or communicate, though his brain functioned like a normal person's.

When guilt ate at me, I buried it deep in my character—Andromeda, who was fearless. Andromeda, who didn't give a shit.

The lesson, though, was seared into my brain like a cattle brand.

When I saw my time coming, I'd make a plan. And stick to it.

I SPLURGED THAT night and took Dylan to a four-star restaurant inside the Peabody. Jon-David secured us a table in a dark, quiet corner. The prices were scandalous. Still, they guaranteed we wouldn't run into Hope.

My filet mignon was pink and tender, but I managed only a few bites before pushing it aside. In contrast, the odd tower of kale-and-beet shavings the chef concocted for Dylan was a huge hit. After dinner, the girl ordered sorbet and I sipped my tea. I was feeling fondly toward Dylan and worried for her. The girl was going to be blindsided by my Graceland plan. I wanted to prepare her somehow. I approached the topic obliquely.

"I know you're excited to meet your father tomorrow, Dylan," I began. "Mine had a profound impact on me." I told the girl a bit more about Dad, how he'd shielded me from my crazy mother, smuggled Elvis magazines and records into the house, helped me hide them in a locked trunk. I described his struggle with ALS, sparing the girl the worst details, but explained how, before he'd procrastinated, he'd planned to take his life.

"Hold on." Dylan squeezed her eyes shut, perhaps battling a brain freeze from the sorbet. "Your father planned to commit suicide? And you thought that was a good idea?"

"People have the right to choose their own end, Dylan."

"My friend Emma volunteers on a suicide hotline. Sometimes people think they want to die, but they just need therapy or drugs."

"You're talking about young people. Healthy people. I'm talking about someone with a disease."

"Mental illness is a disease."

The girl had clearly been brainwashed by her friend. "I'm not going to argue with you, Dylan, but I, for one, plan to choose my time. I refuse to spend my final days on earth slowly suffocating."

"But how do you know when that will be?" she persisted. "I mean, what if the doctors can do some procedure or give you some new meds, and you're fine for another five years."

"I'm sure that's what my father thought and that's why he waited too long. You simply have to pick a time and stick to it."

Luckily, the server arrived just then with our check, providing an easy out from the conversation. I could see now that the girl was too young. She hadn't seen enough of the world's cruelty. I'd done what I could to prepare her. One day, Dylan might think back on our conversation and understand.

THE GIRL INSISTED on getting a souvenir for Emma—a rubber duck or some other nonsense—in the shop that sold Peabody duck paraphernalia. I waited outside, thank you.

As I leaned against the wall in front of the duck store, a crowd of people in black tie and cocktail dresses approached the elevator. I turned to see others ascending the marble staircase and peering over the mezzanine balcony. Tuxes. Gowns. Everywhere.

Oh dear Lord. Breckenridge's fundraiser.

How had I forgotten the event was at the Peabody? Dylan couldn't know. That would be a disaster. She'd want to go, and for the love of God, $250 a person? If the child wanted to hear her father speak, she could do it Saturday evening, at the university, for free.

I scanned the lobby. Unlikely the man himself would parade through, but who knew? And what if Dylan saw him? The girl was nothing if not unpredictable. We needed to leave.

As I swiveled my oxygen cart to enter the store, I felt a tap on my shoulder. A woman's voice. "Excuse me?" I pivoted back, surveyed the tapper. The woman's red dress didn't drape flatteringly, but her shoes were pricey. Her enraptured, awestruck look, though, was classic. My fans did pick their moments.

"Aren't you Olivia Grant?"

"Yes." No point in lying. I was too well-known in Memphis.

"Back in town for a visit? With family?"

How nosy! I gave a pursed-lip half smile and cut to the chase. "I'm afraid I don't have any paper." The woman looked puzzled. "For an autograph?"

"Oh!" she said, as if that hadn't been her goal from the start. She hesitated, then reached into her bag and pulled out a folded program and handed it to me with a pen.

Dylan was in a checkout line behind a dozen people, so I took pity on the poorly dressed woman. On top of everything else, she had the largest nostrils I'd ever seen that weren't on a horse. "To whom should I autograph this?"

"Oh!" she said. "To Veronica."

Chapter 23

Hope

As we drove into Memphis, I stared out the window, gripping the armrest. The river, the Pyramid, the graceful curves of the New Bridge. Everything was at once achingly familiar and oddly unreal. Home. Not home. Mine. Not mine.

Once Jordan exited the highway, I rolled down the window, trying to take it all in. Even a fleeting glance down familiar streets showed me a different Memphis. Instead of boarded-up store fronts, restaurants offered outdoor-seating where couples sipped wine and poked at arugula. The change from eighteen years ago wasn't seamless—on some corners, homeless people still slept in doorways—but overall, it was remarkable. As we waited for the light, a convertible beside us shared Al Green's "For the Good Times."

It had taken a few phone calls to learn the schedule for that night's fundraiser. Aaron wouldn't arrive until after the dinner, thank God, when he'd take the stage with a handful of candidates for local and state office and give the keynote address.

My goal was to figure out if Dylan and my mother were at

the event. If they weren't, fabulous. I'd sneak out as quickly as possible. If they were . . . that was trickier. I had to prevent them from getting anywhere near Aaron.

This was all hypothetical, of course. Who knew if my mother and daughter had even arrived in Memphis yet? Or what they had planned. After mulling for two days over what I'd say when I finally confronted them, I'd concluded my best defense was a strong offense. A new lie. I wasn't sure who Dylan's father was. I'd been dating more than one man at the time. Three, in fact. I felt a bit sheepish about the number before realizing this detail formed the plot of *Mamma Mia!*, and no one had called Meryl Streep's character skanky. In any case, the story could work.

I checked into my room while Jordan parked. I showered in five minutes, blow-dried my hair in two, and threw on the simple black dress I'd packed, a no-iron shift I'd worn to everything from cocktail parties to funerals. It was perfect for a dimly lit fundraiser where I needed to be invisible. I'd forgotten to pack any nice jewelry, so I texted Jordan to ask if I might borrow her pearls.

"Only if you take the earrings, too," she wrote back. "I'm not going to have you pair my pearls with that dangly Jody Coyote stuff you wear."

The woman I'd spoken to said over three hundred people were attending—a reassuring number. Obviously, I couldn't let Aaron see me, but I wasn't worried. Based on my limited experience with such events, the lights would be low, and afterward, Aaron would have people pressing in from all sides, wanting a word. His staff would make him scarce as quickly as possible.

I dreaded hearing Aaron speak, even from a distance. At the Tater Tot, when I'd clicked on a YouTube video of him touring a VA hospital, I'd turned it off at the sound of his warm chuckle. What would it feel like, being in the same room with him? What emotion would win out? The anger? The hurt? The regret? The longing?

Jordan met me at the elevator, and I lifted my hair so she could fasten the necklace. She pressed the earrings into my palm, hugged me for luck, then zipped back to her room. She was having dinner with one of her sisters, then would wander the touristy areas, keeping an eye out for our fugitives. I used the hallway mirror to put on the earrings, pinched my cheeks for color, and reminded myself that the point was not to look attractive, but invisible. No problem. That was my superpower.

THE NOTES FROM the piano ragtime progression faded as I climbed the stairs to the Peabody's mezzanine and strode down a long hallway. A folding table blocked access to the Grand Ballroom. With the dinner over, I hoped to talk my way in for a reduced donation. After that, I'd have to play it by ear. I prayed the room had a dark corner where I could sit and scan for Dylan's pink hair or my mother's white updo.

A young woman wearing a hijab typed on a laptop, while an older woman with spiky silver hair shuffled through papers. I waited for the young woman to look up. Instead the silver-haired woman did. Her head jerked back.

"Hope?"

My stomach dropped straight through to the lobby. "Shelley!" I forced some enthusiasm. "Hi!" I'd been so focused on avoiding Aaron, I hadn't considered running into someone else I knew.

She detoured around the table to give me a hug. "Wow." She

was clearly struggling with what to say. And why wouldn't she? I'd worked closely with her for five months and then disappeared. "You look great. What's it been? Twenty years?"

"Just about." To buy myself time to think, I said, "Your son must be grown now." It worked. She pulled a phone out of her jacket pocket to show me Owen's new baby. No doubt Shelley, too, felt relieved to have something to talk about. Eventually, though, common courtesy dictated she ask me something.

"And how about you? What have you been up to?" Shelley was a master of small talk and wouldn't acknowledge the elephant in the room: *What the hell happened?*

"I work for a small publishing company, in marketing."

"That's great. Where?"

"Oh . . . Seattle." I hated lying to Shelley, but I couldn't have her search for me online or try to friend me on Facebook. A burst of laughter and applause inside the ballroom provided the perfect segue. "To be honest, I'm only in town for a few days and heard about this fundraiser. If I make a small donation, would you let me slip in and listen to the speakers?"

She waved a hand. "Screw the donation. You put in your time. You can have my seat." To my protest, she replied, "No worries. My candidate has already spoken." Shelley nodded toward the woman with the laptop. "I need to help this young lady close up shop. I'll stick my head in later for Aaron's speech." She motioned for me to follow her to the double doors and leaned her head in close to hear the murmur of the speaker. "Hold on while this guy finishes, then I'll sneak you around back."

That sounded perfect. "You don't work with Aaron anymore?" I was praying I'd heard that right. I didn't want her mentioning she'd seen me.

"No, I stay local. Aaron needs the big guns. Now Veronica—you remember her, right? She still works in Aaron's Memphis office. She's here."

Veronica, I thought. *Shit*. I didn't want to run into her, either.

Shelley cracked open the door and listened, raising a finger. I felt a rush of warmth for her. She'd been a good friend to me all those years ago and I hadn't thanked her or even said goodbye.

"Shelley," I whispered, "I'm sorry about the way I left. It was a personal issue . . ."

"Hope," she said, closing the door and resting a hand on my shoulder. "No worries, compadre." Her direct eye contact told me she had a pretty good idea what the issue had been. Shelley had always been a talented reader of people. No doubt I'd done a terrible job hiding my feelings for Aaron.

The audience applauded, and Shelley motioned to follow her inside. I took a deep breath and focused on my task—scouting for my mother and daughter. The ballroom was dimly lit and packed with round tables of eight people. I kept my head down as Shelley led me behind the last row. Out of the corner of my eye, I saw men in black tie and women in tight gowns, but no one with pink hair.

Instead of staying in the back where staff and volunteers usually sit, Shelley turned and proceeded along the left wall toward the front. I stopped, shaking my head no, but she waved me forward. People at nearby tables turned. Eyes lowered, I slunk down the aisle.

Thankfully, Shelley's chair was in the farthest corner of the room, so close to the stage it couldn't be seen by the person at the podium without some serious *Exorcist*-style head spinning. As I sat, Shelley patted my back and waved before hurrying off.

Eventually, I found the courage to raise my eyes to the stage. If Aaron was there, he was seated on the other side of the podium. I exhaled.

The throaty woman speaking had rehearsed some great one-liners, and the audience howled with laughter. I pasted on a smile and followed their cues while scouring the ballroom for my daughter or mother. From my corner I had a decent vantage point, and after a few minutes of craning my neck to see around my tablemates, I concluded my fugitives weren't there. When I sat back in my chair, the unshaven young man on my right smiled quizzically and imitated my head tilts. I rubbed my shoulder and whispered, "Stiff neck."

"And now, here he is," drawled Representative Throaty, "our own native son, a champion for the state of Tennessee, and one of our country's great beacons for the future, Aaron Breckenridge!" The room rose to applaud. I stood, backing deeper into the dark corner, and pulled at my dress, which clung to my damp skin. I made a final sweep of the room.

As the crowd sat, I scooted my chair back to where I could see only part of Aaron's profile. Occasionally, when it felt safe, I leaned forward to sneak a glance. I'd seen recent photos of Aaron, of course, and caught glimpses of him on TV. His face wasn't as narrow as it had been, as one might expect from a man no longer thirty-two, and he'd grayed at the temples. On the plus side, he'd clearly hired someone to do his tailoring. For once his suit fit.

Aaron had been dealt a tough hand following the throaty comic—he wasn't as entertaining. He seemed sincere, though, and far more polished than the man I remembered. He spoke without notes, his gaze lingering on different tables. Even in the far corner, I feared Aaron might look my way, and I kept bending down, pretending to adjust the heel strap on my shoe. The unshaven man next to me turned.

"Need something?" he whispered.

For you to mind your business, I thought. But I smiled and mouthed no. I tipped my chair back against the stage and closed my eyes, as if reflecting deeply on Aaron's points about health care and immigration. His pleasant, modulated voice transported me back to that tiny campaign office over the sporting goods store, where after long days canvassing, we'd chatted about John Grisham novels and climate change, job creation and Bob Dylan's *MTV Unplugged,* whether Walmart would save Memphis or kill it. He'd listened to me, and I'd felt seen.

The creak of a door opening in the back of the ballroom forced open my eyes. Someone sneaking in late. My mother? Dylan? No, even in silhouette, the well-heeled woman was taller than Dylan, younger than my mother. At the podium, Aaron spoke about the issues facing Tennessee and the country at large: the need to stimulate growth, add jobs, repair infrastructure, and provide health care for all its citizens. He ended with climate change. The need to address it immediately. "This should be a bipartisan effort. Few issues are as pressing. We have to invest in sustainable energy and cut back on carbon emissions, or our children and grandchildren will have no earth to inherit."

At the words "our children," a shiver ran down my back. I'd been carried along by his voice, lulled into remembering the man I'd fallen for. But Aaron wasn't that person. Whatever he said, however he presented on the outside, he had an unattractive, ambitious side. He hadn't just rejected me, he'd rejected his child. He'd lured me into an agreement

I regretted. He'd hired that creepy little man on the park bench. *You've made a good choice, Ms. Robinson.*

Aaron was wrapping up, encouraging the crowd to support the candidates onstage with him. He ended with one of those political lines cravenly designed to catapult people from their chairs: "May God bless the state of Tennessee and the United States of America."

The audience did as scripted and leaped to their feet. I followed suit. In the back, someone gave a loud, fingers-in-your-teeth whistle. Shelley. I could make her out, standing by the woman who'd slipped in late. That woman raised a phone to her ear and opened the ballroom door. The light from the corridor illuminated her. Veronica.

Shit. Had she seen me? Had Shelley told her I was there?

I stood too long wondering. The candidates had come forward in a line to wave to the crowd. Now only a few yards away, Aaron turned in our direction, applauding the volunteers at our table and—I realized later—probably looking for Shelley. His gaze passed over me briefly, then returned and held mine for a couple beats.

Shit. Shit. Shit.

Time to go. I reached down to snatch my bag from under the table, and when it resisted, I yanked.

The unshaven man yelped and gave a surprised hop. "Hold on!" he called out, reaching down to disentangle his leg from my purse strap. He brushed off the bag, but instead of giving it to me, he clasped the hand I'd held out and shook it. "I'm Tim, nice to meet you."

"Hope." I glanced right to see if I could exit the side doors. Two men blocked the nearest.

Tim gripped my hand, leaning in to be heard over the hubbub. "You work with Shelley?"

"Not anymore." I twisted away. "Sorry, I need to run. Nice to meet you."

Tim didn't answer. He pointed behind me, his eyebrows raised. I pivoted.

"Hope," Aaron said. "What a surprise. Do you have a minute?"

SHIT, SHIT, SHIT.

Without a glance at the people pressing in around us, Aaron took my elbow and guided me toward the side exit, ignoring calls of "Senator, Senator." The two men guarding the door opened it and blocked for us. Out in the hallway, hotel staff rushed by in both directions. We climbed a few stairs to another hall. The pounding in my ears drowned out everything else.

Aaron opened a door labeled "Dressing Room" and led me in. The small space was empty except for a wool dress and fox-fur shawl hanging on a clothes rack. Not his, I assumed, though I'd learned you never know. He turned and spoke to someone outside the door.

I could think of no explanation for my being there. Seventeen years ago, I'd taken Aaron's money and promised never to return to Memphis. Yet here I was, not just in Memphis, but sitting front row at one of his events. Not simply in violation of our deal but flaunting it.

My breath caught. *Oh my God.* Aaron thought I was there to extort him! At this critical juncture in his career, I'd resurfaced to demand more money. Brilliant. For a confused second, even I was impressed by my cunning. No wonder Aaron had to get me alone. He needed to contain the damage.

Aaron closed the door, opened his mouth to say something, then scratched his head, looking at the ceiling for help.

From habit, my hand flew to my hair, yanking it back from my forehead. "This is not how it looks."

He frowned. "How does it look?"

Someone knocked on the door. Aaron cracked it open, and a voice whispered to him.

"Five minutes," he said. More muttering from without. "No, I'm too tired. We'll deal with it tomorrow." Aaron closed the door, and someone knocked again. He raised both hands as if to say *Welcome to my life*. "Is this okay?" he asked. "You're not trying to catch a movie or something?"

I shook my head a fraction of an inch. My mouth may have been open.

Leaning in through the barely open door, a balding man with tiny, red ears murmured something to Aaron, who raised an index finger and opened the door wider. "This probably looks bad," he told the man, "my ducking into a closet with a woman. Hope is an old friend. A volunteer on my first campaign, in fact. Oh, wait." He stepped back, revealing behind the bald man someone in a red dress and Prada pumps. "Hope, you remember Veronica, don't you?"

The woman bent sideways to see around the man, like a Von Trapp child popping out to say, "Cuckoo." Veronica was more matronly than the college graduate I recalled. She wore reading glasses low on her nose.

"Great to see you again, Hope." She didn't seem surprised, though, so Shelley had spilled the beans. It no longer mattered.

I responded in kind, but she was back listening to Aaron and the bald man. To give them space, I turned and focused on the only thing in the room, the hanging fox fur. Real, it turned out. The poor creature's tail was shoved in its mouth. I empathized.

Aaron closed the door and turned back to me, exhaling loudly. "Let's start over. It's good to see you, Hope."

His tone was confusing. I knew this conversation would eventually turn ugly. In movies, the most spine-chilling villains speak soothingly at first.

"I get it," he said to my silence. "You must hate me."

I had no idea how to respond. I hated him. I loved him. I regretted him. I'd do it all again. Pick a card.

"It's fine," he said. "I don't expect you to forgive me, but God, Hope, I would have liked the chance to talk to you after that night. I turned around and you'd . . ." He made a sweeping hand motion.

"Disappeared," I whispered hoarsely.

"Yes! And not just a little." An edge had crept into his voice. "You vanished like a pro."

I didn't know what he was implying. I remembered Detective Fish hinting that my pregnancy hadn't been an accident. "You make it sound like I was the one who did something wrong."

"No," he said. "Only that . . . I wish I'd had a chance to explain."

Now I was pissed off. "You knew where I lived."

His mouth opened and closed. "I don't know what you mean. Your roommate—that hair stylist—said you'd gone to stay with a friend and then vanished."

"You talked to Ashlee?"

"*And* all three of her boyfriends! I tried everything . . ." Another knock at the door. "Jesus!" He ran a hand through his hair.

"Clearly we need more than five minutes." He cracked the door and barked, "What?" Then: "Crap." A pause. "No, no. Fine. Give me thirty seconds." He turned back to me. "I'm sorry. The governor wants to talk to me. You know how it goes."

"Of course," I said. "He hates it when I duck his calls."

His grin was tight-lipped. "I'd really like to talk to you, Hope." He glanced at his watch. "Can you meet me somewhere in an hour? Are you staying locally? Christ, do you still live in Memphis? Maybe all these years you've been hiding in plain sight."

I squinted at him. Was he gaslighting me? His stooge had been mailing me a check since 1999. "I can meet," I said.

"Great. My condo complex has some social rooms. It's probably the only place I can be right now without paparazzi. I'll get you the address. Meet me there around ten?" He pulled a phone from his jacket pocket. "What's your number?"

I wasn't sure I wanted Aaron to have my number, but couldn't think of an excuse, so I gave it to him. He punched it in and sent the call, and I answered so it would save to his phone.

"Fabulous." With his hand on the door, he stopped. "Needless to say, a lot of people would like my phone number, so please keep it to yourself."

"Of course." Keeping things to myself was just one of the many services I offered.

"Text me if anything comes up. I do want to talk to you, Hope. It would mean a lot to me."

"Sure," I said, struggling to make sense of what had just happened.

As Aaron opened the door, his phone beeped and he glanced at it, smiled. "My son, A.J. He likes to check in after big events." His eyes met mine. "Do you have kids, Hope?"

My frown and slow headshake weren't meant as a lie, or even an answer, but rather an expression of utter bewilderment. *How can you say that?* I opened my mouth to ask, but the bald man grabbed Aaron by the shoulder, pulling him from the room while handing him a different phone. Aaron raised it to his ear. "How are you, Governor?" He waved at me and cocked his head in apology before striding away.

That was when I finally understood. He didn't know.

I SLAMMED THROUGH the hotel doors and took off down the street. I didn't think about where I was heading, didn't know I could walk that fast in heels. My thoughts sprayed out in all directions, like Coke from a dropped can.

I speed-dialed Jordan. Words tumbled out in an incoherent jumble.

"Hope, calm down," she said. "You're not making any sense. You saw Aaron?"

"Yes." I was panting. "Well, he saw me. It was an accident. He put me in a closet."

"What?"

"Not a closet. You know, one of those little rooms with clothes . . ."

"Sweetie, have you been drinking?"

"Jordan." I gasped for breath. "He doesn't know about Dylan. At first, I thought he was just fucking with me, but I could tell by his face."

From her silence, I thought I'd dropped the connection. "Hope," Jordan said slowly, "you told me Aaron *did* know. You said he wanted nothing to do with her."

Of course I'd told Jordan that. I'd believed that. "Hold on. I'm . . . crossing an intersection." I wasn't, but I needed time to think. How could I explain that Aaron didn't know without telling Jordan about the creepy little man on the park bench? How I'd been bought. How I'd willingly taken the money he offered and promised to lie to everyone for the rest of my life. The most shameful of my secrets. "Actually, you know what?" I said. "You're right. I just figured it out. It was a misunderstanding."

"Sweetie," Jordan said. "You sound muddled. Come back to the hotel. We'll get you some coffee. And maybe a blood-alcohol test."

"No, no, I'm good. I'll explain later." I insisted she tell me about her evening.

I tried to focus on Jordan's play-by-play—she'd had dinner with her sister, Angie, who'd had a nose job that didn't go well—but my mind was elsewhere. How could Aaron not know about Dylan? If he hadn't made that agreement with me, who had? Who knew about the park, the tree, our kiss? Had Aaron told Carly those intimate details? That alone felt like a betrayal.

Jordan planned to walk around Beale Street looking for Dylan and my mother. As she ran through the places she'd check, I realized where my feet had taken me: the park where Aaron and I had first kissed. Our park. The sun had set, and the place seemed smaller than I remembered. I stood in the center and rotated, slowly, full circle. Two teenagers canoodled on a park bench, a pregnant woman pushed a double stroller, and an old man lumbered up the walk with a stiff knee.

Jordan was silent. I realized she was waiting for a response to some question I hadn't heard. "Hope, are you sure you're okay? Should I come meet you?"

"No, I'm going to wander around a bit. Don't wait up."

"If you're sure."

"I am, thanks," I said, as a shiver ran up my neck. The old man approaching me didn't have a stiff knee. He was bowlegged.

I lowered my phone as the man stopped and tipped his hat.

"Ms. Robinson," said Marlin Fish. "It's been some time."

Chapter 24

Dylan

I wanted to punch a hole in the window of the duck store when I realized how Olivia had tricked me.

I was in the Peabody lobby, face pressed to the glass of the dark and shuttered store. A few hours earlier, I'd been waiting in line to pay for Emma's duck socks with only four people ahead of me, when Olivia had burst into the store and insisted we needed to go *right then* to see that Memphis Pyramid. Like the monument was going away or something.

There's no arguing with Olivia when she sets her mind on something. Plus, I was using her Amex to buy Emma's gift. So I drove her to the freaking Pyramid. We rode the elevator to the twenty-eighth floor and stood on the observation deck for an eternity, looking out at the river and that double-humped bridge decked out in red lights. The view was nice, but enough already! Then Olivia decided she wanted to see her old house again, so I took her to East Memphis, where we drove by her husband's old car dealership, a park, a cemetery, and—I kid you not—their favorite grocery store. I wanted to rip my face off.

Finally, we returned to the hotel, and while Olivia showered, I slipped back downstairs to find the store closed. A spray-tanned woman in a sparkly dress stopped to peer in the window beside me. She whispered to her husband, "I didn't think Breckenridge's speech was all that special, did you?" My scalp went all tingly.

The guy yawned. "He's watching every word these days. He wants that VP spot." He put a hand the woman's shoulder and steered her toward the lounge. "Come on, let's have that martini."

I spun around. More tuxes and gowns were squeezing into the lounge. Had Breckenridge's speech been here tonight? The Peabody? Jesus . . . had Olivia known?

Of course she had.

It all made sense. That's why Olivia had dragged me from the Peabody and kept me away all evening. So I wouldn't realize my father was there, in the same building.

I took the elevator upstairs and slammed the door to our suite. Olivia, in a Peabody robe, emerged from the bathroom.

"You knew it!" I shouted. "You knew he was here!"

"Of course I did."

Olivia had a knack for throwing me off my game. "Why?" I sputtered.

"You need to trust me, Dylan," she said, moving back into the bathroom, but leaving the door open. "We follow the plan."

"It's just . . ." I crossed my arms and leaned against the door frame. "Sometimes I don't know whose side you're on."

"Side?"

"You keep making excuses for my mother, a pathological

liar, and you don't even tell me my father's in our hotel. Seems like we're not on the same team anymore."

"Oh, for goodness' sake, Dylan." Olivia squeezed toothpaste from the travel-sized tube of Crest onto her toothbrush. "Stop trying to divide everything into sides and teams, or good and bad. Only the most ignorant people see the world that way." She fluttered a hand to shoo me out of the bathroom doorway. "Do you know what the word 'nuance' means?"

I scowled.

"Look it up!" she demanded and shut the door.

I wasn't in the mood for word games. My father was in town, and he might be out there, somewhere, having a late dinner or shaking hands on that famous Beale Street. I waited until it was quiet, then gently opened Olivia's door and heard her soft breathing. I slipped out of the suite.

Outside, even at nine thirty p.m., the humidity smacked me in the face. A bass guitar thundered from a few blocks away, so I headed in that direction.

Beale Street, with its bright lights and flashing signs, smelled of tacos, beer, and cigarettes. The touristy shops were closed, but the bars were alive with clinking glasses and rowdy laughter. How stupid to think I might run into Breckenridge here. Even if he were inside one of the nicer restaurants, I wouldn't know. I hated to admit it, but Olivia was right. I needed to follow the plan.

A block past the hubbub, in a small park, was a statue of Elvis rocking out on his guitar. I took a photo for Olivia that didn't come out well even with the flash, then sat on the cement steps at its base. After a few minutes, I stretched out and lay on my back. I needed to think things through.

Tomorrow I'd meet my father. He'd believe I was a reporter for that newspaper. Shit, what was the name? *The Daily Helmet? Hemsworth?* Never mind, I wouldn't say it. In fact, once I was alone with Breckenridge, did I need to pretend? I'd just get to the point. Did he remember a woman named Hope Robinson? As long as he said yes, the rest would be easy. I pictured the scene. Breckenridge, who'd been studying my face, struggling to figure out who I reminded him of, would frown in confusion, disbelief, then—gradually—understanding. The corners of his mouth would curl up in a smile. Maybe his eyes would fill with tears. Awkward, but I could handle it.

I had another fantasy that I knew was stupid, but whatever, it made me happy. Maybe if I went to his speech Saturday night, Breckenridge would call me up onstage. Introduce me to the audience. Man, the rush of that moment. People would see us together and think, of course, that fits. Bold politician, activist daughter. Nut doesn't fall far from the tree, or whatever that expression was.

There was another possibility, of course. One I hadn't thought about much. What if Breckenridge *did* know about me? What if Mom had told him to stay away, and he had? Or perhaps there'd been some misunderstanding between them. Maybe he'd wanted to be in my life, but Mom had made it too hard. I wouldn't judge the man until I heard him out.

"Miss, you can't sleep there."

I jumped up. A police officer stood on the sidewalk.

I almost cursed her out since she'd nearly given me a heart attack. Instead I muttered "Fine" and headed back down the street. A little self-control, I was learning, could save you some trouble.

I wandered back down Beale. The band I'd heard earlier, playing in a space between two buildings, was taking a break, and I wound my way into the crowd of folks sitting at picnic tables, waiting for the next set. I sat on a bench beside two young women holding hands, one with a nose ring and the other with a baseball cap and tattoo sleeve. The nose-ring girl smiled, so I smiled back.

A folded newspaper lay on the table. The nose-ring girl said it wasn't theirs, so I opened it. Sure enough. Front page. A story about Breckenridge that focused on the Peabody fund-raiser and his speech at the university tomorrow.

The nose-ring girl was reading over my shoulder. Rude, but I let it go. I said, "I guess this Breckenridge guy might get to be vice president."

"Yeah." She grimaced. "Not a fan."

The girl may as well have hit me. I blinked. "Really? Why not?"

"Do you know how long it took him to come out in favor of equal marriage? Even Hillary beat him."

I felt sick. *No. Not possible.*

Her baseball-capped friend shook her head. "This is Tennessee. He can't seem too liberal, or he won't get reelected."

Nose-ring pointed a thumb at her friend. "She was raised Republican, so she cuts him slack. I don't. He's a weenie."

The band was picking up their instruments again and I mumbled something about the time and stood. I asked the nose-ring girl, "Do you happen to know Breckenridge's position on trans rights?"

She didn't take her eyes from the stage, just repeated, "Weenie."

THE IMPORTANT THING was not to overreact, I told myself, kicking sideways at a low cement wall. You can't trust random people sitting on the street. Even ones with cool body art.

It had grown darker. I'd never walked alone in a city at night, but the moon was out and the streetlights kept it from being creepy. As I approached the Peabody, I slowed as a tall figure strode toward me. She wore a lavender dress and was whistling "Pretty Woman."

Jordan.

I considered running, but what could Jordan do—hold me down until Mom came? Besides, Jordan and I had always been buds. Sometimes I shared stuff with Jordan that never got back to my mother. I knew because Mom would have flipped out.

Jordan stopped short, surprised. "Hey there, young lady." Her smile was friendly, nonthreatening.

I kept my distance. "You're a long way from Stoneham."

"I'm here with your mom."

"No duh."

"You need to talk to her, sweetheart."

"Why? She lies to me."

Jordan sighed. "Well, I'm not going to get into it with you, Dylan, but people bend the truth for a lot of reasons, and not all of them are bad. Maybe she felt she had to."

"Why?"

"*Why, why, why?* Jeepers, how old are you? Two?" Jordan was trying to make me laugh.

I wasn't having it. "Guess I don't understand liars."

Jordan stepped aside to let a group of teenagers pass. One stared at Jordan, and I glowered back until he looked away. "Look, you've learned stuff about your father recently. Am I right?"

"How long have you known?"

Jordan huffed out a laugh. "Not as long as you, trust me. And I get that you're eager to know more, but you need to slow down and think. Your mother loves you. She would never do anything to hurt you. If she kept certain things secret, maybe, just maybe, she had a good reason."

I kicked a stone down the sidewalk. "What is it you know?"

"Sweetheart, you need to talk to your mom, not me."

"She doesn't want me to meet my father. Why does she get to choose? She's not always right, you know."

"That's true, but she does always have your best interest at heart."

"Not seeing it."

"Dylan, stop." Jordan sounded angry and a passing couple twisted to watch. Jordan motioned us closer to the building and lowered her voice. "Consider for a minute. The man is a public figure, at a key point in his career. Any questionable behavior from his past—it's not something he'd want to come out right now."

I glanced back toward Beale. "You know what's funny?" I tapped my fist against the hotel. "In health class, they teach kids to take responsibility for their actions. But apparently if you're a white, cisgender male politician, you don't have to."

Jordan held up both hands. "Preaching to the choir here, Dylan. All I'm saying is that the timing, perhaps, isn't ideal."

"Yeah. Wow. Maybe he should have thought of that." I

skirted around Jordan, moving toward the Peabody door. "Well, thank you for this chat. Any chance you can avoid telling Mom you saw me?"

"I'm not going to lie to her."

"I hope she gives you the same consideration." Did Jordan raise her eyebrows at that?

"Just speak with your mother, Dylan. That's all I'm asking. It's not hard."

I burst out laughing. "Not hard? Talking to her about my father? Where've you been?"

Jordan stepped forward, like she had good news to share. "Things have changed. Your mom understands she needs to be more . . . forthcoming. In the last few days, she's really opened up."

"That so? What did she say?"

I could tell from the droop in Jordan's smile she wished she could take it back.

"Spill the beans," Dylan said. "I'd rather hear it from you."

"Dylan."

"Huh. Bad news, then."

"No . . ."

"Let me guess. It was a one-night stand, and she never told Breckenridge she was pregnant?" Jordan had pursed her lips, and I couldn't tell if that meant it wasn't true, or she simply wouldn't say. "Worse?" Here I let loose with a new possibility, one I hadn't fully considered before. "Maybe he *does* know about me and doesn't want anything to do with me. Maybe he *told her* to say he was dead. Is that it?"

Jordan looked at her shoes. My stomach dropped. Mom always joked that when Jordan didn't want to tell you something to your face, she stared at her shoes.

Shit. That *was* it.

"Dylan . . ."

"No, it's okay," I whispered, opening the hotel door. "Good talk."

I'd stepped inside before I realized what I'd done. Now Jordan knew where Olivia and I were staying.

Fuck it. Nothing mattered.

I dropped my head against the back wall of the elevator. Clearly, without realizing it, I'd carried this ugly scenario about my father inside me all this time. And fuck, I wished it didn't make so much sense. What if, all along, Mom had been protecting me from the ugly truth that my father was a jerk and didn't want me? Or worse, protecting Aaron Breckenridge from having a little stain on his flawless character.

What kind of a hypocrite must Breckenridge be? Hiding the truth because it was inconvenient? Rejecting your own child? Well, I had a history of dealing with jerks like him, and I had the ammunition.

I'd blow the asshole up.

Chapter 25

Hope

The handkerchief in Fish's suit pocket was folded into a triangle, as it had been the first time I'd met the detective, all those years ago. That same straw hat. His face was more deeply creased, and his pants hung a little too loosely. How had this little man intimidated me back then? Now outrage trumped my fear.

"My goodness," I said. "It doesn't take Carly long to release her winged monkeys, does it?" It was only a guess, but it was all I had.

"We live in a world with eyes, Ms. Robinson. I assume everything I do is watched. I recommend others do the same."

"You lied to me, Mr. Fish. You led me to believe Aaron had sent you."

"I told you my client's identity was a private matter."

"A park by the river, you said. A shingle oak tree."

"I did say those words. It's interesting to think about what constitutes a lie. Do you ever think about that?"

I wasn't about to be insulted by this shit weasel. "You tricked me. I thought Aaron knew about his child. I thought . . ." My voice quavered and I fought to steady it. "I thought he didn't want her." Despite my efforts, tears spilled over. Fish reached into his breast pocket and offered his handkerchief, but I waved it away and rummaged in my purse. "I don't know how people do jobs like yours." I found a balled-up tissue. "How do you sleep at night?"

He took off his hat, rubbed a spot on his head. "Like most folks, rather poorly. I do what I'm paid to do, Ms. Robinson, regardless of whether I think it's right, wrong, or somewhere between. In truth, I find most things are in the middle."

I blew my nose and said, "You can twist anything so it seems like it's the middle."

"Sounds like you've had experience with that."

He didn't seem to be smirking, only mulling, but I lashed out. "You know what? I haven't always chosen well. I've made mistakes. But that doesn't mean there wasn't a right or wrong—it means I fell short." Snot was dripping from my nose, and he again offered his handkerchief. This time, I had to accept. I wiped and blew. "If everyone throws their arms up and says there's no right or wrong, then we've lost our compass. We're on a road to nowhere." I wiped under both eyes and handed him back the soggy handkerchief.

Fish slid it into a pocket, which made me feel worse. "You're surely right about that, Ms. Robinson. You're a thoughtful person and I regret having to bother you again." He put his hat back on his head. "Nevertheless, here we are. I'm retired now," he continued. "I only came here tonight as a favor to a client who paid me well over the years."

"Carly." I wiped my nose with the back of my hand this time. "I should have guessed."

"Well, as you say, perhaps I stacked the deck. Regardless, you're in violation of the agreement you signed."

"Look, Mr. Fish, I can't afford to break that agreement. I don't have the money to pay her back." My phone quacked and I lifted it from my bag to glance at the home screen. A text from a Memphis number I didn't recognize.

"Then why are you *here*, Ms. Robinson? You do understand, don't you, that you're risking everything by being in Memphis?"

I sniffled again. "I don't *want* to be here. My mother and daughter took off without telling me . . ." As soon as the words left my mouth, I realized my mistake.

"Why are your mother and daughter in Memphis?"

"My mother is an Elvis freak," I said, hastily. "She's ill and wanted to see Graceland one last time. I wouldn't take her, so my daughter did."

"Is that so? Well, I certainly hope that's the case. I spoke to my client tonight about cutting you some slack. After all, Memphis is your hometown, and you've stayed away for almost eighteen years. But I'm not sure I can help you if you've violated both parts of the agreement. If other family members know . . ."

"I haven't told my mother or daughter anything about Dylan's father," I said, truthfully. Which wasn't to say they didn't know.

"And the reason you were at Senator Breckenridge's event tonight?"

Fish knew that, too? Damn. "Stupid curiosity," I said. "I shouldn't have gone." Did he know Aaron had seen me? Spoken to me?

"Very well, Ms. Robinson. As I said, my job is to make sure we're on the same page. The agreement is specific. At a minimum, it prohibits you from revealing the identity of your child's father. To anyone. I'm afraid I need to emphasize this point. An-y-one."

"I get it," I said, brushing away a fallen leaf with my shoe. "Not even the father."

"No one. And may I suggest it would be in everyone's best interest if you left Memphis in the next twenty-four hours?"

"I'll try. I can't promise."

"I like you, Ms. Robinson. So please try. Try really hard."

I HURRIED AWAY from my meeting with Fish, back toward the Doubletree, not stopping until a passing trolley on North Main Street forced me to catch my breath. I stepped into a doorway, checking my phone. It was getting low on battery. The text message alert I'd heard earlier was for a link to Aaron's condo complex with "as promised" typed below it. No time for chatty messages in his world. I saved his number in my contacts simply as Aaron.

Tilting my head against the cool brick of the dark doorway, I closed my eyes. Aaron didn't know about Dylan. He'd never known. I wasn't sure how Carly had managed that, but regardless, I had a decision to make. Should I tell him?

I didn't take long to decide. The answer was no. Neither of us could afford the fallout. Fish would try to recover the $260,000 I'd been paid over the years—money that had gone toward my maternity bills, a down payment on our house, childcare, Dylan's braces. Money I didn't have. I'd probably lose our house, and how would that help my daughter? And for Aaron, could the timing be worse? According to the political commentators, a hangnail could tip the scales on the VP pick. An affair with a staffer and secret child was bad enough. What if they found out about the hush money? No matter what Aaron said, it would look like he and Carly had paid me off.

And finally, there was Dylan. Already she hated me for lying to her. What would happen when she found out I'd done it for money?

I double-checked the condo address Aaron had sent and stepped out of the doorway. I wasn't sure I could look Aaron in the eye, but I needed to hear what he had to say. His tone had been oddly apologetic, not accusatory. Was it possible Carly had kept her promise to me and not told Aaron I'd been expelled from the U of M? If so, why had he chosen Carly? Why hadn't I been enough for him? These were things I both dreaded hearing and ached to know.

Aaron's high-rise condo building was new since my time in Memphis. Gleaming white, with row upon row of balconies, it sat on a bluff facing the Mississippi. Inside, the lounge and an adjoining room were jam-packed with a wedding after-party. The security guard at the front desk called up to Aaron and handed me the phone. "I didn't realize those rooms were booked," Aaron said. "I hope this doesn't sound like a ploy, but would you be willing to come up?" I said I trusted him.

Aaron's condo had more furniture than his apartment years earlier, but the same look of someone with no time to decorate. I recognized a photo of the Memphis skyline at night and a framed print of hazy peaks in Great Smoky Mountains National Park. Maybe Carly had sent him packing with only the artwork that he'd brought to the marriage. Or maybe he had a nicer place in DC.

Aaron asked me to have a seat in the living room and returned with a bottle of Chardonnay and two glasses. "Wine?"

I nodded. Truthfully, a fifth of vodka sounded good, but I'd stick to one glass of wine. I'd listen to what Aaron had to say and not offer much. Far too easy to slip and mention my daughter.

"Excuse the mess." He lifted a stack of paper from the coffee table and dropped it on one of the chairs. "I'm rarely in Memphis long enough to unpack. So where's home for you, Hope?" he asked, pouring us both some wine.

I hesitated for a second, remembering what I'd told Shelley. "Seattle."

Maybe that lie wasn't necessary. If all went well, I'd leave Memphis soon with my mother and daughter and Aaron Breckenridge would have no reason to seek me out. But I wasn't taking any chances.

"Oh." He seemed surprised. "I thought maybe you'd ended up in LA, with your mom."

"No. In fact, she just moved to be near me. In Seattle," I added, unnecessarily.

"And you like it there?"

"Seattle?" *Jesus, how many times was I going to say that?* I shrugged. "Kinda rainy, but otherwise fine." I wanted off this topic, so I asked about his kids. He pulled out his phone and showed me photos. They were good-looking teenagers, though the younger boy, maybe thirteen, needed a couple years to grow into his nose. Googling Aaron over the years, I'd learned his sons' names, and yet when he said, "And that's Dylan," my heart fluttered uncomfortably in my chest.

"They're good kids," he said. "Dylan's going through a phase right now. The divorce didn't help."

"Divorces generally don't."

"Are you . . . divorced?" he asked, adding quickly: "I don't mean to pry. You're not wearing a ring."

I'd forgotten that men notice that. "No, not divorced. Well, not married, either. Just dating." I paused, realizing that the last date I'd had was over eight months ago. "Actually, not really dating either. I'm sort of . . . between disasters."

He laughed. "That surprises me. I've always pictured you living on a cul-de-sac with an architect, five kids, and a collie."

I was amazed he'd thought about me at all. What I mustered was: "A collie?"

"Maybe it was a golden retriever." He shrugged. "I've never been good with dogs."

Aaron asked what brought me back to Memphis and I said my mother was visiting an old friend. Not entirely untrue if you considered Elvis her friend and a trip to his memorial a visit. I changed the subject to Shelley. How great it had been to see her.

Aaron rubbed a thumb across the stemless wineglass, as if trying to remove a smudge. "She must have been surprised," he said. "Did you say anything about why you'd left?"

"I mumbled something about personal issues."

He wiped again at the smudge. "In the interest of complete transparency . . . she knows."

"What?"

"I went a little nuts after you disappeared. She guessed about us. Or at least, she told me what she suspected, and I didn't deny it."

My turn to wipe at an invisible smudge.

"I looked everywhere for you, Hope," Aaron said, quietly. "You gave me nothing to go on. Not a word to Shelley or Veronica. I finally found a number for your mother."

I shook my head in disbelief. "Wait. You spoke to my mother?"

He squinted a bit, struggling to recall. "I left a message. I think it was her agent who called me back."

This was new information. "What did you say?"

"Nothing personal. I mean, I didn't say, 'I slept with your daughter, and she disappeared.'"

No, but clearly that's what she took from it.

"Anyway, according to the agent, your mother didn't know where you were. Traveling the country, or something."

At least my mother had covered for me. I could see, though, how she'd eventually pieced things together. "Aaron, look, I'm incredibly flattered that you asked around . . ."

"Asked around?" He made a face like I didn't get it. "Hope, I hired a detective."

"A detective?" A chill ran up my spine. "Do you remember his name?"

He looked at me oddly. "Lincoln James. He was a hunting buddy of my dad's. Why?"

"Sorry." I waved a hand. "Doesn't matter." I took a big sip of wine. "I appreciate everything you did to try to find me, Aaron. And truly, I don't blame you for what happened. You had a tough decision to make."

"You don't understand. Please. Let me explain."

Something clawed at my chest that made me fear, oddly, that I might cry. To keep control, I stared at my wineglass. Thinking I was looking for more, Aaron poured me another.

He said, "Let's start with the morning I last saw you."

AFTER OUR NIGHT together, Aaron had asked Carly to meet him at his apartment. It was the morning of the Fall Festival. As soon as Carly walked in the door, he blurted that he needed to end their engagement. Just as she had before, Carly remained calm. She said, "I understand you have cold feet. Lots of guys do." Then she asked if there was someone else. Aaron didn't want to lie, so he'd said, "There may be." Cool as a cucumber, she said, "Well, I'm completely certain I want to marry you. But if you're not sure, then take the time you need."

I held up a hand. "Did you tell her the other woman was me?"

"She didn't ask. She kissed me on the cheek and said I knew where to find her when I'd decided. That was it."

Interesting. The Carly who'd confronted me in the park a few hours later had been a teary, vitriolic mess.

Aaron continued: "I didn't see Carly for a couple days, while I was looking for you. Between that and the campaign, I was a little crazed. I'd left my apartment to meet with that detective when Carly appeared in the parking lot. I'll cut to the chase. She was pregnant."

I frowned at my wineglass. He'd just showed me photos of their sons. The oldest was fifteen—two years younger than Dylan.

Aaron plowed ahead. Carly said she'd have the baby regardless of what he decided. "I didn't know what to say, what to think, which way to turn," he said. Late for his appointment with the detective, he made some excuse and rushed off. As he drove, he asked himself what his father would have done. "He would have told me to do the right thing. Keep my promises, own up to my responsibilities. But another part of me felt it was wrong. You shouldn't marry someone if you're in love with someone else."

I kept my eyes on the table. Was he aware of what he'd just said?

"I was so confused. I was driving along this winding road and it was drizzling and foggy. Out of nowhere, this deer leaped across the road. I slammed on the brakes and turned the wheel hard. I must have come within an inch of hitting its tail and ended up on someone's lawn." He coughed, took a sip of wine. "I turned to see where the deer had gone, but it had vanished. Just, poof." He paused, looking at me, willing me to understand, to interpret it as he had.

"You saw it as a sign from your father," I said.

"How could I not?" Aaron sipped his wine. "I sat there, stunned, asking, *What are you trying to tell me, Dad?* A pickup had stopped behind me, and the driver came over to make sure I was okay. What he said was 'Wow. You stopped just in time.'"

AARON'S PHONE HAD beeped, and he went into the kitchen to make a call. I heard him rattling around in the refrigerator, saying he'd deal with it tomorrow. When he returned with a new bottle of wine, he poured us more and sat back on the sofa, running his fingers through his hair. "I never met with the detective. I drove to Carly's and told her I'd honor my commitment to her and responsibility to our child. She agreed we'd do some counseling." He gave a wry laugh. "Somehow that never happened. She wanted to be married quickly, before the pregnancy showed. All her life, she'd dreamed about her wedding. I thought I could at least give her that. We were married three weeks later."

"And it turned out she wasn't pregnant."

"No, she was. She had a miscarriage. On our honeymoon, in fact."

"I'm sorry," I said, but I must not have sounded sincere, because his expression changed to one of curiosity.

"You don't believe me."

I bit my lip, wondering if I was being catty. "I believe *you*, Aaron. If Carly had a miscarriage, then truly, I'm sorry for the loss. It just seems a little . . ."

"Convenient?" He twirled his wineglass. "I hear you. I had a moment where I wondered. But she was *so* upset afterward." He got up to pour himself some water. "I don't know. Maybe I needed to believe her. To convince myself I'd done the right thing." He took a long drink. "It doesn't matter. I can't regret my marriage to Carly because it gave me two wonderful kids. What ate at me over the years was what happened with you." His phone was ringing, and he glanced at it, pushed a button. "I figured you'd heard about our engagement—that's why you didn't come back. Or maybe you'd decided you were better off without me. Regardless, I regretted not having the chance to see you and explain."

Aaron excused himself again and this time went into his bedroom to return the call. I ran a finger around the rim of my wineglass and thought of the irony. He'd agreed to marry Carly thinking she was pregnant, while at the same time, I really was pregnant, though I didn't know it yet. What he'd said should have made me feel better. After all, I'd assumed his feelings for me hadn't been that strong, that they'd crumbled under Carly's insistence that I was a liability, not good enough for him. When he'd had to choose between me and his future in politics, he'd chosen the latter, and taken as a consolation prize the pretty, charming, and wealthy wife.

Instead, I felt bereft, though whether for the lost opportunity years ago, or the one now, I couldn't be sure. I would have enjoyed staying in touch with Aaron if I could have. Again, I tested the idea of being honest with him. Telling him about Dylan. I'd spoken so self-righteously to Fish. Shouldn't I consider moving toward what I knew was right?

I didn't have a choice. I'd made too many shitty decisions that shaped this one—choices that provided no way out. For now, my parting gift to Aaron Breckenridge would be to leave him in peace.

AARON AND I talked for two more hours. I wasn't sure I could carry on a conversation for that long without mentioning Dylan, but I spoke carefully, considered my words. My stories about Gary and his nutty slogans made Aaron nearly choke on his wine, and he told me crazy, insider tales of the DC scene. I admitted to disliking politics. "I'm not surprised," he said. "I'm sure I did that to you"

Aaron told me about the two-day camping trip he'd squeeze in with his sons that coming week. They'd drive to Gatlinburg, hike in the Smokies, fish in the Little Pigeon River. As he spoke so proudly of his kids, an ache settled in my chest. This is what I'd cost Dylan.

Around midnight, I decided I should go. His condo was only a few blocks from the Doubletree, and I turned down his offer to walk with me. As I opened the door, though, he pushed it closed again.

"Hope," he said. "I just want to say again how sorry I am for everything."

I turned to face him. I hadn't planned it, but I put one hand on the side of his face and kissed him gently. I was saying good-bye, but he grasped the hand and didn't let go. We stood there, silently, and he ran his hand softly down my other cheek, Then he kissed me back, longer. When we separated, I noticed the lines under his eyes.

"Not a good idea?" I said before he could.

"Not in the least." He rolled his eyes. "But when has that ever stopped us?"

I knew it was crazy. I knew it was just one night and I'd never see him again. He believed I lived in Seattle. But when he pressed me up against the door to kiss me passionately, the same way he had eighteen years earlier, I realized that I hadn't felt this way about a man for exactly that long, and I let myself enjoy it. For once, I didn't worry about pleasing anyone but me.

Chapter 26

Olivia

After that first visit to Graceland years ago, I never went back. Yes, it was the King's home, and it held special meaning to me, impossible to express. It was also, though, a mecca for free-range nutters.

I'd always been a *devotee* of the King, not some wackadoo fan. You'd never find me wearing Elvis pajamas, drinking from an Elvis teacup, or owning an Elvis wall clock with wildly swinging legs. No, I appreciated the man in all his complexity. His humble passion for his music. His dazzling, showman's soul. The inevitability of his self-destruction.

And so, when a family of six clambered aboard the shuttle bus at Graceland wearing identical hound-dog T-shirts, I nearly lost my mind.

Dylan was seated next to me, her eyes closed, her head resting against the bus window. I elbowed her gently. "Really?" I whispered. "You're telling me that those toddlers are going to appreciate Priscilla's china?"

Dylan grunted and twisted away. Fine. Probably didn't sleep well after her little escape from our suite the night before.

Oh, I knew the girl had stepped out. She carelessly let the door slam on her exit, and when she returned to the suite, she was swearing a blue streak. I didn't intend to ask her about it and didn't have to. In the morning, a red message light blinked on our suite phone. Jordan. Begging me to please stay put. Hope needed to speak to me.

So the girl had taken an extracurricular stroll and bumped into Jordan. Well, good to know. Thank you, Jordan, for that heads-up. I'd wanted to get to Graceland early—to beat the crowds and confront Ann Abernathy before she'd had her coffee. Now, all the more reason to decamp immediately.

Once I'd shaken Dylan awake, her mood was as black as the T-shirt and shorts she threw on. She didn't utter a word during our stop for breakfast, and at Graceland, she disappeared into the restroom during my loud negotiations with their ticket sellers. After we arrived at the mansion, though, she gave me nonstop lip. What was so special about Elvis's cupboards? she grumbled as she carried my oxygen cart up the steps. Why would she want to see his toilet? She'd rather stick sharp things in her eye. That kind of talk.

Inside the foyer, it became unbearable.

"This is it?" she asked, surveying Elvis's living room with its grand piano and stained-glass peacocks. "I've seen bigger homes on *House Hunters*."

I ignored her. I'd worn sunglasses and a scarf to conceal my identity and was examining the roped-off staircase to the second floor, where Elvis's bedroom was, when a young man materialized out of nowhere.

"Please don't touch, ma'am," he said. His blue polo shirt had a Graceland logo.

I removed the hand I'd rested on the rope and muttered to no one in particular, "This place is crawling with docents."

Clearly, the girl didn't know what a docent was. She jumped back and scanned the floor.

By the time we reached the Jungle Room, I'd had it with Dylan's attitude. She took one look at the green-shag carpet on the ceiling—which Elvis had installed on purpose so he could record there—and fake vomited. I lost my temper.

"For heaven's sake, Dylan! If you visited Mahatma Gandhi's house you wouldn't make fun of the straw mats or rice bowls. That's not what the experience is about."

Dylan scowled and went quiet. Probably trying to figure out if Mahatma Gandhi was the same Gandhi she knew about.

Finally, we entered a room filled with glass cases that displayed the King's bejeweled outfits, his records, and video clips of his movies and TV appearances. In the third case, I saw it instantly. The *Life* magazine cover with the photo of Elvis and me after the LA Forum concert. I leaned in closer, pressing my fingers to the glass.

Another blue-shirted docent stepped out of the shadows. "Please don't touch the glass, ma'am."

I was amazed to hear Dylan leap to my defense. "That's *her* in that photo with Elvis," she snapped.

The woman peered into the case, then at me. I removed my scarf as if in a movie reveal.

"Oh my goodness!" The woman almost tripped backward. "You're Andromeda! I was such a fan of your show!"

I dipped my head graciously.

"Our new curator added that photo. She couldn't believe it wasn't in the exhibit before."

"The picture did get some play in its day," I allowed. "Speaking of Ann, can you tell me where I might find her? The person at the ticketing area said she was here, at the mansion."

"I saw her, not that long ago." The woman unhooked a walkie-talkie from her belt and stepped outside, returning after a few minutes. "If you wait outside by the pool, Ann will be over in a bit."

I TOLD DYLAN I needed to speak to Ann Abernathy alone. The girl threw up her arms and stomped over to the Meditation Garden. After she lowered herself onto the concrete steps that formed a graceful semicircle around the burial plots for Elvis and his family, I thought she might reflect on the lovely inscriptions, or even—harkening back to our conversation the night before—on life and death itself. Instead, she keeled over backward and covered her face with her hoodie.

I seated myself on a stone bench facing a large white statue of Jesus flanked by two praying angels, with a cross behind him and "Presley" etched into the base. Jesus had both arms raised to the side, palms up. Oddly, the pose reminded me of an actor taking the stage on *The Tonight Show*, flapping his arms skyward and prompting the audience to cheer.

Oh, how my mother would have hated that comparison.

Then again, Mother would have liked nothing about my being here.

WITH MY EARLY *Light Within* earnings, I was able to place my mother in one of the better mental asylums. And yes, back then, that's what they were called. I didn't visit often. The asylum was in New Jersey, and I was in LA, and even this top-of-the-line institution smelled of Lysol and pee. Plus, my presence agitated my mother, who still had an unfortunate tendency to call me a whore.

The last time I visited was just before I eloped with Harold. My mother looked ancient, drugged. She stared at a crucifix on the wall.

"Here's your daughter, Mrs. Grant," gushed the aide. By that time, Andromeda had become a household name. "We see her on TV, don't we? You must be so proud."

My mother refused to speak. After the aide left, I prattled on about the weather, the news, and all sorts of nonsense, then told her I planned to marry Harold and move to Memphis. There was a long silence. When my mother finally spoke, it startled me.

"Jesus Christ is famous," she said.

"That's true, Mom. About as famous as you get."

"He will be remembered forever." She turned to me. "Elvis Presley will be forgotten tomorrow. *You* will be forgotten tomorrow." She closed her eyes and tilted her head back in a way that made me think she was fainting, then lurched forward to spit at me.

"Okay, Mom." I rose, wiping at the saliva on my blouse. "We'll see about that."

WHEN ANN ABERNATHY appeared by the pool, I hardly recognized her as the cute little girl who'd played with Hope. She'd grown into a praying mantis of a woman, with large, wide-set eyes and a triangular face. Nowhere near as attractive as Hope, who inherited my lovely oval face and sparkling blue irises.

After the required pleasantries—my condolences on her father and requests to remember me to her mother—our business was transacted in under a minute. Ann had made room in her schedule to see me later that day. In truth, it was the least she could do, but I expressed my thanks.

When, for the second time that day, I shook Dylan awake, I said we could be on our way. I was coming back to see Ann at four.

"But I have that interview with Aaron Breckenridge at five. And we're going to his speech tonight."

"I can't come to the interview, Dylan. The man would recognize me." She clearly hadn't considered this and nodded slowly. "And in terms of the speech tonight, you'll be better on your own, not dragging an old lady."

Dylan remained silent as we made our way back to the shuttle bus. I expect she felt a little abandoned. In truth, this was not how I'd planned things, but there was nothing I could do, or wanted to do. To be honest, in many respects, the timing was perfect.

Chapter 27

Hope

In the condo elevator, Aaron kissed me and held our foreheads together. He was tied up in meetings all day at the Sheraton but hoped we could get together after his speech tonight. He'd be in touch, maybe late afternoon.

"Seems unfair that your Washington and my Washington aren't closer," he whispered.

I thought it was some joke about politics before I realized: *Seattle, stupid.* How badly I wished geography were the biggest problem separating us. "We really screwed this up, didn't we?" I said as the doors opened.

Aaron's phone buzzed. His taxi was waiting. He hugged me quickly and left, his phone pressed to his ear. We'd agreed I'd sit in the lobby for a minute and let him exit the building alone. Neither of us wanted a photo of us leaving his condo together, looking scruffy and sleep-deprived.

I collapsed into a wingback chair and checked my phone. I'd run out of battery sometime that night and commandeered Aaron's charger in the morning. Just before boarding the elevator, I noticed I had messages from Jordan, and opened them now. She'd found Dylan. I called her, ecstatic.

"Where the heck are you?" she shouted. "When you didn't respond to my texts, I started banging on your door at seven a.m."

"I went for an early walk," I said. "My phone died. I should have left you a note." I couldn't tell if any of that made sense. After all, I was talking on my phone.

Luckily, Jordan was too preoccupied with her news. "They're staying at the Peabody. I saw Dylan go in there."

I dropped my head into my hands. Another bad call. I'd told Jordan not to bother checking the Peabody because my mother was too cheap to stay there.

Jordan was at the hotel already, searching the parking garage for Dylan's car. Could I come right over?

I started to say yes, then realized I was still wearing the dress I'd worn to the fundraiser. Why hadn't I just admitted to Jordan that I'd spent the night with Aaron? Here she'd been out late finding Dylan, and what had I been doing? Having a good time. "Actually, I wandered farther than I meant to," I said. "I'll be there as soon as I can."

"Okay," she said, perhaps a bit puzzled. "Text me when you get here."

I took off for the Doubletree as quickly as my idiotic heels would allow.

WITH NO TIME to shower, I rolled on enough deodorant to choke a horse and threw on a clean skirt and blouse. I wanted to look nice in case I saw Aaron again. Not that it mattered, of course.

Jordan was seated in the Peabody lounge, her eyes closed and her head thrown back over the top of the sofa. Not a good look for someone doing surveillance—or trying to downplay an Adam's apple for that matter. I collapsed next to her. Without raising her head, she said, "They left." After checking the parking garage, she'd spotted the Bug at a light two blocks down.

We thought they might be headed to Graceland. It was, after all, my mother's excuse for coming, though it might well have been only that. At least I knew they weren't seeing Aaron, since he was in meetings all day. Would they go to his speech tonight? Try to talk to him afterward? Getting face time with Aaron couldn't be easy, but I was never sure what connections my mother had, especially in Memphis.

Jordan sat up straight. "Say, what in the world were you telling me on the phone last night? You saw Aaron? Spoke to him?"

"Just briefly, in his dressing room. It was fine, actually. All good."

"*Good?*" Jordan's eyes were huge, struggling to reconcile this with what I'd told her about Aaron. "He didn't mind you were in Memphis?"

"No, no, he's over that."

"You said something about Dylan, too. That Aaron didn't know—"

"That she's here," I interjected. "Aaron doesn't know she's in town. And we need to keep it that way."

"You're right." Jordan recounted her sidewalk meeting with Dylan. "I may have left her with some less-than-positive feelings about her father, but it's for the best. Maybe she'll think twice about wanting to meet him."

I prayed Jordan was right. I knew Dylan, though. When she set her mind on something, she didn't let go.

Jordan and I settled on a plan. There was no point trying to follow my mother and daughter to Graceland, even if we knew for sure that's where they were headed. Aaron had told me the Elvis attractions had expanded to both sides of the street, and the mansion could be accessed only by shuttle bus. I planned to hang out at the Peabody and catch our fugitives when they returned. Jordan, who was eager to visit some of her old Memphis haunts, promised to check in periodically.

I POSTED UP by the Peabody elevators, snagging a waitress for some coffee. The lounge didn't serve food, only little silver trays of nuts, and after I finished mine, I pinched the remnants off a deserted table nearby. I tried to do research for my EduLearn proposal on my phone but found I couldn't work and still watch the elevators. I crossed fingers that the memo I'd sent to Gary from the Tater Tot was enough to satisfy him until Monday.

Around ten, the Peabody grew crowded as people arrived for the duck parade. I cursed the hotel guests who blocked my view of the elevators. Random tourists plopped down beside me, and a few tried to strike up a conversation. I told them I had impetigo and they might want to sit elsewhere. For the most part, they did.

Around one p.m., I ordered a Memphis Blues Martini to keep me going. I was beginning to wonder if my mother and daughter planned to return at all. At some point, I'd have to shift my surveillance to outside the auditorium where Aaron would speak. That would be their last chance to catch him in person. After that, he was going camping with his sons.

I'd just drained my second martini and was fantasizing about jamming something in the player piano when I heard the familiar squeak of my mother's oxygen cart and saw her pulling it toward the lobby. I bolted from my chair, steadying myself after the drinks, then skirted a table and two armchairs, nearly knocking over one of the waitstaff. The commotion caught my mother's attention. She hesitated, then moved toward me with a big smile.

"Hope! So glad you decided to join us."

"Mother," I said through gritted teeth. "How dare you?"

She took me by both shoulders and embraced me, then circled to my side, as if to take a seat and chat. "Dylan and I are having a marvelous time. I don't know why you haven't been back to Memphis in so long." My mother cocked her head. "Then again, maybe I do." She held one arm oddly behind her back, as if brushing something away. I glanced behind her to see Dylan halt midstep, her eyes flitting from her grandmother to me. She spun around and dashed for the exit.

"Dylan!" I shouted, loud enough to turn heads. I zigzagged around my mother's cart and sidestepped a chair when something behind me crashed. Several people gasped and one called out, "Oh my God." I pivoted and couldn't find my mother. Only when I followed people's eyes did I see her ankles sticking out from behind the sofa.

Racing back, I pushed aside bystanders and dropped to my knees. I righted her oxygen cart and straightened the cannula, worried it might have cut off her air. Her eyes were closed, but she was breathing. Had she fainted?

"Mom, are you okay?" I gently patted her face. "Can you hear me?"

Someone shouted that they were dialing 911, and I called back my thanks. "Does anyone see a girl with pink hair?" I asked. The crowd had enclosed us, blocking my view, and I prayed Dylan had heard the commotion and returned. As I turned back to my mother, I could have sworn her eyes opened a slit, then closed quickly.

Noooo, I thought. *She wouldn't.*

Followed immediately by *Of course she would.*

"Mother," I whispered, leaning in close. "Open your eyes or I'll strangle you."

A woman hovering over us gasped. "What did you say?"

My mother moaned. It was a moan I knew well. On one mid-nineties season of *The Light Within*, Andromeda popped too many pills and drove her car off one of the Swiss Alps. My mother was feuding with the producers at that time, so no one—not even the writers—knew if Andromeda would survive. She did an entire month of episodes lingering on death's door, waiting for the volume of fan mail needed to save her character.

"She's fine," I told the crowd. "My mother's a bit of a drama queen."

"I saw her go down," the hovering woman said. "That didn't look fake to me."

A voice behind me cried, "That's Antigone!"

"Andromeda," I corrected.

The hovering woman whispered to someone, "Looked to me like she was *knocked* down."

The bartender elbowed his way into the circle. An ambulance was on the way.

"I'm not sure we need it," I said. "My mother is fine."

"Someone should call the *police*," muttered the hovering woman.

My mother groaned again, blinking her eyes in a bit of overacting so cringeworthy I couldn't believe everyone in the crowd wasn't embarrassed. A few people videoed her with cell phones.

"Please, no photos," I said.

"Take 'em," said the hovering woman. "It's a crime scene."

"Mom," I lowered my face to her ear. "Please tell these people you're okay. Otherwise, you're headed to the hospital."

She raised a shaky hand. "No hospital," she croaked. Everyone applauded.

"Just relax, ma'am," said the bartender. "Don't move until the EMTs get here."

I twisted to check for Dylan. My mother clutched my arm. "Hope. Don't leave me."

"Of course not, Mom," I said, leaning down, my jaw clenched. "I won't let you out of my sight. Ever. Again."

She closed her eyes and went limp. A ray of light from the chandelier caught her loosened white hair and made it glow, like an angel's.

I had to hand it to her: the woman was good.

BY THE TIME the EMTs arrived, the bartender and I had hoisted my mother into a chair, and the crowd had dispersed, though the hovering woman had staked out a sofa nearby and kept her narrowed eyes on me. My mother basked in the attention of the male EMT, telling him how she'd only gone light-headed once before, after winning her first Daytime Emmy.

The EMT squatted in front of my mother's chair, raising

her lids and examining her pupils. "Did you see your mother faint?" he asked me.

"Yes." My mouth was tight. "A classic faint. Just like in the *movies.*"

"I don't believe you were watching, Hope," my mother sniffed. "You had pushed me aside to get to Dylan."

The EMT felt around the back of my mother's head. "Is it possible you knocked her off balance and she hit her head?"

I counted to five. "I did not knock her down."

"My daughter thinks I'm doing this for attention," my mother interrupted. "Perhaps I had another MI. The doctor mentioned that recently."

His eyes narrowed with concern. "You've had a heart attack recently?"

"What doctor?" My voice had entered the squeaking range. "I've been to all your appointments."

"I saw a doctor on Thursday," my mother said. "I think we can agree you weren't with me then."

I had to give her that one.

The other EMT was chewing a wad of gum. Juicy Fruit, by the smell. She said, "If a doctor evaluated you for a myocardial infarction yesterday, we should take you in."

"Oh," my mother said. "I didn't mean MI. I meant MRI. Too many acronyms."

The gum-chewing EMT looked to me for confirmation. I couldn't speak. The nerve. Had my mother just insinuated she'd suffered a heart attack? I glared at her.

In the end, the EMTs insisted on escorting my mother back to her room, to observe how she managed being on her feet. I trailed behind, fuming silently while she nattered on about her visit to Graceland that morning.

My mother's suite was on the top floor. Her bathroom had a freaking chandelier. As the EMTs gave me final instructions, my mother used a gilded mirror to smooth her mussed hair.

Then I was alone with my mother for the first time since our lunch five days earlier. I fought to keep my voice steady. "Where's Dylan, Mother?"

"How would I know?" she said. "Out exploring, I assume." She removed her Elvis scarf and draped it around her photo, proudly displayed on the entryway table. "I don't expect her back until late."

"For God's sake, have you no shame? You've made me chase you halfway across the country."

She cut me off. "Whose fault was that? I begged you to come, Hope."

"You didn't mention that you planned to kidnap my child."

"Now there's an interesting narrative. Dylan came of her own free will."

"She's sixteen, Mother. She's a teenager. *You're* the adult." I couldn't stop myself from adding, "In theory."

"Dylan is almost an adult, but you don't treat her like one. You were lying to her, Hope. She deserves the truth."

"Oh, and it was your job to provide it?"

"Well *you* certainly weren't." The hotel phone rang, and she moved to the table where it sat. "Exactly when were you planning to tell her?"

Only my mother lifting the receiver stopped me from yelling, "Never!" Because that was the truth. I wouldn't deny it. I'd have never found the right time to tell my daughter I'd lied to her. Whenever I did it, however I did it, I knew she'd be horrified, sickened—as repulsed by me as I was by myself. I'd been right.

"Oh, hello, Jon-David," my mother said. So that's how she'd scored this suite! "No, I'm fine. A little dizzy spell. Your staff was all over it." She paused, laughed gaily. "Oh really? Do tell!"

Somehow, I'd imagined all I needed to do was catch up to my mother and explain things. I'd been certain she wouldn't go against my express wishes. But I was wrong. As always, my mother was convinced she knew best.

I needed to find my daughter.

"Hope?" my mother called out as I unlatched the door.

I slammed it behind me.

Chapter 28

Dylan

I pressed a hand to the stitch in my side as I jogged toward the river. Glancing back, I didn't see anyone following. Phew.

Clearly Jordan had ratted me out. Told Mom where Olivia and I were staying. Well, what had I expected after waltzing into the Peabody right in front of her? Why not just hand Jordan a room key? Stupid, stupid girl.

I'd hesitated for just a second back at the Peabody, when Mom called after me in that croaky, pleading voice. Nice try, but I wasn't falling for it. I didn't drive halfway across the country to be stopped now. For better or worse, I planned to meet my father, to size the man up. I'd decide on my next move after that.

Ignoring the "Don't Walk" signal, I trotted across the divided road, toward the river. Olivia insisted this river was the Mississippi, but it didn't seem as mighty as those grade-school books had made it out to be. Or maybe that was just me. I tended to build things up in my mind, and then they disappointed me. Concerts I begged to attend that, in the end, weren't *all that*.

Boys I'd crushed on, hard, until I kissed them, and then, ick. Even things like my beautiful Bug had warts. Next on my list of disappointments? My father.

Until Jordan slipped and told me the truth, I'd never imagined that my father might be a jerk. Why would I? Olivia had made it seem like he was a great guy—that eighteen years ago, when he'd called and left that message, Breckenridge had been heartbroken and desperate to find my mother. She'd made it seem almost romantic. Ha! What if all Breckenridge had wanted, in finding Mom, was to shut her up?

Sweat dripped down the center of my T-shirt and I flapped my elbows to help dry my pits. A long patch of green park ran along the river with a path crawling with runners, bikers, and hand-holding couples. In the distance was the Pyramid and that curvy bridge Olivia said reminded people of Dolly Parton's boobs. Maybe I'd head the other way. Hide out until my appointment with Breckenridge.

"Hey there, little lady!" called out a deep Elvis-like voice.

Whirling around, I saw three college-age guys in Elvis jumpsuits. The guy who'd spoken stepped forward. He had a cheerful, chubby face, and his white jumpsuit was stretched tight around his midsection. He waved a cell phone. "Would you mind taking a photo?"

With a final glance behind me, I trotted over and accepted the phone.

"Thank you, darlin'. Thank you very much," he said. It had to be the worst Elvis impression of all time.

The second Elvis looked more authentic, with dark, wavy hair and a bejeweled jumpsuit that highlighted his broad shoulders. The third was red-haired and freckled. He had a Hawaiian theme going on, with a lei and a flower in his belt. The trio posed sideways, as if balancing on surfboards. I snapped several photos, calling out "Say 'Vegas'" or "Say 'Lisa Marie,'" to show off my Elvis smarts. When the dark-haired one stepped forward to take back the phone, he looked me up and down in my sweat-stained shirt and shorts. I wanted to squirm, in a good way.

"Someone chasin' you, Pink?" he asked. "You runnin' from the law?"

"Just my mother."

The Elvises found this hysterical.

"Come on over to our house," the chubby one said. "It's our Elvis competition tonight. I'm gonna win." When the dark-haired Elvis fake coughed, he added: "It's not the looks, it's the moves." He wiggled his hips.

The Elvises—or was it Elvi?—said they lived in Tupelo House at the University of Memphis. They were taking courses this summer because, well, some of them hadn't done so well in the spring. The dark one's name was Brett, but I didn't catch the others'. One might have been Wayne.

I was meeting Breckenridge at this office at five p.m. and planned to attend his speech at seven thirty, but how often did I get invited to a college party? Like, never. When I mentioned how much my grandmother would enjoy the Elvis contest, though, there was an awkward silence. I quickly explained how Olivia once went on a date with Elvis. That just got a lot of whoops and a few comments about my grandmother that weren't quite appropriate.

"Whaddaya say, Pink?" Brett moved close. He smelled all sweaty. "Wanna be my guest? Come over now for the preparty." He winked. "I'll show you my Jungle Room."

They whooped again like this was a great joke. I didn't mind. I gave them my most adorable shrug. "Sure, why not?" Anything that would make my mom freak the hell out, like partying with college guys, sounded great.

Chubby Elvis threw his arms around Brett's shoulders and jumped up and down chanting, "Pink, Pink, Pink." Hawaiian Elvis joined in, forming a tight circle around me. I begged them to stop without meaning it for a second.

When they broke apart, Brett pointed at three motorcycles tucked away down a little path and leaned in close, his breath hot on my ear. "Take you for a ride?"

Mom despised motorcycles. I was absolutely forbidden to ride one.

"You bet," I said.

Chapter 29

Hope

B ack in the Peabody lounge, I ordered another Memphis
Blues Martini and kicked at the table leg.

On a cold weekend in early 1998, as I'd been starting my
last semester at college and my mother was packing for a quick
visit to Memphis, my father had phoned her in LA complaining of stomach pain. Probably indigestion, he said, but it could
be the flu. My mother couldn't risk being sick, not with her
filming schedule, so she canceled her flight. Two days later,
my father's housekeeper found him on the bedroom floor, dead
from a massive heart attack.

My mother flew home then, of course, and I endured the
usual media-flurry around anything involving Memphis's beloved Soap Queen. She gave phone interviews with the *Commercial Appeal* and *Soap Opera Digest* and sat for a horrifying
People photo session, gazing at my father's portrait.

What broke me, though, was hearing from my mother's
mouth how she'd discouraged my father from calling his

doctor. "Oh, for God's sake, Harold," she'd said, "take a Tums." When she relayed this, my jaw dropped.

She'd gotten all huffy at me. "Well I'm not a doctor! Your father never listened to me. How could I know he'd pick that moment to start?"

I barely spoke to my mother after that. For years. No doubt it was unfair to blame her for my father's death, but my grief was bottomless and irrational. Besides, making her the villain kept me from turning the anger on myself. I'd been only ten minutes away at school, after all, and hadn't phoned my father that weekend.

So when my mother fake fainted at the Peabody and had the gall to imply she might be having a heart attack, it didn't sit well with me. Not at all.

I CALLED JORDAN to ask for her help, and twenty minutes later, she breezed into the Peabody lounge, a vision in turquoise. Her matching skirt, jacket, and pumps reminded me of some of the gorgeous church-lady outfits I'd seen years earlier when Shelley had taken me to Al Green's Full Gospel Tabernacle one Sunday morning.

"Reporting for duty," Jordan said, taking a seat beside me. She lifted my drink, examining it curiously.

"Memphis Blues Martini. Help yourself."

Jordan took a sip as I told her about my mother's theatrics. I asked if she'd be willing to take turns watching my mother's suite, in case she tried to leave, or Dylan returned. Whoever wasn't doing that could comb the streets for Dylan.

Jordan volunteered for the first shift of suite-watching. "Honestly, I could use a little quiet time," she said.

BEALE STREET WAS humming in the midafternoon heat, smelling of barbecue and weed. Outside a touristy shop, a bearded man was playing "Fire and Rain" on guitar, and I almost didn't hear my phone ringing. Shoving a finger in one ear, I answered and speed-walked up the street.

"Hope," Gary bellowed without so much as a hello, "the ideas you sent were terrible. Dull. Boring. No student is going to rip apart a textbook for free copies at Staples."

"You said you wanted coupons."

"Yes, coupons! You know! Coffee, donuts, fries. Stuff kids want."

Thank God Gary couldn't see me slap my forehead. "Do we really want to encourage that, Gary? What about something healthier?"

"For Pete's sake, Hope! Students aren't going to destroy a $150 textbook for a fruit-and-nut plate."

I'd arrived at an intersection and pushed the walk button. "Let me play around with some different ideas. I can't talk right now," I said as a truck roared by. "I'm on a street corner."

"You volunteered for this, Hope. You said you could put in the hours. Then you skip town, and every time I hear from you, you're closer to the border. Are you on the lam?"

He was joking, right? "Give me until Monday. It's the weekend."

I stopped midstep as a group of motorcycles crossed the intersection. The riders were in Elvis jumpsuits and the last had a girl clinging to his back. Her helmet didn't completely hide her pink hair.

Noooo!

"Dylan," I shrieked, frantically waving an outstretched arm. "I need to go," I yelled into the phone, and hung up.

The motorcycles stopped at the next intersection. I raced down the sidewalk, dodging pedestrians. There were too many, so I veered into the street, sprinting alongside the parked cars. By the time I saw the car door opening, it was too late. I caught the edge hard with my hip and went sprawling onto the pavement. My phone flew out of my hand and into the middle of the street, where a cab, swerving to avoid me, ran over it.

"Oh my God!" said a woman's voice. From where my cheek rested on the pavement, I saw navy sandals leap from the car. "I didn't see you. I'm so sorry!" A young woman squatted down, grabbing my elbow as I peeled myself from the ground. She looked both ways to be sure no cars were coming and ran out to grab my phone. I limped around her car to the curb.

"I'm okay," I said, though the facts spoke otherwise. I was bent in half, holding my hip with both hands. When I looked down, my skirt was ripped, my hands were raw, and blood was dripping from one knee. My elbow burned like the skin had been scraped off.

The woman handed me my phone and I hobbled a few steps to get a clear view of the street. The motorcycles were nowhere in sight. Several people had paused on the sidewalk, clutching their cells, no doubt wishing they'd captured my dooring to share on Instagram.

"Not your fault," I called back to the woman whose car door I'd tried to remove with my hip. My phone screen was shattered in a spiderweb pattern and vibrated erratically. The term "death rattles" came to mind. Was that a call coming in? Had

Dylan seen me fall? I gently pressed the hint of green at the bottom and held it to my ear.

"Hope, don't ever hang up on me. That's the one thing I won't tolerate."

"I can't talk, Gary." I headed down the sidewalk in a furious limp. "That's why I hung up. Because I can't talk." I could feel my voice breaking and fought to steady it.

"Hope, I'm warning you . . ."

My phone made a noise like a duck being strangled.

"You're breaking up, Gary," I lied, pushing something red.

I shuffled away from the stares of passersby, fighting back tears. Not only did I hurt like hell, but Dylan was gone, no telling where, on the back of a motorcycle with Elvis.

Another pathetic duck sound. By scrolling carefully along the side, I could read most of the message, which appeared below the link to Aaron's condo. He asked if I could meet him in Memphis Park in ten—or was it fifteen?—minutes. No matter how I scrolled, I couldn't be sure of the second number.

I took in my ripped clothes and bloody shins. Not my best look, but it would have to do. The sooner I could get to Aaron and the closer I could stay to him, the more likely I could intercept Dylan.

On the shattered keypad, I pecked out what I hoped was "Okay."

THE TROLLEY DRIVER looked me up and down, taking in my Girl, Doored look.

I plopped down in a front seat for some triage. The gash on one knee was deep, and blood had dried in rivulets down my shin. The cut was no longer bleeding, just . . . gaping. My skirt had torn, and a corner of fabric hung near my hip bone. The front of my white blouse looked like someone had driven over me.

It was only a few blocks to my stop. Waving off the driver's hand, I gripped the rail and tottered down the trolley stairs.

As I approached the park, the smell of fresh-cut grass and crepe myrtle filled the air. Carousel music drifted up from a passing riverboat: "Dixie." When I'd lived here, I'd never realized the park had a name, but last night, Aaron had set me straight. It had been Confederate Park—now temporarily renamed Memphis Park while the city chose a permanent name—and the orator statue was Jefferson Davis. Both the sculpture and Civil War cannons were scheduled for removal.

I cut across the grass and gingerly lowered myself onto a bench beside the oak tree Aaron and I had claimed as ours. My phone shuddered in my bag, and when I checked, I'd missed a call from a Boston number. I poked blindly at a few spots, trying to navigate to voicemail. A flash of blue moved in front of me, and I looked up, letting the phone drop into my lap.

The skin around her eyes was deeply lined, but Carly's strawberry-blond hair was still chin-length, as it had been when she'd surprised me here eighteen years ago.

"You're gonna have to teach me this trick," I said.

Chapter 30

Olivia

I peered out the suite's peephole and cursed my bad luck. The large figure in the turquoise jacket and skirt was clearly Jordan, pacing back and forth in the hallway. No doubt Jordan meant to follow me wherever I went. Well, that wouldn't do. My meeting with the Graceland curator was in forty-five minutes.

On any other day, I'd have invited Jordan in and complimented her stunning outfit. Jordan had such a lovely color sense—far better than Hope, who favored beiges and grays that washed her out. Unfortunately, this wasn't any day. It was *the* day. And Jordan was in my way.

I lifted the room phone and asked for Jon-David. I needed a favor.

Ten minutes later, the elevator dinged, and I heard voices in the hall. Angry voices. Someone rapped on my door, making me flinch.

"Olivia, it's Jordan!" Her voice was muffled through the door. "Tell these people you know me."

The voices grew louder, higher pitched. Yelling unnerved

me. That shrieking boy on set. I went into the bathroom and turned on the shower full blast to drown out the noise. I felt badly for Jordan, but Jon-David could be counted on to handle this appropriately. I couldn't let anything interfere with my plan. Not this day.

JON-DAVID HAD CALLED a cab and escorted me down on the elevator.

"I'm sorry to be so much trouble," I said. "That lady in the hallway—you don't suppose she's waiting outside, do you?" I dreaded an awkward scene with Jordan.

Jon-David's face was solemn. "I don't want to alarm you, Olivia, but that was no lady." He peered over his glasses, giving me a meaningful look.

"Well, I'm sure she's a lovely person. She just wants to follow me, is all."

"No worries," he said, holding open the lobby door. "We've taken care of it."

Once I was in the cab, though, and the driver had rounded the corner onto B.B. King Boulevard, I noticed a huge commotion at the Peabody's side entrance. Two patrol cars had lights flashing. The cabbie zipped past, and I twisted in my seat to watch an officer shove someone into the back of the cruiser. Someone wearing turquoise.

Dear God. No.

"Stop!" I yelled.

The driver glanced in his mirror. "Stop?"

"Go back!" I pointed behind us. "I need to speak to those police officers."

"I'll have to circle the block," the driver explained. "It's one way."

"Fine! Just hurry."

When we arrived back at the Peabody, though, the cruisers were gone.

No, no, no, no.

The driver pulled to the curb. He watched me in his rearview mirror.

I found Jon-David's card in my wallet and called. It went to voicemail. Dear Lord, why today, of all days? "Jon-David, it's Olivia. I'm terribly upset. I did not intend for that woman outside my room to be arrested." I paused, unsure what to say next without admitting I knew Jordan. The mailbox beeped and clicked off. I checked my watch. I'd have to figure this out on the fly.

"Go, please!" I fluttered my fingers.

"To?" The cabbie was confused.

"To Graceland."

The cab took off again, and I dialed 911. I was transferred to the nonemergency number and then to a different precinct. Both dispatchers denied sending anyone to the Peabody. On the third transfer, I was disconnected.

I bent forward and dropped my head into my hands. We were now minutes from Graceland. No time to go through it again. I wrestled with myself, then gave in and dialed Hope. Praise God, it went to voicemail.

"Hope, there's been a terrible misunderstanding. Jordan may have been arrested. Please do your best to straighten it out."

I hung up, closed my eyes, and dropped back against the

seat. I tried to calm myself. Hope would take care of it. The situation shouldn't be that difficult to explain, and in truth, Hope was more capable than even she herself realized. The whole thing would make an amusing story someday. Hope and Jordan would have a good laugh at my expense.

As confident as I felt of this scenario, I wanted to do something to make it up to Jordan. I found a pen in my bag and wrote on the back of Jon-David's card.

Hope,

I would like Jordan to have the antique amethyst necklace in the third drawer of my jewelry case.

I tucked the card back in my purse.

That was better. Not perfect, but . . . something. Once again, I leaned back and tried to assume the feeling of peace I'd hoped for on this particular day. At least the weather was cooperating, the late-afternoon sun peeking out from behind wispy clouds. I took out my credit card to pay for the ride. I liked to estimate the tip in advance to avoid the exorbitant percentages offered on the screen. Next to the credit card gizmo was the cab driver's information card. I blinked, refocused. Really? I studied the driver, then examined his card again.

I leaned forward. "Your name . . . is Harold Waites?"

The man nodded.

Harold. My husband's name. The man who loved to proclaim that there were no coincidences, that everything happened for a reason.

I still believed that idea was bullshit. There was no grand

plan, things were not foreordained. Olivia Grant directed her own life, thank you very much. Oddly, though, in recent weeks, the world had seemed full of signs—signs that had led me to this day, that had come together to form this plan. A screaming boy's cries telling me it was time to move on. A beloved photo proclaiming that some souls are never forgotten. A teenager's pink hair and pink car—Elvis's favorite color—providing an unexpected lift.

No, it wasn't that things happened for a reason, exactly. I didn't believe that. What I did believe was that we could make meaning out of what happened. That, in fact, we must.

I squinted again at the cab driver's name. Harold Waites. Here I was, on my way to Graceland, and my husband had reached out to give his blessing.

I was on the right road.

Chapter 31

Hope

Carly smoothed her skirt and lowered herself onto the park bench beside me. "Oh, it wasn't hard to find you," she said. "You've been texting with Veronica."

I frowned, hating to look as dull-witted as Carly imagined me to be.

"She handles everything for Aaron in Memphis. His phone contacts are her contacts."

"And her contacts are yours, apparently."

Carly had a deep laugh that I had to admit was attractive. She cradled a Starbucks iced cappuccino. "Honestly, when I first hooked up Veronica with Aaron's campaign, I had no idea what a gold mine that girl would be. She can't stay out of anyone's business. And loyal! I've known German Shepherds less devoted."

I recalled Veronica's narrow-eyed looks when she popped into the office after hours to see if Aaron and I needed help. Her annoyance when we grabbed sandwiches to eat in the park, leaving her to manage the phone volunteers. I'd brushed it off as envy. She'd chased after us once, stopping us at the edge of the park and saying she'd forgotten the password on my computer.

Carly seemed to read my thoughts. "Really, Hope, there's a lesson in this for all of us. It's important to invite people to lunch now and again."

I picked up the phone in my lap and dropped it into my bag. Of course. So much made sense. Veronica had guessed why I'd ditched her that night and followed me into the park. She wouldn't have had to hover long in the darkness before seeing Aaron pull me behind the tree, our two figures merging into one. That's how Carly had known I was the other woman. And how Fish had known those words—a park, a shingle oak—I'd believed could only have come from Aaron.

"Veronica called you from the fundraiser, I assume?"

"Hadn't heard from her in years! So good to catch up." Carly took in my ripped clothes, bloody shins. "Are you okay, Hope? You look like you were hit by a bus."

"If not, I'm about to be."

She laughed again and patted my leg. "You're funny. It's too bad we've always been on opposite teams. Wanted different things."

"Once we wanted the same thing."

"True! And I won. So I get it—you're not a fan. But you think I'm a bad person, and really, Hope, I'm not." I snorted and her mouth tightened. "Maybe you're not aware, but I run a charity that provides massage therapy for terminally ill children. I founded another that offers therapeutic horseback riding for kids with autism. I've spent my entire life looking out for other people's best interests. Including yours."

I flicked a glance in her direction. Her jaw was set. She was serious.

Carly continued: "Think about it. How many women would provide for their husband's illegitimate child?"

"You tricked me," I said. "You made me believe Aaron knew."

She laughed. "Seriously, Hope? Is that the hill you want to die on? Because, let's face it, honesty is not your strong suit."

That stung and I lashed out. "This from the woman who faked a pregnancy to get Aaron to marry her?"

Her eyebrows shot up. "Fascinating." She thumbed a drip from the side of her iced cappuccino. "Is that what Aaron believes?"

I'd regretted the words as soon as they'd left my mouth. "No, he didn't say that." I fumbled, trying to get back that feeling of righteous indignation. "But let's be honest, Carly. How much of a coincidence . . ."

"Oh, no coincidence at all." She held up a palm. "I saw you coming a mile away. Two weeks after you started canvassing with Aaron, all I heard was 'Hope this' and 'Hope that.' I knew what I had to do. Circle the wagons. Protect what was mine."

I traced a line in the grass with the toe of my shoe. So Carly *had* been pregnant. She'd gotten pregnant on purpose. And miscarried on her honeymoon. "I'm sorry," I whispered.

Carly wasn't one to waste an advantage. "What other private matters did you and Aaron discuss at his condo last night?" My stomach dropped. "That's right, Detective Fish followed you there. Did you enjoy yourself? Relive old times?"

I inhaled deeply, taking a moment to pull myself back together. "May I ask what your stake is in this, Carly? Aren't you and Aaron divorced?"

"Unfortunately. I wasn't happy about it. I'm not used to failing. Oh, I played nice, went quietly, as they say. If you act sweet when men dump you, often as not they come crawling back, tail between their legs. I knew Aaron would change his mind." She took another pull from the straw in her drink. "I finally had to let go of that idea. Earlier today, I managed to get five minutes of his precious time, and he was an incredible dick to me. He straight up told me we are never, ever, getting back together." Carly shook her head, stared off into the distance. "I wasn't even aware he knew that song."

Something in her oddly detached tone made me shiver. "Look, Carly, I haven't told Aaron anything about his daughter or the agreement. The truth is, I can't afford to break it. I can't pay you back. And I don't want Aaron or my daughter to know about it. I'm ashamed of that choice. It came from a bad place, and it's forced me to live in a bad place, but that's my problem." I turned to her. "All I want to do is collect my mother and daughter and get out of Memphis."

Carly was shaking her head. "Too late," she said, sadly. She stood and hoisted her Burberry handbag onto her shoulder. "I'm tired of being the good guy while you and Aaron sneak around and break things—promises, engagements, agreements. He needs to learn a lesson."

"Wait." Something stuck in my windpipe. "You wouldn't do anything to hurt Aaron. Not right now . . ."

"Me? Oh, no, it won't be me who takes Aaron down. Probably not even you, Hope. I'm thinking it will be your pink-haired felon of a daughter."

"Leave my daughter out of this."

Carly stepped back and shrugged. "Karma's a bitch, Hope."

She picked up her coffee and started to turn, then pivoted back with a smirk. "By the way, you never answered my question about last night. Since you and I are being so honest with each other, did you enjoy your time with Aaron? Did you sleep with him?"

I looked up, giving her my best smile. "Yes," I said. "And it was fabulous."

In one motion, Carly pulled the top off her iced cappuccino and tossed it at me. It splashed on my face and blouse, the cubes falling into my lap. "You know," she said, "all those years ago, I could tell Aaron was buying your bullshit. He thought you were such a good person. What a laugh. When you think about it, Hope, which of us has been more dishonest?"

I rose stiffly, brushing the ice cubes off my skirt. "You want to know what's even funnier, Carly? The whole time I've been sitting here, I've been wondering the same thing."

I STOOD THERE for a long time, until Carly had disappeared into the parking lot on the other side of the park. Then, remembering the missed call, I checked my phone. There were two missed calls, and one voicemail. I tapped the broken screen gently.

The message was from my mother, in a shaky voice that raised the hair on my arms. Jordan had been arrested.

Chapter 32

Dylan

The half-mowed patch of dead grass in front of Tupelo House swarmed with every kind of Elvis imaginable. A tall, skinny Elvis in army fatigues. An unshaven Elvis sporting a karate black belt. Zombie Elvis with a papier-mâché toilet attached to his ass. As I followed Brett to the porch, a Chihuahua in a curly black wig and aviator sunglasses yipped and circled my ankles. "Don't Be Cruel" blasted through the windows.

My legs wobbled a bit. The way Brett had dipped his motorcycle around corners and gunned it at lights had scared me shitless. I'd clung to his jumpsuit and nearly choked from his pit odor. Somehow my walk on the wild side to piss off Mom hadn't been a great decision. What I wanted, I realized, was some time alone, to figure out what to do about Breckenridge. Everything else seemed . . . immature.

"Now that we're here," Hawaiian Elvis said, slipping a sweaty arm around my back, "you get to pick your King."

Gross.

Brett yanked me away and hissed, "Back off." He turned to Chubby Elvis. "You, too, Wade."

Okay, so not Wayne. Wade. And, again, gross.

Inside Tupelo House, it smelled like they'd mopped the floor with Budweiser. The furniture had been pushed aside, and a tattooed girl perched on the ratty sofa, using a Sharpie to draw sideburns on a pompadoured King. Hawaiian Elvis led the way through a swinging door to the kitchen, where the table was piled high with pizza boxes and topped with a bag of Cheetos, like a flaming volcano. Crap. What were the chances they had anything vegan?

The deafening music had switched to "Burning Love."

"Want some punch?" Brett yelled in my ear.

"Does it have alcohol?" I shouted back.

Brett roared. Looping an arm around my waist, he told me it had grain alcohol. I'd drunk beer before, but whole-grain alcohol sounded kind of healthy, so I said sure. My meeting with Breckenridge wasn't for two hours. I'd need to be stone-cold sober for that.

Using plastic cups, Brett scooped punch from the vat in a way that seemed vaguely unsanitary, but I was thirsty and took a big gulp. It tasted like paint thinner stirred into Kool-Aid. I coughed and Brett thumped me on the back, grinning like I'd passed a test. Without breathing through my nose, I downed the rest.

The three Elvi pummeled me with questions as they showed me the house. Where was I from? What was I doing in Memphis? When I mentioned I was only sixteen, Brett threw his plastic cup on the floor and stomped on it. "Crap! Why does this keep happening to me?"

As the horrid-tasting punch kicked in, the top of my head felt like it was floating out through my hair. I clutched the stair railing and thought I might puke. The music was hurting my ears, the boys smelled, and nobody responded when I asked for water. I needed out.

When we ended back in the living room, Brett said he wanted more punch and pushed through the kitchen door, Hawaiian Elvis in tow. I saw my chance and bolted for the front door. I was halfway down the street when Wade caught up to me, holding out a cold bottle of water.

"I apologize for those two," Wade said. "Care to take a walk?"

I shrugged. The water bottle was plastic, but whatever. I'd recycle it.

WADE AND I walked past some dilapidated frat houses to a shady park, where we sat side by side on saddle swings. Wade was studying journalism. I didn't dare ask if he wrote for the *Daily Helmet*. We chatted about everything—my Bug, his bike, my Graceland tour, his Elvis contest. The punch had made me talkative, and I let slip how I'd come to Memphis to meet my father for the first time. No name, just that I'd see him later that afternoon. "Trying to keep an open mind," I said. "I've heard a few things about him that aren't great."

"Like what?"

"He's a weenie."

Wade laughed. "My father could be an asshole sometimes. He yelled a lot. But he also took me to Redbirds games, and we had a blast there, yelling at the umpires." He twisted his swing around in a circle. "I guess he just liked to yell."

I dug my sneaker in the dirt. "Maybe it's my fault. I had this picture of my dad. I wanted him to be a hero. Like in *Die Hard*. Someone who'd walk across broken glass for me."

"Love Bruce Willis!" Wade said, letting his swing spin back around. "You're right, though. Most dads aren't like that. Mine sure wasn't."

"I'm nothing like my mom, so I thought I must take after my dad. I kind of modeled myself on him. What I imagined he was like. But if he's not who I thought he was . . ." I trailed off, drawing an X in the dirt with my toe.

"Look," Wade said, "all this guy did for you was donate a few genes. You don't have to be like him. Think about Elvis. His dad went to jail for forging checks, and he had this weirdly smothering mom. He didn't let his parents define him."

"Huh." Olivia hadn't told me that.

"I mean, even if there was a yelling gene and I inherited it from my dad, I still could use it however I want. I could yell at the CEO of Exxon for fracking." He glanced skyward, shading his eyes from the sun. "Maybe my father didn't think of that."

"Dude!" A voice shouted from across the park. Hawaiian Elvis bent forward, hands on knees, panting. "Been lookin' for you!" He waved at Wade to come.

"Right back." Wade jumped off his swing and jogged over. I watched them argue, two Elvis impersonators on a street corner. Memphis was bomb.

I stretched back in the swing, let the sun warm my face, and thought about Aaron Breckenridge. For the zillionth time that day, I replayed my conversation with Jordan. In the light of day, I couldn't be absolutely certain what Jordan had been trying to say—or rather, trying not to say—about my dad. Sure, maybe Breckenridge was a jerk—that was one possibility. Or maybe Jordan had it wrong. Jordan didn't know everything.

If this trip had taught me anything, it was that adults in general didn't know as much as they pretended to. Olivia acted like she had everything under control, but she'd screwed up badly with her oxygen. And Mom, geez! Even when she wasn't lying, sometimes she was flat-out wrong. Mom thought Olivia was selfish. And okay, Olivia could be, now and then, but not always, and she made up for it by being fun. Plus, Mom told me Olivia wasn't much for physical affection. Not true. Olivia might not know when to give hugs, or how to ask for them, but that didn't mean she was opposed to them.

No, I couldn't trust anyone on the Breckenridge issue. I'd keep a semi-open mind and go with my gut. In all honesty, I was having trouble letting go of the idea that my dad would be excited to meet me. It felt right. For once, I'd take things slow, not rush to conclusions. I had a decent bullshit meter.

I checked my phone. Three p.m. Would Mom still be hanging out at the Peabody? I wanted to change my outfit before my appointment with Breckenridge. I texted Olivia, asking if the coast was clear.

Wade trotted back and apologized. He needed to get back to the preparty. Brett and Hawaiian Elvis, whose name I finally learned was Donny, wanted to rehearse their act. Did I need a ride back to my hotel?

I explained my dilemma to Wade. My mom was a little— how to put it?—unstable. She'd followed my grandmother and me on this trip and had been stalking me around Memphis.

She might be at the Peabody now, hoping to nab me. I needed to avoid her and get to my room.

Wade thought for a moment, then grinned. He had an idea. Back at Tupelo House, he took Brett and Hawaiian Elvis aside. The Elvi huddled together and burst out laughing.

"A distraction?" Brett cackled, turning to me. "Oh, little lady, you picked the right guys."

THE ELVI ENTERED the Peabody first. I slipped inside the door and hovered in a hallway as I scanned the lobby for my mother. Still no message from Olivia. What if my grandmother couldn't respond? What if Mom was holding her hostage in our suite?

Across the lounge by the duck fountain, the three Elvi took their places. Wade called out something about free entertainment and dropped onto one knee. Rotating his arm like a propeller, he belted out the opening of "Blue Suede Shoes."

Wade wasn't bad! Behind him, Brett and Donny thrust their hips left and right and sang backup. Everyone in the lounge stared, stood, or aimed their phone. Time for me to move. Hugging the wall, I ducked into the elevator, pressing the door-close button until it shut.

Once outside our suite, though, I checked my phone one last time. Thank God, I had a response from Olivia. It said, "At Graceland. Don't worry about your mother. I created a little problem that will keep her busy. 😊 Good luck tonight. Love you. O."

That was the first time Olivia had said she loved me. I screenshotted the text and saved it.

Inside the suite, I changed into my gray camo miniskirt, gray T-shirt, and black hoodie with knee-highs and ankle-high black boots. The outfit was fire if I did say so myself. It honored Breckenridge's military background while showing me as someone who meant business. I dumped out all the bumper stickers in my bag, stuffed in a pad and pen, and raced back to the elevator.

Down in the lobby, the Elvi were surrounded by two security people and Jon-David. Brett pointed to me. "There she is! Pink said your hotel would love our act." Jon-David gave me a pained look.

I said we needed to get going.

"Good," he whispered.

The Elvi walked me to the Peabody garage and begged for a spin in my pink Bug. Wade called shotgun, and the others dove into the back. I circled the block and cruised down this long street with the Elvi hanging out the windows, hooting at passersby. When we stopped for a light, I noticed a woman on the next block, half running, half limping along the sidewalk. Her clothes were a mess.

"Jesus. That's my mom."

In the back seat, Brett nearly climbed on top of Donny to stick his head out and look.

"I didn't believe the crazy mom part," Brett said after we drove past. "I do now."

BRECKENRIDGE'S MEMPHIS OFFICE was in a tall white building, nothing special, but the security inside was like an airport, with a conveyor belt and body scanner. Would these people question me? Demand credentials? Thank God I'd cleaned out my bag. My bumper stickers weren't subversive, exactly, but the ones with f-bombs weren't to everyone's taste.

I placed my bag on the belt and held my breath as I stepped

through the portal. On the other side, the security people ignored me and kept chatting. Phew.

Alone in the elevator, I gripped the handrail and gave myself a pep talk. I had this. I'd ask Breckenridge a few questions, make him feel comfortable, then drill down on the past. Mention Hope Robinson. Watch his face. I imagined Breckenridge squinting at me, like I was someone familiar he couldn't place. Maybe he'd feel pinpricks, or a shiver. If he really was my father, wouldn't he have to feel *something*?

Breckenridge's office door had a blue and gold seal that said "United States Senate." The doorknob wouldn't budge. Shit. I noticed an intercom on the wall and pushed the speaker button. When I said my name, the door clicked open.

A middle-aged woman stood behind a desk, her eyes glued to a computer monitor with the concentration of an air-traffic controller landing a plane. She held up a finger. Without turning to look at me, she said: "Just . . . one . . . teeny sec. If I don't write this down, I'll forget."

The woman wore her hair in a bun, and either it was pulled too tight, or she had a really unfortunate nose. Probably this was the office manager Olivia had spoken to. Behind her was an interior office with cloudy glass you couldn't see through. The shadowy figures inside erupted in laughter.

My father was behind that door. The corner of my mouth wouldn't stop twitching. I bit down on it.

The office manager scribbled something on a Post-it and slapped it on her monitor. When she finally looked up, she did a double take. The hair. I was used to it.

"Thank you for coming, Dylan," she said. "I'm sorry to tell you, the senator won't be able to meet with you."

I gripped my bag tighter and stared at her. "I have an appointment."

The woman gave several exaggerated nods, acknowledging I was right. "He was supposed to appear on the Memphis morning show tomorrow, but some local celebrity has shown up out of the blue, so they're taping his segment this afternoon, over at the university. That fit his schedule better, anyway. He's leaving in five minutes."

I fought to focus. "He can't. I've got to talk to him."

"Well, I know, sweetheart. I left several voicemails at the number your adviser gave me."

Shit. I never listened to voicemail. "There must be some other time." I struggled to control the quiver in my voice. "You can move things around."

"I'm afraid not. He has an event tonight, and tomorrow he's leaving on vacation with his sons."

For some reason, this made me furious. "I need to interview him. It's important."

The woman sighed audibly, turned back to her computer, and hit a few keys. She scanned the screen, shaking her head. I assumed she was searching Breckenridge's schedule, though perhaps she'd returned to work and was ignoring me.

What would Olivia do in this situation? Charm, threats, cash. I had no patience for doing things in order. "I'll give you a hundred dollars."

The woman pivoted, her hand on her heart. "Gracious." She laughed. "That won't help. I'll tell you what. You're coming to the speech on campus tonight, right? Senator Breckenridge will do some Q&A afterward, and if you sit up front, I'll make sure he calls on you."

That wasn't the same at all. I needed to speak to him privately. But how could I explain? "I have a bunch of questions . . ." I tried.

"I'm sure other folks in the audience will have the same questions."

I tended to doubt that. Just then, the door to the inner office opened. Two men and a woman in business suits stepped out. Behind them was Aaron Breckenridge, shaking hands and saying he was glad they stopped by while herding them to the door. I slunk back against the wall, heart banging in my chest. As the suits left, Breckenridge turned and gave me a polite smile.

Don't you recognize me?

The office manager jumped in. "This young lady is from the *Daily Helmsman*. I've explained your schedule conflict and said we'd seat her up front this evening, so you can call on her."

"Perfect," Breckenridge said. "I'm so sorry this didn't work out. I'll try to give you a couple questions tonight."

I searched his face, fixed on his one-sided dimple. Like mine.

Breckenridge stuck out his hand, and I offered mine tentatively, like I wasn't familiar with this strange custom. His grip was firm, damp. "Your name again?"

"Dylan," I whispered. *Look at me. You have to feel our connection.*

"Well that should be easy to remember. I have a son named Dylan."

"I know." *Please. Something.*

"Excellent! You've done your research."

"Senator, the car's waiting." The office manager thrust a briefcase into his hand.

His back to me, Breckenridge touched his forehead and asked the name of the TV interviewer he was meeting. The office manager clicked her mouse and found the name. Breckenridge had the door half-open when he turned. "Oh, Veronica?" She lifted her head from her screen. "Call Tom and reschedule our meeting tonight. I'm going to try to see Hope again, while she's in town."

Hope? My insides turned to ice.

Veronica's face dropped. He couldn't cancel, she said. This was the only time possible. Breckenridge strode over and stood behind her as they reviewed the schedule. Their words were muffled and unintelligible to me. I couldn't hear them over the sound of my heartbreak.

See Hope? Again?

Somehow it was resolved, and Breckenridge pointed his briefcase at me. "I'll see you this evening, Dylan. Bring some good questions." Was he mocking me? Had my mother already gotten to him?

I forced a half smile. *Be careful what you ask for, motherfucker.*

Chapter 33

Hope

As I listened to my mother's message, another voicemail popped up. It was from Jordan and told me where the police had taken her. I'd already guessed. Everyone in Memphis knew 201 Poplar. The downtown facility housed a police station, courts, and a jail. When I was in college, frat boys who drank illegally and got unruly in the downtown bars ended up there. The complex wasn't far from the park, so I limped across Front Street in an awkward hitch-trot, like a child riding an invisible stick pony.

Something buzzed around my hip, and I swatted it. Not an insect—my phone, in my skirt pocket, vibrating even more faintly. I pulled it out and poked at a hint of green to answer.

"Just so you know, Hope, I was ready to fire you."

Shit, shit, shit.

Gary continued. "No one hangs up on me once, never mind twice. Terry had to pour me a drink. It took her half an hour to calm me down, but she convinced me to listen to your explanation."

"I hung up on you, Gary."

Silence. "Sorry?"

"I said I hung up on you. I'm in the middle of a family emergency, and I have to prioritize things."

"Hope, you assured me . . ."

"I know I did. And I was wrong. Wrong to take on an idea I thought was goofy to begin with, wrong to think I could turn it into something that wasn't ethically bankrupt, and certainly wrong in imagining I could make you understand how slimy . . ."

"You're fired, Hope."

"I know, Gary." I laughed like a madwoman. "This is my moment." I hung up.

Shoving my phone back in my pocket, I looked up just in time to see Dylan's pink Bug speed by, Elvises hanging out of every window.

By the time I reached 201 Poplar, both my heels had blisters. The security woman checking bags stared at my ripped, stained clothes but let me through. Inside, the concrete complex was as cavernous and depressing as I remembered, and I spent twenty minutes being shuffled from one long, dark corridor to another. When I finally reached the right office, I learned Jordan was being held for trespassing and resisting arrest. Bail had been set at $2,000. The woman who took my credit card moved so slowly I was still waiting for my receipt when Jordan, her right eye black and swollen, came flying through the door, landing on her knees.

Later, Jordan would explain that she'd received the black eye not at the jail, but in a scuffle at the Peabody, where she'd also severed the heel of one of her pumps. The broken shoe had caught on the jail doorjamb, causing her to trip. In short, what I witnessed was a police officer grabbing at Jordan's back to keep her from falling. What my brain saw was my friend, beaten by the police, being pushed to the floor.

Simple misunderstanding.

I'm pretty sure I screamed, "Get your hands off of her." Jordan says I f-bombed the officer. In the end, it didn't matter. What did was the way I elbowed the cop out of the way as I dropped to the floor to help Jordan. Apparently, touching police officers is a no-no, and—this part I should have guessed—especially elbowing one in the boob. I was on the floor myself in seconds, my arm twisted behind my back, my bottom lip smashed on the tile, the taste of dirt and blood filling my mouth. Jordan shouted and grabbed the woman's arm, which got her back in Dutch. All in all, if I hadn't had a good working definition of a clusterfuck before, I did now.

ONCE WE'D BEEN interviewed and processed, two officers came to take Jordan and me to separate holding cells. I pleaded that they keep us together. They seemed amused, but it must have been a slow night, because they walked Jordan and me to a cell with four bunks—a snoring, rumpled woman on one of them—and a sink and toilet at one end.

"You sure?" asked the cop who'd tackled me. She had gorgeous violet eyes, which, for some reason, made me feel worse.

I said I was sure, and Jordan shrugged. I prayed neither of us would need to use the toilet.

As the cop closed the cell door, I asked when I could make my phone call. She sighed, like I should have asked earlier. Like I did this every Saturday night. She escorted me into a room with a table, chair, and old telephone with square push buttons, and helped me find the number for the Peabody. The front desk refused to confirm that an Olivia Grant or Dylan Robinson was staying there. They asked for a room number, and my description of a "really nice suite with a chandelier in the bathroom" wasn't enough. I replaced the receiver, terrified that I'd forfeited my one call. The cop said she'd wait until I reached someone or could leave a message. When I told her the number I needed was on my cell phone, she had someone retrieve it. That was kinder than I expected for someone who'd just slammed my face into the floor.

Calling Aaron was a gamble. His speaking event was in two hours. But I didn't know who else to try. Dylan wouldn't answer my call and certainly wouldn't listen to voicemail. I didn't know any lawyers, or how in God's name I'd find one on a Saturday night. And I had to believe that Aaron, if he got the message, would surely be able to help.

"You've reached the office of Senator Aaron Breckenridge. We can't take your call right now . . ."

Shit. That didn't sound right. He'd told me the number was his personal cell. Confused, stressed, unable to imagine what else to do, I left a message.

THE WEATHERED AND bedraggled woman sleeping across the cell reeked of alcohol and BO. I blocked my nose so I wouldn't gag. Sitting next to Jordan on the lower bunk, I let my head fall into my hands. When I glanced sideways, Jordan was staring straight ahead, her jaw clenched.

"Are you okay?" I whispered. I didn't want to wake the sleeping woman.

"No, I am *not* okay." The anger in her voice made me cringe. "Jesus, Hope, what the fuck were you thinking?"

"When?" I wasn't clear which fuckup she meant.

"Wrestling with that police officer."

"She pushed you!"

"I fell!" she nearly shouted, whipping off her right pump. "Could you walk in this?" She told me what had happened, earlier, at the Peabody, and how she'd tripped. "That police officer was *decent* to me. She was kind," Jordan grumbled. "Everything was going to be fine until you took a swing at her."

"I didn't take a swing! I just tried to . . . move her."

"You call it what you want. By the time this gets to court, you took a swing." Jordan put the broken pump back on her foot, which I didn't think was a great idea.

"Jordan, I don't know what to say. I'm so, so sorry." Across the cell, the woman moaned in her sleep.

"Did you call your mother?" Jordan muttered.

"I tried. No one answered." I hesitated to say more but had no choice. "I called Aaron."

"Aaron Breckenridge?"

"I know that sounds crazy, but last night, we . . . reconnected."

I watched the slow shift in her face, from angry to appalled. "Jesus, Mary, and Joseph. Tell me you didn't sleep with that guy."

"No, it's okay! I was wrong about him."

"Oh. My. God." Jordan rose, batting away the fumes from the sleeping woman.

"Jordan, it's not what you think."

"What I *think*? What I *think*?" she repeated. She was pacing the cell, occasionally lurching sideways on the broken heel. "How in hell would I know what to *think* anymore?"

"Aaron didn't know about Dylan. He didn't know she existed."

"Hope." She bent down, putting both arms on my shoulders. "We discussed this. You said, very clearly, he wanted nothing to do with her. Did you lie to me?"

"No, that's what I thought! I was wrong." I dropped my head. "I didn't lie . . . I just didn't tell you everything."

Jordan flung both arms into the air. "Well, *there's* a surprise. How unlike you to tell partial truths. I guess I should feel privileged that I got half the story, right?" I'd never seen Jordan this angry. She was in a white rage. "That's one of the *perks* of being your best friend?"

"I'm sorry. It's not that I enjoy lying. I've had to."

"Well that's interesting, because I keep looking around, and I've yet to see a gun held to your head."

"Sometimes, when people don't tell you the whole truth, it's because the truth is too painful or embarrassing." My forehead throbbed. "Surely, you of all people can understand that."

Her eyes grew wide. "Ex-cuse me? Is that what you think? That I've kept secrets because my truth is painful? Because I'm embarrassed by the truth?"

I tried to play back what I'd said. Had I said that? Had I meant that? "No, of course not."

"Because, for your information—and I didn't imagine I'd ever have to say this to you, Hope—I'm happy with who I am. It's the rest of the world who has problems with it. *That's* why I've had to keep secrets. Whereas you, my friend, you're not happy with who you are."

Jordan walked over to the bars of the cell and called for the police officer.

"Jordan! What—"

She cut me off, her voice cold. "That's the difference between us, Hope. I like who I am, even when I've had to hide it."

I didn't know what to say. I pulled a George. Looked at my shoes.

Jordan wasn't waiting for my response. She was on a roll. "You're afraid to let people get close to you because they might see who you are. You push them away. Or run away—I guess you've done that, too." Jordan leaned into the bars, trying to see around the corner. "You know what I think? You didn't disappear eighteen years ago to give Aaron Breckenridge the freedom to choose you. You disappeared so he *wouldn't* choose you. Because you didn't think you were worth it."

She called through the bars again, and a distant voice yelled back. "Coming, already!"

Jordan returned to me. "Here's something I've learned, Hope. You can't conceal your own truth. If you hold it under water, it'll float to the surface. If you bury it, it'll bust out of the ground like Carrie's freakin' bloody arm. So if that's what you want to do? Keep your truth buried? Then I'm done helping you with that."

The violet-eyed officer appeared. "What's the problem?"

Jordan said, "I made a mistake. I don't want to be in this cell."

"Figured," the officer said, glancing my way.

The sleeping woman struggled to raise her head. Pointing at me, she hissed, "Take that one! She smells!"

"Sorry, Diana," the officer said as she opened the door to let Jordan out. "Just hold your nose."

I CURLED INTO a fetal position on the bunk. My upper arm ached where the cop had yanked it back. My bottom lip, ragged and swollen, felt detached. I longed for a blanket to throw over my head and shut out all light.

What an idiot move to call Aaron! With his speech in an hour, he might not even check his messages. Probably some staff member screened his calls.

I jerked upright, recalling what Carly had said. *Shit. Shit. Shit.* The text message I'd saved as "Aaron" was from Veronica. She, not Aaron, would get the pathetic, sniveling message saying I was in jail. Oh, Lord, what fun she and Carly would have with this one.

Sleeping Diana convulsed and resumed snoring. I gagged, tasting bile, and thought I might be sick, but I couldn't bear the thought of my bruised knees on that rough floor by the toilet. I collapsed back onto the hard mattress, chin pressed to my chest.

Jordan was right. As a twenty-two-year-old, I hadn't believed my luck that Aaron preferred me over someone like Carly. I believed it *was* luck. I'd somehow blinded him to who I was, and my darkest fear was that he'd learn the truth. As I'd driven away from Tennessee, mixed in with gut-wrenching pain was also the tiniest whisper of relief. I wouldn't have to witness his disappointment.

The jail-cell pillow was rough and hurt my ear. I had no idea how much time passed, and it hardly mattered. I'd miss

Aaron's speech. I'd lost my chance to find Dylan beforehand, talk to her, convince her . . . to what? Come home with me? Believe me? Trust me to know what was best for her? It all sounded so ludicrous.

I'd failed as a mother, daughter, friend. My mother and Jordan had both used the same words: I pushed people away. I'd even done it with my daughter. My worst nightmare had always been that she'd discover my secret—not that her father wasn't worthy of her (though at the time, I'd believed that, too), but that I wasn't. To prevent her from finding that out, I'd kept my daughter at arm's length. Now I couldn't reach her.

Graceland

Chapter 34

Olivia

I removed the small cotton throw I'd stuffed in my oxygen cart. Bending down, I spread it across the embossed metal that covered the grave, pulling the blanket higher, so only the name "Elvis" was visible. Like tucking a child into bed. I lowered myself gently until I was seated on the rectangular slab. Elvis's grave, like the others in the Meditation Garden, sat just inches above the surrounding grass. I thanked God for my natural flexibility and years of vinyasa yoga. Not many women my age could still hold a warrior pose, never mind maneuver like this.

Pulling the cart closer, I removed the pill bottle from my bag. Tipping it into in my hand, I took the pills, two at a time, with sips from the Dasani water I'd found in the hotel minifridge. I reclined back on the stone and gazed at wisps of clouds overhead. On this day, in the middle of July, there was still some time before sunset.

TWO HOURS EARLIER, I'd been in the office with Ann Abernathy as the final tourists made their way around the Meditation Garden.

Ann, it turned out, was a rigid, controlling type. She had no interest in my childhood fascination with Graceland, my clandestinely purchased records and hidden magazines, or the letters I'd written Elvis while he was in the army. Instead, she pushed for intimate details on my date with Elvis. After I related how Elvis brought me to his suite, where I partied with him and his entourage, Ann interrupted constantly with questions. "How did Elvis react when you said that?" "What was Elvis doing when you were chatting with Sonny?" "Did Elvis get involved in the argument with Red?" I responded patiently to these inane questions, then resumed where I'd left off. Wresting the interview from Ann Abernathy had been an exhausting tug-of-war.

Indeed, I could tell by the number of times Ann glanced at her phone that the interview was taking longer than expected. No matter. The Elvis biography by Peter Guralnick had required two volumes, *The Godfather* saga three films, and the Bible both an Old and New Testament. Some stories simply can't be rushed.

When I came to the part where the party broke up and Elvis's entourage retreated to their own rooms, I folded my hands.

Ann blinked. "What happened after that? Did Elvis invite you to his bedroom?"

"As I'm sure you'll understand, there are some things I need to keep private, out of respect for the King."

Ann prodded, but I refused to reveal anything more. Oh, I had juicy stuff all right, but how could I share that without hinting at the rest? How Elvis had begun slurring his words, slipping in and out of consciousness. I'd gone into the bathroom for some water and seen the pill bottles, lined up rows deep on the vanity. Even then, seven years before Elvis died, I could tell he'd gone too far down that road. There'd be no turning back. I'd slipped out of his hotel room with the heartbreaking thought that he probably wouldn't remember my being there.

Ann Abernathy was clearly frustrated by my discretion. Still, as we called it quits, I felt emboldened to ask for what I really wanted.

Ann smiled, shaking her head. "I'm so sorry, Olivia. No one but Priscilla, Lisa Marie, and the curator are allowed in Elvis's bedroom. It's been that way since Graceland opened. I'd lose my job if I so much as let you climb the stairs." She glanced down at my oxygen tank, a subtle reminder that getting to the second floor was perhaps more than I was up to, in any case.

"And yet, we've all heard rumors that Nicolas Cage was up there." I sniffed. "Even lying on Elvis's bed."

"Well, if you marry Lisa Marie, you might get an invitation, too. I'm afraid I know of no other way."

As hard as it was to admit defeat, I had a backup plan, and truthfully, some aspects of that plan were preferable. In gratitude for my interview, Ann granted my request for time alone in the Meditation Garden after Graceland closed. Ann would remain in her office, completing paperwork, and come get me at six thirty, before setting the alarms.

I hated to think of Ann's horror when she came for me.

Or maybe I didn't.

THE RAISED LETTERING cut into my shoulder, so I shimmied closer to the edge of the grave. Not exactly what I'd dreamed of as a teenager, when I'd fantasized about being with Elvis at Graceland. Then again, very little ended up being what you expected.

Water burbled in the fountain behind me. Leaves rustled in the breeze. Cars passed outside the gates on Elvis Presley Boulevard. Everything was going as planned. I took a long, slow inhale and closed my eyes. I recited Psalm 23, a prayer my mother had taught me as a child. Though never fond of imagining myself as a sheep, I'd been enchanted by the other images: green pastures, cups running over, the valley of the shadow of death. I wasn't worried about dying. I believed in an afterlife. Oh, nothing like the one my crazy mother had described: choirs of angels, God as an old man with a beard. Something more . . . ineffable. My life energy would merge with that of people who'd gone before me. I'd be with them again: Harold. Beth. Elvis.

I waited for the pills to take effect. As added insurance, at the last possible moment, I planned to remove my cannula. Ideally, I hoped to experience no more than a touch of breathlessness as the pills pulled me under. The timing had to be just right.

Where would Hope and Dylan be, I wondered, when they got the news? They'd be upset, of course, but they'd get over it. It wasn't like I'd been an award-winning mother or grandmother. Still, I was sorry I couldn't share in Dylan's joy at meeting her father. And witness Hope's gratitude for dragging her to Memphis. Maybe not at first. Eventually, though, Hope would realize the journey had been for her, even more than for Dylan. It was my gift to them. I'd embraced my role as mother and grandmother a tad late, but in the end, as always, I'd nailed it.

I had a harder time picturing my fans' reaction to my departure, struggling to put a face to any of them. That windbag waitress in the diner would turn the conversation to herself, how I'd been rude to her and hadn't tipped. The shriveled old gecko in the wheelchair at Subway wouldn't understand, and her son, being a priest, couldn't approve of my exit. Even Frances, my fan-club president, would resent having to find a new hobby. Any tears that woman shed would be for herself. In truth, when I considered the lot of them, all the fans I'd met over the years, I couldn't recall anyone whose opinion I valued.

Dylan had said something similar the night before, as I struggled to supply Frances with the perfect retort for @WhatWouldAndromedaDo? She'd asked why I bothered.

"It's the price of fame, Dylan. You must feed the fans."

"But you don't even *like* those people."

"What do you mean, I don't like them?"

"Everyone we've met you've found annoying."

The child had a point. Ironic, wasn't it? Though I'd never thought of it in this way, fame meant being loved by a lot of people you wouldn't invite over for dinner. Half of them would read the news of my demise over their morning coffee and then turn to the gossip section for more dirt on Kevin Spacey. How odd this hadn't occurred to me before.

Well, Dylan would miss me. We'd had quite the journey together. Sure, the girl's harebrained decisions had created challenges, but wasn't that what made life such a wild ride? Just like Andromeda on *Light Within*, Dylan made things happen, stirred things up. Hope didn't understand that Dylan's recklessness, her impulsive nature, was simply a coping mechanism. By not thinking before she acted, Dylan could pretend she didn't care. I only wished I could have helped the child more. Perhaps the father would step up.

And then there was Hope. I'd brought my daughter this far. Hope could figure out the rest on her own, couldn't she? Face whatever heartache had paralyzed her for so long? Get on with her life? Get unstuck?

A gray fog was seeping into my brain. I heard a sigh and turned toward it. No one there—only that tall statue of Jesus and the little angels beside him, shifting, transforming. The pills were taking effect. I needed to stay alert and remove the cannula, but suddenly here was Dylan, wavy and ethereal. The child was lying down with me, wrapping her arms around me, squeezing me so tight I could hardly breathe.

And now there was a terrible racket, a girl shrieking. Beth. No, not Beth. Hope. As a small child, Hope had hidden in the kitchen and wailed inconsolably each Sunday as I packed my bag for LA. How strange. Perhaps my intolerance for scream- ing hadn't been from the accident, after all? Had it always been Hope's crying I couldn't bear?

In my mind, I was back on the threshold of our Memphis home, bag in hand, taxi idling in the driveway. I could walk through that door as I always had, or I could return to my daughter.

The sound of the wind in the trees stopped. The wailing quieted. My mother's voice whispered, "You'll be forgotten tomorrow."

Yes, Mother, I will. By almost everyone, and by no one who matters.

I closed the door and put down my bag. I wouldn't leave. Not this time.

My eyes snapped open, and I grabbed at my face, pinching it, trying to jiggle feeling back into it. I struggled to sit up and succeeded only in propping myself on one elbow. Rolling to my side, I clawed in the grass for my cell phone. I had to act fast. The cannula was still in place, but for a woman of my age, in my health, the pills would probably be enough.

The gray fog rolled in again, dragging me under. I was searching . . . but for what? My hand slowed, and I combed my fingers through the grass the way I once had through Harold's hair. A breeze whispered through the trees. The last thing I saw was a little girl—Hope, wrapped in a towel, after a bath. The girl was reaching out, begging me to lift her up.

Chapter 35

Hope

The clanging of the jail door made me heave myself upright. Had I dozed? The violet-eyed cop unlocked the cell door and motioned for me to come out. She seemed intent on not waking Diana, which I appreciated. She locked the door behind us and gestured for me to walk in front of her. "You've been released."

I kept my mouth shut. My father used to joke, "When the judge says not guilty, just say thank you and leave." As I limped down the hallway, my banged-up knee stiffer than before, a wave of excitement washed through me. Aaron must have received my message. He'd be at the university now, about to give his speech, but he'd sent someone.

Then I remembered. The person I'd messaged wasn't Aaron, it was Veronica.

Please God, don't let Veronica be waiting for me.

The officer steered me into a room where a clerk handed me a box with my purse and cell phone. We returned to the dark hallway, and she fumbled with the door lock. I needed a moment for my eyes to adjust to the fluorescent light of the waiting area. I stepped carefully over the doorjamb that had tripped Jordan.

The cop closed the door behind me, and I blinked several times. Across the room, rising from a bench, was Marlin A. Fish.

"Ms. Robinson." He advanced toward me. "You are a very trying woman."

"And you barely know me." I scanned the lobby to see if Carly or Veronica had come for the humiliation party. But no, only Fish, grasping his straw hat. "You bailed me out?"

"I've secured your release, yes."

I shuffled over to speak to the woman behind a bulletproof enclosure, tapping the glass to get her attention. "I need to go back. I can't accept this man's money."

She called to someone through an open door behind her: "Sherise, I ain't never had someone refuse bail before. What do I do?"

Fish touched my arm and motioned for me to step away from the glass. "Please. Let me explain."

"No need," I said, brushing dirt from my clothes. "I get it. You gave me twenty-four hours to leave town. I'm almost out of time, and Carly is giving me a little push. Unfortunately, I can't accept your help."

"I no longer work for that client."

My legs wobbled, no doubt a delayed stress reaction. I limped to the bench and plopped down. "I got you fired, didn't I? You would not believe the streak I'm on."

Fish rotated his hat in his hands. "It was my decision, Ms. Robinson. I terminated the relationship."

I made the face Dylan pulls when she thinks I'm full of shit.

"No, it's true," he went on. "I wasn't kidding when I said I liked you. I thought a lot about our conversation in the park."

Fish noticed my confusion. "What you said about that murky middle. It's true. Not everything is black and white, but that doesn't mean I can't figure out what's right."

"I said that, huh?" I pulled at a loose thread in my ripped skirt. "I should listen to myself."

Fish said after he'd sent Carly packing, he'd received a call from a former associate of hers, a woman he'd spoken with many years ago, named Veronica. "My goodness but she talks fast. I couldn't catch everything she said—something about not recognizing your daughter this afternoon, then getting a call from Mrs. Breckenridge—but the point was, you were in jail, and she needed you out. She wants you to retrieve your daughter."

"Veronica said that?"

"With some urgency! Seems she's quite a loyal employee of the senator," Fish said. "Had more than a few choice words to say about Mrs. Breckenridge. Well, you and your daughter, too."

No doubt. "This is all fascinating, Mr. Fish," I said, "but I'm not comfortable taking your money."

"Oh, no money involved. I served on this police force for thirty years. The chief is an old friend."

"That must be helpful for parking tickets."

"Boy, don't I know it!"

I grinned and thanked Fish for his trouble. "I'd love to accept your offer. There's someplace I desperately need to be right now," I told him. "Unfortunately, I can't leave."

IT TOOK ANOTHER thirty minutes to get Jordan released. By the time we got to Fish's car, parked illegally in front of a fire hydrant, it was seven forty-five. Aaron's speech was underway.

"Where to?" Fish asked.

"The Doubletree, I guess." I twisted toward the back seat. "Jordan, may I use your truck to get to campus? Or should I call a cab?"

Jordan had said barely a word since our release. "Take it," she said to the window.

I had a lot I wanted to say to Jordan, beginning with "I'm sorry," ending with "I'm sorry," and with a lot of "I'm sorrys" in the middle. But from her close examination of the car window, Jordan wasn't ready to hear it yet. I'd schedule some groveling for later that night.

In the meantime, I needed to get to the university. If I hurried, I might make it before Aaron's speech ended. My phone, shattered though it was, showed no enraged texts from Aaron Breckenridge, so at least Dylan hadn't found him before the event. That left me a little time. Not that I had a plan, exactly. Just a better compass.

The parking garage was dark and silent when Fish dropped us by Jordan's truck. "I realize I helped get you into this mess," he offered as we got out. "I hope in some small way I've made up for it." I thanked him and admitted I wasn't sure how things would play out. "Don't worry," he said. "You'll know what to do."

Jordan clicked the key to unlock her truck and handed me the keys.

"Do you want to come?" I asked.

"I'll sit this one out."

I opened the door. "I'm sorry, Jordan," I said, rapidly. "For everything. You've been an incredibly loyal and supportive friend and I've been a shitty one."

"Yes," she said. "You have."

I swung myself up into the driver's seat. "We'll talk later."

"Go do whatever you have to do," she said. I heard the judgment in her words.

Throwing the truck in reverse, I headed out of the garage. I still didn't know what lay in front of me, but I felt a new determination, born in a rank jail cell on a scratchy mattress. I needed my daughter and mother back. To get that, I was prepared to lose everything else.

Chapter 36

Dylan

A Chipotle parking lot may not be the ideal place for a meltdown, but it worked for me. I turned off the Bug and grabbed my throbbing head with both hands.

What in goddamn fucking hell was going on? Had Breckenridge been messing with me? He was "seeing Hope," he said, "while she's in town." How many people could that possibly describe? Not only that—he was seeing her *again*. Clearly Mom had gotten to Breckenridge first, but what did that mean? Had they been plotting together for years to keep me in the dark? To keep their little secret out of the public eye?

And what about the smooth way Breckenridge had pretended not to recognize me? His disarming grin and casual banter. He had to know who I was. Why else would he so pointedly mention Hope? Was he warning me to keep my mouth shut? Well, we'd see about that. There was a special circle in hell for that level of asshole.

The meltdown made me hungry. I bought a Chipotle salad with guacamole and ate in the Bug, then drove to the

University of Memphis campus and parked on a side street.
I wandered around campus for the better part of an hour, my
fury feeding on itself. Around seven, I headed to the auditorium. Standing out front of the door was that office manager, the one Breckenridge had called Veronica, her nostrils
flared and mouth tight. She glared as I walked up to her.

"I know who you are now," Veronica hissed. "And you are
not getting in."

I LURKED IN the shadows of the parking garage and pulled my
hoodie over my hair, waiting for the right moment.

Veronica hadn't said more, just pointed to two security
guards by the auditorium doors and told me they had strict orders not to let me in. I guessed Breckenridge had told her who I
was. I backed away, feigning surrender, and circled around the
brick building, checking the doors. All were locked, including a steel delivery entrance at the very back, up a small flight
of cement stairs. I considered knocking on that door, to see if
someone would let me in, but that seemed risky. Who knew
where Veronica was? So I waited. One thing I'd learned from
Olivia: a little patience and planning could pay off.

Within minutes, a FedEx truck pulled into the alley near
the rear entrance. The driver grabbed two boxes from the back
and climbed the steps, then knocked on the door. I trotted up
behind him.

"Let me help," I said, grabbing the door as someone opened
it from the inside.

While the driver entered and handed off the boxes, I slipped
behind him into the backstage area. I headed toward the wings
and peeked out into the audience. Cameras were set up in the

back. Making a beeline for an empty seat in the third row, I scooted in between a whispering couple and a student with his bare feet draped over the seat in front of him.

People poured into the auditorium from two doors in the back. Some were college age, some older. A middle-aged woman with hair like Mom's made my heart flip-flop in my chest. I kept my head down, pretending to read my phone, until the lights dimmed, and some university bigwig took the stage.

The guy gave background on Breckenridge, then introduced him like he was a rock star: "Your senator and—who knows—maybe next vice president of the United States . . ."

Or not.

I ducked down as Veronica slid into the front row.

Breckenridge took the stage to thunderous applause. I listened to his speech without hearing it. He seemed a little stuck on himself and I wondered if he practiced in front of the mirror. I doodled an exploding star on my notepad, then wiped my sweaty palms on my sweatshirt. After about forty minutes, Breckenridge began winding up, using those catchphrases politicians love: hard work, reaching across the aisle, our children's future. When he finished, people applauded, and a few stood. He motioned them to sit down, saying, "We have time for some Q&A. Who has a question?" A thousand tiny needle pricks zipped through my chest, out to my fingertips.

Would Breckenridge even call on me? Without looking in my direction, he pointed to someone halfway up, on the center aisle. A volunteer ran over and thrust the mic so close to the young woman's face, she lurched back. She asked something about #MeToo and sexual harassment.

Breckenridge professed support for the victims of sexual

harassment and spoke about the importance of listening to their stories. I wondered if "listening to" was the same as "believing." I wished the woman would push him for something concrete, like proposed legislation. Instead, he asked for another question. I raised my hand too late. Breckenridge pointed to a far corner of the room. "Yes, in the back?"

The question was about climate change. As I turned to see the questioner, a door opened, and my mom slipped into the rear of the auditorium. I slouched down in my seat.

"He won't see you," the barefoot guy next to me whispered. "Take off the hoodie."

I pushed back the hood and kept my hand into the air. I was barely listening to Breckenridge's answer and didn't realize he'd finished. My barefoot friend stood and pointed at me, and suddenly, Breckenridge looked my way.

"Yes, down front."

The guy with the microphone ran over. I stood up, not looking in my mother's direction. Sweat dripped down my neck.

"Oh, yes, the reporter," Breckenridge seemed oddly pleased to see me. "I promised you a couple questions. It's Dylan, right?"

In the front row, Veronica rose from her seat, shaking her head madly at Breckenridge. He saw her and looked confused. I looked back to see a figure moving slowly down the aisle. My mother. Limping? Breckenridge glanced in that direction as well.

"Yes," I said, taking the mic from the kid. "Dylan Robinson." I flicked a finger toward Mom. "You may remember Hope Robinson, who worked on your first campaign, eighteen years ago? I'm her daughter." I took a deep breath and spoke boldly, channeling my grandmother, the actress, Olivia Grant. "And, as I understand it, your daughter, too."

Silence, then a low buzz rose in the auditorium. Veronica waved at the kid with the mic, hissing "Take it away."

Breckenridge frowned and looked toward my mom. I turned, too. Mom's face looked anguished, as if being my mother were the saddest thing she could imagine.

The kid snatched the mic from me as the crowd's confusion grew louder: "What did she say?" I heard someone ask: "His daughter?" In my peripheral vision, I noticed two guys with shoulder-mounted cameras moving closer, but I kept my eyes fixed on Aaron Breckenridge and wiped my hands on my skirt.

That should do it.

Chapter 37

Hope

A murmur blanketed the auditorium.

"Hope?" Aaron mouthed at me. He wanted to know if what Dylan had said was true. No doubt my appearance—ripped, bloodied, cappuccinoed—added to his confusion. I felt horrible for Aaron. He had the look of a swimmer caught in a riptide, suddenly aware he might not make it back to shore.

I turned to my daughter. Seeing her made my throat tighten, my eyes fill.

I turned back to Aaron and nodded. "Yes," I said. It was true.

Much later, that daughter would dispute the way I'd tell the story. She'd claim the choice to tell the truth wasn't mine. She'd already spilled the beans, after all. Even if I'd denied it, the truth would have come out. Nothing turns the media into rabid sleuths like a good denial.

And if you look at it like that, she was right. For me, though, it *was* a choice: to stop hiding. To stand there in front of my daughter, Aaron, the cameras, the world, with a full understanding of what it would cost. My personal life, including every humiliating mistake of my past twenty years, was about to become tabloid fodder. Worse, my daughter and I had unpinned a grenade and chucked it at Aaron's career with no idea of the damage it would inflict.

I won't say that none of that mattered. What I will say is that I needed my daughter back, and that had to start with what was true.

I'd never seen Aaron flounder publicly before. He'd lost control of the event, and for a politician, that was disastrous. "Folks, I apologize," he said. "Given the disruption, we're going to call this a wrap. Thank you all for coming." A few nervous claps were drowned out as the murmur in the auditorium became a roar.

Aaron crouched down and with one arm on the stage, jumped off, and pushed his way through the crowd toward Dylan. TV crews closed in on her, pointing cameras in her face. She reeled back and shaded her eyes from the lights. Aaron touched her elbow and she turned to look at him. He put a hand on her back and guided her up a short flight of stairs to the right of the stage. He looked back, caught my eye, and motioned for me to follow.

The cameras and cell phones turned on me as I muscled my way through the clogged the aisle. When I reached the stairs, I was face-to-face with two burly security people who didn't seem to understand my pivotal role in this shit show.

Veronica hoofed it back down the stairs and whispered to one of them to let me through. Her mouth drawn tight, she led me backstage at a brisk clip, slapping through a second door and into a hallway where Aaron and Dylan were waiting. Dylan's face was drained of color, though whether from anger or fear, I couldn't say. Aaron, though, was scarlet with rage. When Veronica went to leave, he grabbed her arm, making her stay.

"Hope," he nearly shouted, his eyes wide and wild. "What the fuck?"

I couldn't imagine the right words for such an occasion.

"Who are you working for?" Aaron asked, his voice cold. "And how much did they pay you?"

Veronica raised a hand to her mouth. I shook my head, feeling sick. "It's not like that."

Aaron looked from me to Dylan and back again. "Well, congratulations, Hope. I don't know how long you've been planning this, but you certainly paid me back."

Whatever I started to say, Dylan shouted over it. "Shut up!" She was shaking. "Both of you make me sick." She whirled around and slammed her hands against the middle bar of the door. It was an emergency exit. Alarms sounded.

I pushed past Aaron to follow her. He grabbed my arm, and I wrenched it away. Crashing through the door, I screamed Dylan's name.

A sea of lights blinded me. I was at the top of a short, concrete stairway, and shadowy figures on the stairs jostled one another, trying to shove a mic in my face. Two guys with TV news cameras on their shoulders pressed in. Raising a hand to block their lights, I searched in both directions for my daughter. "Dylan!" I called out again.

"Was that your daughter? With the pink hair?" someone asked.

"Yes! Where did she go?"

A student filming with a cell phone pointed toward the parking garage.

I pushed my way through the crowd. A tall blond woman

shoved a mic in my face. "Your daughter said Aaron Brecken-ridge was her father." When I didn't respond, she and several others followed alongside me. They had no trouble keeping up with my limping. I arrived at Jordan's truck, which, after driving over the grass to avoid the parking lot gate, I'd parked illegally behind a dumpster.

I heaved myself into the truck and found the keys in the ignition, where, apparently, I'd left them.

"Is it true?" the blonde with the mic shouted over the others. "Is that girl Senator Breckenridge's daughter?"

I paused to look the woman in the eye. "Yes." How easy this truth-telling was!

Throwing the truck into reverse, I backed up, slowly but determinedly, forcing reporters to dive in all directions. I rolled down the window and yelled to the lady with the mic: "Please don't be too hard on Aaron. He didn't know until ten minutes ago, either."

I cranked it into drive and sped away.

I KNEW IT was a waste of time to circle the campus, looking for my daughter. She'd be long gone. I did it anyway.

I'd passed the U of M's giant Ramesses statue for the third time when my phone gave a couple pathetic shudders. I pulled into the parking lot to navigate the shattered screen. After some fiddling, I could see it was a Memphis number, and while not the one Aaron had given me, I was certain it would be him. It wasn't.

It was the hospital. They had my mother.

THE NURSE BLOCKING my mother's hospital room assured me she was doing fine. He wouldn't explain what had happened, only that the doctor was with her. I followed his eyes to my stained blouse and ripped skirt, the dried blood below my knees.

"You should see the other guy," I quipped half-heartedly, then cringed. The other guy was Aaron.

I stationed myself in a plastic chair across the hall to catch the doctor. I started to text Jordan, to ask if she'd keep an eye out for Dylan, then dropped the phone back in my bag. Jordan owed me no favors.

Nice work, Hope. Is there anyone you haven't managed to piss off?

A middle-aged woman with a paper coffee cup rounded the corner and rushed over to ask if I was Hope. She introduced herself as Ann somebody, the curator at Graceland. Apparently, we'd known each other as children, though I had no memory of her. She then launched into a confusing narrative that included my mother, Elvis, and a cotton throw.

"Hold on." I had to raise my hand to eye level before she stopped. "You found my mother where?"

After some back-and-forth, Ann realized I knew nothing about the interview or my mother's request for time alone in the Meditation Garden. "We sometimes grant little favors like that for dignitaries and celebrities. Allow them private tours, after hours. But when I glanced at the surveillance camera, she wasn't standing by the grave, she was lying on top of it! Naturally, I called security."

"She fell?"

"That's what I thought at first. Or maybe she'd passed out."

I recalled my mother on the floor of the Peabody lounge earlier. Could she have pulled that stunt twice in the same day? My mother wasn't shy about reusing her best material, so it was in-character to a point, but she hated hospitals. Mom wouldn't have let anyone bring her here if she'd had any say in it.

My second thought was more frightening: What if she hadn't been faking earlier? What if something really was wrong with her?

Ann continued: "The blanket, though."

"Blan-ket," I repeated phonetically.

"Yes, a little throw. It was draped over the grave. Almost as if she'd placed it there, laid down, and gone to sleep." Responding to my confused expression, she nodded. "I know! But she wasn't sleeping. Neither the security people nor I could wake her, so I dialed 911." She held a hand on her chest. "I nearly had a heart attack myself." I caught the displeasure in her voice. She hadn't appreciated this stunt, whatever it was. "I don't think I did anything wrong."

I was lost again. "I'm sure you didn't . . ."

"As you can imagine, I'd like to keep this between us, if possible. I don't think Graceland has any liability."

I understood then: she was afraid we'd sue. I assured Ann that whatever my mom had intended to do was not her fault.

Clearly eager to hand off responsibility, Ann pressed a business card into my palm and told me to call as soon as I knew anything. After she left, I pulled out my phone and was struggling to type a brief message to Jordan when the doctor emerged and said I could see my mother. He lowered his voice. They'd had to pump her stomach. Apparently, my mother had taken sleeping pills.

"Sleeping pills?" I wasn't aware my mother had any.

He fished around in the pocket of his lab coat then handed me the empty bottle. The prescription was from three months earlier. A doctor at UCLA.

"Your mother claims it was a mistake," he said. "Says she thought they were baby aspirin." The doctor was watching me carefully, trying to read my expression. "Does your mother sometimes get confused?"

"Not really," I said. "Her hobby is confusing me."

He patted my shoulder, gave a once-over to my clothes, and said, "Well, best of luck . . . with everything" before hurrying away.

My mother's bed was cranked nearly upright, but her eyes were closed, her hands folded on the blanket. Her face looked almost as white as her hair. As I gingerly lowered myself into the chair beside her, my arms shook.

Without opening her eyes, my mother said: "Well, that didn't go very well, did it?"

I leaned forward. "No, Mom, it didn't. What in God's name were you thinking?"

"Me?" Her eyes opened. "I meant *you*." She reached beside her on the bed and lifted the remote to click on the TV. It was tuned to one of the local news stations. Across the bottom of the screen: "Breaking News: Breckenridge speech disrupted by paternity allegations." When the image shifted from the anchor, it showed Aaron jumping down from the stage and me climbing into Jordan's truck, surrounded by reporters. "Channel 11 also offered some nice footage," my mother said, clicking off the TV. "You might want to give more thought to your outfit next time."

"Thank you," I said. "I'll certainly consult you going forward. Assuming you don't off yourself in the meantime."

Her head dropped back as her eyes implored the ceiling. "I opened the wrong bottle. My lower back was acting up."

"Stop it, Mom. Just stop. I'm calling a moratorium on bullshit."

"Fine. Your bullshit, too? Or only mine?"

"Everyone's bullshit," I said. "We'll start with yours, though. What were you trying to do?"

She fiddled with her blanket, sighed. "Write my own script."

"Not following," I said. "Use more words."

"I never wanted to be old, Hope. I wasn't designed for it. People like me . . . we should go like Elvis did, in our prime."

I couldn't help myself. "That was his prime?"

She shot me a look. "Close enough." She ran her thumb, almost lovingly, down the side of the TV remote. "I've already lived too long. So few people recognize me anymore. I can go anywhere—grocery shopping, the hair salon! No one looks twice at a woman with a cantaloupe strapped around her face."

"Cannula."

"I know what it's called! You never did get my humor." She reached for her water. "I'm on my way out. I simply wanted to do it with . . . panache." She smiled, pleased with the word.

"You saw nothing worth hanging around for, Mom? Not Dylan? Not . . ." *Why was it so hard to say this?* "Me?"

"You don't need me, Hope. Never have." I started to protest, but she waved me off. "No, let's face it. I've not been much use as a mother." Her voice was growing scratchy, and she coughed to clear her throat. I fished around on the tray, and finally, inscrutably, handed her a napkin. She wiped her mouth before continuing. "I thought in Memphis we could all stop pretending. I'd reconnect with Elvis. I'd help you stop hiding from Dylan, from whatever happened in your past. It was my parting gift."

"I don't recall asking for your help."

"You were pushing Dylan away. You weren't there for her."

That was a bridge too far. "Mother, how can you, of all people, say that to me?"

"How can I say it?" She lifted a shoulder from the bed to turn to me. "How do you think I *recognized* it?" When I didn't respond, she leaned back against the pillows and fiddled with her rings. "I've already admitted I wasn't a good mother to you, Hope. What more do you want? We didn't work well together."

If I was supposed to protest, I wasn't going to. "No, we didn't," I said. "But thank you for your honesty. This is a conversation I've wanted to have for years."

She snorted. "And now, being a Christian woman, you can't?" I frowned, trying to place the familiar words. "*The Wizard of Oz*," she explained. "When Auntie Em tries to tell off Miss Gulch." She brushed some imaginary crumbs off her blanket. "I thought I'd help you by casting myself as the witch."

"Give me a break, Mom. You chose Miss Gulch because she's the most interesting character. Naturally, you'd see me as Auntie Em."

"I didn't make you Auntie Em. You were *born* Auntie Em."

"Plain? Colorless?"

"Reserved. Inscrutable. Kept everything to yourself. Even as a toddler, you gave me no clues, nothing to work with."

"Well, I'm sorry, Mom. If I could do everything over, I'd be more like Beth." I'd never spoken Beth's name in her presence, and I expected some reaction. A surprised look, at least. When she gave me nothing, I pressed on. "I'm sure it was easier to be a good mother to her."

"No." My mother sighed. "I pretty much sucked with her, too."

I studied my mother's face, waiting for her to acknowledge

the joke. Of course she'd loved Beth more. I'd seen the photos. My mother beaming as she pushed Beth on the swings, holding her in the pool, posing with her in a new Easter outfit. I'd been so different from Beth. Hard to love. "You don't have to lie, Mom," I said, finally.

"No, it is true." She coughed again and handed me her empty water cup. "I tried with both of you. Acted the part as best I could. I wanted to do well for Harold's sake. He was so awfully good with children." I filled the cup with water and handed it back to her. She took a long sip. "By the time you were a toddler, studies were starting to show that depressed mothers raised depressed children. I decided it was better for you if I wasn't around."

I wasn't letting her go that far. "Come on, Mom. You wanted to be back on TV. Admit it."

"Well of course I did! I loved acting. That's what you do when you can't stand to be yourself—pretend to be someone else." She put down the cup and smoothed the blankets around her legs. "But it doesn't work forever. And it never works at all for some people."

"Yes, Mom, I know. I'm a terrible actress."

"Dreadful."

A nurse interrupted to check my mother's vitals. I took out my phone. Nothing from Dylan or Aaron, but every news organization in the country somehow had my email. It was going to be a long night.

I asked my mother if she'd heard from Dylan. To my astonishment, she reached over to the nightstand and retrieved a cell phone. When I shouted, "What the hell?" she explained she'd bought it for the trip. "It's a safety issue, Hope. You need a phone to do almost anything these days." I closed my eyes and counted to twenty.

My mother messaged Dylan, and we waited a few minutes with no reply. "Go check the Peabody, and see if Dylan is there," she said. "Just be sure to come back soon. I may need your help getting out of here." Her fleeting look toward the window made me nervous.

"Don't move until I get back," I warned. In my hand, my phone quacked half-heartedly. A text from a Memphis number.

"Can you meet me somewhere?" it read.

THE NIGHT WAS warm, and the earthy smell of mud wafted up from the river. Aaron leaned over the wrought iron fence, his back to me, staring out at the Mississippi. I hobbled over and stood beside him. He kept his eyes on the river.

"I'm going to need some genetic testing," he said flatly.

"I understand."

"I've contacted a friend, a doctor, who says he can have the results back in twelve hours. It would go quicker if he could have a sample from you as well as Dylan."

"Of course." If I could find Dylan.

His head was down, his eyes heavy. "It's not that I don't believe you, Hope. The truth is I do. Though God knows why since you've given me every reason on earth to mistrust you." My turn to look at my shoes. "But other people are demanding proof." I could imagine: his campaign advisers, his financial backers, the DNC. "So that's where we are. I've postponed my camping trip so I can make a public statement about this before I go."

"Aaron, just to be clear: no one is paying me. No one is be-hind this . . ."

He held up a hand and tilted his head to the sky. "If I seemed a little upset back there, you have to imagine my"—he bit down hard on the word—"surprise."

"I didn't want this to happen. I was doing everything I could to prevent it. When I ran into you at the fundraiser, I was try-ing to find Dylan, to convince her to come home . . ."

"*Home?*" Even in the dwindling light, I could see the set of his jaw. "You mean *Seattle?*"

"Oh God," I whispered.

"Or maybe it's *not* Seattle, but actually as far from Seattle as possible. Perhaps *Boston?*"

I tapped my fingers on the railing. "I've got nothing. Can't even explain that one."

He turned toward me, his face full of rage. "Hope, why didn't you tell me?"

I took a deep breath. The truth. "At first, because I was heartbroken. You'd chosen your path, and your wife, and it wasn't me." I held up a hand. "I know, my disappearing didn't help. We don't need to go there again. But I was devastated and didn't want to speak to you ever again." I turned and rested my back against the rail. "I planned to keep the baby. I assumed you wouldn't want me to. So, better if you didn't know."

He held out a hand again, asking me to stop. "You're going to have to give me a minute here, because honestly, I can't re-call when I've been this furious with someone I cared for." His use of the past tense made me cringe. "I mean, we spent last night together. A really nice time, I thought. And you didn't even mention you had a daughter, never mind that it was *my* daughter."

"Aaron, I'm not asking for your forgiveness. Just let me explain."

On the way over, I'd debated whether to tell him about Carly and the money. On one hand, Carly was still the mother of his children. On the other, it was the truth. Whenever possible, I would let that guide me, even when it didn't show me in the best light. So I started from the beginning. How Carly had confronted me in tears almost eighteen years ago. How she'd known about us. Veronica's spying. How I'd lost my pills when I left Memphis in a hurry, and later discovered I was pregnant. I told him about Fish and the money.

I could tell by his white-knuckled grip on the fence that he'd been blindsided by the stuff about Carly and Veronica. When I got to the part about the agreement, he kicked the fence and let out an enraged "Jesus F. Christ."

"I understand this makes things worse for you."

"Worse? No, not worse. A fucking nightmare. Even if Carly comes forward and says I had no part in this contract, no one will believe it. Christ, even I wouldn't believe it." What could I say? He was right. "I'm not trying to blame you, Hope, but when this man offered you money and wouldn't say who was behind it, did you even think of calling me?"

"You *are* trying to blame me, Aaron," I said with some warmth. "And I get it. This sucks for you. But no, I didn't consider contacting you. I thought you'd chosen to marry the rich girl, keep her father's backing, and make your inconvenient child disappear. I believed you'd sold your soul."

"Yeah, well, thanks for your faith in me."

"Put yourself in my shoes. I'd just read how someone leaked that dirt on your opponent, right before that election." I glanced over at Aaron. He looked stricken. "I'm sorry, I know now you wouldn't do that. But at the time . . ." My words trailed off as I watched him close his eyes. It took a moment before I understood. "You *did* do that."

His head dropped. "I lost Shelley over that," he said. "I justified it to myself. I wouldn't have won otherwise." He scuffed the toe of his shoe back and forth in the dirt. "And here it is, back to bite me. We never know what some decisions cost, do we?"

He asked if I'd give him a minute and I nodded. He walked the path to the other end of the park, by the remains of an old wall, where two stone tablets were carved with the Ten Commandments. Surely the irony didn't escape him. He ran his hands through his hair, then squeezed both elbows together, covering his face.

I shuffled over to the bench under the oak and checked my phone. *Dylan, where are you? Please, please, be safe.*

Aaron returned and dropped down beside me. He lifted a fallen twig from the bench and twirled it, as he used to do with pens. "I'm sorry about your run-in with Carly. It took me a long time to accept that her mean streak wasn't going away, no matter how much I tried to love her." He said Carly had called him earlier, after the speech fiasco, to insist he have nothing to do with Dylan. She wasn't his real family. "I hung up on her," Aaron said.

I thought of the financial ruin I faced if Carly chose to enforce our agreement. Could Aaron calm down his ex? Hanging up on her wasn't a good start. I brushed a bug off my ripped skirt. When I lifted my head, he was staring at my clothes.

"You know, I didn't want to ask . . ."

"Yeah, don't." I pulled at my coffee-stained blouse. "Though Carly's iced cappuccino was a nice touch."

The night was growing darker, a few stars visible despite the park lights. A couple wandered down the path holding hands. Aaron's phone beeped and he checked it, said he needed to go. This might surprise me, he said, but he had a public relations disaster to attend to. "Thank you for explaining everything," he added, then did a double take. "That *was* everything, right?"

I nodded.

"Even if I don't agree with it, I'm glad there was a reason you kept my daughter from me. I've been struggling with whether you thought that little of me."

Aaron said he'd walk me to my car, which I had to explain was a truck, and not mine. I also admitted, hesitantly, that I didn't know where Dylan was at the moment but would text him as soon as I found her. *Please God, let me find her.*

As we reached the truck, he said: "I'm going to need time to process this all." He wondered if I could stay in Memphis until they completed the genetic testing, and he issued a press statement. Given I was unemployed, I could. He said he'd be in touch and raised a hand to wave, then hesitated. "I meant to ask. Her name? Dylan?"

"What was the line? Something about staring straight ahead and trying hard to do what's right?"

He nodded. "I thought so."

He waved again and I climbed into the truck. I rolled down the window and closed my eyes, leaning back against the headrest. At the sound of his voice, I jumped.

"Sorry." Aaron's hand rested on the window. "One more

question. When you disappeared all those years ago and I couldn't find you, I thought maybe I'd made more of our relationship than had really been there."

"No," I assured him.

As Aaron walked away, he threw up both hands and called out, "What is it with me and difficult women?"

Chapter 38

Dylan

The Peabody lounge was full of overdressed people sipping cutesy cocktails. The ducks were gone, though, tucked away in their private rooftop villa. Sounded heavenly. As bone-tired as I felt, I couldn't go back to the suite. Olivia would be there and want to hear about my meeting with Breckenridge. I couldn't talk about it. My father was a douchebag. Both my parents were seriously messed up, but of the two, he was worse. The blowhole wouldn't even cop to being my father.

I spotted an open seat at the bar. Well, almost open. A woman in a dress cut down to her ass had left her clutch on the chair next to her while jabbering to her date. I hovered close by and, when the woman leaned in to whisper to her companion, pushed the bag off the chair and squeezed onto it. I could tell the guy on my right, in a T-shirt and jeans, was staring at me. I refused to look his way.

The bartender lifted his chin. What was I having?

"Michelob," I said with the kind of authority I hoped might keep him for asking for ID.

The guy to my right said, "She'll have a Shirley Temple. On me."

My head jerked around. It was George, his hands cupped around a beer. I turned back. "Jesus. What does a girl have to do to be left alone in this town?"

"Been wondering that myself," George said.

The lady with the low-cut dress spun around, searching for her clutch. I pointed at the floor, then stared her down until she bent to retrieve it. The bartender added a cherry to my drink and passed it to me. How much more humiliating could the night get? I hadn't had a Shirley Temple since I was ten.

I twirled my glass, keeping my eyes on the bartender while speaking to George. "Didn't go well tonight."

"So I heard."

My back went up. "Mom told you?"

"No." He pulled his phone out of his pocket, swiped across the screen, and clicked on a saved video called "WREG Breaking News." It showed Aaron Breckenridge jumping down off the stage, a swarm of reporters enveloping him, glimpses of my pink hair through the crowd. Then it cut to Mom outside the auditorium, squinting and trying to block the lights shining in her face. Across the bottom of the screen: "Teen and mother allege paternity at Breckenridge speech."

"Jesus." I rummaged in my bag and pulled out my earbuds. "Can I listen?"

"Be my guest."

I inserted the earbuds and jacked up the volume. A reporter outside the auditorium said she had no information yet about the girl, who said her name was Dylan Robinson. The studio anchor wondered if this revelation, if true, would affect Breckenridge's chances of being chosen as the presidential running mate? Certainly, the reporter replied. While an illegitimate child wasn't necessarily a career killer, it raised a lot of questions. Had Breckenridge cheated on his wife? Did he know about this child? Had he tried to hush it up? "A circus like this couldn't have come at a worse moment for Breckenridge," she concluded. "No presidential candidate wants this dominating the news cycle."

I removed my earbuds and slid the cell back to George. "Well, Aaron Breckenridge deserves it. He's a jerk. He went apeshit at Mom and me."

"Really! Apeshit, you say?"

I flicked him a look. "Yes! He screamed at us."

"Imagine that."

"Not appreciating the sarcasm." I wouldn't let Mom talk to me this way, but I'd always taken it on the chin from George. "Breckenridge is a weenie. That's the word on the street."

"You're right, not good father material. He's got emotions, opinions. Flaws, even. Almost like a real person."

"Enough. I get the point. You weren't there." I sipped my drink. The damn thing was delicious.

"He's not your fantasy dad anymore, Dylan. While he was in your head, he could be anything you wanted him to be. Not so much now."

"I didn't expect him to be perfect."

"Really?"

"Why are you defending him? This guy who, according to you, didn't want anything to do with me?"

"Did I say that?"

"You looked at your shoes."

George frowned—no doubt wondering about the shoes—but admitted, "Yeah, I guess I believed that. Turns out, I didn't know the whole story."

According to George, Mom never told Breckenridge about me. There'd been some . . . miscommunication. That was all George knew, and he was withholding judgment until he learned more. "No doubt Breckenridge could have handled it better, sweetheart, but maybe cut the guy a little slack. You blindsided him. He had no idea whether you're his daughter or some attention-getting troll. You dropped a public bomb-shell during arguably the most pivotal weekend in his life. I dunno . . . maybe not ideal?"

I drained my Shirley Temple, then tapped the glass on the counter to get the bartender's attention. I'd have another. This new information, that Breckenridge hadn't known about me, was making me feel a little shitty. "Politicians do worse stuff all the time. He'll be fine."

George shrugged. "Probably. What gets politicians in more trouble is the cover-up. He'll have to prove he wasn't hiding you all these years." He picked up my earbuds, wound them around his hand, and slid them back to me. "All I'm trying to say is that you took the man by surprise. Slow down. Give him a chance."

I swiveled my chair to face George fully and forgot what I was going to say. His right eye was bruised and swollen. "Jesus, what happened? Did someone hurt you?"

"I believe the person most directly responsible is your

mother," he said, "but I'm over it." George recounted the mix-up at the police station.

I was almost afraid to ask. "Is that . . . why you're dressed like that?"

"Naw. My clothes needed dry cleaning. Jordan will be back tomorrow."

Chapter 39

Hope

I street-parked near the Doubletree and limped across the intersection toward the Peabody. Inside the lobby, as I waited for the elevator, I scanned the lounge. No sign of Dylan. The elevator dinged, and as I moved aside to let a man using a cane exit, a flash of pink caught my eye. My sixteen-year-old daughter sat at the bar, her head on the shoulder of an older man with his arm around her. I speed-hobbled over, ready to sucker punch the asshole.

George glanced up first, which gave me a moment to register the situation before Dylan pivoted to see what he was looking at. A lump the size of Texas lodged in my throat, and I couldn't get out the right words. "Thank God," I wanted to say. Or "I'm so glad you're safe." Or even "I fucked up." Instead, I lurched forward to hug my daughter, who stopped me with a raised hand.

"*So* not ready for that," she said.

George slid off his bar seat, professing a long-held desire to visit the penthouse home of the Peabody ducks. I mouthed a *thank you*, and he raised his eyebrows. *Good luck*, they said.

I slipped onto the chair George had vacated. The bartender, wiping the counter, asked if I'd like another Memphis Blues Martini.

Dylan scowled. "You two know each other?"

"I'll have whatever she's having," I said, pointing to her Shirley Temple.

As the bartender walked away, Dylan balled up her cocktail napkin in her fist. "I don't want to talk about it."

"Okay." I'd take things slow.

Barely a second later, she blurted, "This is all your fault, you know. Why did you lie to me?" She trained her eyes on the bartender as he shook a cocktail. "You could have just said, 'Your father's a jerk. That's why I don't want you to meet him.' I would have accepted that."

"Would you, now!"

Dylan exhaled in disgust. "You sound like Olivia," she said.

I flinched. Dylan didn't know about her grandmother. I'd have to tackle that next. One dumpster fire at a time. "Look, Dylan, Aaron Breckenridge is not a perfect human being. He can be pretty sure of himself. He sometimes loses his temper. Occasionally, he takes political positions that I find convenient. But for the past eighteen years, I've blamed him for things that weren't his fault. That was my mistake, not his."

Dylan fiddled with the paper straw. "Well he sure acted like a flaming asshat tonight."

"I know it seems that way. You may not have caught him at his best."

She pushed her glass forward and twisted in her seat, planning her escape. "I've already been over this with George. I don't need another lecture."

"Okay." I held up a hand. "What *do* you need?"

"How about the truth? Do you think perhaps I deserve that?"

"Yes," I said.

So I told Dylan the truth. When I got to the part about Fish and the money, she gave a little head jerk of surprise. I braced myself for her judgment, but she simply said "Huh" and sipped her drink. I ended with my meeting with Aaron, barely a half hour earlier. "He's still a bit unhappy about how it all unfolded, but he's angry at me, not you."

Dylan used her crumpled cocktail napkin to wipe at something on the bar. "He's not mad I hurt his chance to be vice president?"

I shrugged. "He probably wishes you'd found some other way—"

"I tried!"

I held up a hand. "But that's not where he'll end up, trust me. Give him some time."

She sat with this for a moment, then flicked her head in my direction. "What happened to your clothes?"

I explained that I'd been doored but got more sympathy when I showed her my shattered phone. For a teenager, a fate worse than death.

"It's been a rough two days," I admitted. "But bottom line—and no, I can't believe I'm saying this—I'm glad you forced me to make this trip."

She put a hand over her mouth to suppress a laugh. "You should tell that to Olivia."

"Never," I swore. "And if you do, I'll deny it."

I took a deep breath before telling Dylan about her grandmother. I explained that she was in the hospital, and why. I held nothing back. Tears pooled in Dylan's lower lids. She turned her face from me as they spilled over, some landing on the bar.

"Olivia wouldn't do that," she protested. "She loves me."

I longed to hug my daughter, but sensed it was still too soon. Instead, I handed her a napkin. My go-to move lately.

"Your grandmother does love you. She has her own struggles, and we'll have to be more attentive to that. *I'll* have to be more attentive to that."

"Not everything is your fault, Mom." Her mouth was still trembling, and she pressed her lips together hard before adding, "I mean, *most* things are. But not everything." She sniffled and gave a little smile. My daughter was so beautiful when she smiled.

WHEN I EXPLAINED to the doctor about my mother's PTSD with overnight hospital stays, he agreed to discharge her to my care. Her tests had shown an irregular heart rhythm and though she was in no immediate danger, he suggested she see her cardiologist in Boston about a pacemaker. Naturally, as soon as the doctor left, my mother nixed the idea.

"What would be the point?" she said.

Dylan was having none of it. "Seriously?" she said. "You're going to die and leave me with Mom?" I wasn't sure I appreciated that particular tack, but when my mother patted Dylan's hand and clasped it in her own, I sensed she was more affected than she let on. As Dylan pressed her face under my mother's chin, I realized I'd never hugged my mom like that. Not that I recalled, anyway. Which, of course, didn't mean I couldn't try.

We brought my mother back to the Peabody and I helped her into bed. Dylan lay on the sofa, clicking through TV news stations. Video of Aaron's speech debacle had been picked up by the national news organizations, who'd wasted no time in figuring out who Dylan and I were and where we lived. The fact that my mother was a legendary soap star didn't detract from the story's interest. All three of us had been forced to silence our phones.

The Boston TV stations had interviewed one of Dylan's teachers, a woman who looked like she'd been hauled out of bed, and the owner of the restaurant where my daughter wait-ressed, who spoke affectionately about her table-clearing skills. When the stories started repeating themselves, I turned off the TV and sat in the chair beside Dylan, a glass of water in hand and an ice pack on my knee.

Dylan was still sprawled on the sofa so all I could see was the back of her head. "I don't know if you remember this," she said. "Once when I was little and you were tucking me in bed, I asked you for a photo of my father. You said you didn't have one."

"I remember." I recalled every question she'd ever asked about Aaron, and the gut-wrenching sensation of lying to her.

"Afterward, I heard you crying in the bathroom. I thought you were sad about him."

I stared at the ceiling. "Maybe," I admitted. "I was also an-gry at myself for the choices I'd made. I've had some trouble forgiving myself."

"For lying to me?"

"Among other things."

"Because I sort of get it now. You were keeping a promise. That's kind of admirable."

Of all the ways I'd imagined Dylan interpreting my actions over the years, it had never occurred to me she might see it like that. She'd made a choice, I understood. She chose to see it that way because she loved me. I started to say thank you, but my voice cracked.

She cut in. "Don't get me wrong. It was a stupid promise to make, lying to everyone about your child's father." This sounded more like my daughter. "But I get why you made it. And once you did, you were stuck." She raised herself to a sitting position and plunked her bare feet on the glass coffee table. I didn't say anything. "So here's my question," she said, still not looking at me. "If you had the chance to do it all over again, would you still sleep with Aaron Breckenridge?"

Okay, we were having this conversation! I took a deep breath. "Honestly? I wouldn't change anything if it meant I wouldn't have you."

She seemed pleased enough with that answer. "So we're only telling the truth from now on, right?"

"Trying."

"Okay . . ." I could hear the grin in her voice. "What do you think of my hair color?"

I took a deep breath. "Hate it. Always have."

"Well," she said, dropping her phone on the coffee table. "That's progress, I guess."

As CEMETERIES GO, this one was lovely: lush, green, with stunning white oak trees and a stream. According to my mother, it was the cemetery where Elvis had been buried before his father moved his body to Graceland. I'd never been there before. My father had chosen to be cremated and my mother—never a hiker—had let me scatter his ashes on a scenic ridge in the Great Smoky Mountains National Park.

I parked Dylan's Bug where my mother directed and walked beside her, pulling her oxygen cart across the uneven grass. Even on the short walk, her breathing was labored. We stopped in front of Beth's headstone, which stood by itself under the shadow of a huge oak, a stone bench close by. My mother lowered herself onto the bench, her spine erect as always. I joined her, reading my sister's stone.

ELIZABETH OLIVIA ROBINSON
August 5, 1971–August 21, 1975
Beloved Daughter

"It's a lovely spot," I said.

"Your father picked it out. I was incapable."

Was it too late to tell her how sorry I was for her loss? Would she brush aside any hint of vulnerability, as she so often did?

My mother broke the silence. "Beth would have hated it here. Too quiet."

"Dad said she was a lively kid."

"Loved music. She was belting out 'Hound Dog' at eighteen months."

I chuckled at the idea that Beth had shared my mother's passion for Elvis. But why not? Beth had been born in 1971, not long after my mother's famous date with the King.

I looked again at the headstone. Not that long at all.

I pulled out my phone and Googled the date of Elvis's Los Angeles Forum concern. November 14, 1970. I did the math.

"Mom." I shifted on the bench to face her. "This is a personal question, so you don't have to answer, but . . . did you sleep with Elvis?"

"Not much sleeping went on with Elvis," she said. "He was quite the insomniac."

"You completely dodged the question."

"I did not."

"You did."

"I said we didn't sleep. I didn't say we didn't have sex."

"Jesus, Mom! You *slept* with Elvis?"

"For heaven's sake, Hope. I wasn't the only woman who did."

"I'm not judging," I said, then added, "Well, maybe a little . . ."

"I know I shouldn't have. I was dating your father at the time. Very seriously. But my God, Hope. It was Elvis. What was I to do?"

I stared at her, shaking my head. "And Beth?" My sister, born—as I could now clearly see—nine months after the LA Forum concert. "Was Elvis her . . ."

She threw her hands into the air. "Oh, who the hell knows? It wasn't like today. You couldn't just spit into a tube."

I was grabbing at my hair again, trying to take in all this information. "What about Dad? Did he know?"

"I confessed everything to your father. Went to him the day after my date with Elvis and spared no details. I said, 'If you don't want anything to do with me, I completely understand.' But he did. Amazingly. It was the early seventies, the time of free love. Nobody really knew what the rules were. His solution was to get married quickly, as people did in those days. Then, if

I was pregnant, we wouldn't know for sure who the father was. Harold never mentioned it again. He loved Beth like he loved you, with his whole being. He had no regrets."

"Yes, but . . ." I hesitated. This was a question I'd wanted to ask for a long time. "Your marriage to Dad . . . wasn't ideal."

"By what measure?" she shot back. "Just because a marriage isn't conventional doesn't mean it's not good. Our marriage was as good as most. Probably a damn sight better." She was playing with her rings again. Was she aware? "I loved your father. He loved me. I know you blamed me when he died—for not being there, for not saying the right thing."

"It was the way you talked about it, Mom. You treated that conversation like a joke."

She waved a hand. "That's the way I talk." She adjusted the cannula around her ears, grew quieter. "Guilt and regret are not emotions that sit well with me. Doesn't mean I don't feel them."

We remained silent for a long time on that bench facing my sister's grave. "So, just to be clear on Beth? Her father?"

"No one knows." She smoothed her skirt. "Not even me."

"But Beth's eyes, Mom," I said, remembering them in the photos my father had showed me. They were haunting, deep-set, icy blue. "Her eyes."

"Yes." She smiled. "Lovely, weren't they?"

THE FIVE OF us wandered around Graceland in groups, sometimes catching up with one another, sometimes hanging back to give people space. Jordan was the only one wearing headphones and listening to the narration. She hung on every word and lagged behind the entire way. I let Aaron and Dylan walk ahead while Mom and I lingered to examine Elvis's ancient microwave, the carved Jungle Room chairs, the photos from his youth.

Aaron had pulled strings to get us this private end-of-day visit. I was frankly amazed that Ann Abernathy would allow my mother back on the property. Perhaps she was still afraid of being sued, or maybe she was eager to use my mother's interview. Since Aaron's speech and its aftermath, Olivia Grant had become quite the media darling again, with more talk-show invitations than she'd had in decades. On Memphis's morning show, she'd seemed a little dismayed that so many of the questions posed were about Dylan and me but answered with more pride than I would have expected. She hadn't committed to any national shows yet, though she'd mentioned twice she was "awfully fond of that Ellen DeGeneres."

Not surprisingly, Aaron wasn't chosen for the VP spot on the Democratic ticket. I'm sure he was devastated, but he told everyone that the senator from Virginia was a great guy. After two days camping and fishing with his sons, Aaron was tanned and more relaxed. He was still a bit abrupt with me at times. I expected he would be for a while. He seemed to have put the gruffness aside that afternoon.

The results of the genetic testing had been no surprise: Dylan was Aaron's daughter. Aaron had held a brief press conference with Dylan and his sons by his side. He wanted to introduce his daughter, Dylan Robinson, a delightful addition to his family and surprise to everyone, including him. The reporters had chuckled, then asked some pointed questions about his relationship with a young staff member given his engagement at the time. He acknowledged his lapse in judgment in falling in love with one person while engaged to another. He said he'd tried to do the right thing by sticking with his original commitment, but that things are often more complicated than any of us can foresee.

Out of all that, it was the phrase "falling in love" that made my stomach twist. The two of us had certainly screwed things up.

Aaron had allowed Dylan to answer a few questions about how she'd come to Memphis and her journey to find her father. I thought she presented herself well, though she seemed a different person because of her hair. While Aaron was away, Dylan had gone to a salon and dyed her hair back to her natural brunette color. She claimed she was tired of being defined by her pink hair, but I suspected she wanted to play up the resemblance to her father. It wasn't only the hair, though. Dylan seemed to move differently, more thoughtfully. She often paused before speaking. Perhaps I was imagining it. Or maybe the seeds of a new maturity had been there before, and I'd failed to notice.

I'd brought Dylan to Aaron's condo before the press conference so he could prep her. The media hadn't caught wind of the money Carly had paid me, so the question was whether to raise the issue ourselves. Aaron voted to get out in front of it. Secrets will bite you in the ass, he said, and given the last several days, I couldn't disagree. Of course, he wasn't happy about the probable fallout for him politically. Even though Aaron had known nothing about Carly's agreement, his complicity would be assumed. We'd both seen it happen before. When the wife of a Massachusetts congressional rep was convicted of tax fraud and her husband denied knowledge of it, no one believed him. The congressman lost the next election to a primary challenger.

Aaron's dilemma was compounded by his desire to avoid a

war with his ex and protect his sons. We finally decided on a strategy that, while not perfect, all of us could live with. Aaron would announce at the press conference that he'd learned, through me, I'd been paid to conceal he was Dylan's father. He'd state categorically that he was neither involved with, nor aware of, that agreement. Any further questions would be directed to me. Aaron didn't hold back in explaining what this would mean. I'd be mobbed by reporters thrusting cameras in my face. I'd be vilified by some people, praised by others. I should stay away from Twitter at all costs.

I dreaded the prospect, but it was the least I could do for Aaron. As expected, reporters swarmed around me after the conference. I didn't duck my head or try to hide. I told them the truth: the only person I'd ever met with, and who'd signed the agreement and checks, was a private detective. And no, I wasn't giving up his name.

The coverage played out just as badly as we feared. Aaron's opponents came right out and accused him of paying me off. "Nothing we can do," he texted back when I messaged him to apologize. "We can't control the media."

Then something surprising happened. Later that evening, a Memphis station aired breaking news. A detective named Marlin A. Fish had come forward and admitted he was the person who'd negotiated my agreement. No, he couldn't say who his client was. The one thing he was willing to say: it was not Aaron Breckenridge. Yes, he was quite sure. His client had gone to great lengths so Breckenridge wouldn't find out.

Most people probably didn't see what I saw. As the reporter badgered Fish, asking, "Was it one of Breckenridge's political backers? Someone in his ex-wife's family?" Fish gave an almost imperceptible smile before turning away.

AFTER THE PRESS conference, Aaron invited Dylan to go out on his boat with him and the boys, and she eagerly accepted. Dylan wanted to grill him on some political issues. Exactly what Aaron was hoping for, no doubt.

When I dropped Dylan off at his condo, Aaron asked to speak to me. He flipped on the TV, told Dylan to make herself at home, and motioned for me to follow him. He opened the door to his bedroom.

"Sorry, it's the only place to talk privately."

I could feel the warmth in my face as I recalled the last time we had been in the room. It didn't help when Dylan called out, "You two behave in there."

Perhaps in response to her comment, Aaron walked to the other side of the room and leaned against the windowsill. "We should discuss financial arrangements."

"I'm sorry?"

"I have a responsibility here."

"I hate to bring this up, but your ex-wife already contributed a fair amount. As long as she doesn't sue me for trashing our agreement."

"No worries," Aaron said. "Carly will never mention that agreement again. And that isn't the point, anyway. This money should come from me."

"I don't want your money," I said.

"Well, it's not for you, Hope." He did an exaggerated eye roll. "I can at least help pay for Dylan's college."

"Fine. You talk to her about college. Good luck with that."

He raised his eyebrows. "Duly noted."

GARY CALLED ME on Wednesday. After seeing the news coverage, he'd felt bad about the way he'd treated me. He didn't apologize, exactly, but if I wanted my job back, he'd listen. He believed in me.

I thanked him and declined.

"No?"

I laughed. "I'm working on a project for a new client."

Gary was appalled. "Who's *that*?"

"Me. And you know what's even funnier? The *project* is me, as well. Turns out, it doesn't matter if you believe in me, Gary. Only matters if I do."

I've made myself sound braver than I was. In the days between the speech debacle and press conference, I'd found career support from an unexpected source: my mother. I shared my desire to join a nonprofit, work for a cause I believe in, as I'd done on Aaron's campaign. When I said I couldn't without a college degree, she puffed dismissively.

"Go back and get it now," she said, as if it were the most obvious thing in the world.

"Easy for you to say, Mom. I have a mortgage. I can't take out loans."

"I'll pay for it."

"Thanks, but I can't let you do that. Not after what happened with Rafe."

"Rafe?" She frowned.

"The guy who took all your money?"

"*All* my money? Did I say that?" she asked. "Oh, dear, no.

The man took everything in that checking account—and it was a sum, I won't deny that—but you didn't think I'd give him access to everything, did you?"

"Oh," I said. Because I *had* thought that. Living as frugally as I had all my life, it never occurred to me someone might have more than one checking account.

"You may not realize this," she continued, "but in the past, I've had trouble parting with money."

"You, Mom?"

She gave me a sidelong glance. "Nothing like lying on Elvis's grave to grant one perspective."

AND NOW WE were back in Graceland's Meditation Garden, my mother and I, reflecting on the graves of Elvis, his parents, and his grandmother, and the memorial to his stillborn twin. As I studied the dates, I realized for the first time that Elvis had been survived by both his father and his grandmother. How sad when a parent outlives a child, at any age.

Dylan and Aaron had finished the tour. She was taking selfies in front of the mansion while Aaron strolled back in my direction. I went to meet him, leaving my mother to commune with Elvis.

"What would you think," he said, pausing to feel out this new coparenting relationship, "about Dylan spending the rest of the summer in DC? She could do intern work for my office. It would look good on her college applications."

I raised my eyebrows. "You've known her for four days and you've talked her into college?"

He grimaced comically. "Well, I'm not sure how you feel about this, but I floated the idea of a gap year between high school and college." He stepped back, unsure whether I might hit him.

I tamped down my inner mama bear. "Keep talking."

"What impresses me is her interest in policy. She and I debated different issues for almost an hour on the boat, until my sons were ready to kill us. It's something she might want to explore." He glanced at me nervously. "Just an idea."

I tried to picture my daughter by herself, in a city ten hours from Boston. Only she wouldn't be by herself. "Let's take this one step at a time," I said. "Pitch me the summer idea first."

Aaron had clearly given it some thought. Dylan could stay with him, or, if he were traveling, with a couple he knew. It would be a great opportunity for them to get to know one another. I tried to focus on the upside but kept imagining my summer without Dylan. I hadn't been prepared to let her go so soon. Maybe I hadn't been prepared at all.

"Be careful what you ask for," I warned. "Dylan can be a challenge."

He gave a little head tilt. "I'd say she comes by that honestly."

"Hope," Jordan called out, emerging from a turn in the path. "Don't leave without me. This place is fascinating."

I waved my reassurance. She was wearing a new tangerine skirt and polka-dot blouse that Dylan had helped her pick out. They'd been shopping.

"By the way," Aaron said. "I like Jordan a lot. But she took a selfie of the two of us in the TV room and it's not flattering. My eyes were closed."

"That's your concern? Your eyes?" I teased. "Not to worry. Jordan would never post a photo without asking."

"Well then, I'm reassured," he deadpanned. "God knows, I can put a lot of trust in you, Hope."

As he jogged back toward Dylan, I thought, Yep, gonna be some time before he forgives me.

My mother untied the red scarf from around her neck and tossed it over the low fence. It caught a breeze and unfurled, dropping on the corner of Elvis's grave. She turned to me. "This is the part where you tell me I was right all along."

"I wouldn't hold your breath on that, Mom."

She adjusted her cannula. "Oh, be honest! A trip to Grace-land was exactly what this family needed."

"Apparently it was what you needed. You got to commune with Elvis, unite Dylan with her father, and meddle in a presidential election. Are you satisfied?"

"For now." She looked to where Aaron was taking a photo of Dylan. "But Hope, you need to be honest with that man about your feelings."

I bristled. "And you know my feelings how?"

"You're a terrible actress."

"Trying to hear that as a compliment."

"He cares for you. I see it in his eyes. Take the initiative. Go after what you want." She removed her sunglasses. "I've been thinking . . . ," she said.

"Oh God." I closed my eyes.

"There are some Elvis artifacts at the Smithsonian." She'd lifted her face toward the setting sun, which gave her cheeks a reddish glow. "And before I die, I'd like to visit Washington, DC, again."

"Nice, Mom. We'll discuss later."

"Well, you know," she said, turning toward the exit, "I don't have much time."

I put my arm around her waist in a way that was unfamiliar, but perhaps not as uncomfortable as I might have imagined, and guided her toward the drive. The two of us stared straight ahead, being extra careful of our footing on the path in the waning light.

Acknowledgments

For me, writing a novel didn't just take a village, it took a small country. Plus a bit of Canada.

I'd been writing short, humorous pieces, and I thought all I had to do was string together, like, eighty of them. Ha! Pride cometh before a workshop. Happily, I had a few great mentors and a lot of amazing friends and fellow writers who were both encouraging and—more importantly—honest.

A thousand thanks and vows of eternal devotion to the following people:

My agent, Paige Sisley, for believing in my writing and laughing at my jokes. I'm sorry I made you spit your tea.

My editor, Asanté Simons, for loving *Graceland*, especially the character of Olivia. Olivia loves you right back, Asanté. She's asking about a road trip to New York City.

The extraordinary Michelle Hoover, who leads a year-long course called the Novel Incubator at Boston's GrubStreet and guides writers from shaky first draft to ready-for-prime-time. Michelle helped me take *Graceland* to the next level while chuckling in all the right places and being an unflagging cheerleader.

My nine compatriots in the Novel Incubator program

offered (and some continue to offer) invaluable insights. Thank you, my dear friends: Shalene Gupta, Madeleine Hall, Eson Kim, Meghana Ranganathan, (Lily) Yichen Shi-Naseer, Richard Sullivan, David Schiffer, Reid Sherline, and Kristin Waites Bennett.

Michelle Wildgen, for an amazing developmental edit that that allowed me to see new possibilities in my work and kill some darlings who, quite frankly, were asking for it.

Michael Lowenthal, who writes critique letters so gorgeous and funny that the Pulitzer people need to create a new category. Mike's brilliance and charm are matched only by his devastatingly good looks. (Ha! Didn't think I would take that bet, did you?)

Henriette Lazaridis and the writers in a twelve-week novel intensive course, who workshopped early chapters and kept me from steering my road trip down some odd rabbit holes.

Mary Carroll Moore and the students in her online course, for helping me breathe through the labor and delivery of newborn scenes. Mary once sat with me at a conference breakfast and offered advice that kept me from stabbing my novel with a butter knife.

Christopher Castellani and his workshop group at the Bread Loaf Writers' Conference in Sicily (yes, that's a thing, and it's fabulous), for a memorable week of critique and pasta. Tricia Crisafulli, your enthusiasm for my story was life changing.

Graceland is a work of imagination, though sprinkled with some real people, settings, and events. Some aspects of the novel required a lot of research, like pinpointing a concert date when Elvis might have been free from other entanglements and available to party with Olivia Grant. Others, like what goes on in a jail cell at 201 Poplar in Memphis, are mostly imagined. (Though I thank the unnamed officer there, who guardedly answered my questions, not buying a word of my "I'm writing a book" story.)

Thanks, too, to the following advisers for their assistance with important details. Any errors are my own.

Sensitivity readers Milo Todd, Declan DeWitt Hall, and Suzanne DeWitt Hall provided invaluable guidance with the character of George/Jordan, and Raina Brown offered amazing age- and era-appropriate insights for Dylan.

Dr. Heather Awad and Dr. Jan Richardson generously advised me on medical issues.

Wayne Dowdy at Benjamin L. Hooks Central Library in Memphis provided background on how the city changed over the eighteen years of this story.

The spunky, unforgettable Betty Pike taught me about COPD and life with oxygen tanks back in 2015. Betty always spoke her mind, though she tended to do so more nicely than Olivia.

Many friends read drafts of the entire manuscript, and I am forever in their debt: Elizabeth Atkinson, Heidi Love, John Mercer, Sharon Adams Poore, Pam Richardson, Julia Rold, and Elizabeth Weinstein. Others read early chapters or shared their expertise: Chuck Latovich, Susan Paradis, Holly Robinson, Cyd Raschke, Adair Rowland, Donna Seim, and Bettina Turner. Cynthia Albrecht and Cynthia Ward helped with eleventh-hour editing questions.

The alumni from twelve years (and counting) of the Novel Incubator program have become a huge family, and many offered mentorship, encouragement, query-critiques, and publishing advice. Pam Loring, Louise Miller, and Cameron Dryden come to mind, though I'm sure I'm forgetting others and will beat myself up later. Julie Carrick Dalton has been an invaluable mentor, generously sharing her publishing experiences. My cohort from a post–Novel Incubator class provided pandemic companionship and critique: Lisa Birk, Marc Foster, Carol Gray, David Goldstein, Rick Hendrie, Rose Himber Howse, Sharissa Jones, Eson Kim, James LaRowe, Emily Ross, Mandy Syers, and Leslie Teel.

Thank you to the Unbound Book Festival for choosing the first page of *Graceland* as a winner in their "First-Page Rodeo" back in 2016. It was, indeed, my first rodeo.

Thanks to my sisters, Carol Dunlop and Jeanne Schmitt, for believing I could do this, and to Mary Rider for cheering me on. To my book group, you are too numerous to name but I love you all, and your champagne toast when I got a book deal meant more to me than you know. To my dear friends Clark Baxter, Sharon Adams Poore, Roy Craig, Rhona Robbin, Lisa Pinto, and Susan and Rob Shaw-Meadow, thank you for ceaselessly buoying me up with emails, Zoom check-ins, phone calls, and pomegranate martinis.

Riding shotgun on my trips to Memphis were two BFFs who also read multiple drafts of the manuscript. My partner-in-crime since kindergarten, Tracy Plass, has always played Butch to my Sundance, and someday we'll end up in Bolivia together. Susan Beauchamp, my Tobacco Princess, you are my ride or die. The next one's for you.

Finally, nothing would have been possible without the loving support of my husband, Paul, and two daughters, Danielle Cantor and Rebecca Crochiere, and their spouses and families. Thank you for your patience, belief in me, and nonstop cheerleading. I'm sure you're just happy I'm no longer writing columns about you.

DARK PASSAGES

The Decadent Consciousness in Victorian Literature

Barbara Charlesworth

Dark Passages

THE DECADENT CONSCIOUSNESS

IN

VICTORIAN LITERATURE

The University of Wisconsin Press

Madison and Milwaukee, 1965

Published by the University of Wisconsin Press
Madison and Milwaukee
Mailing address: P.O. Box 1379, Madison, Wisconsin 53701
Editorial offices: 430 Sterling Court, Madison

Printed in the United States of America
by the North American Press, Milwaukee, Wisconsin

Library of Congress Catalog Card Number 64–7724

For my parents

. . . many doors are set open—but all dark—
all leading to dark passages—
We see not the ballance of good and evil.

John Keats,
Letter to John Hamilton Reynolds,
3 *May* 1818.

Acknowledgments

This book was originally a thesis written under the direction of Professor Jerome Buckley, and I am happy to have the opportunity now of thanking him for all the help he gave me. I am grateful too to Professors Douglas Bush, W. J. Bate, Howard Mumford Jones, and Clark Emery for their encouragement and advice. Professor Denis Donoghue's suggestions aided me greatly in my revision of the manuscript—a revision made possible through a summer faculty fellowship from the University of California—and many other friends have made helpful suggestions: particularly Professors Edgar Bowers, Adele Emery, Albert Gelpi, Robert Kiely, Joel Porte, Jill Conway, and Dennis Chaldecott.

The librarians of Houghton Library and of the Widener Collection as well as those at the University of Miami, the University of California at Santa Barbara, and the William Andrews Clark library have all made my way easier. Indeed, given the book's theme, it seems ironic that while working on *Dark Passages* I have met with nothing but help and human kindness and at every step of my way have time and again had pleasant conversations about Decadence, self-centeredness, isolation, and despair.

B. C.

Santa Barbara, California
July, 1964

Contents

> The heart should have fed
> upon the truth, as insects on a leaf, till it be tinged
> with the colour, and show its food
> in every . . . minutest fibre.
> *S. T. Coleridge*

Introduction

Perhaps the term "Decadence" is useful only to mark off boundaries: to delineate a period in English literary history between approximately 1890 and 1900. For if it is used to describe the characteristics of literature or of writers during that period the word obscures thought. It carries the implication that the Romantic tradition came to a whimpering end in the nineties and that modern poetry began in, say, 1910. Such a patterning of literary history, given our awareness of the intellectual and emotional involvement which such modern poets as Yeats, Pound, Eliot, Stevens, and Frost had with the ideas and feelings of the nineties, is naïve. The 1890's, like the 1790's, was a period of change, and if part of that change was a gradual stiffening of old forms and old ideas, part of it was also the growth of new ones. The term, in other words, conveys only half, the less important half, of the process. And yet, like the words "Gothic" and "Romantic," it has acquired a certain authority and grace through usage and thus communicates more than a newly coined word might.

Anecdotes about the colorful personalities of the nineties are often delightful, but beneath them, as beneath the lives of the people whom they describe, one has a sense of sadness and frustration. Graham Hough captures that sense when he describes the period as one of "an immense number of false starts and blind alleys, and not a few personal tragedies, all directed to finding some sort of accommodation between art and a bourgeois industrial society."[1] The problem for these artists might be described as one of self-definition in a society whose values they felt they could not accept.

G. H. Mead gives this explanation of the way in which a self is created: "The human self arises through its ability to take the attitude of the group to which he belongs—because he can talk to himself in terms of the community to which he belongs and lay upon himself the responsibilities that belong to the community; because he can recognize his own duties as over against others—that is what constitutes the self as such."[2] His definition of self offers a means of understanding the dilemma in which the artists of the late nineteenth century found themselves: they could not accept the religious, social, or economic attitudes of their society. In religion their choice, as they saw it, lay between an overly rational "muscular Christianity" and an anti-intellectual fundamentalist faith; in economics between the harshness of *laissez-faire* and the sentimentality of philanthropic works. And the society created by such economic attitudes and upheld by such religious beliefs was spiritually, emotionally, and intellectually confused. It offered no community to which they wished to belong and no responsibilities which they felt they should undertake.

It is not necessary, however, that a man approve of his society in order to create a self by taking its attitudes. Matthew Arnold is a case in point. Although painfully aware of the faults of his own age, he found a role in it by seeking to reform those faults. The same is true of Ruskin, Morris, Shaw, and other Victorian "reformers." In order to effect changes in society, these men were obliged to communicate with its members, and they could do so only by putting themselves in the place of those whose attitudes they wished to modify or correct. Through that dialogue with society each created a self.

But there were those who believed that such a dialogue was impossible. The most succinct and influential statement of their position is Walter Pater's "Conclusion" to *The Renaissance*. Its premise is that nothing outside the mind has any meaning save that given it by the mind. Everyone creates for himself a reality which is personal, incommunicable, and imprisoning. However, each individual has sensory experience as a means of escape to the world outside the mind. Such experience may be an illusory escape, but the question of its truth or falsehood simply does not apply, for the mind gives it reality.

Only one of the senses receives no mention in Pater's "Conclusion": hearing. For each individual is a "solitary prisoner," and there is no communication from cell to cell. Nevertheless, each can turn his attention to forms momentarily beautiful and discipline himself to catch them at precisely that moment of perfect beauty: "Every moment some form grows perfect in hand or face; some tone on the hills or the sea is choicer than the rest; some mood of passion or insight or intellectual excitement is irresistibly real and attractive to us,—for that moment only."[3]

It is possible, then—even if somewhat arbitrary—to divide Victorian society into three groups: the Philistines whose ideal was the attainment of wealth, power, and physical luxuries and whose selves were formed by the attainment of those things through social institutions; the Reformers whose ideal was the attainment of the good, the humane life and whose selves were formed in the attempt to apply that ideal within society; the Decadents whose ideal was the attainment of as many moments as possible of heightened sensory experience, enjoyed within the mind outside the society. Members of the first group, with its solid objectives, created solid selves—although in doing so they led their society into the First World War. In the end, then, they worked more harm to society than did the Decadents. But although the Decadents were correct when they believed the Philistine ideals to be false, their own alternative ideal was a destructive one which led them into personal disaster. In the "moment" they had not a proper basis upon which to form a self. The consequence of their attempt to put it to that purpose was the Decadent self, impermanent and insubstantial, a self dependent upon the moment, a series of selves, separate and distinct from one another, appearing and vanishing on the continuum of time.

This state closely resembles that which George Santayana describes as the condition of the sceptical solipsist:

> He will see the masked actors (and he will invent a reason) rushing frantically out on one side and in at the other; but he knows that the moment they are out of sight the play is over for them; those outlying regions and those reported events which messengers narrate so impressively are pure fancy; and there is nothing for him but to sit in his seat and lend his mind to the tragic illusion.
>
> The solipsist thus becomes an incredulous spectator of his own romance, thinks his own adventures fictions, and accepts a solipsism of the present moment.[4]

None of the figures who appear in this study is a consistent sceptical solipsist, but all subscribed at least in part and for a time to what Arthur Symons describes as the ideal of Decadence: "to fix the last fine shade, to fix it fleetingly; to be a disembodied voice, and yet the voice of a human soul."[5] They do not, of course, represent the whole company of those who shared the ideal; even such important figures as Ernest Dowson and Aubrey Beardsley are absent. My purpose, however, is not to consider every Decadent in the light of the ideal but to study the ideal as it affected some who lived by it.

Since my concern is primarily with the 1890's, it may seem quixotic to devote so much of the book to a discussion of D. G. Rossetti, A. C. Swinburne, and Walter Pater. None of these men belonged to the Decadent generation; Rossetti died in 1882, Pater in 1894, and Swinburne, although alive throughout the nineties, had only the slightest personal connection with any of the Decadents. It is not, however, the physical absence or presence of these three that is significant but rather their intellectual, moral, and emotional influence upon the men of "the tragic generation." The latter were so conscious of being disciples that any attempt to understand them must begin with a consideration of their masters.

DARK PASSAGES

The Decadent Consciousness in Victorian Literature

It is bad enough when there
is a gifted and powerful opposition to the teaching of the
best minds in any period: but when the best
minds themselves are on a false tack,
who shall stem the tide?
D. G. Rossetti

Chapter I

Dante Gabriel Rossetti

The first number of the Pre-Raphaelites' short-lived magazine
The Germ, which appeared in January, 1850, contains a parable
by D. G. Rossetti called "Hand and Soul." It is a story about
Chiaro dell 'Erma, a young artist of extraordinary sensibility, who
passionately loved the outward aspect of all natural things and
in his love for them wanted to depict them worthily: "The extreme
longing after a visible embodiment of his thoughts strengthened
as the years increased . . . until he would feel faint in sunsets and
at the sight of stately persons."[1] He was ambitious for worldly
fame as well—and indeed he quickly achieved it—but in his work
he tried always to offset his ambition by making his art a means
by which to worship God. Even so, he came to feel that "much
of the reverence which he had mistaken for faith had been no
more than the worship of beauty." And he reacted by creating
works of art which had moral instruction as their conscious aim.

These were large "public" paintings, allegorical depictions of virtue.

Then one day, as he looked out from the window of his room, Chiaro saw the large allegorical fresco of Peace which he had painted on a church wall spattered by the blood of townsmen fighting among themselves in the square. In despair he felt that religious belief and ambition and even morality had failed him. At that moment a beautiful woman appeared in the room. She called herself the image of his own soul and told him to distress himself no further over whether or not he was fulfilling God's will: "What He hath set in thy heart to do, that do thou, and even though thou do it without thought of Him, it shall be well done." It is, in other words, God's will that the artist work for art's sake. And she concluded: "Chiaro, servant of God, take now thine Art unto thee, and paint me thus, as I am, to know me . . . . Do this; so shall thy soul stand before thee always, and perplex thee no more" (*CW*, I, 394–95).

A strange story, one that creates more perplexities than it solves. Rossetti's conscious desire, one gathers, is to make a statement through it about the relationship between art and morality. That art which has a consciously moral intention will be bad because it imposes a pattern on life instead of discovering a pattern in life; in his depreciation of Chiaro's cold allegories, Rossetti is repeating the "organic" theories of Romantic criticism. His conception of good art, however, shows his own modification of those theories: such art is created by a man alone in his room who paints the picture of his own soul. But there are questions which his theory leaves unanswered: if a man's soul stands always before him, will it no longer perplex him? is a man's own soul all that he can ever know? can he, for that matter, know his soul? And so around again. Like the phrase "art for art's sake" the questions turn back upon themselves; they encircle and imprison the artist whom it was the story's conscious intention to set free.

To the Decadents Rossetti was himself a Chiaro dell 'Erma, type of the ideal artist. Their descriptions of him, then, are also further definitions of that ideal, and it is noteworthy that they put special stress upon his isolation from society. Wilde describes him as "a pillar of fire to the few who knew him, and a cloud to the many who knew him not."[2] Arthur Symons thinks of him as one who never cared to leave the dream world of his own imagination, but who lived, wrote, and painted in an interior world "like a perfectly contented prisoner to whom the sense of imprisonment is a joy." Symons mentions another characteristic by which Rossetti exemplifies the true artist: his desire to live, as much as possible, in a state of heightened awareness amounting to ecstasy. In his own interior world, conscious only of "the love of beauty, the love of love" he lived an imaginative life in which at every moment he might hope for some new revelation of love or of beauty.[3]

As it worked out in practice, Rossetti's conception of the artist's life is very close to that which Tennyson had symbolized in "The Lady of Shalott," one of the Pre-Raphaelites' favorite poems. Its central image is that of a lady who, though forbidden to look directly at the scenes of life, weaves into her "magic web" images of the world which she sees reflected in a mirror. Like her, the artist creates beautiful forms from those "magic sights" mirrored in his imagination. But if he has the gift which enables him to do this, he may not turn his gaze from the mirror to the world; he must live, like the Lady of Shalott, in a world of shadows, separated from the common life of men. "Here is a fine saying of Keats's in one of his letters," Rossetti wrote to his mother; " 'I value more the privilege of seeing great things in loneliness than the fame of a prophet.' "[4] Pater echoes his approval of solitude when he writes of the glimpses of landscape one catches in Rossetti's poems, "not indeed of broad open-air effects, but rather of a painter concentrated upon the picturesque effect of one or two selected objects at a time . . . as he sees it from one of the windows, or reflected in one of the mirrors of his 'house of life.' "[5] His identification of Rossetti with the Lady of Shalott is clear; so too is his intimation that in writing as he did Rossetti had accepted a thought which lesser souls might not be able to bear: that we are each of us enclosed in a room lined with mirrors.

There remains, however, the question: if the artist's gaze is necessarily fixed upon the mirror of his imagination, by what standard is he to judge the reality of what he sees? Behind that question lies the possibility of a loneliness in which the only "great things" before him are vast shadows of himself. Coleridge described it at the conclusion of "Constancy to an Ideal Object." Writing of his love for a woman, he wonders whether the woman as he thinks he knows her and the love he believes himself to feel for her are not both creations of his own imagination:

> And art thou nothing? Such thou art, as when
> The woodman winding westward up the glen
> At wintry dawn, where o'er the sheep track's maze
> The view-less snow-mist weaves a glistening haze,
> Sees full before him, gliding without tread,
> An image with a glory round its head;
> The enamoured rustic worships its fair hues
> Nor knows he makes the shadow he pursues![6]

Yeats brings together many of these ideas as he considers the tragic lives of Dowson and Johnson. He wonders whether the poetry of Coleridge and of Rossetti might not help to explain that tragedy. First he alludes to the conflict between art and morality by describing Lord Burghley's objection to Spenser's islands of Phaedria and Acrasia, and he continues, "In those islands certain qualities of beauty, certain forms of sensuous loveliness were separated from all the general purposes of life, as they had not been hitherto in European literature." Most poets, including Spenser, have had some means of sharing in the life of their time, "some propaganda or traditional doctrine to give companionship with their fellows":

But Coleridge of the *Ancient Mariner*, and *Kubla Khan*, and Rossetti in all his writing made what Arnold called that "morbid effort," that search for "perfection of thought and feeling, and to unite this to perfection of form," sought this new, pure beauty, and suffered in their lives because of it.[7]

The story of Rossetti's search is found in his sonnet sequence, *The House of Life*. It describes his purpose, his method, and the result of his quest.

Rossetti, as we have noted, wanted to live continuously in a state of heightened perception. Such a life is, of course, not feasible, and so he contented himself with striving for as many moments as possible in such a state. With a theory somewhat resembling Wordsworth's doctrine of "recollection in tranquillity,"

he made of the sonnet both a talisman by which the moment
might be prolonged and a memorial in which its passing might
be commemorated. "I hardly ever do produce a sonnet," he wrote
to William Bell Scott, "except on the basis of special momentary
emotion." [8] And the introductory sonnet of *The House of Life*
stresses the occasional aspect of the work:

> A Sonnet is a moment's monument,—
> Memorial from the Soul's eternity
> To one dead deathless hour.

Had the moment not passed, there would be no need for the
poem. Each sonnet of *The House of Life* recalls a "deathless
hour," but each is a monument to a *dead,* deathless hour.

Rossetti begins, then, with a dignified admission of defeat, and
the same proud submissiveness motivates his demand that the
moment be described with all possible care and ceremony. Like
Pater, he insists on a clear hard outline, not for the form's sake
alone but for the better preservation of the moment:

> Look that it be
> Whether for lustral rite or dire portent
> Of its own arduous fulness reverent:
> Carve it in ivory or in ebony,
> As Day, or Night may rule; and let Time see
> Its flowering crest impearled and orient.
> (*CW,* I, 176)

Rossetti's emphasis upon the "moment" is related to his painting as well as his poetry. A sonnet written in very early Pre-
Raphaelite days shows his belief in the revelatory power of the
moment's insight; the painter's depiction of a particular scene
caught at a specific time becomes, by a process resembling
metonomy in language, a "tangible equivalent" (in Kenneth
Burke's phrase) of a spiritual reality. Tracing the history of art,
Rossetti makes its climax that period in which

> soon having wist
> How sky breadth and field-silence and this day
> Are symbols also in some deeper way,
> She looked through these to God and was God's priest.
> (*CW,* I, 214)

The step from this doctrine to the theories of Symbolism is a short one, and Arthur Symons, who was to make that step, took special note of the interest of the Pre-Raphaelites in life's critical moments.[9]

Prosper Mérimée criticized the Pre-Raphaelite brotherhood for failing to distinguish properly between poetry and painting. In his opinion they had not read Lessing's *Laocoön* with sufficient care; they attempted to record a conversation, when painting should confine itself to a single instant of time.[10] But Mérimée's criticism has only a reverse application to Rossetti's work. It is true that Rossetti makes little distinction between the temporal and spatial arts, but he confuses them not so much by attempting to make time a part of his canvas as by trying to describe in poetry that single instant which sculpture and painting are, but poetry is not, equipped to render.

In 1849 Rossetti visited the Louvre and wrote a sonnet about Giorgione's "Venetian Pastoral"; for half a century after that the picture was a symbol of the "exquisite moment":

> Water, for anguish of the solstice:—nay
> But dip the vessel slowly,—nay, but lean
> And hark how at its verge the wave sighs in
> Reluctant. Hush! beyond all depth away
> The heat lies silent at the brink of day:
> Now the hand trails upon the viol-string
> That sobs, and the brown faces cease to sing,
> Sad with the whole of pleasure. Whither stray
> Her eyes now, from whose mouth the slim pipes creep
> And leave it pouting, while the shadowed grass
> Is cool against her naked side? let be:—
> Say nothing now unto her lest she weep,
> Nor name this ever. Be it as it was,—
> Life touching lips with immortality.
>
> ("For a Venetian Pastoral, by Giorgione," *CW*, I, 345)

This revised version of the sonnet appeared in *Poems* of 1870; originally the last line had read, "Silence of heat and solemn poetry." William Rossetti expressed a preference for the earlier version, thinking the revised one too "ideal," but Rossetti disagreed, saying that his revision gave "the momentary contact with the immortal which results from sensuous culmination, and is always a half-conscious element of it."[11] The moment of most intense sensuous perception is at the same time a moment of spiritual insight, perhaps of vision.

Such was Rossetti's faith. His difficulty lay in the fact that it *was* faith. What link could he posit between objects in experience and a spiritual reality of which they are symbols save that of his own imagination? As we shall see, the possibility that "God and the Imagination are one" did occur to Rossetti—and later to Symons—as it had to Coleridge, but in the face of such a thought they had none of Stevens' calm.

Pater, who worked out the aesthetic theory of the moment far more elaborately than did Rossetti, made Rossetti his exemplar of one to whom "life is a crisis at every moment."[12] Symons expanded and intensified that thought in describing Rossetti's central motivations, those which gave his life its pattern: "Here [in Rossetti] all energy is concentrated on the one ecstasy, and this exists for its own sake, and the desire of it is like a thirst, which returns after every partial satisfaction. The desire of beauty, the love of love, can be but a form of martyrdom when, as with Rossetti, there is also the desire of possession."[13] His vision of Rossetti's life has its justification in the poem "Soul's Beauty." There Rossetti describes himself as a Romantic wanderer pursuing an ideal of love and beauty which constantly eludes him. The pursuit is "a form of martyrdom," and there is no suggestion that the wanderer will ever come to the end of his journey:

> This is that Lady Beauty in whose praise
> Thy hand and voice shake still—long known to thee
> By flying hair and fluttering hem—the beat
> Following her daily of thy heart and feet,
> How passionately and irretrievably,
> In what fond flight, how many ways and days!
> (*CW*, I, 215)

But in earlier sonnets of *The House of Life* there are moments in which the quest seems to have gained its end. The beauty of an earthly woman is incarnation, symbol, proof of ideal beauty:

> Sometimes thou seemest not as thyself alone,
> But as the meaning of all things that are;
> A breathless wonder, shadowing forth afar
> Some heavenly solstice, hushed and halcyon;
> Whose unstirred lips are music's visible tone,
> Whose eyes the sun-gates of the soul unbar,
> Being of its furthest fires oracular;—
> The evident heart of all life sown and mown.
>
> ("Heart's Compass," *CW*, I, 190)

Just before "Heart's Compass" is a sonnet, "Mid-rapture," which describes the poet's worship of Beauty made manifest:

> What word can answer to thy word—what gaze
> To thine, which now absorbs within its sphere
> My worshiping face, till I am mirrored there
> Light-circled in a heaven of deep-drawn rays?
>
> (*CW*, I, 189)

At first the beloved is described in terms usually applied to transcendent beauty; she is a beatific vision in which the poet loses all consciousness of self; then, in front of one's eyes, as it were, the sense of a human face disappears, to be replaced by a mirror reflecting upon the worshipper an idealized image of himself. Here, as in Coleridge's poem, is "an image with a glory round its head," a magnified shadow of the self, but the tone of "Mid-rapture" and of "Heart's Compass" following it does not suggest that Rossetti intended to give the image that meaning. His thought, rather, is that in the contemplation of love and beauty the self is at once lost and glorified. But the image he uses to express his idea is significant.

Such ecstatic moments are not the only ones which Rossetti finds meaningful and desires to commemorate in verse. Often he wishes to hold fast those times in which he is suddenly conscious of the warmth, safety, and comfort of love in a world ordinarily harsh and unfeeling. He writes in "The Monochord" of the love that "draws round me at last this wind-warm space" after "the lifted shifted steeps and all the way" (*CW*, I, 216). With the sudden harmony and sense of communion that it brings, the moment serves as might a small shelter in the lee of the wind to a mountain-climber.

Remembered afterward the moment is a sanctuary; while it is experienced it is a "sensuous culmination." A poem like "Silent Noon" shows how both aspects of the moment may create together a perfect instant of time, a heaven-haven. In "Silent Noon" the impersonal appreciation of Giorgione's "Venetian Pastoral" becomes personal description of an earthly Paradise:

> Your hands lie open in the long fresh grass,—
> The finger-points look through like rosy blooms:
> Your eyes smile peace. The pasture gleams and glooms
> 'Neath billowing skies that scatter and amass.
> All round our nest, far as the eye can pass,
> Are golden king-cup fields with silver edge
> Where the cow-parsley skirts the hawthorn hedge.
> 'Tis visible silence, still as the hour glass.
>
> Deep in the sun-searched depths the dragon-fly
> Hangs like a blue thread loosened from the sky:—
> So this wing'd hour is dropt to us from above.
> O! clasp we to our hearts, for deathless dower,
> This close-companioned inarticulate hour,
> When two-fold silence was the song of love.
>
> (*CW*, I, 186)

Though Rossetti evokes a scene of perfect silence, harmony, and peace and, as it were, fills the center of his mind and his emotions with these qualities, still time and change move menacingly around the outskirts; they show themselves in the "billowing skies that scatter and amass," in the hour-glass which, though motionless itself, is a symbol of mutability, and in the knowledge that this hour is "wing'd." And yet time and change may not be such dreadful enemies, for by the contrast they provide to its permanence and eternity within the mind they serve to deepen the intensity of the moment within the poem. This "sensuous culmination" has no violence in it; the passion is *there* in the poem, but it is mingled—as so often in Pater's work also—with a deeply inward, quiet melancholy. A similar melancholy characterizes Rossetti's comment on Blake's designs: "If they be for him, he will be joyful more and more the longer he looks, and will gain back in that time some things as he first knew them, not encumbered behind the days of his life; things too delicate for memory or years since forgotten; the momentary sense of spring in winter-sunshine, the long sunsets long ago, and falling fires on many distant hills" (*CW*, I, 448). Even the style of the passage fore-shadows the slightly weary cadences of Pater.

The idea implicit in "Silent Noon" is that the moment's perfection will act as shoring against the ruins of daily life. Other poems —"The Lovers' Walk," for instance, and "Youth's Spring Tribute"— carry the same thought, and "Lost Fire" makes it explicit:

> Many the days that Winter keeps in store,
> Sunless throughout, or whose brief sun-glimpses
> Scarce shed the heaped snow through the naked trees.
> This day at least was Summer's paramour,
> Sun-coloured to the imperishable core
> With sweet well-being of love and full heart's ease.
>   (*CW*, I, 191)

But it is easy to see that, with only a slight darkening of his mood, Rossetti may become more aware of the moment's passing than he is of its permanence. In that state of mind, escape from his own consciousness, even for a short time, seems impossible, and the silence of perfect communion becomes the silence of utter isolation: "Two separate divided selves . . . . Such are we now," he writes in "Severed Selves." And he tries to comfort himself, as so often before, with the thought of a future time, even though it be only "one hour" when the sense of isolation will be lifted. He tries, but the comfort fails:

> One hour how slow to come, how quickly past,
> Which blooms and fades, and only leaves at last
> Faint as shed flowers, the attenuated dream.
>   (*CW*, I, 196)

Worse than his consciousness of the moment's passing (which mars his happiness even as he feels it) is Rossetti's fear that he cannot really trust the validity of the moment. Those questions implied by the mirror image of "Mid-rapture" demand an answer when the ecstasy has passed. Perhaps such moments cannot serve as proof or even as sign of an ideal of love transcending the self; perhaps the sense of communion with another was an illusion created by that self which was one's only real companion all along. Thus the sonnet "Love and Hope" begins, typically enough, with images of mutability and isolation and, still typically, describes "one hour at last" when the lovers may escape into their private world. Then suddenly the very force of his desire to have that hour be the reflection of some permanence lessens his hope that it really is so:

> Cling heart to heart; nor of this hour demand
> Whether in very truth, when we are dead,
> Our hearts shall wake to know Love's golden head
> Sole sunshine of imperishable land;
> Or but discern, through night's unfeatured scope,
> Scorn-fired at length the illusive eyes of Hope.
> (*CW*, I, 198)

The final image, like that of "A Superscription"—"Sleepless with cold commemorative eyes" (*CW*, I, 225)—takes its forcefulness and horror from the sense it gives of a malevolent Watcher in the darkness, inescapable because he is oneself. "Lost Days" makes that horror explicit:

> I do not see them here; but after death
> God knows the murdered faces I shall see,
> Each one a murdered self, with low last breath;
> "I am thyself—what hast thou done to me?"
> "And I—and I—thyself," (lo! each one saith,)
> "And thou thyself to all eternity."
> (*CW*, I, 220)

Part of Rossetti's difficulty may be that the moments he treasures are those which serve as an escape from reality, not those which bring greater awareness of it. Both the dark, quiet moments of love, those experienced "Beneath her sheltering hair / In the warm silence near her breast" (*CW*, I, 97), when the sense of self is lost in one way, and the moments of blazing light like the one described in "Mid-rapture," in which that sense is lost in another, serve as escapes from the true self. A passage in Rossetti's poem "Dante in Verona" helps to define the escapist tendency of a Rossettian moment by the implicit contrast it gives with a Dantean moment.

In the poem Dante, lonely and misunderstood at the Court of

Verona, is comforted by the memory of Beatrice:

> For then the voice said in his heart,
> "Even I, even I am Beatrice";
> And his whole life would yearn to cease:
> Till having reached his room apart
> Beyond vast lengths of palace floor,
> He drew the arras round his door.
>
> At such times, Dante, thou hast set
> Thy forehead to the painted pane
> Full oft, I know; and if the rain
> Smote it outside, her fingers met
> Thy brow; and if the sun fell there
> Her breath was on thy face and hair.
> (CW, I, 7)

The line "Even I, even I am Beatrice" is a translation of "Guarda-mi ben: ben son, ben son Beatrice" from the scene which one might consider the emotional center of *The Divine Comedy*. Having climbed the Mount of Purgatory, Dante at last meets Beatrice, but she appears to him veiled and stern, like Christ in judgment. Her words "Guardami ben . . ." are not a comfort, they are a stern reproach, and in telling Dante to look well upon her, she forces him also to see himself. With the "harsh pity" of genuine love she turns him from the self-involvement of remorse to the self-awareness of repentance, and in that revelation of self, Dante moves closer to beatitude:

> Gli occhi mi cadder giù nel chiaro fonte;
> ma, veggendomi in esso, i trassi all 'erba
> tanta vergogna mi gravò la fronte.[14]

The words which for Dante were a challenge, love's demand that the lover come to clarity of vision, become in Rossetti's poem an invitation to escape into temporary oblivion. Because the beloved is not for Rossetti a "presence" (in Gabriel Marcel's sense of the term), his fear that their moment of communion may have been factitious is perfectly reasonable. Or to put it another way: Rossetti attempted to transcend the consciousness by merging with the consciousness of another. Such a desire sounds altruistic, seems so indeed as one feels it, but the force which impels it is an egotism in which one must inevitably become more and more deeply entangled as one struggles.

So it was with Rossetti. His frustration lay in the fact that no moment, however intense, really gave the sense of escape from self that he desired. And at times, like Keats and like Poe, he brooded upon the thought that one moment at least might serve as escape, as illumination, as the end of all conflict: the moment of death. William Bell Scott describes an afternoon in 1869 when he and Rossetti visited a black pool called the Devil's Punch Bowl, deep in a ravine. As Rossetti gazed down upon it, he looked so fascinated that Scott believed him to be thinking, "One step forward, and I am free!"[15]

About that time Rossetti was working on a poem called "The Orchard Pit," for which he wrote a prose outline, though he finished only a few, fragmentary verses. The poem was to tell of a siren singing in an apple-tree which screens from view a pit filled with the bodies of dead men. She offers an apple which brings death to any man who tastes it. The story's narrator, although he is betrothed to a beautiful young girl, is drawn irresistibly to the siren, toward a meeting he has always feared and yet always desired. At first her song is "Come to Love," and next she sings "Come to Life." Then the narrator says, in words which echo the conclusion of Keats' sonnet "Bright Star": "But long before I reached her, she knew that all her will was mine: and then her voice rose softer than ever, and her words were, 'Come to Death;' and Death's name in her mouth was the very swoon of all sweetest things that be" (*CW*, I, 430).

If that were the end of the story as Rossetti planned it, one might suppose that he hoped for some revelation in death, but his outline concludes:

And one kiss I had of her mouth, as I took the apple from her hand. But while I bit it, my brain whirled, and my feet stumbled; and I felt my crashing fall through the tangled boughs beneath her feet, and saw the dead white faces that welcomed me in the pit. And so I woke cold in my bed; but it still seemed that I lay indeed at last among those who shall be my mates forever, and could feel the apple still in my hand (*CW*, I, 430).

The siren echoes his own desires—for life, for love, for death. As an emanation of his own consciousness, she gives him the promise of escape from self through those things which, when grasped, are seen to be illusions. He is still enclosed within the self; he has always been so.

Rossetti was a divided man. His emotions cried out for the existence of a transcendent realm while his reason questioned its existence. Yeats expresses the division by saying that "Coleridge, and Rossetti, though his dull brother did once persuade him that he was an agnostic, were devout Christians."[16] And it is true that the last sonnet of *The House of Life* expresses the thoughts of a Christian agnostic:

> When vain desire at last and vain regret
> Go hand in hand to death, and all is vain,
> What shall assuage the unforgotten pain
> And teach the unforgetful to forget?
> Shall Peace be still a sunk stream long unmet,—
> Or may the soul at once in a green plain
> Stoop through the spray of some sweet life-fountain
> And cull the dew-drenched flowering amulet?
> (*CW*, I, 227)

His vision is modelled upon Dante's earthly Paradise, a green plain in which the soul, after long imprisonment, breathes clear air. But the poem's questions and uncertainties, its conscious lack of rational foundation, change Dante's vision to day-dream.

Rossetti was also divided between his commitment on the one hand to introspection and self-discovery—to painting his soul as it was—and his belief on the other hand that the ideal of the self must not lie within the self. There must be an external ideal around which it can move in order and harmony. "Seek thine ideal anywhere except in thyself," he wrote in his notebook. "Once fix it there, and the ways of thy real self will matter nothing to thee, whose eyes can rest on an ideal already perfected" (*CW*, I, 152). Arnold, feeling the same need for an external standard, found one in the vision of a good society and turned his energies toward making a part of that potential good actual. His answer, however, was not really a synthesis between the self and the world outside the self. Feeling that he must choose and that no

synthesis was possible, he chose the latter, thinking it less dangerous. And he was right; it *was* less dangerous.

Rossetti was faced with a similar division, but the world of
social action had no interest for him. The world outside the self
to which he looked for a standard was a spiritual, eternal realm
of love and beauty. Through the concept of the moment he tried
to establish a link between that realm and the mind; his·thought
was that in a state of heightened perception the consciousness
recognizes in objects and persons the spiritual reality of which
they are a reflection. He never gave up his emotional commitment
to that reality, but he never succeeded in answering the question
Coleridge had raised: "And art thou nothing? . . ."

That doubt threw him back constantly upon himself and made
his effort an unhappy one. There was, moreover, a danger in-
herent in the effort itself. Writing of Edgar Allan Poe, D. H.
Lawrence makes a comment which might, word for word, be
applied to Rossetti—not surprisingly, since the two men have
much in common: "The root of all evil is that we all want this
spiritual gratification, this flow, this apparent heightening of life,
this knowledge, this valley of many-coloured grass, even grass
and light prismatically decomposed, giving ecstasy. We want all
this *without resistance.* We want it continually. And this is the
root of all evil in us."[17] It is "the root of all evil" because its
object so easily becomes a magnification of the self attained
while all consciousness of self seems lost. The moment takes
on more reality than the consciousness which experiences it, and
the real self becomes liable to disintegration.

In Swinburne's reaction to Rossetti's work one sees that process
beginning to take place. Swinburne describes the "angels and
virgins" of Rossetti's early canvases and the "strange visions" of
his later work: Venus, Helen, and Cassandra. He takes from
this change in Rossetti's subjects the thought that

any garden of paradise on earth or above earth is but a little of a
great world, as every fancy of man's faith is a segment of the truth
of his nature, a splintered fragment of universal life and spirit and
thought everlasting; since what can he conceive or believe but it
must have this truth in it, that it is a veritable product of his own
brain, and outcome for the time of his actual being, with a place

and a reason for its own root and support to it through its due periods of life and change and death?[18]

The paradisal moment has become a "segment," a "splintered fragment," given temporary validity by a consciousness which is itself splintered and fragmented. What had been to Coleridge and to Rossetti an awful possibility was to Swinburne a simple matter of fact: the "Lady Beauty" whose "fluttering hem and flying feet" Rossetti had pursued, was a shape within his own imagination, subject, like his imagination, to "life and change and death." Thus interpreted, Rossetti's moment became the Decadent moment.

Chapter II

Algernon Charles Swinburne

"It was blue summer then, and always morning, and the air sweet
and full of bells."[1] That is the way Edward Burne-Jones describes
the months from August to December, 1857, when D. G. Rossetti
and his disciples came down to Oxford to fresco the walls of the
Union debating hall. In October young Algernon Swinburne
came up for the fall term of his second year at Oxford, and on
November 1 he met Rossetti, Burne-Jones, and Morris in the
rooms of a friend. A few days later he went to the debating hall
to watch the work.

There are so many accounts of those days in the Union that it
is easy to imagine the scene into which Swinburne entered.[2] High
up on a scaffolding, a paint-spattered Morris was drawing
medieval animals all over the ceiling. Burne-Jones was frescoing
the ceiling too—with pictures of fat little William Morrises.
Models in medieval armor or flowing draperies were posing for

the fourteen-foot frescoes of Val Prinsep and John Pollen amid
a litter of overturned paint buckets, soda water bottles, and odd
bits of scaffolding. Beside Rossetti himself, as model for Guinevere, stood the darkly beautiful Jane Burden, soon to marry
William Morris. Her face was to haunt Rossetti all the rest of his
life. The fresco on which Rossetti was working depicts Sir
Launcelot asleep before the chapel of the Holy Grail. Between
him and the shrine there rises the dream-image of Guinevere,
barring his entrance; her arms are extended in the branches of an
apple tree, and in one hand she holds an apple.³

A dark subject, prefiguring the still darker theme of "The
Orchard Pit"—but the atmosphere in the Union was anything
but gloomy. Swinburne was swept away by the delight of it all:
the boyish comradeship, the laughter, the romantic medievalism.
He was brought into that company immediately and dubbed
"Little Carrots," and since he could not paint even so much as
a medieval animal, he set himself to the writing of Arthurian
romances and border ballads.

Those poems are apprentice work and are not in themselves
significant, but they served as preparation for the poems which
Swinburne wrote "for art's sake." In the latter, as a disciple
of Rossetti, he followed the master's injunction to look inward
for the sources of poetic inspiration. The "studies of passion and
sensation" which resulted (for it is thus that Swinburne described
*Poems and Ballads*⁴) are fantasies which express the conflicting
ideas and emotions of his consciousness.

During the time in which he was concerned with the portrayal
of these inner states, Swinburne was drawn to the work of
Charles Baudelaire, who had the same purpose and whose poetry
described internal divisions closely resembling those which
Swinburne felt. In an article on Baudelaire which introduced that
poet's work into England, Swinburne wrote:

His perfect workmanship makes every subject admirable and re-
spectable. Throughout the chief part of this book he has chosen to
dwell mainly upon sad and strange things—the weariness of pain and
the bitterness of pleasure—the perverse happiness and wayward sorrows of exceptional people. It has the languid and lurid beauty of
close and threatening weather—a heavy, heated temperature with

dangerous hot-house scents in it; thick shadow of cloud about it, and the fire of molten light.[5]

This paragraph gives Swinburne's version of the doctrine of art for art's sake. The only demand one may make of a poet is that of "perfect workmanship." His subject matter is his own concern—in two senses of that phrase: he may write whatever he chooses, and what he chooses will be to depict the divisions he finds within himself. Baudelaire's purpose was serious, and so—even in the midst of all the boyish skylarking of his younger days—was Rossetti's. Swinburne, although he could describe its results enthusiastically, never really understood the purpose of this introspection, and as a result he was always of two minds about the worth of his own erotic poetry.

Of course, he was easily swayed by the opinions of those whom he admired, and comments like the following from John Ruskin may have given him pause:

For the matter of it [*Poems and Ballads*] I consent to much—I regret much—I blame, or reject nothing. I should as soon think of finding fault with a thundercloud or a night-shade blossom. . . . There is assuredly something wrong with you—awful in proportion to the great power it affects, and renders (nationally) useless. So it was with Turner, so with Byron. It seems to me to be the peculiar judgment-curse of modern days that all their greatest men should be plague-struck. But the truth and majesty which is in their greatest, causes the plague which is underneath, in the hearts of meaner people, smooth outwardly, to be in turn visible outside while there is purity within. The rest are like graves which appear not—and you are rose graftings set in dung.[6]

Any comfort Swinburne might take from knowing that he was not a whited sepulchre was effectively cancelled by the image of himself as a rose grafted in dung beside the sepulchre. And so, one gathers, he often wanted to get out of the graveyard altogether.

He wrote this little quatrain of self-mockery:

> Some sinners delighting in curses,
> Though sinful, have splendidly sinned;
> But my would-be maleficent verses
> Are nothing but wind.[7]

The ironic tone of the quatrain makes it possible, of course, for him to enjoy describing his verses in this way without really taking the description seriously himself or expecting his reader to do so. Yet time and again, even before his "reformation" in 1879, he writes that *Songs before Sunrise,* a volume given over mainly to philosophic or political poems—and very heavy-handed ones at that—is the best expression of his true self and of his most genuinely poetic mode.[8]

At the same time, Swinburne took a very personal pleasure, a schoolboy's delight, in shocking people. One sees it in this ingenuous sentence to Charles Howell: "I have added yet four more jets of boiling and gushing infamy to the perennial and poisonous fountain of Dolores" (*Letters,* I, 122). Then too, he insisted on the publication of *Poems and Ballads* (in the face of advice to tone down the work from Ruskin, Rossetti, William Bell Scott and many others who so often worried over "What to do about Algernon") and did courageous battle with reviewers because the cause of "art for art's sake" was identified in his mind with his own integrity. William Bell Scott wrote to Lady Trevelyan when Swinburne was about to publish *Chasterlard:*

> You will perhaps see certain things there—the total severance of the passion of love from the moral delight of loving or being loved, so to speak, and the insaneness of the impulses of Chasterlard—for example, which may give you a text for writing to him. With all his boasting of himself and all his belongings he is very sensitive about society, and I certainly think you will do him the very kindest of actions if you can touch his sensibility on his vanity—a little sharply (*Letters,* I, 135–36).

Scott was shrewd but—for his purposes—not shrewd enough. Swinburne's very vanity made it a matter of personal honor to him to publish his work; moreover, the fact that he knew he would be victimized for doing so acted as a stimulus rather than as a deterrent to his masochistic nature.

So much for his motives in insisting upon free expression for his imagination. The important thing about the poems themselves is that when Swinburne allowed his imagination such freedom he came to more truth than he knew. In writing this kind of poetry he was facile, and that facility could be dangerous; nevertheless, the poems that resulted were much more genuine than those "nationally useful" poems in which he consciously set himself to the expression of high thoughts. Paradoxically, he found the latter sort of poem very difficult to write and complained of the problem in a letter to William Rossetti:

If I do finish this poem ["A Song of Italy"] at all to my satisfaction, there will be a bit of enthusiasm in verse for once—rather. After all, in spite of jokes and perversities . . . it is nice to have something to love and believe in as I do in Italy. It was only Gabriel and his followers in art (l'art pour l'art) who for a time frightened me from speaking out . . . . Only, just as one hears that intense desire has made men impotent at the right (or wrong) minute, my passionate wish to express myself in part, for a little about this matter [of Italian nationalism] has twice or thrice left me exhausted and incompetent: unable to write, or to decide if what has been written is or is not good. I never felt this about my poems on other subjects (*Letters,* I, 195–96).

The passage is full of the most astonishing paradoxes. Swinburne feels that his temporary belief in "art for art's sake" frightened him from "speaking out"; it was at that time that he wrote the "jokes and perversities" which the Victorians found so shocking. Now he intends to pluck up his courage and thunder out republican sentiments which, as it turns out, will interest very few, alarm even fewer. Swinburne should have been warned by his difficulties in writing those nationalistic poems. They were almost unwritable; they are now unreadable. But the poems which were simply "self-expression," written for their own sake—the poems about whose sentiments one might say he scarcely *thought* at all have, in spite of all their very obvious faults, something significant to say about human experience.

What Swinburne had to say in these poems will be made clearer by stopping to consider another work which he wrote purely for its own sake, his unfinished novel *Lesbia Brandon.* The fragments of *Lesbia Brandon* are really more a series of fantasies than a coherent story, but Swinburne has written enough to show the plot that he had in mind. It is very close to the plot of the first half of *Wuthering Heights,* one of Swinburne's favorite novels: "It may be true," he wrote, "that not many will ever take it [*Wuthering Heights*] into their hearts; it is certain that those who

do like it will like nothing very much better in the whole world
of poetry or prose" (*Works,* XIV, 54), and when attempting his
own novel he paid *Wuthering Heights* the compliment of
imitation.

The real heroine of *Lesbia Brandon,* as Swinburne's letters
show[9] (for not he but Thomas Wise or Sir Edmund Gosse gave
it that title), is Lady Margaret Wariston. She and her brother,
Herbert Seyton—an idealized Swinburne—are the book's central
figures. And Lady Wariston is placed in a position precisely
analogous to Catherine Earnshaw's. She is married to a man who
gives her affection, kindness, material comfort—but not passionate
love: "Her husband did not embitter and did not enliven her
life. . . . He had for her a little love, and she had much liking for
him. He could fill up his life with little satisfactions, but she could
find no single expression of her wants and powers. In those years,
a maiden at heart, she had a vague and violent thirst after action
and passion. . . . Of one thing only she never thought: of love."[10]
Breaks in the manuscript make it necessary to piece her later
history together: she falls passionately in love, we gather, with
a man named Denham, her brother's tutor, who we know has
been in love with her for years. Denham discovers, however, that
he is in reality her half-brother; the only fragment relating to the
love affair is a scene in which Margaret Wariston and Denham
decide that they must part. Shortly afterward he is brought back
to the house, shot through the heart in what is reported to be an
accident.

Herbert Seyton (Lady Wariston's brother), meanwhile, has
fallen in love with Lesbia, who dies in a bizarre and "decadent"
manner from an overdose of opium and eau-de-cologne. And the
end of it all—like the end of Swinburne's other novel, *Love's
Cross-Currents*—is emotional deadlock. Lady Wariston and Herbert Seyton both become people to whom nothing will ever
happen: "As for him [Seyton] I cannot say what he has done or
will do, but I should think, nothing. This may certainly be
affirmed of his sister, whose husband, one of our happiest country-
men, is content to farm, to shoot, to vote in the House where he
never speaks, and to adore his family" (p. 353).

Lady Wariston, one might say, is as much an ancestress of

Lady Chatterley as a descendant of Catherine Earnshaw. There is, however, an interesting point of difference between *Lesbia Brandon*'s theme and that of a typical novel by Lawrence. Lawrence's heroines must always learn to rejoice in their separateness from the men they love: it is only by an understanding of *that* division that they may achieve harmony within themselves and peace with their men. In order to escape self-division, Lawrence preaches again and again, one must conquer the narcissism which would use another simply as a means for loving oneself. His vehemence shows that he thinks it no small temptation; the important point here, though, is that he is consciously concerned with it as a temptation. *Lesbia Brandon* might serve as an exemplum for a Lawrentian sermon. The passionate feelings of all the principal characters are narcissistic, and their result is barrenness and sterility.

The central pair of divided lovers in *Lesbia Brandon* are Lady Wariston and her brother Herbert. The book opens with an elaborate description of both which repeatedly stresses their resemblance to one another, while emphasizing at the same time their difference in sex. And the most harmoniously sensual passage in the book describes an evening in Herbert's boyhood when Margaret kissed him, pleased with his courage in saving a young neighbor from drowning. It is a scene with scarcely a hint of the torment and violence which characterize the other love affairs of the book:

"I say, let your hair go," said Herbert, pressing his arms under hers: she loosened the fastenings, and it rushed downwards, a tempest and torrent of sudden tresses, heavy and tawny and riotous and radiant, over shoulders and arms and bosom; and under cover of the massive and luminous locks she drew up his face against her own and kissed him time after time with all her strength (p. 265).

When he discusses *Wuthering Heights* and *Jane Eyre*, Swinburne picks out for special comment the passage in which Catherine Earnshaw says: "I *am* Heathcliff," and that in which Jane Eyre answers Rochester's question "whether she feels in him the absolute sense of fitness and correspondence to herself which he feels to himself in her, with the words which close and crown the history of their twin-born spirits—'To the finest fibre of my nature, sir'" (*Works*, XIV, 9). Swinburne's choice of those particular incidents in other novels when placed beside the incidents of his own novel shows what he believed to be passion's driving impulse: the desire to unify the self through love. But Swinburne begins with the knowledge that such a desire can meet only with frustration and self-division, and these are the "passions and sensations" he chooses most often to describe.

One of the poems in which he does so very movingly is "Laus Veneris," Swinburne's version of the Tannhäuser legend. He begins his poem at what is usually the story's conclusion, after Tannhäuser's return to the Hörselberg; the reason he gives for doing so is interesting: "The immortal agony of a man lost after all repentance—cast down from a fearful hope into fearless despair—believing in Christ and bound to Venus—desirous of penitential pain, and damned to joyless pleasure—this in my eyes was the kernel and nucleus of the myth . . . . The tragic touch of the story is this: the knight who has renounced Christ believes in him; the lover who has embraced Venus disbelieves in her" (*Works*, XIV, 353).[11] The poem has no logical development; nor has it really any emotional development. One simply joins the knight in spirit as he moves through the conflicting emotions which obsess him. There is no escape from them and no hope of bringing them into unity. From stanza to stanza—sometimes from line to line—the speaker's mood changes, and the only real constant is that change. The very pattern of a stanza like the following shows all these fluctuations obviously enough:

> Alas, Lord, surely thou art great and fair.
> But lo her wonderfully woven hair!
> And thou didst heal us with thy piteous kiss;
> But see now, Lord; her mouth is lovelier.
> (*Works*, I, 147)

That stanza shows that even Swinburne's analysis was an oversimplification. The knight still desires Venus, still clings to her, although at times he thinks her fearful. With one hysterical image of torture and imprisonment after another he describes her torments: "Her little chambers drip with flower-like red . . . ," but suddenly his mood changes:

> Yea, all she slayeth; yea, every man save me;
> Me, love, thy lover that must cleave to thee
> Till the ending of the days and ways of earth,
> The shaking of the sources of the sea.
>   (*Works,* I, 151)

The change is obvious not only in the sudden shift of tone to gentle melancholy but also in the change from indirect description of a terrifying Venus to direct address of a pathetic one. Nor does the knight always desire the heaven he has lost:

> Ah love, there is no better life than this;
> To have known love, how bitter a thing it is,
> And afterward be cast out of God's sight;
> Yea, these that know not, shall they have such bliss
>
> High up in barren heaven before his face
> As we twain in the heavy-hearted place,
> Remembering love and all the dead delight,
> And all that time was sweet with for a space?
>   (*Works,* I, 161)

The knight's only harmonious, whole-hearted desire is for total oblivion:

> Ah yet would God this flesh of mine might be
> Where air might wash and long leaves cover me,
> Where tides of grass break into foam of flowers,
> Or where the wind's feet shine along the sea.
>   (*Works,* I, 148)

The last line of the stanza refers specifically to the sea, but the images of the two preceding lines describe the earth as if it were a sea. For to Swinburne death's symbol is not the earth, which reminds man of his duality by its identification with the body, but the sea, which is at once the origin of all life and an element alien to human life.

"Anactoria," another dramatic monologue, has an emotional pattern which closely resembles that of "Laus Veneris." Sappho is the speaker. Through her imprisoned consciousness circle the obsessive thoughts and desires created by her love for Anactoria. Neither this poem nor "Laus Veneris" has the character of a Browning monologue; they do not catch the speaker at a partic-

ular spatial and temporal moment but—as in Tennyson's "Titho-
nus"—in what seems to be an eternal moment. "Anactoria" is a
more violent poem than "Laus Veneris"—the division it describes
is more bitter—but it is clearer too. The mingled love and the
hatred which Sappho feels for Anactoria are not emotions which
really relate to any object outside herself. She is caught by the
dualities of self-love and self-hatred:

> Yea, though thou diest, I say I shall not die,
> For these shall give me of their souls, shall give
> Life, and the days and loves wherewith I live,
> Shall quicken me with loving, fill with breath,
> Save me and serve me, strive for me with death.
>
> (*Works*, I, 198)

So it seems as if her thoughts will drift off, but with a sudden
revulsion she abandons the desire for any sort of immortality in
her longing for oblivion:

> Alas, that neither moon nor snow nor dew
> Nor all cold things can purge me wholly through,
> Assuage me nor allay me nor appease,
> Till supreme sleep shall bring me bloodless ease;
> Till time wax faint in all his periods;
> Till fate undo the bondage of the gods,
> And lay, to slake and satiate me all through,
> Lotus and Lethe on my lips like dew
> And shed around and over and under me
> Thick darkness and the insuperable sea.
>
> (*Works*, I, 198–99)

As "Anactoria" shows, one of the moments which Swinburne
wishes to capture in verse is that of desire just before it reaches
its limit to become pain and frustration in the consciousness of
limit. The difference between this moment and a similar Rossettian moment is clearest in Swinburne's description of Rossetti's
"Venetian Pastoral": "In the verse as on the canvas there is the
breathless breath of over-much delight, the passion of overrun-
ning pleasure which quivers and aches on the very verge of
heavenly tears—tears of perfect moan for excess of unfathomable
pleasure and burden of inexpressible things only to be borne by
Gods above" (*Works*, XV, 31). Rossetti's moment passes as he

becomes aware once more of time and of self: its passage leaves a deep but very quiet melancholy, as quiet as the moment itself. But there is violence even in the pleasure of Swinburne's moment, and the violence increases as the frustration implicit in Rossetti's description becomes explicit in Swinburne's.

As frustration at the "otherness" of the beloved increases, the moment of love and near-communion becomes one of consuming hatred—of the beloved, of oneself, of life and its limitations. Thus in "Anactoria," Sappho's desire for total possession of Anactoria changes into the desire to kill her and afterward to kill herself; at least by destruction of all consciousness she can come to a negative communion:

> O that I
> Durst crush thee out of life with love, and die,
> Die of thy pain, and my delight, and be
> Mixed with thy blood and molten into thee!
> (*Works*, I, 194)

The limitations of love become identified with all human limitation, so that it is with an analogous feeling that Sappho turns upon God:

> Him would I reach, him smite, him desecrate
> Pierce the cold lips of God with human breath,
> And mix his immortality with death!
> (*Works*, I, 195)

In such a moment God and Man would be mixed, God would become mortal, Man God-like, and both would be destroyed—as if in one instant *both* Jupiter and Semele were shattered. This is love's desired consummation, and so it is that in Swinburne's mind love and death are not opposites: they are identical.

In his quasi-autobiographical poem "Thalassius," Swinburne describes an innocent boy, child of the sun and the sea, who on an April day meets the God of Love. The god's form is child-like, and he wanders helpless and blind; in pity Thalassius guides him, thinking himself the stronger of the two. But as they travel the god becomes huge and terrifying. He turns on Thalassius suddenly and mocks him: "O fool, my name is sorrow; / Thou fool, my name is death" (*Works,* III, 297). With those words he vanishes.

From the bitter hopelessness of love Thalassius turns to a life of violent pleasure, the life described in "Dolores." In his "Notes on Poems and Reviews" Swinburne describes the same change of feeling: "I have striven here [in "Dolores"] to express that transient state of spirit through which a man may be supposed to pass, foiled in love and weary of loving, but not yet in sight of rest; seeking refuge in those 'violent delights' which have 'violent ends,' in fierce and frank sensualities which at least profess to be no more than they are" (*Works,* XVI, 360). Swinburne also writes that the placing of "Dolores" within *Poems and Ballads* is significant: "Dolores," "The Garden of Proserpine," and "Hesperia" should be considered as a trilogy—an arrangement which reflects the self-division and longing for death that one finds in the book's individual poems. For "Hesperia" and "Dolores" are expressions of opposite states of mind, the one dominated by a Diana-like goddess that redeems, the other by an Astarte that consumes. Hesperia is "a bride rather than a mistress, a sister rather than a bride" (*Works,* XVI, 362) to whom the speaker flees. He is one who "has loved overmuch" in his life and turned from the pain of love to the respite which lust at first seemed to offer:

Was it myrtle or poppy thy garland was woven with, O my Dolores?
Was it pallor of slumber, or blush as of blood, that I found in thee fair?
For desire is a respite from love, and the flesh not the heart is her fuel.
                    (*Works,* I, 306)

Nevertheless, Dolores has cruelties of her own, and the speaker has fled from her, Our Lady of Pain, to seek refuge with Hesperia:

Let her lips not again lay hold on my soul, nor her poisonous kisses
To consume it alive and divide from thy bosom,
Our Lady of Sleep.
Ah daughter of sunset and slumber, if now it return into prison,
Who shall redeem it anew? . . .
                    (*Works,* I, 307)

The speaker's address to Hesperia as "Our Lady of Sleep" and his identification of her with sunset suggest that Hesperia is Death. If she is, does Swinburne's analysis of the poem make sense? It

does if one thinks of Hesperia as that lost innocence which, emotionally if not intellectually, it seems possible to regain—but only
by death. For the poem concludes with a fantasy in which the
speaker and Hesperia ride across the landscape which resembles
the Northumbria of Swinburne's boyhood: they ride furiously,
pursued by "the goddess that consumes":

And our spirits too burn as we bound, thine holy but mine heavy-laden
As we burn with the fire of our flight; ah love, shall we win at the last?
(Works, I, 308)

Between "Dolores" and "Hesperia" comes "The Garden of Proserpine," which describes that state in which the spirit "without fear
or hope of good things or evil hungers and thirsts only after
perfect sleep" (*Works*, XVI, 362). In the poem's final image that
sleep of death is identified with the sea; there the human spirit
is promised a blessed release from consciousness and an end of
all dualities.

In "The Triumph of Time" the sea also grants unity of spirit
but of a slightly different kind: it returns the poet to that innocence which was destroyed by the divisions of love. Nevertheless
the sea's singleness and freedom are unattainable except in
death; the sea's gift is one of her "pure cold populous graves"
(*Works*, I, 177). When he wrote "Thalassius" in 1879–1880, however, Swinburne described a return to innocence and unity of
spirit which is attained without suffering death. Thalassius simply
leaves his revelling companions and returns to the sea, his
mother:

> The tidal throb of all tides keep rhyme
> And charm him from his own soul's separate sense
> With infinite and invasive influence.
> <div align="right">(<i>Works</i>, III, 302)</div>

Herbert Seyton, like Thalassius, is brought up beside the sea
and finds in it the deepest pleasure he will ever have. There he
can keep his identity without all the conflict of love and at the
same time can merge his identity in an overpowering force.
Swinburne describes the boy after he has been swimming as "wet
and rough, blown out of shape and beaten into colour, his ears
full of music and his eyes of dreams: all the sounds of the sea

rang through him, all its airs and lights breathed and shone upon
him."[12] The echo of "and the glory of the Lord shone round about
them" (Luke 2:9) emphasizes the visionary quality of the experience. Swinburne uses a similar vocabulary in a letter to his sister:
"The whole sea was literally golden as well as green—it was liquid
and living sunlight in which one lived and moved and had one's
being. And to feel that in deep water is to feel—as long as one is
swimming out if only a minute or two—as if one was in another
world of life, and one far more glorious than even Dante ever
dreamed of in his Paradise" (*Letters*, V, 275).

The moments in which the sea gives him a sense of infinite
expansion are those which Swinburne most prizes, but, like
Rossetti's moments of supreme peace in love, they can bring no
genuine revelation. Using Blake's terms, one might say that
Swinburne rejects Experience and returns to the state of Innocence. He does not come into the state of imaginative maturity
which makes it possible to understand and therefore to accept
Experience, the state which Yeats described in "A Dialogue of
Self and Soul" when he wrote:

> I am content to follow to its source
> Every event in action or in thought;
> Measure the lot; forgive myself the lot![13]

Instead Swinburne retreats into fantasy, withdrawing from all that
is not the self, expanding the self into infinity. The sea is his
Paradise because as he swims in it, he can enjoy the illusion of
solitary existence, and as he identifies with it, he can make that
existence seem infinite.

Swinburne's legacy to younger poets was, first of all, his career
itself, already legend even as he lived it, and secondly *Poems and
Ballads* which captivated generation after generation of adolescents—Oscar Wilde, Ernest Dowson, and Arthur Symons among
them. Its images, surrounded by a haze of undefined but powerful
emotion and described in language whose effect was virtually
hypnotic, created for its readers a separate world—a realm of
fantasy "separated from the general purposes of life." T. S. Eliot
was thinking of the book in this way when he wrote that in

Poems and Ballads "the object has ceased to exist . . . because language, uprooted, has adapted itself to an independent life of atmospheric nourishment."[14] His words recall Yeats' thought that "these images grow in beauty as they grow in sterility." That is to say, *Poems and Ballads* provided no link between the fantasies of the mind and a reality outside the mind, and because it was, therefore, at least potentially imprisoning, it was a dangerous book for those adolescents who best appreciated its effects.

At least as important as his influence upon the adolescents of his time is Swinburne's effect upon a contemporary, Walter Pater. The two men seem to have stood off from one another; they were acquaintances, not friends. But Pater was quick and gracious in admitting a debt to Swinburne when the latter complimented him on his first essays in the *Fortnightly*. "He replied," Swinburne writes, "that he considered them as owing their inspiration entirely to the example of my own work in the same line" (*Letters*, II, 241). Perhaps it was as well that Pater was so courteous, for Swinburne and Rossetti had, in fact, remarked between themselves on certain likenesses. "I liked Pater's article on Leonardo very much," Swinburne wrote to Rossetti. "I confess I did fancy there was a little spice of my style as you say, but much good stuff of his own, and much of interest" (*Letters*, II, 58). Although the tone of his comment is slightly patronizing—and one gets the impression that neither Rossetti nor Swinburne *liked* Pater—its truth is unquestionable. Indeed, there are similarities of material as well as of style between Swinburne's "Notes and Designs of the Old Masters at Florence" and Pater's "Leonardo da Vinci." This, for instance, is Swinburne's description of a study by Michelangelo: "But in one separate head there is more tragic attraction than in these: a woman's three times studied, with divine and subtle care; sketched and re-sketched in youth and age, beautiful always beyond desire and cruel beyond words; . . . In one drawing she wears a head-dress of eastern fashion rather than western" (*Works*, XV, 159–60). The mixture of beauty and cruelty in the subject, the emphasis upon care in its portrayal, and even the hint of connections with the East all appear in Pater's description of the Mona Lisa.

But Pater's dependence on Swinburne's previous criticism for

such details is not as important as the similarity of critical attitude which one finds in the two men. In "Notes on Some Pictures
of 1868" Swinburne described several works by Rossetti: pictures
of Lilith, of Proserpine, and of Beatrice. He has of each a different
impression; Lilith's "sleepy splendour" as she contemplates herself
in a mirror gives him pleasure, as do Proserpine's "sacred eyes and
pure calm lips" and "the symbolic and ideal head" of Beatrice.
Each of these works, however different, shows the artist's "love of
beauty for the very beauty's sake, the faith and trust in it as in a
god indeed." The critic's function is to worship this beauty "trans-
formed and incarnate in shapes without end" (*Works,* XV, 215–
16). But the manner of Swinburne's worship shows that he is not
loving those works of art for their own sake; he uses the art work
as material for fantasy. His descriptions are not so much of the
paintings themselves as of the different fantasies and resultant
moods which they evoke in his consciousness.

Pater's method, as he describes it in the preface to *The Renaissance,* sounds more scientific; the aesthetic critic's function is "to
distinguish, to analyse, and separate" the particular qualities of
a work of art. But the questions upon which that analysis is based
are these: "What is this song or picture, this engaging personality
presented in life or in a book, to *me*? What effect does it really
produce on me? Does it give me pleasure? and if so, what sort or
degree of pleasure? How is my nature modified by its presence or
under its influence?"[15] Such a method of criticism is, like Swinburne's, solipsistic in that it makes no clear separation between
the observer and the art work. All objects outside the self, whether
in art or in immediate experience, are, in one sense, equally removed from the self: their meaning is that which the self imposes.
All are, in another sense, part of the self, since they have meaning
only as they contribute to its fantasies. And yet, ironically, the
criticism of both Swinburne and Pater sets consciousness itself
adrift in the flux of experience; before each new object—Beatrice,
Lilith, or Proserpine—the observer is a different man. The end
result is that the enjoyment of an object takes on more reality
than either the object itself or the observing consciousness. Pater
was to come to such a point in the "Conclusion" to *The Renaissance* when he described the enjoyment of "strange dyes, strange

colours, and curious odours, or the work of an artist's hands,"
as a way of grasping at life "while all melts under our feet."

Of the two men Pater was the better critic in that he gave
intelligent expression to concepts that remain darkly implicit in
Swinburne's work, and it is doubtful that Swinburne himself
could have done so. He had the incapacity for ideas of a genuine
Barbarian. But he had as well the Barbarian charm and high
spirit. Causes not ideas interested him, and if the cause were his
own or a friend's, he was thereby convinced of its justice and
impatient for battle. Thus, for the ten years from 1857 to 1867 he
was proud to think of D. G. Rossetti as, so to speak, his general
and of himself as a captain, leading a charge of young recruits to
battle against the Philistines. Had the combat been in fact so
physical, he would have acquitted himself bravely, for he had a
gallant heart. But in that "mental fight" he was a confused and
therefore a dangerous leader.

Chapter III

Walter Pater

In the late spring of 1884, close to the publication date of *Marius the Epicurean*, William Sharp came to Oxford to visit Walter Pater. There, as they walked in the spring sunshine, the talk turned to William Blake, and Pater said, "I never repeat to myself without a strange and almost terrifying sensation of isolation and long weariness, that couplet of his:

> "Ah, sunflower, weary of time,
> Who countest the steps of the sun."[1]

Pater's singling out of that particular couplet as well as his reaction to it is a clue to what he himself might call his "formula," his principal preoccupation, perhaps one could even say his obsession: the consciousness always with him that time—with all the events, friendships, and sense impressions contained within it—was moving past him, and, worse still, the knowledge that he too

36

was caught up in the movement so that he could not take even himself as a point of rest. Yet neither could he float simply in the consciousness that "everything flows," for—to continue the metaphor—in such turbulent water he might well not float but drown. Pater believed that there must be an answer, a possibility of order, and though he changed his ideas of what that ordering principle might be, it always had its foundation in a moment of insight, a moment in which the flux was formed into a pattern within the consciousness of the observer. In Pater's changing attitudes towards the "moment" one finds a key to an understanding of his thought, and the changes are clearest in *Marius the Epicurean.* There Pater summed up and commented upon his earlier opinions and showed the direction of all his later thought.

A year after his visit, Sharp reviewed *Marius* in *The Athenaeum.* It was the enthusiastic review of a fervent disciple, but some of its sentences show that he had missed his master's point: "There are . . . some pages here and there in these two volumes which unmistakably present the personal opinions of the author, and these conjointly with portions of Mr. Pater's other published writings, constitute sufficient basis for the assumption that he does, indeed, recognize the teaching of Epicurus as—in its quintessential doctrine—not unworthy . . . of serious consideration as a practical philosophy of life."[2] Rather inconsistently he went on to say that if Pater had intended to show the Epicurean philosophy as futile and Christianity alone as "really responsive to man's deepest needs" he had hardly been successful. John Pick has pointed out that of all Pater's disciples only Lionel Johnson followed or seemed even to understand the changes that took place in their master's thought;[3] Sharp is clearly among those who stuck with the Pater of *The Renaissance.* In order to do so he had to disregard facts that would be clear even in a quick reading: first that Marius is a Roman mask for Pater himself and second that Pater recognized his earlier Epicurean philosophy as inadequate and, while still working from its basic principles, made it more spiritual without really making it Christian.

Heraclitus' philosophy was always important to Pater; he used a line from Heraclitus as an epigraph for the "Conclusion" of *The Renaissance,* and, much later in his life, he began his lectures on

Plato and Platonism with a discussion of the phrase Πάντα ρεῖ, all things are in flux.[4] The same philosophy serves as a point of departure in *Marius the Epicurean*. When Marius, shocked by the death of his friend Flavian, begins to consider the meaning of that experience and of his whole life, he turns first to the philosophy of Heraclitus—or, more precisely, to that of Protagoras, since Marius accepts Heraclitus' description of the problem without following him when his intellectual ladder "seemed to pass into the clouds."[5] Pater himself had shown much the same attitude as a young man when he objected to Coleridge's attempt to escape the phenomenal world into a world of pure being, an absolute world beyond change. In an early essay entitled "Coleridge's Writings," he pointed out that any metaphysical hypothesis remains only and always hypothesis; it is a sad expense of spirit, therefore, to turn away from physical experience in order to walk in the grey world of the abstract. The case of a potentially great artist like Coleridge is especially sad, because the artist, with his extraordinary sensitivity to real objects and emotions, will find a better answer to life's meaning through them than the philosopher ever can: "The true illustration of the speculative temper is not the Hindoo, lost to sense, understanding, individuality; but such a one as Goethe, to whom every moment of life brought its share of experimental, individual knowledge, by whom no touch of the world of form, colour, and passion was disregarded."[6] Pater could scarcely even understand the tension between metaphysics and art that Coleridge felt and that Yeats was later to feel. The lectures on *Plato and Platonism* allow for the necessity and even the virtue of abstraction but not for metaphysical speculation—and even abstraction or generalization has as its final end only the illumination of the particular. "Converse with the general," as Pater understands it, is worthwhile for the sudden vision it can bring, when once mastered, of the concrete: "By a kind of short-hand now, and as if in a single moment of vision, all that which only a long experience moving patiently from part to part, could exhaust, its manifold alliance with the entire world of nature, is legible upon it, as it lies there in one's hand."[7]

Pater believed that Coleridge failed as an artist because he turned metaphysician, whereas Plato was the best of philosophers because he was actually an artist, not lost in the light of the invisible but turning that light upon the visible in order to fuse the material and the spiritual into unity. "While in that fire and heat, what is spiritual attains the definite visibility of a crystal, what is material on the other hand, will lose its earthiness and impurity."[8] And so, interestingly enough, Pater finally adopted the same principles as those of the abstract Coleridge and even used the same image in explaining them: the beautiful image of crystal. Coleridge had written: "Something there must be to realize the form, something in and by which the *forma informans* reveals itself: . . . An illustrative hint may be taken from a pure crystal . . . . The crystal is lost in the light which yet it contains, embodies, and gives a shape to."[9] Yet it is unfair to quote a man against himself, and the Pater of *Plato and Platonism* was in many ways very different from the Pater who wrote "Coleridge's Writings." The latter, like the young Marius, clearly balked at an attempt to fuse material and spiritual because, though exquisitely conscious of the material world, he questioned the existence of a spiritual one.

Marius disliked an attempt at metaphysical ordering of the universe for yet another reason, the one given by Pater in the preface to *The Renaissance*. There, as we have noted, counting metaphysical ponderings on the abstract nature of beauty as worthless, he makes the critic's first question: "What is this song or picture, this engaging personality presented in life or in a book, to *me?*"[10] Ruth Child has interpreted this to mean that the critic must first define himself to himself—must, in a word, find his own "formula." [11] Certainly that seems true; yet we should remember as well that Pater wrote those words with a consciousness of every man's imprisonment within himself. He explains that Marius stopped at the threshold of philosophy because he saw that every system attempting to reflect "reality" could use but the mirror of the human mind and personality creating it, and that "the little knots and waves" of that mirror's surface would destroy the truth of the reflected image.[12] Moreover, there is not only the problem of a perfect reception of reality; there is also the problem of its communication. Since each man's vision of the world is hopelessly personal, he cannot really find common terms with which to express his feelings about it to others or by which he can be sure to understand theirs.

Implicit too in the awareness of isolation which the preface to *The Renaissance* expresses is an idea which was to have as great an impact on Oscar Wilde's thought as the "gem-like flame" passage of the "Conclusion." It is, if you will, a secular Calvinism which encloses every individual in the cocoon of his own heredity and his personal history, yet does not allow for that grace through which God releases the elect. In the "Conclusion" the idea forces its way into expression in a terrifying image: "Experience, already reduced to a group of impressions, is ringed round for each one of us by that thick wall of personality through which no real voice has ever pierced on its way to us, or from us to that which we can only conjecture to be without. Every one of those impressions is the impression of the individual in his isolation, each mind keeping as a solitary prisoner its own dream of a world."[13] Pater, as Ernest Tuveson has shown,[14] was carrying one of John Locke's ideas to a perfectly logical conclusion; Tuveson compares Pater's image of the mind as a prison with a passage in which Locke compares the mind to a dark room: "for methinks the understanding is not much unlike a closet wholly shut from light, with only some little opening left, to let in external visible resemblances, or ideas of things without."[15]

Those "ideas of things" were much more fleeting, more evanescent to Pater than they were to Locke; nevertheless, when the young Marius had thought himself down and down into the prison of himself he (like the young Pater) found in them a secret spring which promised release: "But our own impressions! —The light and heat of that blue veil over our heads, the heavens spread out, perhaps *not* like a curtain over anything!— How reassuring, after so long a debate about the rival criteria of truth, to fall back upon direct sensation . . . how natural the determination to rely exclusively upon the phenomena of the senses, which certainly never deceive us about themselves, about which alone we can never deceive ourselves."[16]

With this as his answer, Marius put aside all abstract speculation and found himself happy in the doctrine of Aristippus of

Cyrene, an "anti-metaphysical metaphysic," which taught that one must live "a full or complete life," a life of various yet select sensation "whose direct and effective auxiliary must be, in a word, Insight." Through a moment's insight he might shape the flux into meaning and so give order and peace to his soul. In order to do so, he must refine and develop his sensations and his intuitions; he must make them into so many sensitive media for reception, trained upon the vision—"the 'beatific vision' if one cared to make it such," writes Pater in a significant aside—of his experience.[17]

The sensations and ideas of Marius at this point in his life are those of Pater when he wrote *The Renaissance*. And, though, as we have seen, Coleridge was to Pater an example and a warning of the wrong way in which to think, Coleridge's theory of art and that of the German philosophers on whose work it was based gave Pater the answer to the question, How to live? The Romantic theory of art also began with an aching consciousness of mutability which must somehow be soothed. More than that, it refused any abstract system which would impose a form by cutting in, somehow, anyhow, to make a pattern through separation. It insisted that the answer lay not in analysis but in vision. Schelling had written: "If, as the excellent man of discernment remarked, every natural growth has only one moment of true and consummate existence, we may say that it also has only one moment of complete existence. At this moment it is what it is for all eternity: beyond this its lot is merely a becoming and a passing away. Art, by depicting the creature at this moment, raises it up out of time and presents it in its pure being, in the eternity of its life."[18] A sentence like the following by Hegel also had its comfort: "Art liberates the real import of appearances from the semblance and deception of this bad and fleeting world, and imparts to phenomenal semblances a higher reality, born of mind."[19]

Pater simply expanded this so that it made every thinking man, every truly conscious spirit—and it was only "choice spirits" to whom he addressed himself—an artist, or perhaps one should say an "aesthetic critic." In Pater's opinion the artist and the aesthetic critic may be equated because the fundamental quality in both is an ability to recognize and catch a perfect moment, a moment which, using the vocabulary of this organic criticism, Pater says has *grown* perfect.[20] Objects in the external world gradually come to their momentary perfection, and the mind gradually acquires the capacity for recognizing that perfection. The sudden meeting of mind and object creates the moment. Simply to recognize it is to endow it with the permanence "born of mind." Thus when he speaks of "life as the end of life" or "the love of art for its own sake," he is saying the same thing: the perfect work of art is the perfection of a moment in life, and the recognition of the beauty in both is the whole of what we may expect in human happiness.

It is easy to understand, then, why Pater shares Rossetti's desire for definition of form and outline in a work of art and why he makes clarity of memory one of the chief characteristics of any artist. Marius, he writes, gave up his youthful attempts to write poetry (as Pater himself did[21]) and labored instead to perfect his prose. Nevertheless, he had always "the poetic temper: by which I mean, among other things, that quite independently of the general habit of that pensive age, he lived much, and, as it were by system, in memory."[22] Pater has come to the same idea which Eliot was later to express in "Burnt Norton":

> Time past and time future
> Allow but a little consciousness.
> To be conscious is not to be in time.
> But only in time can the moment in the rose garden,
> The moment in the arbour where the rain beat,
> The moment in the draughty church at smokefall
> Be remembered: involved with past and future,
> Only through time time is conquered.[23]

Like Eliot he makes it the poet's function to hold the moment "out of time" in his memory so that gradually its significance may become as clear as the experience once was.

So it is that in his writing Pater almost makes physical objects of his memories, twisting them this way and that so that a moment caught in the mind may in a new light or a different place reveal something of itself that was hidden before. He writes of his childhood over and over again, setting it in different countries perhaps, and at different historical periods, yet remembering always the clean white house, the sunlight, his own religious devotion: in *Marius the Epicurean* itself, in "The Child in the House," *Gaston de Latour,* and "Emerald Uthwart."[24]

Of all these the most appropriate for this discussion is "The Child in the House," first published in 1878, because it is not so much a story as an attempt to recall certain moments of childhood. "Memory" is perhaps too simple a word for the process by which this is done; the heightened recollection takes on an almost visionary light, not supernatural perhaps, but preternatural. Pater writes of "the finer sort of memory" which brings its object to mind with great clarity, "yet, as sometimes happens in dreams, raised a little above itself, above ordinary retrospect."[25]

Florian, the little boy who serves in this story as a persona for Pater's childhood self, found the garden gate open one evening. He walked through it with a sense of excitement, for ordinarily the gate was closed, and saw before him a beautiful red hawthorn in full flower:

> Was it some periodic expansion of soul within him, or mere trick of heat in the heavily-laden summer air? But the beauty of the thing struck home to him feverishly, and in dreams, all night, he loitered along a magic roadway of crimson flowers which seemed to open ruddily in thick, fresh masses about his feet, and fill softly all the little hollows in the banks on either side. Always afterwards, summer by summer, as the flowers came on, the blossom of the red hawthorn seemed absolutely the reddest of all things; and the goodly crimson, still alive in the works of old Venetian masters, or old Flemish tapestries, called out always from afar, the recollection of the flame in those little petals, as it pulsed gradually out of them kept long in the drawers of an old cabinet.[26]

To attempt to hold the vision by keeping the petals in a drawer is hopeless, as Pater the man knew—and Marcel Proust after him —though Pater the child had still to learn it. Only the memory can hold the color fixed. And looking ahead for a moment to the death of Marius, we find memory again as the finest hope, the best, perhaps the only comfort. After all his questioning of how to live Marius finds as he is dying that he can rest his mind only by gazing inwardly at the remembered faces of those whom he has loved, "like a child, thinking over the toys it loves, one after another."[27]

All this is some comfort perhaps, but come at it how one will, it is not much, as Pater knew. Of course—though this is by the way—the recognition of what one feels to be a grim truth and the consciousness of bearing it bravely can give a self-satisfaction which almost makes up for the mental bleakness that goes with it. And Pater will comfort himself this way often enough.[28] Nevertheless, though in his consciousness of the moment's passing he relied on memory to "hold Beauty back," he knew, like Hopkins, that the attempt was unrealistic, and there comes even into his earlier, more agnostic work a longing to believe that moments of perfection might be kept safe for us in a drawer where they will not fade. In the original version of the essay on Giorgione, Pater writes:

Who, in some such perfect moment, when the harmony of things inward and outward beat itself out so truly, and with a sense of receptivity, with entire inaction on our part, some messenger from the real sound of things must be on his way to one, has not felt the desire to perpetuate all that, just so, to suspend it in every particular circumstance, with the portrait of just that one spray of leaves lifted just so high against the sky, above the well, forever? A desire how bewildering with the question of whether there be indeed any place wherein those desirable moments take permanent refuge. Well! in the school of Giorgione you drink water, perfume, music, lie in receptive humour thus for ever, and the satisfying moment is assured.[29]

And he has Marius think to himself: "Could he but arrest, for others also, certain clauses of experience, as the imaginative memory presented them to himself! In those grand, hot summers he would have imprisoned the very perfume of the flowers."[30] At this time in his life Pater, like the young Marius, believed that the work of art, by reincarnating the moment held in the memory, offered sufficient permanence, or at least as much as one might demand. It was for this reason that the clear form and the definite outline were so important. The object of memory must be brought into that clear, preternatural light and held there, whole.

That quality of Marius' prose which Pater singles out as pri-

mary is "a certain firmness of outline, that touch of the worker
in metal amid its richness."[31] The phrase brings to mind the
central image in an "Imaginary Portrait" called "An English
Poet." The sensitive boy described there, who lives in the rough
Cumberland country in surroundings he cannot see as beautiful,
finds one object which at once excites and satisfies his imagination:
in a church there is a wrought-iron grille worked in a honey-
suckle pattern. In time he becomes a poet, and his verse is noted
for "a peculiar character, as of flowers in metal," the strength and
elasticity of his language blended with a subtlety that can follow
"a tender, delicate feeling as the metal followed the curvature of
the flower."[32] There was such a grille on the door of Pater's room
in Brasenose College; one can see that Pater took pleasure in it
as an image of his aesthetic theory because it brings together the
ideas of form as organic, growing by necessity from within the
thing it expresses, and of form as that which makes permanent,
capturing beauty laboriously by chiselling and rubbing until the
form within reveals itself. Like the French Parnassians and like
Rossetti, Pater believed that the moment must be carved "in
ivory or in ebony."

This paradox of the way form is achieved is almost impossible
to express except through symbol; nevertheless one feels that the
symbols used do express a real process. Certainly Pater understood the symbol and the process which it revealed—understood it
so well that he could manipulate it at will and apply it to the
creation of a work of art or of a view of life. For instance, in this
passage from *Plato and Platonism* one sees an early expression of
what Hulme and Pound were to say in a few years about "the
form within the stone":

Κόσμος; order; reasonable, delightful order, is a word that became
very dear, as we know, to the Greek soul, to what was perhaps most
essentially Greek in it, to the Dorian element there. Apollo, the Dorian
god, was but its visible consecration. It was what, under his blessing,
art superinduced upon the rough stone, the yielding clay, the jarring
metallic strings, the common speech of every day. Philosophy, in its
turn with enlarging purpose, would project a similar light of intelligence upon the at first sight somewhat unmeaning world we find
around us;—project it, or rather discover it, as being really pre-

existent there, if one were happy enough to get one's self to the right
point of view. To certain fortunate minds the efficacious moment of
insight would come, when, with the delightful adaptation of means to
ends, of the parts to the whole, the entire scene about one, bewildering, unsympathetic, unreasonable, on a superficial view, would put
on, for them at least, κοσμιότης, that so welcome expression of fitness,
which it is the business of the fine arts to convey into material things,
of the art of discipline to enforce upon the lives of men.[33]

The passage brings together all the points we have discussed so
far: the whirl of impressions seen and ordered differently by
each individual; the moments of insight which give at least a
temporary escape; the process through which those moments are
caught and held in art work where they may offer the consolation of their coherence in an incoherent world.

Marius sets off for Rome, rather serious and severe in his ways
considering his age, but possessed in his soul of something like
cheerfulness once he has thought his way through to the "new
Cyrenaicism"—a philosophy we have noted to be close to that of
Pater when he wrote the "Conclusion" to *The Renaissance.* Yet as
the years pass Marius discovers that he has not found an answer
that will do once and for all; the moments of intensity for which
he had found it sufficient to live, these remain, but they are
changed into sudden, vivid realizations of pain until "his 'observation of life,'" says Pater, "had come to be like the constant telling
of a sorrowful rosary, day after day."[34] It is difficult to understand how, having read that, William Sharp could suggest that
Pater was putting Epicureanism forward as a "practical philosophy of life." On the contrary, three-quarters of the book is taken
up with demonstrating that the philosophy of Epicurus is insufficient for the human happiness which it makes its end.

Pater does not denounce his earlier philosophy as evil—perhaps
that was how the misunderstanding arose in the minds of his
disciples. He simply counts it as a partial truth, one for which
the young have a special affinity, "based on a vivid, because limited, apprehension of the truth of one aspect of experience—in
this case, the beauty of the world and the brevity of man's life in
it."[35] Pater has every sympathy with the young who continue to

come to this answer, but if they fail to grow out of it by realizing its limitations, they will themselves remain limited.

The reason for the failure of Cyrenaicism lies in the very principle on which it is based: that the individual has no knowledge beyond his own experience, and no sense of an external order, either metaphysical or moral, save that of which he himself is aware in his happiest and best moments. Now from the moment he makes the Cyrenaic philosophy his own, Marius understands that the desire for a life full of every kind of experience might lead to acts which, if not sinful according to this relativist philosophy, could still be harmful to oneself and painful to others. He has no real answer to this save his own early conditioning at "White Nights," the "first early, boyish ideal of priesthood" which made him desire always "hieratic beauty and order in the conduct of life."[36] For stability Marius really needs the precepts of a religion in which he no longer believes. Or rather, as B. A. Inman has pointed out, Marius takes from Cyrenaicism only those precepts which are congenial to his "temperament,"[37] and that temperament was formed in part by the religion in which he was raised:

He hardly knew how strong that old religious sense of responsibility, the conscience, still was within him—a body of inward impressions, as real as those so highly valued outward ones—to offend against which, brought with it a strange feeling of disloyalty, as to a person. And the determination, adhered to with no misgiving, to add nothing, not so much as a transient sigh, to the great total of man's unhappiness, in his way through the world:—that too was something to rest on, in the drift of mere "appearances."[38]

What, though, of those who had not that "sense of responsibility"? Pater never answered that question;[39] or perhaps it is truer to say that his criticism of Cyrenaicism is based on a moral concern at once subtler and broader than that of simply doing good and avoiding evil. His concept of morality, like that of Matthew Arnold and of Henry James, centers upon the individual's development of all his finest human attributes. Marius feels that his nature is becoming cramped, narrowed, one-sided—and sees suddenly that this is true of the Cyrenaic philosophers too:

If they did realize the μονόχρονος ἡδονή, as it was called—the pleasure of the "Ideal Now"—if certain moments of their lives were high-pitched, passionately coloured, intent with sensation, and a kind of knowledge which, in its vivid clearness, was like sensation—if, now and then, they apprehended the world in its fullness, and had a vision, almost "beatific," of ideal personality in life and art, yet those moments were a very costly matter: they paid a great price for them in the sacrifice of a thousand possible sympathies, of things only to be enjoyed through sympathy, from which they detached themselves, in intellectual pride, in loyalty to a mere theory that would take nothing for granted, and assent to no approximate or hypothetical truths. In their unfriendly and repellent attitude towards the Greek religion and the old Greek morality, surely, they had been faulty economists.[40]

So Marius, conscious of his spiritual barrenness, casts off the Cyrenaic ordering of the world and sets himself again, as he had after Flavian's death, to the task of making his experience meaningful. But the "formula" has not changed: he is still conscious only of the flux of events, unable to believe in an absolute order *there* objectively within it, and still aware that his world vision must always be entirely personal.

The danger of holding such a position, the danger to which Marius is particularly liable, is that of falling into the state of Decadence. Nor is it just the wisdom of hindsight which says so, for Pater himself was perfectly aware of the possibility. In his essay on Prosper Mérimée he described the effects of the philosophy which would make all speculation about the unseen world nonsense; the state of consciousness which results is the Decadent one:

The désillusionné, who had found in Kant's negations the last word concerning an unseen world . . . will demand, from what is to interest him at all, something in the way of an artificial stimulus. He has lost that sense of large proportion in things, that all embracing prospect of life as a whole (from end to end of time and space, it had seemed), the utmost expanse of which was afforded from a cathedral tower of the Middle Age . . . . Deprived of that exhilarating yet pacific outlook, imprisoned now in the narrow cell of his own subjective experience, the action of a powerful nature will be intense, yet exclusive and peculiar. It will come to art, or science, to the experience of life itself, not as portions of nature's daily food, but as something that must be, by the circumstances of the case, exceptional; almost as men turn in despair to gambling or narcotics, and in a little while the narcotic, the game of chance or skill is valued for its own sake. The vocation of the artist, of the student of life or books will be realised with something—say! of fanaticism, as an end in itself, unrelated, unassociated.[41]

And yet Pater himself had expressed the point of view of the "désillusionné" in the "Conclusion" to *The Renaissance*. This passage, by describing so grimly the dangers of his own earlier philosophy, is as strong a retraction of that philosophy as one finds anywhere in Pater's writing. It also disproves Arthur Symons' theory that Pater was "quite content that his mind should 'keep as a solitary prisoner its own dream of the world.' "[42] Perhaps Symons confused Pater's withdrawn and distant personality with his philosophy of life, or perhaps he read the "Conclusion" but did not take sufficient notice of this passage about Mérimée or of another which describes Gaston de Latour climbing the tower of Jean de Beauce at Chartres. Gaston enjoys as he does so the "exhilarating yet pacific outlook" which Pater praises in the essay on Mérimée: "At each ascending storey, as the flight of birds, the scent of the fields swept past him, till he stood lost amid the unimpeded light and air of the watch-tower above the great bells, some coil of perplexity, of unassimilable thought or fact, fell away from him."[43] Gaston may still be isolated, but he is not confined in the narrow prison of the self; he stands in a watch-tower from which he can see and share in all human life. "And with that vision he can guess the secret of some older, deeper, more permanent ground of fact" (p. 52).

Marius has a similar moment of insight while he enjoys the quiet of the Sabine hills. There the answer, so far as there is an answer, comes to Marius in a moment of clearer understanding than he is ever to have again and on a day in which he seemed, like Shelley's ideal poet, in "possession of his own best and happiest self."[44] On this day Marius was considering a sentence from Marcus Aurelius: " 'Tis in thy power to think as thou wilt," which leads him to wonder whether a bold willingness to accept "the hypothesis of an eternal friend to man, just hidden behind the veil of a mechanical and material order," might not lead the

intellect eventually into certitude of that being's existence. It is
the philosophy of a divided man—emotions, will, and intellect
each operating in him separately—but of a man who desires internal unity and coherence. And indeed for a moment at least
the very possibility of such an internal harmony mirroring a
universal coherence frees Marius: "The purely material world,
that close, impassible prison-wall, seemed just then the unreal
thing, to be dissolving away all around him."[45] With the thought
that the world of material things may be only a reflection of the
divine mind—this making it not less but much more permanent—
Marius feels comforted: no longer solitary but companioned by
the divine assistant, no longer aware of time passing so much as
of the moment made permanent:

How often had the thought of their brevity spoiled for him the most
natural pleasures of life, confusing even his present sense of them by
the suggestion of disease, of death, of a coming end, in everything!
How had he longed, sometimes, that there were indeed one to whose
boundless power of memory he could commit his own most fortunate
moments, his admiration, his love, Ay! the very sorrows of which he
could not bear quite to lose the sense: . . . And he had apprehended
to-day, in the special clearness of one privileged hour, that in which
the experiences he most valued might as it were take refuge.[46]

The speculation which leads Marius into his moment of vision
reminds one of the philosophy of William James—and, looking to
the end of the story, one might even think of Marius as a prag-
matic martyr, for though he cannot assent completely to the
truths of Christianity, he acts *as if* they were true. Given a crucial
choice, he goes to the side of the believers.

By generously taking for granted the hypothesis that there is
a transcendent reality, Marius saves himself from the Decadent's
vision in which all activity is "unrelated, unassociated." With it he
finds a way to enjoy and even to preserve the perfect moment
without a sense of desperation as he does so. It is true that his
answer, like the conclusion of the novel, is still tenuous and
even melancholy—Marius would not be one to shout "alleluia"
even if he were suddenly convinced of salvation. As it is, his
attitude is more a provisional assent to a hypothesis than an active

assertion of belief. But it is sufficient to give him an "outlook," an escape from the prison of the self.

Thinking of the book only in relation to *The Renaissance* one might say that Pater had a negative and a positive purpose in writing *Marius the Epicurean:* on the one hand, he wanted to show the insufficiency and even the danger of the point of view he had expressed in the "Conclusion" to *The Renaissance;* and on the other, the positive side, he wished to offer a possible escape from the ultimate dissolution of the self which was the threat of a skeptical impressionism. The book, though an achievement in other ways, did not fulfill either of these practical purposes; of all the young writers who looked to Pater for guidance, only Lionel Johnson heeded the warning in *Marius the Epicurean.* Of course, simple chronology can explain the fact that *Marius* had very little effect upon Oscar Wilde. He came to Oxford the year after *The Renaissance* was published, read the book while he was there, and was strongly influenced by it. But by the time *Marius the Epicurean* was published Wilde was no longer a docile student, ready to change opinions as Pater changed his.

What, though, of someone like Arthur Symons? He was still a very young man when Pater first wrote to him in 1886, a year after the publication of *Marius.* Why was he also influenced by *The Renaissance* and not by *Marius the Epicurean?* The reason may lie in the fact that Pater's first discussion of the problem, his description of modern man's situation, was masterful, unforgettable, but his later solution of it was tentative and vague. The sentences of the "Conclusion," with their clear images and urgent tone, are forceful even now when their ideas and their phrases are perfectly familiar: "Not to discriminate every moment some passionate attitude in those about us, and in the very brilliancy of their gifts some tragic dividing of forces on their ways, is, on this short day of frost and sun, to sleep before evening."[47] We need only compare that sentence, or any sentence from the "Conclusion," with this passage from the essay on Mérimée: "Fundamental belief gone, in almost all of us, at least some relics of it remain—queries, reactions, after-thoughts; and they help to make an atmosphere, hazy perhaps, yet with many secrets of soothing light and shade, associating more definite objects to each

other by a perspective pleasant to the inward eye against a hopefully receding background of remoter and even remoter possibilities."[48] This is Pater's answer, the same answer as that of
Marius the Epicurean, but in writing it Pater manipulates his
prose almost with cunning, as if he wished to cover the tracks of
his thought. When the sentence finally drifts to an end, "we are
in a Mist." Thus the answer that Pater offered, though it seems to
have been useful to him personally, could not guide others
through the labyrinth, and Pater's disciples were left where
Pater himself had begun, "ringed round . . . by that thick wall
of personality."

Man is least himself
when he talks in his own person. Give him a mask,
and he will tell you the truth.
Oscar Wilde

Chapter IV

Oscar Wilde

In *A Vision* Yeats used Oscar Wilde as one of his examples of
those who live in the nineteenth phase of the lunar cycle, the
phase which marks the beginning of "the artificial, the abstract,
the fragmentary, and the dramatic." The man of this phase is
forced "to live in a fragment of himself and to dramatise that
fragment."[1] Others have had the same sense of Wilde's fragmentation. Arthur Symons describes him as one who made for himself
many souls "of intricate pattern and elaborate colour, webbed
into infinite tiny cells."[2] Then he modifies the image: Wilde is not
only a craftsman but also a skilled juggler who amuses people by
whirling his separate "souls" before them. Later he uses yet another metaphor, clearing the theatre and making Wilde the only
spectator of his own performance: "One sees that to him everything was drama, all the rest of the world and himself as well;
himself indeed always at once the protagonist and the lonely

53

king watching the play in the theatre emptied for his pleasure."[3]

On the basis of a somewhat similar theory about Wilde, Arthur Nethercot made a study of *The Picture of Dorian Gray* and of Wilde's plays in which he suggested that "he [Wilde] split himself into two parts, into two types of self-representative."[4] The later discovery of a letter from Wilde to an otherwise unknown admirer, Ralph Payne, helped to prove that both his theory and Symons' were correct: that is to say, that Wilde, even more consciously than most writers, split himself into various characters and saw in all of them some portion of his actual or potential self: "I am so glad you like that strange many coloured book of mine [*The Picture of Dorian Gray*]: it contains much of me in it. Basil Hallward is what I think I am: Lord Henry, what the world thinks me: Dorian what I would like to be—in other ages, perhaps."[5] This letter suggests the way in which it might best be possible to understand Oscar Wilde: by separating him, as he separated himself, into several selves (each, however, watching the other selves and offering comments upon or even engaging in dialogues with the self at stage-center), remembering always that the man and his work are inextricable, though the work too is a mask.

1 *The Mask of Dorian Gray*

In the opening scene of *The Picture of Dorian Gray* Basil Hallward and Lord Henry Wotton discuss Dorian Gray's physical beauty and his innocence: these are his given characteristics, but when he himself appears, the qualities in him that seem more striking are his quickness and docility—he is a good student. When Lord Henry "with that graceful wave of the hand that was always so characteristic of him" (and of Wilde) tells him that "the aim of life is self-development," Dorian understands immediately, just as a good student in the humanities might, the relevance of the doctrine to actual experience. And Oscar Wilde, like Dorian Gray, was also in this sense a good student. In his first term at Oxford in 1874, Wilde attended Ruskin's lectures on the "Aesthetic and Mathematic Schools of Art in Florence"; he became such an enthusiastic follower of Ruskin's teaching that he was one of the group which helped to build—or attempted to build—a road between Upper and Lower Hinksey. "Art and the Handicraftsman," one of Wilde's American lectures, gives his version of the story; in it he becomes one of the students with whom Ruskin first discussed the project. And, after all, he made it a good story, although the road-work had already begun when Wilde arrived in Oxford. Wilde's telling of it is only a slight elaboration, nothing to compare to the splendid lie with which he begins his account: "Well, let me tell you how it first came to me at all to create an artistic movement in England, a movement to show the rich what beautiful things they might enjoy and the poor what beautiful things they might create."[6]

While he was still a student Wilde wrote an essay on the Grosvenor Gallery exhibition of 1877 that showed a truer sense of intellectual history. There he mentioned "that revival of culture and love of beauty which in great part owes its birth to Mr. Ruskin, and which Mr. Swinburne, and Mr. Pater, and Mr. Symonds, and Mr. Morris, and many others, are fostering and keeping alive, each in his own particular fashion."[7] The review itself is written wholly under the influence of Ruskin: Wilde praises all the pictures done in the Pre-Raphaelite manner and gives Whistler only a slighting mention; moreover, his criticism itself tends, like Ruskin's, to be anecdotal. For instance, Wilde praises a painting called "Afterglow in Egypt" for its coloring, but, he says, "It is difficult to feel a human interest in this Egyptian peasant."[8]

It was partly as a result of this essay that Wilde began to move from the orbit of Ruskin towards that of Walter Pater: Wilde sent Pater a copy of his essay and received a cordial reply in which Pater suggested that they meet to discuss certain points about which they were not in agreement, "though," he continued, "on the whole I think your criticisms very just, and they are certainly very pleasantly expressed" (*Letters*, p. 47).

In *De Profundis* Wilde says that it was in his first term at Oxford, the term in which he trundled stones for Ruskin's road, that he read Pater's *The Renaissance*, "that book which was to have such strange influence over my life"[9] (*Letters*, p. 471). Of course, it may be an oversimplification—more than that, an affectation—to say that the course of one's life has been changed by a book; nevertheless, it is possible that, like many of Wilde's dramatic simplicities, this "explanation" is true in essentials.[10] A single book could change the whole course of a man's life if it expressed all the things that he was already prepared to believe. And Pater's uncanny ability to catch and hold the drift of intellectual experience in his time gave his work extraordinary power. Arthur Symons, for instance, also writes about *The Renaissance* as a book which "opened a new world to me, or rather, gave me the secret of the world in which I was living," and with a single detail he gives his comment the ring of truth: he says that he read *The Renaissance* in its first edition on ribbed paper—"I have the feel of it still in my fingers."[11]

In the world of art, in any event, such things are possible, and Lord Henry Wotton changes Dorian Gray's life within the space of an afternoon by preaching a sermon based on the "Conclusion" to *The Renaissance,* beginning with the horror of time's passing, the loss of youth, the short time in which strong sensation is possible, and ending with the exhortation: "Live! Live the wonderful life that is in you! Let nothing be lost upon you. Be always searching for new sensations."[12] As he preaches, Lord Henry notices the strong effect of his words, and his memories make it clear that he is not meant to represent Pater; he is the older Wilde remembering what he himself had once learned: "He [Lord Henry] was amazed at the sudden impression that his words had produced, and, remembering a book that he had read when he was sixteen, a book that had revealed to him much that he had not known before, he wondered whether Dorian was passing through a similar experience" (p. 23). The point is an important one because of the changes which Lord Henry makes in the message of *The Renaissance;* the words he uses may almost paraphrase Pater's, but the doctrine is Wilde's.

A scene from *The Ambassadors* shows the difference. The situation is very like that in *The Picture of Dorian Gray:* an older man, Lambert Strether, is giving a younger one, Little Bilham, the philosophy taught him by his own experience. The very words echo Lord Wotton's: "Live all you can; it's a mistake not to. It doesn't matter what you do in particular, so long as you have your life."[13] But the difference between Lord Wotton and Lambert Strether lies in Strether's belief that he must desire nothing, save his impressions, for himself. In his selflessness he is a Paterean saint, while Lord Wotton, whose search is not for "impressions" but for "sensations," is among the damned. Strether finds his pleasure in his vision of others; Lord Wotton is interested in the effects of external stimuli upon his own consciousness. His gaze is fixed upon himself. Pater had written, "We may well grasp at any exquisite passion, or contribution to knowledge that seems by a lifted horizon to set the spirit free for a moment."[14] The moment of great intensity, whether sensual, emotional, or intellectual, serves as an escape from imprisoning self-consciousness. Dorian Gray, under the tutelage of Lord Wotton, takes pleasure not so much in enjoyment of the moment as in watching the effect of the moment upon himself.

Gray makes another important modification of Pater's doctrine when he uses evil acts as a means of achieving "sensations." His hope as he does so is to come to ever deeper self-knowledge, ever wider self-expression. And so it fascinates him to think that he can watch the gradual process of his own corruption in the portrait: "He would be able to follow his mind into its most secret places. This portrait would be to him the most magical of mirrors. As it revealed to him his own body, so it would reveal his own soul" (p. 128).

But the portrait really gives only a partial revelation; it presents no vision of the "best self," and by taking its partial revelation for the whole truth, Dorian Gray narrows his consciousness. Pater in his review of the book makes that point and protests at the same time against the interpretation put upon his theory—if so strong a word as "protest" may be used for his blandly remote comment: "A true Epicureanism aims at a complete though harmonious development of man's entire organism. To lose the moral sense, therefore, for instance, the sense of sin and righteousness, as Mr. Wilde's hero—his heroes seem bent on doing as speedily, as completely as they can, is to lose, or lower, organization, to become less complex, to pass from a higher to a lower degree of development."[15] And indeed, although his first letter to Wilde was flatteringly cordial, Pater came in time to find his young student just as distressing as he later found the fictitious Dorian Gray.[16]

André Gide's account of one of the stories Wilde often told
(though from behind the Lord Henry mask) makes Pater's distrust understandable. Wilde had noticed that Gide listened with
intensity to all that was said: "You listen with your eyes," Wilde
commented, and he went on to tell of the flowers which had
asked the river for water that they might weep for Narcissus, who
had just died. The river refused, saying that all the drops of
water it contained were not enough for his own tears, so much
had he loved Narcissus:

"'Oh!' replied the flowers of the field, 'how could you not have loved
Narcissus? He was beautiful.' 'Was he beautiful?' said the river. 'And
who could know better than you? Each day, leaning over your banks,
he beheld his beauty in your water . . .' "

Wilde paused for a moment . . .

"'If I loved him,' replied the river, 'it was because, when he leaned
over my water, I saw the reflection of my waters in his eyes.' "

Then Wilde, swelling up with a strange burst of laughter, added,
"That's called *The Disciple.*"[17]

This, however, is the attitude of a different Oscar Wilde; his
youthful change from following Ruskin to following Pater was
much less conscious and not at all cynical. By the time he wrote
another criticism of a Grosvenor Gallery exhibition, that of 1879,
he showed a difference in his views by the praise he gave to
Whistler;[18] in "L'Envoi," written in 1882 while he was in America,
Wilde formally avowed his withdrawal from Ruskin's sphere of
influence and made his presence in Pater's apparent by his generous (though unacknowledged) quotation from the master.

Although Wilde says that "we of the younger school have made
a departure from the teaching of Ruskin,—a departure definite,
and different and decisive," he realizes at least partially the effect
Ruskin's teaching had had upon Oxford. Wilde's opinion of the
nature of his achievement is interesting in that, with some
justice, it relates Ruskin's work more closely to Pater's than
either man might have liked; he writes that Ruskin "taught us at
Oxford that enthusiasm for beauty which is the secret of Hellenism." But Ruskin cannot be an acceptable master, "for the key-
stone of his aesthetic system is ethical always."[19]

Wilde posed in "L'Envoi" as the acknowledged leader of his

generation. Indeed, his high-handedness offended Rennell Rodd, the author of *Rose Leaf and Apple Leaf* for which this essay served as preface, because Wilde, as self-appointed editor, cut out of the book two poems Rodd had intended to publish and then wrote himself a fulsome dedication in Rodd's name.[20] But Wilde's lofty tone and loftier actions show that he would have liked to be what later he attempted to make of Dorian Gray: "Indeed there were many . . . who saw, or fancied that they saw, in Dorian Gray the true realization of a type of which they had often dreamed in Eton or Oxford days—a type that was to combine something of the real culture of the scholar with all the grace and distinction and perfect manner of a citizen of the world (pp. 155–56). It may have been Wilde's desire to be the man of this new Renaissance—a Renaissance patterned by Pater— that moved him in 1881 to issue his *Poems*. It is hard otherwise to explain how a man who wrote so fine a critical essay as "The Critic as Artist" would not recognize his own poems as bad art.

A good many of the *Poems* are simply schoolboy exercises in which Wilde wrote patriotic, hortatory sonnets in the manner of Milton and Wordsworth; wistful, Catholic sonnets in the manner of Rossetti; lush, pagan effusions in the manner of Swinburne.[21] Nevertheless, the general pattern of the book parallels Wilde's account of Dorian Gray's "search for sensations." In the section of *Dorian Gray* modelled mainly upon Huysmans' *A Rebours* Wilde says that Dorian, desiring experience "that would be at once new and delightful, and possess that element of strangeness so essential to romance . . . would often adopt certain modes of thought that he knew to be really alien to his nature" (p. 159). He was, for instance, attracted for a while to the Roman Catholic ritual, as well as to mysticism ("and the subtle antinomianism that seems to accompany it") and to the materialism of the *Darwinismus* movement in Germany. "Yet as has been said before, no theory of life seemed to him to be of any importance compared with life itself" (p. 160).

Now as it happened there seemed also the possibility around the year 1877 that Wilde might become a Catholic,[22] and several of the earlier poems in the book describe the Church's fascination for him: "Rome Unvisited," "Urbs Sacra Æterna," and "Sonnet on

hearing the Dies Irae sung in the Sistine Chapel." Following the
section of the book which contains these poems comes "The
Burden of Itys," which rejects Catholicism and celebrates the
return of a splendid new Hellenism:

> Poor Fra Giovanni bawling at the mass
> Were out of tune now, for a small brown bird
> Sings overhead, and through the long cool grass
> I see that throbbing throat which once I heard
> On starlit hills of flower-starred Arcady.[23]

A later poem, "Panthea," takes the position that human happiness
lies in the recognition that we shall "through all æons mix and
mingle with the Kosmic Soul!" (*Poems,* p. 191)—while further on
"Humanitad" asserts that "That which is purely human, that is
Godlike, that is God" (*Poems,* p. 228). Of course, it is possible to
argue that Dryden's *Collected Works* would show just as many
changes of opinion: the opinion itself is poetically not of importance so much as the truth of its expression, its truth, so to
speak, to itself. But this is precisely where Wilde fails: he is not
true even to his changing opinions; he is much more conscious of
himself as Wilde the Catholic, Wilde the pagan, Wilde the
humanist, than he is of the Catholicism, paganism, or humanism
he professes. Knowing that such an objection is possible, he gives
this justification for the "insincerity" of Dorian Gray:

Is insincerity such a terrible thing? I think not. It is merely a method
by which we can multiply our personalities.

Such at any rate was Dorian Gray's opinion. He used to wonder
at the shallow psychology of those who conceive the Ego in man as a
thing simple, permanent, reliable, and of one essence. To him, man
was a being with myriad lives and myriad sensations, a complex
multiform creature that bore within himself strange legacies of
thought and passion, and whose very flesh was tainted with the
monstrous maladies of the dead (pp. 171–72).

As the passage continues, it becomes obvious that the adoption
of a new idea or belief serves only as the opportunity for acting
a different role, for Wilde moves from a discussion of Dorian
Gray's changing opinions to a description of his imaginative identification with different personalities, first those of his historical

ancestors and then those of his "ancestors in literature." It is worth noting that he is drawn only to depravity, but what is really more important is that his imagination shows a reverse, a Decadent "negative capability." Instead of losing himself in other people or ideas, he brings them into himself until indeed only his own ego exists: "There were times when it appeared to Dorian Gray that the whole of history was merely the record of his own life, not as he had lived it in act and circumstance, but as his imagination had created it for him, as it had been in his brain and in his passions" (pp. 173–74).

Wilde's poem "The Sphinx" and the play *Salomé* are both marred by qualities which resemble those of Dorian Gray's reveries. Both are sexual fantasies which dwell on the morbid and even the depraved, but although the subject matter itself can partially account for the atmosphere of decay which pervades them, it is its manner of presentation which throws around these works an even more lurid, phosphorescent light. The meditations on the strange half-bestial lovers of the Sphinx or on Salomé's passion for John the Baptist are auto-eroticism, not negative capability. There is no question of Wilde thinking himself into the soul of Salomé, understanding her motivation, suffering her passion; he is simply using Salomé imaginatively in order to experience a new *frisson*. And, when Herod turns at the end of the play and gives orders, "Tuez cette femme,"[24] the act itself means nothing save that the reverie is over: Salomé has fulfilled her function.

When Dorian Gray, frightened by the near success of Jim Vane's vengeful attempt to kill him, decides that he will reform his life, his first act of virtue is to spare the honor of a country maiden—an act which shows Gray's lack of originality in virtue as well as in sin. But Lord Henry Wotton makes him realize that even goodness is now only another form of self-consciousness for him, still another *frisson* for one to whom every sort of vice has now become monotonous. Dorian begins to wonder: "Had it been merely vanity that had made him do his one good deed? Or the desire of a new sensation, as Lord Henry had hinted with his mocking laugh? Or that passion to act a part that sometimes makes us do things finer than we are ourselves? Or perhaps all of these?" (p. 269). At last he concludes that it was, indeed, all of these, and utterly trapped, he stabs the portrait and kills himself.

One of the reasons that *De Profundis* makes such painful reading is that Wilde there shows himself equally trapped within the mask of Dorian Gray. Though he may wish and intend repentance, he cannot keep himself from dramatizing the wish at the same time, so that it becomes unreal, perhaps even to himself. Repentance itself becomes a new and different kind of "moment":

I remember that as I was sitting in the dock on the occasion of my last trial listening to Lockwood's appalling denunciation of me . . . and being sickened with horror at what I heard, suddenly it occurred to me, *How splendid it would be, if I was saying all this about myself.* I saw then at once that what is said of a man is nothing. The point is, who says it. A man's very highest moment is, I have no doubt at all, when he kneels in the dust, and beats his breast, and tells all the sins of his life (*Letters*, p. 502).

But Lord Henry Wotton, watching such a performance, would have given his mocking laugh.

ii *The Mask of Lord Henry Wotton*

Throughout the trials, but especially in the first, Wilde retained the mask by which he was at the time best known: that of the dandy—calm, intellectually acute, remote and almost cynical (for even outright cynicism would imply too much emotion) —in the tradition described by Barbey d'Aurévilly. He was the aphorist, the creator of paradoxes which, however light-hearted and even light-minded they might seem, showed the ability to detect and expose affectation in a moment. Moreover, he could expose evil or weakness without professing to be either good or strong—only indifferent. This was the mask of Lord Henry Wotton, which Wilde said was "what the world thinks me."

Wilde put on the mask of Lord Henry very early; at least it is possible to catch glimpses of him wearing it even on his trip to America, when his part was more often that of a young man living for the sake of intense experience, a Dorian Gray. Lord Henry's attitude toward experience, though it possesses similarities, is really quite different: " 'I have known everything,' said Lord Henry, with a tired look in his eyes, 'but I am always ready

for a new emotion. I am afraid, however, that, for me at any
rate there is no such thing' " (p. 95). George Woodberry, who
met Wilde in Lincoln, Nebraska, wrote a long letter to Charles
Eliot Norton describing him; in it he mentions a very similar pose
of world-weary remoteness from vital experience, a self-conscious
abstention from life instead of a self-conscious desire to enjoy it:
"He [Wilde] told every[thing] of his early life to show that he
had developed, and he may keep on; but I am sorry for the man
who loves Ruskin and says that 'like Christ he bears the sins of
the world,' and who straightway speaks of himself as 'always, like
Pilate, washing his hands of all responsibility.' The contrast is
unfortunate."[25]

It is possible to think of all the essays in *Intentions*, including
"The Soul of Man under Socialism," as spoken through the mask
of Lord Henry Wotton, not so much for the ideas expressed in
them as for the way in which they are expressed: the pose of the
writer, or of the main speaker in the dialogues, is in all of them
that of the detached ironist, the aristocratic observer. The necessary separation between art and nature is the first premise of
Wilde's mature criticism: it was an old doctrine, but it had been
given a new interpretation, its truth revealed in a new way by
Baudelaire when he insisted that "la première affaire d'un artiste
est de substituer l'homme à la nature et de protester contre elle"[26]
and that "Tout ce qui est beau et noble est le résultat de la raison
et du calcul."[27] Even as early as 1882, Wilde with his enormous
capacity for the fruitful combination of ideas, if not for their
creation, had brought this theory into harmony with the doctrine
of Rossetti and Pater on art's capturing of the "moment":

For him [the poet] there is but one time, the artistic moment; but one
law, the law of form; but one land, the land of Beauty—a land removed
indeed from the real world yet more sensuous because more enduring;
calm, yet with that calm which dwells in the faces of Greek statues,
the calm which comes not from the rejection but the absorption of
passion.[28]

Wilde wrote whimsically in "The Decay of Lying" and "The
Critic as Artist," but his theory is the same: out of the flux of
experience art must create form, for raw experience is meaning-

less—the only pattern possible is that made within the human mind. Wilde also takes the next logical step to a position which superficially resembles Arnold's on the poet's role as "myth-maker" in the society of the future[29] but actually stands Arnold on his head—Arnold intended that poetry serve as a bridge between man and the world surrounding him; Wilde makes it a defense, a drawbridge: "I am certain that, as civilization progresses and we become more highly organized, the elect spirits of each age, the critical and cultured spirits, will grow less and less interested in actual life, and will seek to gain their impressions almost entirely from what Art has touched. For Life is terribly deficient in form."[30]

One of Wilde's most interesting paradoxes allows for a relationship between art and nature but reverses their usual order of precedence, saying that, if the truth of the matter is properly understood, it is obvious that nature does her fumbling best to imitate art. The Impressionists created "those wonderful brown fogs that come creeping down our streets"; Rossetti and Swinburne have made "the long throat, the strange square-cut jaw, the loosened shadowy hair" common attributes in women;[31] that is to say, the artist by making us aware of objects, brings them into existence for us. Along with this rather simple psychological point, however, goes a more mysterious interpretation of art's function:

The Greeks, with their quick artistic instinct, understood this [art's influence on life], and set in the bride's chamber the statue of Hermes or Apollo, that she might bear children as lovely as the work of art she looked at in her rapture or her pain. They knew that Life gains from Art not merely spirituality, depth of thought and feeling, soul-turmoil or soul-peace, but that she can form herself on the very lines and colours of art, and can reproduce the dignity of Pheidias as well as the grace of Praxiteles.[32]

Yeats read that sentence while "The Decay of Lying" was still on galley sheets,[33] and although he may also have found the doctrine elsewhere, especially in the work of the Symbolists, it is interesting to see it appear, relatively unchanged, even in his very late poems. In "The Statues" he refers to it—and mentions Phidias—in the lines:

> when Phidias
> Gave women dreams and dreams their looking-glass.[34]

His final poem, "Under Ben Bulben," has this stanza:

> Poet and sculptor, do the work,
> Nor let the modish painter shirk
> What his great forefathers did,
> Bring the soul of man to God.
> Make him fill the cradles right.[35]

Wilde, at least in his character of Lord Henry, would not have liked to see the matter put so strongly. He always insisted on art's inutility; and yet his interest in art as the mirror of the creator's personality led him to give much less importance to form and style than, say, Gautier would have given, even when he seems to be repeating Gautier's ideas. For instance, in a review of George Sand's letters Wilde writes that "art for art's sake is not meant to express the final causes of art but is merely a formula of creation." The review continues: "She [George Sand] thought Flaubert too much preoccupied with the sense of form and makes these excellent observations to him—perhaps her best piece of literary criticism. 'You consider the form as the aim, whereas it is but the effect. Happy expressions are only the outcome of emotion and emotion itself proceeds from a conviction.'"[36] George Woodberry even questioned the real strength of Wilde's feeling for form: "He speaks of form; it seems to me he has more sense of color. He spoke of prose style, but he cared for its iridescence, as in Pater."[37] And it is true that Wilde's interpretation of "art for art's sake" carries none of the overtones of an almost grim dedication to the careful chiselling of a line, the arduous polishing of a phrase. Wilde's doctrine is really "art for the artist's sake": "*A work of art is the unique result of a unique temperament. Its beauty comes from the fact that the author is what he is. It has nothing to do with the fact that other people want what they want.*"[38]

As early as 1882 Wilde's eclectic talent had established a relationship between the ideas of "art for art's sake" and of "self-realization":

For it is not enough that a work of art should conform to the aesthetic demands of its age: there must be also about it, if it is to affect us with any permanent delight, the impress of a distinct individuality, an individuality remote from that of ordinary men.

La personalité, said one of the greatest of modern French critics, *voilà ce qui nous sauvera.*[39]

Admittedly, Baudelaire had already done much of Wilde's work for him when he established two principles: first that the thought of the artist dominates his model, and second that an artist must work with enormous fidelity to his craft.[40] However, Wilde makes an extremely important change in the theory by linking it with his own interpretation of Pater's impressionism. When Baudelaire writes of an artist's "naïveté"—his ability to express his essential nature—he makes that nature a constant, perhaps the only constant in the artist's work. Wilde, however, like Anthony Beavis in Aldous Huxley's *Eyeless in Gaza,* thought the permanence of personality "a very subtle metaphysical problem";[41] the "chameleon poet" thus has his counterpart in a Wildean "chameleon critic," but just as Wilde reversed the direction of negative capability, bringing all outside experience into himself, so he makes the process of appreciation "the record of one's own soul" and criticism "the only civilized form of autobiography," one which deals with "the spiritual moods and imaginative passions of the mind."[42]

Nevertheless, any change Wilde makes in Baudelaire's theory is the result of a difference in emphasis and not in theory—the outcome of Wilde's tendency to link critic and artist more closely than Baudelaire would have done, for Wilde's impressionism is very closely related to Baudelaire's belief that "la meilleure critique est celle qui est amusante et poétique . . . un beau tableau étant la nature réfléchie par un artiste,—celle qui sera ce tableau réfléchi par un esprit intelligent et sensible. Ainsi, le meilleur compte rendu d'un tableau pourra être un sonnet ou une élégie."[43] Wilde entirely agreed—as had his aesthetic masters Pater, Rossetti, and Swinburne—though when he himself attempted such critical set pieces (as he did, for instance, when describing *A Rebours* in *The Picture of Dorian Gray*), he was not really successful at all: his very self-consciousness, his desire to do a piece of "fine writing" came between the art work and his "esprit intelligent et sensible." When he reached for less, as he did in the essays of *Intentions,* he achieved more real insight, and if he was not poetic, he was very amusing. Moreover, he was, willy-nilly, instructive; his two sentences on Wordsworth are the equal of several paragraphs on the "egotistical sublime": "Wordsworth went to the lakes but he was never a lake poet. He found in stones the sermons he had already hidden there."[44]

Of the names which have appeared so far as influences upon Wilde, only one might cause a slight start of surprise—Matthew Arnold—and yet he is, one might say, the guest of honor in Wilde's criticism. In "The Critic as Artist" Wilde (or rather, Gilbert, the Wildean character in the dialogue) speaks of Arnold as one "whose gracious memory we all revere" but adds that Arnold's definition of the aim of criticism—"to see the object as in itself it really is"—is "a very serious error, and takes no cognizance of Criticism's most perfect form, which is in its essence purely subjective, and seeks to reveal its own secret and not the secret of another."[45] But although Wilde and Arnold may begin by describing their ideal critic in opposite terms, their concepts of his role within society are surprisingly similar. Wilde's individualist critic, like Arnold's man of culture, is not active but contemplative. He is devoted to the principle of beauty, just as the Arnoldian perfect man is devoted to "sweetness and light," and as a result of his disciplined devotion he has a similar order, harmony, and breadth of mind: "The true critic will, indeed, always be sincere in his devotion to the principle of beauty, but he will seek for beauty in every age and in each school, and will never suffer himself to be limited to any settled custom of thought, or stereotyped mode of looking at things."[46] Wilde, like Arnold, must defend the contemplative vision of the individualist's "good life" from those who would charge that in remaining aloof from all philanthropic and humanitarian activity, in refusing to be socially useful, the critic is not only unsocial but anti-social. He makes a very telling point: philanthropic activity, if carried on unthinkingly, only serves to increase social injustice because it glosses over and sentimentalizes but does not eradicate social evil:

*The proper aim is to try to reconstruct society on such a basis that
poverty will be impossible.* And the altruistic virtues have really prevented the carrying out of this aim. Just as the worst slave-owners were
those who were kind to their slaves, and so prevented the horror of the
system being realized by those who suffered from it, and understood by
those who contemplated it, so, in the present state of things in
England, the people who do most harm are the people who try to do
most good.[47]

Summing up the world in a phrase, Wilde concludes: "There
is also this to be said: It is immoral to use private property in
order to alleviate the horrible evils that result from the institution of private property. It is both immoral and unfair." Philanthropic endeavor is individually as well as socially harmful in
Wilde's opinion: its necessary activity and emotion have the bad
effect of beclouding what might otherwise have been a clear
mind: "The sure way of knowing nothing about life is to try
to make oneself useful."[48]

Gilbert says, "But perhaps you think that in beholding for the
mere joy of beholding, and contemplating for the sake of contemplation, there is something that is egotistic. If you think so,
do not say so."[49] And Wilde's analysis, through Gilbert, has been
so intelligent that the reader, like Ernest, is silent—but is he
convinced? The difficulty is that Wilde, when he writes of the
good life for the individual and for society, is writing in the
spirit of Lord Henry Wotton: that is to say, his intellectual understanding of society's problems carries with it no desire "to make
reason and the will of God prevail." Sometimes one senses even
in the Arnold of *Culture and Anarchy* a latent wish to remove
himself from society, a latent fear of Victorian society's violent
growth and change: Wilde makes both the wish and the fear
overt by transforming the Arnoldian man of culture into a Baude-
lairean dandy: "Calm and self-centered and complete, the
aesthetic critic contemplates life, and no arrow drawn at a
venture can pierce between the joints of his harness. He at least
is safe, he has discovered how to live."[50] The dark side of that
statement finds its expression in Lord Henry's comment: "I can
sympathize with everything except suffering . . . . It is too ugly,
too horrible, too distressing. There is something terribly morbid

in the modern sympathy with pain" (pp. 47–48).

To the Romantics' sense of isolation from society and Arnold's distrust of "the masses," Wilde added the contempt of Gautier and of Baudelaire for "la marée montante de la démocratie" which is one of the most important elements in both *Dandyisme* and Parnassianism.[51] Or, it would be more truthful to say, Wilde seems at times to have wished that he could be capable of a dandy's lofty contempt. Time and again, however, his desire to win approval, his extraordinary dependence on the good opinion of the whole society, shows through the mask of Lord Henry. When he writes privately, as in this note to Lord Alfred Douglas, it is obvious: "Please *always* let me see *anything* that appears about myself in the Paris papers—good or bad, but especially the *bad*. It is a matter of vital import to me to know the attitude of the community" (*Letters*, p. 591).

Although Wilde's desire for others' good opinion may seem a "happy fault," no matter how ridiculous it might occasionally make him appear, it is necessary to remember that, in part of his nature at least, he himself regarded it as a terrible weakness; though he could not always preserve the mask of Lord Henry, he would have liked to do so, as he confessed to André Gide: "It is not through excessive individualism that I have sinned. My great mistake, the error I cannot forgive myself, is having, one day, ceased to believe in it in order to listen to others, ceased to believe that I was right to live as I did, doubted myself."[52] Nevertheless a part of Wilde's nature always doubted the "self" of Lord Henry; the spokesman for that part is Basil Hallward.

III *Basil Hallward*

Basil Hallward is, on the surface at least, a much less interesting character than either Lord Henry or Dorian Gray. Yet it is of him that the flamboyant Wilde writes, "Basil Hallward is what I think I am." His comment adds greatly to the significance of Basil's murder, which otherwise has the air of a plot device that is both awkward and ineffective, and it also gives yet another possible explanation for Wilde's decision to remain in England and face trial for homosexuality. It is now almost a tradition for those who write on Wilde to offer an explanation for his

refusal to flee the country when flight was still possible: Frank
Harris says that Wilde's cowardice made it impossible for him
to face a decision, so that, in a lethargy of fear, he stayed; Yeats
believes that Wilde showed his greatest courage in remaining and
makes his doing so a proof of the theory that Wilde really was
a man of action; Hesketh Pearson thinks Wilde's resolution the
result of his incurable love of self-dramatization, itself caused by
his emotional immaturity; Robert Sherard believes that Wilde
was caught in the grip of megalomania.[53] What is interesting
about every one of these theories is that each is a reflection of
the particular biographer's ordering vision of Wilde's character.
And although every one of them might be partially true in the
case of a personality as fragmented as Wilde's, none offers the
explanation hidden in the character of Basil Hallward: that there
was in Wilde an "ordinary man" who felt terrible guilt for the
sins of that part of him represented by Dorian Gray and who
could never really be convinced, as Lord Henry Wotton was
convinced, that sin is merely another form of self-realization.

Conversations between Lord Henry, Basil Hallward, and
Dorian Gray become very interesting, then, if one thinks of them
as an internal dialogue.[54] First Dorian Gray, the student, the one
given over to influences, asks:

> "What do you mean by good, Harry?"
> "To be good is to be in harmony with oneself," he replied, touching
> the thin stem of his glass with his pale, fine pointed fingers. "Discord
> is to be forced to be in harmony with others" (p. 93).

Lord Henry continues with an exposition of the philosophy of
individualism, and in the course of it makes a telling point: the
dandy, by making himself the center of his morality, is at least
without illusions. He is not acting from a pretended belief in a
code no longer in existence: "Modern morality consists in accepting the standards of one's age. I consider that for any man of
culture to accept the standard of his age is a form of the grossest
immorality." Lord Henry had adjusted to a world without
absolute values by making himself his own absolute. But Basil
Hallward still believes in objective absolutes of right and wrong
and even gives society the right to punish those who transgress

them, not because society really understands either the sin or the sinner but because society's vengeance is the sinner's purification:

"But surely, if one lives merely for one's self, Harry, one pays a terrible price for doing so?" suggested the painter.
"Yes, we are overcharged for everything nowadays . . . Beautiful sins, like beautiful things, are the privilege of the rich."
"One has to pay in other ways but money."
"What sort of ways, Basil?"
"Oh! I should fancy in remorse, in suffering, in . . . well, in the consciousness of degradation" (p. 94).

There is another conversation which gives the impression of interior dialogue: it is held between Basil Hallward and Dorian Gray not long before Basil's murder: " 'I owe a great deal to Harry, Basil,' he [Dorian Gray] said at last—'More than I owe to you. You only taught me to be vain.' 'Well, I am punished for that Dorian—or shall be some day' " (p. 131). And later Dorian says: "I am changed, but you must always be my friend. Of course, I am very fond of Harry. But I know you are better than he is. You are not stronger—you are too much afraid of life—but you are better" (p. 133). Basil seems weaker than Lord Henry only because his conscience makes him vulnerable as Lord Henry is not.

Still another point is illuminated by thinking of Hallward as a reflection of Wilde. The sins with which Dorian Gray experiments are left vague, though the suggestion that homosexuality is the chief of them is clear enough, and Lord Henry talks much about self-realization through sin but never seems to commit any (with the single, but terrible, exception of Hawthorne's unforgivable sin[55]): as the book was originally written, however, it is Basil who openly confesses to homosexuality and regards it as a sin that he must expiate. At the suggestion of Walter Pater, the whole passage was much toned down in the book's final version, with the result that Basil's central explanation falls a little flat; he explains only the obvious. In the earlier version, this was not so; Basil there says to Dorian Gray:

It is quite true that I have worshipped you with far more romance of feeling than a man usually gives to a friend. Somehow, I have never loved a woman. I suppose I never had time. Perhaps, as Harry says, a really "grande passion" is the privilege of those who have nothing to do, and that is the use of the idle classes in a country. Well, from the moment I met you, your personality had the most extraordinary influence over me. I quite admit that I adored you madly, extravagantly, absurdly. I was jealous of every man to whom you spoke. I wanted to have you all to myself. I was only happy when I was with you. When I was away from you, you were still present in my art. It was all very wrong and foolish. It is all wrong and foolish still.[56]

André Gide is of the opinion that, although Wilde always "insisted on the mask" in his work, yet "always he managed in such a way that the informed reader could raise the mask and glimpse, under it, the true visage (which Wilde had such good reasons to hide)."[57] His description of a reading of Wilde's work is unfortunate, however, if not unfair; it creates such an ugly picture of the knowing, rather prurient reader who, with an insinuating leer, can enjoy a special peep show of the soul—whereas in actuality, Wilde is like an elegant Ancient Mariner who fixes his readers with a glittering eye and demands that they hear his confession over and over again.

Gide's interpretation of the reasons behind Wilde's use of the mask is also open to question. In his opinion "this artistic hypocrisy was imposed on him by respect, which was very keen in him, for the proprieties, and by the need of self-protection."[58] Gide does not take into account the possibility that Wilde's respect for propriety may have had its basis in a respect for morality. Wilde can repeat as much as he pleases that "the artistic critic, like the mystic, is an antinomian always";[59] he remained in his heart a Manichean, nonetheless. His Manicheanism sometimes turns up unexpectedly, in fact, to contradict points he has carefully made about the complete separation between aesthetics and ethics; for example, it does so in his letter to the *St. James Gazette* about *Dorian Gray*. In defending his book he describes the sin committed by each of the main characters and the inevitable punishment it brings. He concludes: "Yes, there is a terrible moral in *Dorian Gray*—a moral which the prurient will not be able to find in it, but it will be revealed to all those whose minds are healthy." Then, catching himself up in the realization that all this talk of morality is beneath his dignity as an artist, he adds: "Is this an artistic error? I fear it is. It is the only error in the book."[60]

The stories told in *The House of Pomegranates* offer further evidence that Wilde was disturbed by a sense of guilt which he attempted to soothe by this partial, hidden confession. Each one of the stories, except "The Birthday of the Infanta," tells of a sin and a resulting fragmentation of personality, of repentance and ultimate healing—though sometimes the last is won only by death. The only mask Wilde uses in telling these stories is that of the style itself: it is a mingling of the ornate "jewelled" style (a mixture of Swinburne, perhaps, and Gautier) which he often uses in *Dorian Gray* and the carefully simple phrasing of Rossetti's *Hand and Soul,* heavily seasoned with the Bible and the *Arabian Nights.*[61] The result is exotic but not really unpalatable, perhaps because, in spite of their artifice, the stories have the quality of parables and carry a genuine human emotion.

"The Young King" describes the dreams by which a young "lover of the beautiful" is made aware of the human suffering necessary to provide him with beautiful robes and jewels; "The Star Child" concerns the long repentance of a beautiful child who in his pride repudiated his mother. But the most interesting of these tales is "The Fisherman and his Soul," which tells of a young fisherman's love for a mermaid. She promises to carry him with her to the caverns of the sea if he first will separate himself from his soul. The fisherman goes to the priest for help in sending his soul away and explains the reason, concluding:

> "And as for my soul, what doth my soul profit me, if it stand between me and the thing I love?"
> "The love of the body is vile," cried the Priest, knitting his brows, "and vile and evil are the pagan things God suffers to wander through His world. Accursed be the Fauns of the woodland, and accursed be the singers of the sea!"[62]

The fisherman finally gets his wish in spite of the priest, though he must use the powers of black magic to do it. He cuts off his soul and sends it away, refusing it the heart it pleads for; then he dives into the sea. Each year the soul attempts to lure him away from his mermaid, once with the promise of wisdom, next with the promise of wealth; each time the fisherman refuses, saying that love is stronger than either, but at the last temptation, which is really only that of physical desire—the promise that he shall see the white feet of a dancer nearby—the fisherman leaves the sea. Then he discovers not only that he cannot return but that his soul, which is heartless, leads him into acts of evil: violence, robbery, and finally murder.

Repentant and horrified, the fisherman binds himself so that his soul may not influence him further and returns to the shore (though always dogged by his soul) to search for the mermaid. Only after her death does he find her; at the sight of her body his heart breaks, and his soul, now purified, can again be united with him. The story has a coda: the priest's vision of the world is changed by the discovery of flowers growing from the grave in which the mermaid and the fisherman are buried:

And in the morning, while it was still dawn, he went forth with the monks and the musicians, and the candle-bearers and the swingers of censers, and a great company, and came to the shore of the sea, and blessed the sea, and all the wild things that are in it. The Fauns also he blessed, and the little things that dance in the woodland, and the bright-eyed things that peer through the leaves. All the things in God's world he blessed, and the people were filled with joy and wonder.[63]

Both Basil Hallward and Lord Henry Wotton have as their ideal the union of heart, soul, and body that "The Fisherman and his Soul" describes. Lord Henry believes that he has found the secret in his new hedonism: "to cure the soul by means of the senses, and the senses by means of the soul" (p. 25), but Basil, while he too says, "The harmony of soul and body—how much that is!" (p. 12) does not feel that such a harmony can be achieved by going against conscience. It is on the question of conscience that he and Lord Henry disagree: " 'Conscience and cowardice are really the same thing, Basil. Conscience is the trade-name of the firm. That is all.' 'I don't believe that, Harry, and I don't believe you do either' " (p. 8)·. The conflict in Basil between his conscience and his love for Dorian Gray is not resolved intellectually at all, though it finds an emotional resolution in his death. Through the more complex character of Sir Robert Chiltern, however, Wilde continues the discussion, the weighing and considering of the validity of conscience.

Sir Robert is the protagonist of Wilde's play, *An Ideal Husband*.[64] When the play opens Sir Robert is presented as a wealthy and very successful, highly respected undersecretary for foreign affairs. The mask he attempts to wear—and until the opening of the play he has been successful—is nothing less than perfection: he appears to be an incorruptible servant of the state, a supremely happily married man, an omniscient financier. However impossible it is to relate the mask to reality (and one of Wilde's points is that it is indeed impossible), the wearing of it proves how conventional Sir Robert is, how much he is bound by the code of society. Very early in the play Mrs. Chevely, an intelligent woman even though the villainess, points out society's hypocrisy:

In old days nobody pretended to be a bit better than his neighbours. In fact to be a bit better than one's neighbour was considered excessively vulgar and middle class. Nowadays, with our modern mania for morality, every one has to pose as a paragon of purity, incorruptibility, and all the other seven deadly virtues—and what is the result? You all go over like ninepins. . . . Not a year passes in England without somebody disappearing. Scandals used to lend charm, or at least interest, to a man—now they crush him.[65]

The whole play turns on Sir Robert's fear of unmasking, his imaginative picturing of "the loathsome joy" with which the newspapers would describe his fall and of the hypocritical dismay which would be expressed by his colleagues who "every day do something of the kind themselves. Men who, each one of them have worse secrets in their own lives" (p. 76). The secret of Sir Robert's life is that at the beginning of his career he had given state information to a Baron Arnheim about the British Government's intention to buy Suez Canal shares; on the strength of that knowledge the Baron had brought into the company when its stock was still very low and had made a fortune; in "gratitude" he gave Sir Robert £110,000.

Sir Robert is described in the stage directions as a man whose very features suggest "an almost complete separation of passion and intellect, as though thought and emotion were each isolated in its own sphere through some violence of will-power" (p. 11). The division becomes clear in his attitude toward the swindle: one side of his nature thinks it perfectly justifiable—more than that, courageous. He describes Baron Arnheim, who rather resembles Lord Henry Wotton and has "a strange smile on his pale, curved lips,"[66] as a man of splendid intellect, and he holds, with the Baron, that to wield power is the one pleasure of which one never tires. When his friend Lord Goring says that he was weak in yielding to Baron Arnheim's temptation, Sir Robert is almost indignant: "Weak? Do you really think, Arthur, that it is weakness that yields to temptation? I tell you that there are terrible temptations that it requires strength, strength and courage to yield to. To stake all one's life on a single moment, to risk everything on one throw, whether the stake be power or pleasure, I care not—there is no weakness in that. There is a horrible, a terrible courage" (pp. 82–83). When Lord Goring only answers that he is sorry for him, Sir Robert says immediately, "I don't say that I suffered any remorse. I didn't. Not remorse in the ordinary, rather silly sense of the word." Nevertheless, the remorse he goes on to describe bears all the characteristics of the ordinary variety, including the uselessness—silliness, one might say—of remorse without repentance: "But I have paid conscience money many times. I had a wild hope that I might disarm destiny. The sum Baron Arnheim gave me I have distributed twice over in public charities since then." (Lord Goring, speaking as one part of Wilde to another, cannot let that pass: "In public charities? Dear me, what a lot of harm you must have done, Robert!" [p. 85].) And later the purely emotional side of Sir Robert cries out, "I would to God that I had been able to tell the truth . . . to live the truth. Ah! that is the great thing in life, to live the truth" (p. 96).

Through the good offices of Lord Goring, who, like the Scarlet Pimpernel, is a dandy with a heart, Sir Robert is finally able to tell the truth, at least to his wife, and to win forgiveness; at the same time he preserves and even increases his position in the world. All this is done, though, in such a whirl of attempted blackmail, intercepted letters, and mutual misunderstandings and reassurances that the central conflict in the principal character is left unresolved—or rather, its resolution is practical, not psychological. Lord Goring is able to convince the puritanical Lady Chiltern that "life cannot be understood without much charity" (p. 101), and he says of Sir Robert: "What you know about him is not his real character. It is an act of folly done in his youth, dishonourable, I admit, shameful, I admit, unworthy of him, I admit, and therefore . . . not his real character" (p. 177). Even granted that this is so, there is nothing in the play to suggest that Sir Robert himself comes to know his own "real character," or that there is any final union between his intellectual amorality and his emotional sense of sin. By the end of the play the relation of the mask to the reality is as great a mystery as ever.

Indeed, *The Importance of Being Earnest* is the only one of Wilde's successful plays in which mask and reality prove to be one; it is possible to think of it (as it is of Mark Twain's *The Adventures of Huckleberry Finn*) as the author's evocation of a never-never land in which the individual, though part of society, is in his essence free of its rule.[67] In their self-centeredness Jack Worthing and Algernon Moncrieff have mastered life; they live remote from any real evil, any scarring emotion, any intellectual problem. But they can only do so in a world specially patterned for them and by them: one in which a broken engagement or a buttered muffin is of equal moment because all the members of it know both engagement and muffin to be at once all-important and unimportant. This knowledge gives all the freedom that life on the Mississippi gave to Huck.

The Importance of Being Earnest has one sort of sincerity; "The Ballad of Reading Gaol" has another. Certainly the poem has any number of artistic faults: it is repetitive, has abrupt and unnecessary changes of style and imagery, and moves equally abruptly from realism to melodrama. Yet in spite of all this the poem works because the emotion behind it is a genuine, not a constructed one, and because in the writing of it Wilde seems more conscious of the situation than of himself describing the situation. The letters Wilde sent to Robert Ross while he was writing the "Ballad" make a delightful collection, because in them too Wilde seems almost self-forgetful. Moreover, his tone is that of a genuine artist-critic: he gives his achievement its proper value. Once he writes whimsically, "I think bits of the poem very good now—but I will never again out-Kipling Henley" (*Letters*, p. 649). He is amusing again when he insists on putting in a few melodramatic stanzas in the style he enjoyed:

I have just sent Smithers four more stanzas for insertion—one of them very good, in the romantic vein you don't quite approve of; but on the whole it will, I think, make a balance in the poem. I can't be always "banging the tins." Here it is:

> It is sweet to dance to violins
> When Life and Love are fair:
> To dance to flutes, to dance to lutes,
> Is delicate and rare:
> But it is not sweet with nimble feet
> To dance upon the air.

On the whole, I like the poem now, except the second and third stanzas of Part III. I can't get that part right (*Letters*, pp. 652–53).[68]

"The Ballad of Reading Gaol" also has a significance beyond itself as the last communication, so to speak, between Wilde and the world outside him, before he became completely enclosed in the prison of himself. While he was still in Reading, Wilde wrote to Robert Ross: "Of course from one point of view I know that I shall be merely passing from one prison to another, and there are times when the whole world seems to me no larger than my cell and as full of terrors for me. Still I believe that at the beginning God made a world for each separate man, and in that world which is within us we should seek to live" (*Letters*, p. 512). When he was released from one prison and found himself indeed in another, he struggled for escape and failed. Then he fell back without hope, resigned to living in "that world which is within us," the world of Walter Pater's "Conclusion" to *The Renaissance*, which now, however, bore a great resemblance to Reading Gaol, where there are "crowds of people, walking round in a ring": "I must reconsider my position as I cannot go on living here as I am doing, though I know there is no such thing as changing one's life—one merely wanders round and round within the circle of one's own personality" *(Letters,* p. 671).

Wilde took the name "Sebastian Melmoth" when he left prison, the first name after the martyred Saint Sebastian, whom Wilde had once identified with Keats: "Fair as Sebastian, and as early slain,"[69] and the second after Melmoth, the outcast of Maturin's novel, doomed to wander eternally through the world. Thus the name itself is a sort of analogue for the title of Yeats' story, "The Crucifixion of the Outcast"; at their last meeting, just before his downfall, Wilde told Yeats that the story was "sublime, wonderful, wonderful."[70] Wilde took a family pride in the fact that Charles Maturin was his great-great-uncle[71]—and indeed the terrible, living portrait of Melmoth may have been in Wilde's mind when he wrote *Dorian Gray*—but in his choice of the name Melmoth he was undoubtedly influenced as well by Baudelaire's comments on "la grande création satanique du reverend Maturin": "Il [Melmoth's laughter] est, qu'on me comprenne bien, la résultante nécessaire de sa double nature contradictoire, qui est infiniment grande relativement à l'homme, infiniment vile et basse relativement au Vrai et au Juste absolus. Melmoth est une contradiction vivante."[72] And although it suited Wilde's melodramatic nature to wrap himself in the great cloak of such a name, playing the part of a "last Romantic," still there is this justice in his using it: his too was a nature of contradictions from which he could find no escape, and in which he finally walked solitary, utterly isolated.

With the intelligence to understand all the conflicts of his age, yet without the ability or the will to resolve them, Wilde was finally broken by them. Arnold had made Empedocles complain because the mirror of his soul caught only glimpses of reality, but at least the mirror itself was whole; in Wilde it was as if the glass were shattered and he set dancing and posturing before its pieces like the dwarf in his own story, "The Birthday of the Infanta"—seeing himself as an aesthete, a member of the Oxford Movement, an artist like Balzac wrapped in a white gown, a disciple of Renan, an aristocratic dandy. All these were, he believed, ways of expressing himself, of multiplying his personality, and all the time his real personality remained as much a puzzle to

him as it was to those who described him. The bewilderment that
one senses beneath all the posing, and the strange quality that
could only be called sincerity—or at least the desire to be sincere,
could he only find a basis for sincerity—these and his very real
humor give Wilde charm almost in spite of himself. Even George
Woodberry, who saw through all the poses, said of him: "I have
seen no one whose charm stole on me so secretly, so rapidly, and
with such entire sweetness. His poems are better than his theories,
and he better than his poems."[73] His charm would not have to be
very impressive to be better than his poems, it is true; however,
Woodberry's statement might be made broad enough to include
all of Wilde's works. His writings, like the costume of a court
jester, were a fantastic patchwork of other men's ideas in which
he walked proudly as a king, thinking himself splendidly attired.
And, like a court jester, he made it his business to amuse his age
—by his wit, if possible; by his antics, if necessary. But it may
well be that at times he caught sight of himself in his own shattered mirror and stopped short.

Chapter V

Lionel Johnson

During Wilde's first trial, Lionel Johnson wrote Yeats a letter
in which he denounced Wilde for his "cold scientific intellect"
and for the triumphant pleasure he took "at every dinner-table he
dominated, from the knowledge that he was guilty of that sin
which, more than any other possible to man, would turn all those
people against him if they but knew."[1] Yeats was saddened to find
that Johnson had "changed with the rest," and yet, given the
differences between his temperament and Wilde's, Johnson's lack
of sympathy is hardly surprising. Wilde became so intent on the
images of himself presented to the world that he lost the sense of
his "true self"—and it is interesting that Johnson places him
imaginatively thus, putting on a performance evening after evening. Johnson, on the other hand, cut himself off so effectively
from all contact with society that by the end of his short life he
was completely alone. Wilde's personality seems best described

by one of his favorite words, "many coloured"; the world in which
Johnson lived, spiritually and physically, was gray, relieved only
by gold, the color he associated with fantasy. In a room which
had curtains of gray corduroy hung over the doors, the windows,
and the bookcases, Johnson slept all day and read during the
night. Yeats asked him whether his schedule did not separate
him from men and women; he replied, "In my library I have all
the knowledge of the world I need."[2]

His answer was confident enough to silence Yeats, but a short
story by Johnson called "Incurable" shows that he himself had
doubts about his relationship with society. On the surface the
sketch pokes fun at aestheticism by describing a young poet who
feels that life holds no more for him. He decides to commit
suicide, regretting only that the river most convenient for his
purpose is waterlily-less. But even without waterlilies he finds it
possible to imagine himself floating down, like a male Lady
of Shalott (in Elizabethan costume), to a heartless and unthinking
London. In the midst of this reverie he falls absent-mindedly into
the river, comes to himself, and swims strongly for shore.

Underneath its satire, the story has a personal quality, a note
of both self-mockery and self-pity. In one passage, for instance,
the poet thinks of his present state: "I am just thirty [Johnson's
age at time of publication] . . . and quite useless. I have a good
education and a little money. I must do something and poetry is
what I want to do. I have published three volumes, and they are
entirely futile. They are not even bad enough to be interesting."
He riffles impatiently through his verses and comes back to the
problem: "And why can't I write better? I know what imagination
is and poetry, and all the rest of it. I go on contemplating my own
emotions, or inventing them; and nothing comes of it but this.
And yet I'm not a perfect fool." Yet no matter how frustrated he
is by his self-enclosure, the poet cannot free himself by taking
part in the concerns of the busy commercial empire which under-
lay Victorian society—he turns away from that: "He would be of
no use: if he went out to the colonies, or upon the stock exchange, he would continue to write quantities of average and
uninteresting verse."[3] Does it not seem possible that this internal
conversation was familiar to Johnson because he had been

speaker and listener in many similar ones?

He was himself from a typical Victorian family, one involved with the fortunes of England, whose men traditionally became officers in the army. Johnson's father was a retired captain; his three brothers were officers who served faithfully in the colonies. But even as a schoolboy Johnson was detached, cut off from any family bonds. The letters he wrote in his last years at Winchester—1883–1885—invariably refer to his family as "Philistine," and when Lord Francis Russell planned to visit him at home, Johnson wrote to J. H. Badley: "A. [Francis Russell] comes to us on the second for a few days: which will be a break in the monotony of spiritual solitude."[4] Later he described the visit to Charles Sayle: "A. [Russell] is with us tasting the quality of Philistia: he rather seems to endure it, and reproaches me with intentional cruelty towards my people—a strange side of the matter."[5] Remarks like these are not at all extraordinary in the correspondence of an adolescent, especially of a very consciously "intellectual" one; as Johnson became less consciously and more truly intellectual, one would expect him in the ordinary course of things to accept his family and his place within it, just because he could accept the many inevitable separations between its ideas and his own. But that was not the pattern of Johnson's development. He may, very occasionally, make a reference that shows some family pride: when reviewing *Barrack-Room Ballads* he writes a little scornfully of those critics who complain of difficulty in reading technical army phrases—"Such criticism is of a piece with the prevailing apathy and ignorance concerning the army"[6]—but with time he turned more and more completely away from his family. By the end of his life, he was living on a pension given him by his mother, but he had no personal connection with his family whatever.

Connected with Johnson's withdrawal from his family's worldly concerns was his rejection of the family form of worship; with his parents' devout, "middle" Anglicanism he had very little patience and wrote to Russell after the latter's visit: "As you see faith in my family is a large element of belief: my father with his 'omnipotent,' my mother with her Churchism—see what faith is. I feel rather bitter in temper, as though selfishness was really more strong than love: it never is. But I seem lonely."[7] The *Winchester Letters* begin with a correspondence between Russell and Johnson in which they both consider Buddhism as a possible substitute for the more Philistine religions; after they read Sinnett's *Esoteric Buddhism,* Johnson publicly announced his conversion. His father replied by forbidding him to write to Russell or to read Buddhist literature,[8] a reaction that seems, indeed, a little pompous as well as unwise, but without doubt it was unthinkable to his parents that Johnson should not follow perfectly naturally in the faith of his fathers. At any rate, Johnson moved very quickly from Buddhism into Shelleyan Platonism, Emersonian Transcendentalism, Whitmanesque Humanism—what you will. Yet the confusion is not as great as it might seem, for all the masters Johnson acknowledges are those whose mental set is towards the transcendental. Just as Yeats would listen respectfully to any doctrine which might help in the overthrow of "Carolus Duran, Bastien-Lepage, Huxley and Tyndall,"[9] so Johnson writes: "Eschew altogether the miserable affectations of Schopenhauer, Hartmann, Comte; hate all systems of that nature: but love the great idealists, Kant, Schelling, Fichte, Emerson."[10]

Johnson's reading was enormously important to him not only as a schoolboy but throughout his life because, having turned away from his family and the social order it embodied and having, therefore, refused the identity which any role in society might offer, he worked at the creation of a self through identification with those authors who attracted him. He searched his library for fragments to shore against his ruin. For Johnson would have been one of those agreeing with Yeats when the latter wrote in 1897: "In our time we are agreed that we 'make our souls' out of some of the great poets of ancient times, or out of Shelley, or Wordsworth, or Goethe, or Balzac, or Count Tolstoy . . . or out of Mr. Whistler's pictures."[11]

When Santayana first visited Johnson in the latter's room at Oxford, he noticed—indeed he could scarcely help noticing—a secular shrine on a center table. A jug of Glengarry whiskey stood between two open books: *Les Fleurs du Mal* and *Leaves of Grass;* looking down upon them were portraits of Cardinal Newman and Cardinal Wiseman.[12] These arrangements have the quality of a still life, an exquisitely careful and conscious patterning of elements with a perhaps unconscious desire behind it to show that the life might disintegrate were the pattern to be disturbed. The element of conscious affectation, however, is not nearly so important as the fact that the two books have an air of holiness, as if two Massbooks were open at once upon an altar. Johnson chooses his influences, one might say, excluding all thinkers of the materialistic sort, and, having done so he thinks of the poets, essayists, or philosophers whom he admires as possible guides to his life. The feeling behind his reading of them often resembles the one he described in his cousin when he wrote to Badley: "Can you tell me where I can get a portrait of him [Shelley], not unworthy of his name. I have hunted all London, and can't light upon what I want. It is for a cousin who almost literally prays to Shelley, having lost all her other gods." [13]

The *Winchester Letters* begin with a series in which, along with their common study of Buddhism, Johnson is encouraging and directing Russell in the latter's "first plunge into the turbid waters of Browning." [14] Browning had the great admiration of all the members of the aesthetic movement, beginning with Rossetti. His introspectiveness and his fascination with the macabre were among the qualities which most appealed to Rossetti, [15] but Johnson revered Browning as a philosopher-poet: "Do read Browning; I feel much more cheerful about things in general when I read him. Read in the volume you are reading, 'Saul,' 'The Guardian Angel,' 'Two in the Campagna,' 'Old Pictures in Florence,' and, above all, 'Evelyn Hope.' " [16] Browning's influence had less effect on Johnson's thought as the latter grew older; there are not the references to him in Johnson's poetry or criticism which would give him a place equal to those men who most formed his mind: Newman, Arnold, and Pater. Nevertheless, in a review of Stevenson's *The Wrecker,* Johnson quotes from Browning, giving the impression as he does so that Browning has captured half the human experience. Comparing Stevenson and Pater, Johnson says:

The one [Pater] is more meditative, more learned, more gentle than the other; but both are men who feel the pathos, the heroism, the living significance of things—Virgil's "sense of tears in mortal things" and Browning's:

"How good is man's life, the mere living!
how fit to employ
All the heart and the soul and the senses
forever in joy!"[17]

The coupling of these quotations from Virgil and Browning is illumined by a further sentence: "The world [to Stevenson] is a pageant of vices and of virtues, to be endured by all means, to be enjoyed if may be." Thus in the end both the tears and the joy become only "literature," both seen from a distance, both meaningless save as they form a pattern in the mind of the beholder.

This is a vision of life very much like Pater's, and indeed Pater was one of the strongest influences on Johnson's thought. The high praise that Johnson gives Pater, higher than that given to Stevenson, is echoed time and again elsewhere in Johnson's criticism: it is Johnson's opinion that Pater's scholarship, taste, and prose style made him the final authority and arbiter of critical taste for his time. Even before he went to Oxford Johnson had read Pater's work; he read *Marius the Epicurean* in 1885 and wrote to Russell praising it ecstatically as "a book to love and worship." At that time he obviously read it, as so many others did, as if it were a repetition, not a development, of the ideas in *The Renaissance*, for his letter to Russell continues in *The Renaissance* manner:

I simply hate the days flying past so speedily. When the endless region of faith and doubt is once entered, life becomes weary of itself: and to remain without that land, contented with the colours of a rainbow and a curtain, the sound of a storm and a sonata, appears the higher, more dignified way. But life is very difficult always and every-way. And this philosophy or want of it is catholic: it allows me to delight in the irreverent cleverness of Orange and the boisterous in-difference of—my brother.[18]

Certainly it is true that Johnson consciously changed his opinion on the higher dignity of watching all life with great but uncommitted interest. In *The Art of Thomas Hardy* he writes of the danger in "vague and dreamy thought" to the man of wide culture, deep knowledge, broad reading. For this man there arises the possibility of thinking that "nothing, not truth itself is at stay"; he may become fascinated by " 'the flowing philosophers,' to whom life is a drifting and a change; the votaries of aesthetics to whom it is a pageant."[19] His tone is disapproving, but his recognition of the danger and his description of the particular kind of man for whom the danger exists might be taken as signs that he had himself experienced the temptation to view life this way—had perhaps succumbed to the temptation. Yeats, after all, said of Johnson that "it often seemed as if he played at life, as if it were an elaborate ritual that would soon be over."[20] Granted the validity, then, of John Pick's argument that Johnson was a much truer disciple of Pater than Wilde was, is it not still possible that Johnson shared Pater's fear that life might indeed be meaningless—though the human mind, to preserve itself, must give life meaning, surrounding it with "elaborate ritual"? And given this interpretation, is it not also possible that Pater's insistence upon *ascesis* may be more melancholy than Pick suggests, not an ordering which is directed to a goal outside itself, but a rigorous care about and insistence upon the details of life so that one may somehow get through the days without madness?

Yet it was Newman's thought, not Pater's, that Johnson really wanted to share, Newman's pattern that he wished to impose upon experience. His effort could only be superficially successful, for in Newman's faith the pattern of the universe is not imposed but revealed; its reality is objective, its order directed toward a definite goal. But Johnson tried at least to make his mind and heart one with Newman's, saying that he knew the thirty-six volumes of Newman's writings better than any other works in literature; more than that, he held Newman's work to be a refuge from modern philosophies of doubt, the sense of futility which they give to life, the "sick and morbid" beauty which they cause in literature. To an age suffering from these ills, Newman "sets forth a solution and a cure."[21]

When Johnson wrote about Matthew Arnold, the third of his major influences, he described an attitude, a quality in him which he found common to all three and took from all three in "making his soul":

Paradoxical as it may sound, there is something very hieratic about Arnold: his apprehension of the beauty of holiness, his love for what is clear and lofty in the pleasures of thought, his constant service of meditation. . . . The false worship of words, the conventional acceptance of phrases, all the spurious wisdom in the world he fought against, and conquered much of it; and there is no one left to take his place in the struggle against vulgarity and imposture: no voice like his to sing as he sang of calm and peace among the turbulent sounds of modern life.[22]

This description of Arnold closely resembles Johnson's lines on Walter Pater:

> Patient beneath his Oxford trees and towers
> He still is gently ours:
> Hierarch of the spirit, pure and strong.[23]

Arnold went out from his books into the midst of the "vulgarity and imposture" against which he struggled. But Johnson found in his work a very different attitude: a lofty, almost contemptuous retreat before a vulgarity that had, in Johnson's opinion, already conquered. *Vicisti et vivimus* was the motto of his family, one that Johnson thought peculiarly appropriate to himself,[24] and so it was, for among the essential qualities in his character were a sense of defeated aristocracy and a contempt far more genuine than Wilde's for the world around him. It was this aristocratic remoteness, this dandyism, in Johnson that most deeply impressed Yeats; it is also the characteristic which Yeats most often associates with all "the tragic generation" who liked to murmur, "as for living—our servants will do that for us."

Johnson's sense of aristocracy was based not on family but on learning, an aristocracy of culture. On the very simplest level his attitude reveals itself in what Katherine Tynan calls "a little haughtiness towards the men who lacked Latin and Greek."[25] Now Yeats was among those with that unfortunate deficiency, and one has the impression that Johnson's aloof manner at times made Yeats feel gauche and uncomfortable; for instance, Yeats' tendency to seize impetuously upon ideas and work them out, his desire to talk to other Rhymers about the world "as a bundle of fragments," met only with Johnson's freezing silence.[26] For what, in Johnson's mind, was the use of noisy opinions, of ideas which were to be put into action? Ignoring that part of Arnold's theory of culture which reflected a hope for social melioration, Johnson envisioned the man of culture as one who stood aside completely from a world intent on its own destruction, a world not worth saving.

Thus, when he writes of Erasmus, Johnson compares him to Arnold but says as well:

Erasmus was an aristocrat of letters, loving their finer spirit, feeling an impatient irritation at the thought and in the presence of those who had not drunk their wisdom and undergone their discipline. In all matters, scholarly or ecclesiastical, his attitude toward the multitude was: "Lord, what fools these mortals be!" . . . He felt that it was easy to be vehement and intense, so hard to be gracious and urbane.[27]

In a paragraph about Pascal Johnson shows by his quotation of Newman's motto—"cor ad cor loquitur"—that he associates Newman as well as Arnold and Pater with a tradition of aristocratic temper, almost of hauteur:

A lover of superiorities, he [Pascal] has pity for their opposites, but mere contempt for the meagre and the middling . . . . France has no writer, certainly no lay writer who resembles him in his superb austerity: *"on mourra seul,"* he said, and in truth he both was and is a man of isolation, dwelling apart. . . . He is one of the voices which at rare intervals come from the heart of a man, and go to the hearts of men: *cor ad cor loquitur,* and deep answers deep.[28]

A similar hauteur may have been one of the elements which turned Johnson toward Roman Catholicism. For, as Newman pointed out in "The Second Spring," Catholicism in England was associated with two groups: Irish immigrants, "coming and going at harvest time, or a colony of them lodged in a miserable quarter of the vast metropolis," and a few members of the very good old families, "an elderly person, seen walking in the streets, grave and solitary, and strange, though noble in bearing, and said to be of good family and a 'Roman Catholic.' "[29] Both of these groups were free in Johnson's mind from any connection with Philistia—and indeed, his discovery of Irish ancestry was, in Santayana's opinion, another of Johnson's ways of rejecting the Philistine world.[30]

But besides its connections with aristocrat and peasant and its remoteness from the middle classes, Roman Catholicism may well have had a link in Johnson's mind with intellectual superiority and wideness of culture; at least one sees it allied to both in works as widely different as "Bishop Blougram's Apology" and Harold Frederic's *The Damnation of Theron Ware.* If Johnson read the latter work, he would have found a reflection of his own feelings in its presentation of the Irish priest, Father Forbes, and the Irish (and aristocratic) girl, Celia Madden, as the two people of greatest polish and intellectual culture in an otherwise narrowly provincial, deeply Philistine small town.[31]

While he approves of its cultured flexibility on the one hand, Johnson is also proud of a deliberately outmoded dignity in Catholicism; in fact, a modern Catholic might almost be alarmed by his pleasure in connecting the Church with the old, the outworn, the cast-off, as it appears in his poem "The Church of a Dream." The poem was written in 1890, only a year before Johnson's conversion to Catholicism, so that its intention, one gathers, was to praise:

> Sadly the dead leaves rustle in the whistling wind,
> Around the weather-worn, gray church, low down the vale:
> The Saints in golden vesture shake before the gale;
>
> .   .   .   .
>
> Still in their golden vesture the old saints prevail;
> Alone with Christ, desolate else, left by mankind.
> Only one ancient Priest offers the Sacrifice,
> Murmuring holy Latin immemorial.[32]

Thus Johnson's acceptance of the Catholic faith, however genuine it may have been, did not really serve as a bond between him and the rest of the world; on the contrary, he made his religion into yet another protective wall. Nevertheless, the very care that Johnson took in using his religion, his culture, even the daily routine of his life, to separate himself from the world argues for the possibility that in his heart he wished for acceptance. His frailty, his short stature, his bookishness, may have set him apart in a family whose men were all expected to be good soldiers, strong believers, and good sports; he, in return, rejected all his

family's values; yet did so with a hidden emotion which suggests
that secretly the values must still have meant a good deal to him.

Lionel Johnson was not a man to take even his closest friends
into his confidence; it must, therefore, be mainly his reading of
Johnson's poetry that makes Yeats say, "much falling he / Brooded
upon sanctity."³³ Yet even those lines, though beautifully succinct
and delicate, especially in their echo of Johnson's "Go from me:
I am one of those, who fall"³⁴—the line that Yeats intuitively knows
as the best expression of Johnson's spirit—do not, save for that
echo, state the truth of the matter in all its negation: Johnson
brooded not on sanctity but on sin. His poetry is much more concerned with damnation than with beatitude:

> That hate, and that, and that again,
> Easy and simple are to bear:
> My hatred of myself is pain
> Beyond my tolerable share.
>
> .　　.　　.　　.　　.　　.　　.
> Darker than death, fiercer than fire,
> Hatefuller than the heart of Hell:
> I know thee, O mine own desire!
> I know not mine own self so well.³⁵

Very often, God seems remote to Johnson, or if He be near, He
comes in vengeance not in love:

> I can die. To quit the light,
> Hide my misery in gloom,
> Well indeed! But in that night,
> At his voice, to meet my doom!
> And Death's Angels, who may fight?³⁶

"The Dark Angel" tries to reach a better and more hopeful solution; yet again most of the poem is taken up with terrible internal
conflict of which the resolution is simply imposed by a change
from Manichean to Neoplatonic theology:

> Dark Angel, with thine aching lust!
> Of two defeats, of two despairs:
> Less dread, a change to drifting dust,
> Than thine eternity of cares.

> Do what thou wilt, thou shalt not so,
> Dark Angel! triumph over me:
> *Lonely, unto the Lone I go;*
> *Divine, to the Divinity.*[37]

Johnson does not believe that he will change to drifting dust, although he wishes perhaps that he did, for a complete materialism would offer him escape; he accepts instead the complete spiritualism of Neoplatonic thought because, paradoxically, it offers a similar escape from all personality and with it all sense of sin.

What all these, his central poems, show is that Johnson, who had of his own will turned away from society, found himself separated as well from a sustaining belief in the presence of God. His attitude to life removed him from society, his conscience and his fear of death made him feel very far from God. As a result, he was left in that state of mind which Eliot describes in "The Waste Land." After the Thunder's word "Dhayadhvam" —sympathize—Eliot describes the fate of the man who has not done so:

> I have heard the key
> Turn in the door once and turn once only
> We think of the key, each in his prison
> Thinking of the key, each confirms a prison.[38]

As it happens, Johnson once used that very image in one of his letters to Russell: "You must forgive my silence, if speech pleases better in this hollow prison vault of a world, where we fumble and grope in the dark to find the keys."[39]

From this loneliness, alcohol served as one escape; his books served as another. For although they could not really help him to "find" himself, Johnson discovered that he could lose himself in books. In his library he could forget the society of his own time, forget frustration, bad conscience, failed hopes, forget loneliness— his books made for him "the good place." Indeed Wilde's prophecy that certain elect spirits would in time seek their impressions not from actual life but from art had its fulfillment in Johnson almost as soon as it was made.[40] For Johnson's "moments" were different from those described by Pater, in that they

did not arise from immediate, strong sensory impressions: they
were moments of sensuous, emotional, and spiritual culmination
lived vicariously, at one remove from the experience itself. Other
men's moments swept Johnson out of himself: "Take me with you
in spirit, Ancients of Art, the crowned, the sceptred, whose voices
this night chaunt a *gloria in excelsis,* flooding the soul with a
passion of joy and awe."[41]

Books carried Johnson to the past, especially the past of
England in the eighteenth century, "the enchanted, the golden,
the incomparable age."[42] It is true that he then brought the past
back with him into the details of his actual life, modelling his
punctuation and even his calligraphy on eighteenth-century style,
often modelling his phrasing on that of Samuel Johnson. But all
these mannerisms served only as props to continue the dream
as long as possible. Johnson did not read of the past in order to
achieve a better understanding of the present; he did so to escape
the present. In "Oxford Nights," after describing his pleasure in
works of the eighteenth century—books read at night while all the
rest of Oxford sleeps—Johnson continues:

> Dream, who love dreams! forget all grief:
> Find, in sleep's nothingness, relief:
> Better my dreams! Dear, human books,
> What kindly voices, winning looks!
> Enchaunt me with your spells of art,
> And draw me homeward to your heart:
> Till weariness and things unkind
> Seem but a vain and passing wind.[43]

Even the Rhymers' Club served Johnson as an elaborate day-
dream. Arthur Symons thought of the Club's meetings as pale
and ineffectual imitations of Bohemian gatherings in the Latin
Quarter,[44] but to Johnson they were re-enactments of the Friday
meetings of Samuel Johnson's Club. If they were subdued and
gray re-enactments, so much the better; the mind might then be
freer to envisage the past and to enjoy its melancholy difference
from the present. Thus in a poem—or rather, in some doggerel
verses—on a modern meeting of the Johnson Club, Johnson imag-
ines the pleasure of the evening if Samuel Johnson were present,
and then sighs:

> If only it might be! . . . But, long as we may,
> We shall ne'er hear that laughter, *Gargantuan* and gay,
> Go pealing down *Fleet Street* and rolling away.
> In silence we drink to the silent, who rests
> In the warmth of the love of his true lovers' breasts.[45]

Perhaps Johnson's tendency to give the world of his books a greater reality than the world around him is one explanation (though admittedly a surface one, resting upon depths too dark and salt for greater exploration) of Johnson's "imaginary conversations." According to Yeats, Johnson would tell anecdotes of meetings with Newman, Gladstone, or Arnold, always with perfect truth to detail, always consistent with an earlier telling, so that Yeats for a long time believed them to have been actual.[46] And though, in fact, these meetings had not taken place, it is possible that Johnson fell so completely a victim to the "dangerous prevalence of imagination" that he himself also believed them real—just as he came to think of himself as Irish. Fantasy changed into delusion.

Related to Johnson's flight to the literary past is his constant returning to his own youth, not the childhood spent with his family—not even were he to simplify it by dreams would he be part of that world—but his youth at Winchester:

> A place of friends! a place of books!
> A place of good things olden!
> With these delights, the years were golden;
>   And life wore sunny looks.
>   They fled at last:
>   But to the past
>   Am I in all beholden.[47]

The mourning of youth and its recollection as a period without struggle, without consciousness of self within or responsibility without, is a major theme in Johnson's poems:

> Pity thyself! youth flies, youth flies.
> Thou comest to the desert plain
> Where no dreams follow in thy train:
> They leave thee at the pleasaunce close;
> Lonely the haggard pathway goes.
> Thou wilt look back and see them, deep

> In the fair glades where thou dost keep
> Thy summer court, thy summer sleep:
> But thou wilt never see them more.
> Till death the golden dreams restore.[48]

And yet, according to the pattern set by Rossetti's artistic isolation and by Pater's cultured retirement in Oxford, a total rejection of life could appear almost noble. Thus when Johnson describes J. C. Mangan's life as one of "dreams and misery, and madness, yet of a self-pity which does not disgust us, and of a weakness which is innocent," when he says that Mangan's was "the haunted enchanted life of one drifting through his days in other days and other worlds, golden and immortal,"[49] he intends a high compliment—the compliment of identification, and the recognition as well that Mangan is living by the code: in artistic terms he has kept himself unspotted from the world. And Johnson's air of high lineage may well have come from his interior sense that he too was doing so: Newman's gentleman, Arnold's man of culture, Rossetti's true artist, Pater's scholar, Wilde's individualist, each represents a very different vision of the good life; nevertheless, out of each of them it is possible to extract a single common element: an isolated pursuit of and pleasure in a beauty which the mass of men cannot enjoy or even understand, a beauty caught momentarily in one's own fantasies. Johnson extracted that element and lived by it to his great unhappiness.

Lord Francis Russell, describing Johnson's influence upon him, writes: "He taught me a lesson I have never forgotten, and that is that all the supposedly real things of life, that is to say the external things, the physical things, the humours, the happenings, disgraces, successes, failures are in themselves the merest phantoms and illusions, and that the only realities are within one's own mind and spirit."[50] Finding nothing in society which he could "love or believe in," Johnson turned his gaze upon himself, but that created "a torment of perpetual self-consciousness" from which he had to escape if he were not to end in "an unnatural state of mind."[51] His escape was fantasy, and so, paradoxically, the "realities of his own mind and spirit" became illusions, daydreams which eventually destroyed what had been a clear mind, a disciplined intelligence.

It was himself, really,
that he had been seeking all the time, conscious at least
of that in all the deviations of the way;
himself, the ultimate of his curiosities.
Arthur Symons

Chapter VI

Arthur Symons

When Arthur Symons came up to London in 1889 he was almost
unknown, though he had put in an apprenticeship by writing
An Introduction to the Study of Robert Browning; he had no
advantage of family name nor even the distinction of being an
"Oxford man," and, unlike Yeats, he was not a genius. Nevertheless, he corresponded with Walter Pater, became a member of
the Rhymers' Club, moved into Fountain Court, where he became
George Moore's "boon companion" and Yeats' friend, and was
what Ernest Dowson called a "standing dish" with *The Academy.*[1]
More than that, he was very busy in Paris as well as in London:
he attended Mallarmé's "Tuesdays," visited Edmond de Goncourt
at his small, exquisitely furnished villa, and waited patiently to
catch Paul Verlaine at the latter's favorite café. It was Symons
who made most of the arrangements for Verlaine's trips to London in 1893 and 1894 and Symons with whom Verlaine stayed

each time.[2] And it was Symons who translated Mallarmé's *Hérodiade* and the poetry of Verlaine for Yeats,[3] Symons who gave Yeats private tutoring in the French tradition, just as it was Symons whose book *The Symbolist Movement in Literature* later became, one might say, a public lecture on the same subject.

A delightful note from Symons to William Rothenstein gives a notion of his itinerary on what appears to have been an ordinary evening. It is written on the back of a printed card which announces Verlaine's intended visit to London and his lecture on "Contemporary French Poetry":

My dear Rothenstein

It is MOST important that I should see you at once, about the Verlaine affair. I shall be dining at Galti's about 7; then I go to the New Gallery, to hear Image's "Arts and Crafts" Lecture, at 8:30; then I shall go to the Alhambra, to see an adorable lady in a new part; finally I shall go to the Crown. Now I depend absolutely on your meeting me at one or all of these places.

Yours

Arthur Symons[4]

He went everywhere and he seemed to know everyone. Thus, when Leonard Smithers planned *The Savoy* to take *The Yellow Book*'s place as an avant-garde quarterly—for *The Yellow Book* had lost its right to that position by taking alarm and dismissing Aubrey Beardsley after Oscar Wilde's downfall—he asked Symons to be editor of the magazine.

Wilde once wrote Vincent O'Sullivan that he knew Symons to be not a man but the trade name of a literary corporation: "I have written to my solicitor to inquire about shares in Symons Ltd. Naturally in mass production of that kind you can never be certain of the quality. But I think one might risk some share in Symons."[5] Symons' career as editor of *The Savoy* had shown Wilde's humorous exaggeration to be very close to the truth, for when *The Savoy* became too poor to pay any contributors, Symons and Aubrey Beardsley put out an entire issue by themselves. Beardsley contributed all the drawings and Symons wrote (1) a poetic sequence on cruel and despairing love, (2) an analysis of the work of Walter Pater, (3) a short story, (4) a translation of

Mallarmé's *Hérodiade,* (5) a travelpiece on the Aran Islands, and (6) an editorial comment.[6]

Because he turns up in so many places and has his head so full of projects, one tends to think of Symons in the half-ironic, half-patronizing way that is reflected in Wilde's comment; he seems a cheerful, bustling Decadent who could talk the prattle of the nineties without really understanding its significance: the casino of Dieppe has some "amusing chandeliers," and a fair held in the town was horrid, but "I managed to snatch a few amusing sensations out of even this discomfort"[7]—that sort of thing. Yet this picture of Symons fades out and must be readjusted, refocussed, as soon as one learns the central fact of his life: in 1908 he went mad. Two years later he recovered his reason, and he even returned to his writing. But his later work is almost painful to read, so much is it dependent on his early writing—old sentences and old phrases reappear in contexts to which they are scarcely applicable, and his essays wander constantly from the point.

His breakdown may have been the effect, at least in part, of an inherited strain of insanity and of the worries caused him by financial difficulties,[8] but his writings show also that he lost his reason because he could not find a "mask" which would adequately define his intense self-consciousness. He was a man who thought much about masks—what friend of Yeats would not?—and his ideas on their significance often have greater lucidity than the rather dark and cryptic oracles of Yeats. For instance, in his "Conclusion" to *Studies in Prose and Verse,* Symons almost seems to be thinking the problem out aloud. He begins by mentioning Barbey D'Aurévilly's famous comment after reading *A Rebours,* that Huysmans had left himself the choice of the end of a gun or the foot of the Cross. In questioning its truth Symons brings together those ideas around which he tried to center his life: "Yet perhaps the choice is not quite so narrow as Barbey D'Aurévilly thought; perhaps it is a choice between actualising this dream or actualising that dream. In his escape from the world, one man chooses religion and seems to find himself; another, choosing love, may also seem to find himself; and may not another, coming to art as to a religion and as to a woman, seem to find himself no less effectually?"[9] That part of the meditation drifts off with a question, a possibility but not a statement of belief. Then Symons turns to think of art, curiously blending the ideas of Rossetti, Pater, and Wilde:

Art begins when a man wishes to immortalize the most vivid moment he has ever lived. Life has already, to one not an artist, become art in that moment. And the making of one's life into art is after all the first duty and privilege of every man. It is to escape from material reality into whatever form of ecstasy is our own form of spiritual existence. There is the choice; and our happiness, our "success in life," will depend on our choosing rightly, each for himself, among the forms in which that choice will come to us (pp. 290–91).

Symons understood perfectly how vital the choice was; he knew that the mask is not separate from personality but a partial reflection of it and realized too that, once habitual, it influences personality. This was the insight that he had into Wilde's nature when he described Wilde making himself many souls;[10] with a truly beautiful clarity and intelligence (for these were new and complex ideas with scarcely a vocabulary fitted to explain them) he expressed a similar thought when he wrote about Mérimée: "Does he realise, unable to change the temperament which he has partly made for himself, that just there has been his own failure?"[11] Later in the essay on Mérimée, Symons describes the process by which the mask becomes inescapable:

Indifference in him [Mérimée], as in the man of the world, is partly an attitude, adopted for its form, and influencing the temperament just so much as gesture always influences emotion. The man who forces himself to appear calm under excitement teaches his nerves to follow instinctively the way he has shown them. In time he will not merely seem calm but will be calm, at the moment when he learns that a great disaster has befallen him. But, in Mérimée was the indifference even as external as it must always be when there is restraint, when, therefore, there is something to restrain? Was there not in him a certain drying up of the sources of emotion?[12]

Yet Symons also knew that the modern consciousness cannot attempt to throw off the mask altogther—even if that were socially possible—and be "natural." So well did he understand Wilde's paradox that "being natural is simply a pose, and the most irritating pose I know,"[13] that he could only listen with amazement when Walter Pater said he believed *Imaginary Portraits* to be his best book because it was the most natural. Symons says wonderingly, "I think he was even beginning to forget that it was not natural to him to be natural." Pater's life and his art were both so consciously, so ceremoniously ordered that "it became a last sophistication to aim at an effect in style which should bring the touch of unpremeditation, which we seem to find in nature, into a faultlessly combined arrangement of art."[14] And in *The Symbolist Movement* he generalizes about any modern writer: "I affirm that it is not natural to be what is called 'natural' any longer."[15]

Symons' history, then, is that of his conscious attempt to find himself by identifying with an ideal or a person outside himself; he tried to do so through religious faith, through love, through the search for sensations, in the "perfect moment," and in the doctrines of Symbolism: every attempt failed, and finally, completely self-imprisoned, he went mad.

Very early in his life he turned away violently from the possibility of self-realization through religious belief. Although Symons himself never mentions it, his father was a Wesleyan Methodist minister.[16] Between 1865 and 1885 he was in charge of nine different circuits, and therefore the family moved often. But even though he does not discuss its cause, Symons attaches enormous importance to this lack of stability, making it the primary reason for his own restlessness and inability to find a center. He mentions it in two autobiographical pieces, *Confessions* and "A Prelude to Life," one of the stories in *Spiritual Adventures;* in the latter he writes: "If I have been a vagabond, and have never been able to root myself in any one place in the world, it is because I have no early memories of any one sky or soil. It has freed me from many prejudices in giving me its own unresting kind of freedom; but it has cut me off from whatever is stable, of long growth in the world."[17]

If we may trust the account he gives in "A Prelude to Life," Symons was even more completely cut off from his family than was Lionel Johnson. He describes his father as a sombre, dryly intellectual man, something of a valetudinarian, "unimaginative, cautious in his affairs, a great reader of the newspapers" (p. 21)— the last perhaps the most cutting point he could make, since Symons thought of newspapers as fit reading only for the very average man.[18] He says that he did not dislike his father, regarding him rather with indifference, but adds, almost as an afterthought, "perhaps a little more than indifference, for if he came into a room, and I did not happen to be absorbed in reading, I usually went out of it" (p. 20).

Symons' description of his mother is very different; as he depicts her, she would have fulfilled Pater's ideal of sanctity, for she had the capacity to appreciate beauty in all its aspects, and Symons even echoes Pater's vocabulary in describing her: "She had the joy of life, she was sensitive to every aspect of the world; she felt the sunshine before it came, and knew from what quarter the wind was blowing when she woke in the morning. I think she was never indifferent to any moment that ever passed her by; I think no moment ever passed her by without being seized in all the eagerness of acceptance" (p. 22).

Even as a boy Symons would willingly have rejected his father's religious beliefs and met his father's solemn attempts to talk to him about his soul only with sullen resentment: "If to be good was to be like him, I did not wish to be good." But his mother too was deeply religious, with a strong and very simple faith which the boy could not but share: "Her certainty helped to make me more afraid." For though she might give him her belief in another world, she could not give him her quiet hope for salvation, and Symons says that as a child he was always convinced that he himself would be damned: "And so the thought of hell was often in my mind, for the most part very much in the background, but always ready to come forward at any external suggestion. Once or twice it came to me with such vividness that I rolled over on the ground in a paroxysm of agony, trying to pray to God that I might not be sent to hell, but unable to fix my mind on the words of the prayer" (p. 19). And with the fear of hell went a terrible fear of death that was always to afflict him.

As he came to adolescence Symons resisted his parents' religious beliefs more and more strongly, and he mentions a revival meeting in which he sat rigid, teeth clenched, refusing to confess his wickedness or to repent as those around him were doing. In "Seaward Lackland," another of the stories in *Spiritual Adventures,* he describes a similar meeting; Seaward, the son of devout Methodists, has been dedicated to the Lord at his birth, but he too refuses in the meeting to succumb to the emotion felt by those around him:

As Seaward saw the preacher coming near him, he felt a horrible fear, he did not know of what; and he rose quietly and stepped out into the night. But there, as he stood listening to some exultant voices which he still heard crying, "Hallelujah!" and as he felt the comfort of the cool air about him, and he looked up at the stars and the thin white clouds which were rushing across the moon, a sense of quiet and well-being came over him, and he felt as if some bitter thing had been taken out of his soul, and he were free to love God and life at the same time, and not, as he had done till then, with alternate pangs of regret. "If God so loved the world," he found himself repeating, and the whole mercy of the text enveloped him. He walked home along the cliff like one in a dream: he only hoped not to awaken out of that happiness (pp. 212–13).

Yet Seaward's tenuous moment of balance between love of God and of the world is very brief, and as the story continues he becomes obsessed with the idea that he has unwittingly committed the unforgivable sin. Symons too would have wished that he could be "free to love God and the world at the same time," but in "A Prelude to Life," he describes no moment at which that ever seemed possible, and given the necessity of choice between his father's God and the world beyond his father's authority, Symons chose the world and risked damnation.

Although the family life that he describes sounds gloomy, even if brightened by his mother's nature, Symons himself must have done very little to add any cheerfulness. He was, if we may trust his account, thoroughly spoiled, completely self-involved, resentful of his parents' poverty and of the fact that they were "surrounded by commonplace, middle-class people, and I hated commonplace and the middle class." It seems almost certain that he exaggerates his egoism, for he makes it very nearly monstrous;

nevertheless, his account of it is interesting for the emphasis it places on his self-enclosure, his inability to go out to others:

From as early a time as I can remember, I had no very close consciousness of anything external to myself; I never realised that others
had the right to expect from me any return for the kindness they
might show me or refuse me, at their choice. I existed, others also
existed; but between us there was an impassible gulf, and I had
rarely any desire to cross it. I was very fond of my mother, but I felt
no affection toward anyone else, nor any desire for the affection of
others. To be let alone, and to live my own life for ever, that was what
I wanted, and I raged because I could never escape from the contact
of people who bored me and things which depressed me (pp. 28–29).

When Symons' father suggested that the time had come for him to have a job, he flatly refused, choosing, he said, rather to starve than to soil his hands with business; he would become an "aristocrat of letters."[19] So he withdrew to his study and not only read but wrote: "I wanted to write books for the sake of writing books; it was food for my ambition, and it gave me something to do when I was alone, apart from other people. It helped to raise another barrier between me and other people" (p. 47).

"A Prelude to Life" concludes with Symons' arrival in London where "alone, and in the midst of a crowd, I began to be astonishingly happy" (p. 49). The whole piece so lacks detail and is so personal in feeling that one could only call it quasi-autobiography, but the emotion with which it is written shows how much an alien Symons felt himself to be in the world, how rootless and drifting, and shows as well why religious belief was of no use to him in his search for something with which he might identify. His early religious belief left him with a permanent fear of death and, perhaps, an unrecognized but continuing belief in life after death—a life in which he found damnation imaginatively much more vivid than salvation. All this was put in the back of his mind, however, as Symons enjoyed his new freedom in London.

He now began to move so rapidly back and forth among several ideals in his search for himself that any attempt to order them must base itself upon logic, not upon biographical fact. It was this tendency in Symons to move quickly from one emotional or intellectual point of view to another that Frank Harris particularly noted; at their first meeting he and Symons struck up a conversation about the London music halls, then just becoming popular, which Symons admired enormously: "In the middle of the animated discussion I reminded him that Plato had called music the divinest of the arts, and forthwith, to my astonishment, Symons changed front in a jiffy and took up this new position."[20] Harris is a notoriously unreliable witness,[21] but here his account is given validity by the fact that Yeats also noted Symons' ability "to slip . . . into the mind of another";[22] the difference between the two analyses is that Harris saw as shilly-shallying what Yeats felt to be an ability to understand "all sides of the question."

Like one of his characters, Christian Trevalga,[23] Symons tried "to find himself, to become real by falling in love."[24] His early poems about women, however, scarcely seem to describe realities: for instance, Rossetti's Lilith, Pater's Mona Lisa, and Swinburne's Lady of Pain come together to form "A Woman":

> They [her eyes] without labour, bought and sold
> Heart's faith, a precious merchandise,
> With tears for silver, blood for gold
> And bargaining of costly sighs
> For the rich treasuries of those eyes.
>
> Dowered with all beauty bodily
> Her soul she meshed in her own snare;
> Beyond herself she might not see
> Infantine—idly unaware
> Of any end but being fair.[25]

Rossetti's ideal woman, his "Soul's Beauty," is also Symons': "Mournful, beautiful, calm with that vague unrest,"[26] she broods "mysteriously alone / And infinitely far away,"[27] or if she be near the poet begs, "Shake out your hair about me."[28] And if she be won, it is with Rossettian passion:

> Spirit to spirit was fused in living flame, and neither knew,
> In that transfiguring ardency of perfect fire,
> Body from body, spirit from spirit, life from death.[29]

Yet the fact that many of Symons' love poems sound like Rossetti processed, put, as it were, through an IBM machine, does not mean that Symons' attitude toward women resembles Rossetti's.

Rossetti idealized women, Symons feared them. Although he found women physically attractive, he used sexual desire as a means of keeping them at a distance and began each love affair by making it already a memory, something passing:

> And every woman with beseeching eyes,
> Or with enticing eyes, or amorous,
> Offers herself, a rose, and craves of us
> A rose's place among our memories.[30]

And when he cannot take love in this way, lightly, as a sensual pleasure without any deeper meaning, then he can think of it only as something painful, an obsession, a disease, in which resentment at his bondage makes his passion as much hate as it is love:

> I have not loved love, nor sought happiness,
> I have loved every passionate distress,
> And the adoration of sharp fear, and hate
> For love's sake, and what agonies await
> The unassuaged fulfilment of desire
> Not eased in the having.[31]

The same poem, "An Epilogue to Love," has a phrase which catches precisely Symons' attitude: "Passionate and untender," and he finally cries out:

> I have not loved love; let me be; O give
> Not love, but life: I would not love but live![32]

All this is not just posing; Symons used the symbols and even the vocabulary of Rossetti and Swinburne because he had not sufficient poetic genius to create symbols of his own, but the emotions behind his borrowed images are perfectly genuine. Yet why did the thought of falling in love cause Symons to suffer such violent conflict? The poems themselves scarcely give an answer: they can only state the emotions, not their cause. In his prose, however, Symons analyzed his difficulty and gave its reason, though he could not find its solution.

It is the stories in *Spiritual Adventures*, especially "Christian Trevalga," "An Autumn City," and "The Journal of Henry Luxulyan," which best explain Symons' fear of the feminine principle: these are not told as autobiography, it is true, but their tone is personal enough to justify our interpreting them as Symons himself interpreted Pater's *Imaginary Portraits:* "Each, with perhaps one exception ["Denys l' Auxerrois"], is the study of a soul, or rather of a consciousness; such a study as might be made by simply looking within, and projecting now this now that side of oneself on an exterior plane."[33] Similarly, Christian Trevalga, Daniel Roserra in "An Autumn City," and Henry Luxulyan are all characters through whom Symons was perfectly consciously describing a part of himself. Of these perhaps the most interesting is Christian Trevalga, the man who had tried to find himself by falling in love. He is a brilliant musician, and at music school he meets Rana Vaughan, who admires him and shares his delight in music. In describing her Symons creates a personality very like that of his mother:

She cared intensely for the one thing he cared for [his music], and not less intensely (and here was the wonder to him) for all the other things that existed outside his interests. For her, life was everything, and everything was part of life. . . . She made no selections in life, beyond picking out all the beautiful and pleasant things, whatever they might be. Trevalga studied her with amazement; he felt withered, shrivelled up, in body and soul, beside her magnificent acceptance of the world; she vitalised him, drew him away from himself; and he feared her. He feared women (p. 99).

The clause "and he feared her" comes as a very deliberate shock; up to that point in the paragraph Rana Vaughan has been presented as a possible salvation, a way of breaking out of the circle of self-consciousness, but suddenly her very presence makes Trevalga only the more aware of being imprisoned: "To live with a woman, thought Christian, in the same house, the same room with her, is as if the keeper were condemned to live by day and sleep by night in the wild beast's cage" (p. 99). To him it is the worst, "the no longer solitary imprisonment." So Christian allows Rana to drift away from him, and the rest of the story describes his gradual descent into madness.

"An Autumn City" is the story of Daniel Roserra, an aesthete, a sensualist, who always said that woman disturbed the even tenor of the aesthetic life and that, like a liqueur, she is "a delightful luxury, to be taken with discretion" (p. 178). At forty,

however, he suddenly fell in love and married; a few months
after the wedding, he took his bride to Arles, a city that Symons
himself particularly liked, that she might appreciate its autumn
beauty, the beauty of decay. When she took no pleasure in the
city's sad, gray peace and begged that they might return to vulgar
Marseilles, Roserra agreed, but in his mind everything about their
marriage had changed. Now for him his wife was a creature from
whom he would take what physical pleasure he could, feeling
even so that he had made a very poor bargain:

A nausea, a suffocating nausea, rose up within him as he felt the heat
and glare of this vulgar, exuberant paradise of snobs and   tourists
[Marseilles]. He sickened with revolt before this over-fed nature,
sweating the fat of life. He looked at Livia; she stood there, perfectly
cool under her sunshade . . . . She was once more in her element, she
was quite happy; she had plunged back into the warmth of life out
of that penitential chilliness of Arles, and it was with real friendliness
that she turned to Roserra, as she saw his eyes fixed upon her (p. 197).

Roserra had been right, at least about himself; for him woman
was a very dangerous luxury. When his contact with her was only
ephemeral and essentially meaningless, he might be utterly self-
centered, but he was not unhappy, nor did he make others unhappy. His attempt to enjoy a relationship with woman that was
meaningful did not simply fail, returning him to his old self-
enclosure; it stirred up in him a resentment and a violence which
had been passive before and left his last state much worse than
his first.

The final "case," Henry Luxulyan, is on the verge of a nervous
breakdown after an unhappy love affair when the story opens.
He is prey to horrible fears, the fear of death and of annihilation,[34]
which he relates somehow to his fear of women:

I realise, on thinking it over in a perfectly calm mood, without any
sort of nervous excitement, that I have always been afraid of women;
and that is one reason, the chief perhaps, why I have always been so
lonely, both when Clare was with me, and before it and after it. Just
as I cannot get it out of my head that there is some concealed con-
spiracy against me, in earthly things, so there seems to be, in the other
sex, a kind of hidden anger or treachery which makes me uneasy. I

was never really happy when a woman sat on the other side of the table, at the corner of the fireplace.[35]

Again one gets the sense of a man trapped, like Christian Tre-valga, in a wild beast's cage. Moreover, although that image is only implicit in this passage, it appears explicitly within a few pages of it: Luxulyan has a moment's respite one afternoon as he sits quietly in Regent's Park, until he realizes that the strange, mournful cry of which he had been vaguely aware was "the crying of the wild beasts, over yonder, inside their bars" (p. 261). That shatters his peace, and he leaves the park.

Luxulyan has been befriended by the Baroness Eckenstein, a woman whom he finds physically repulsive, because one side of her face is badly scarred, but who catches his interest and his pity; little by little his friendship for her draws him out of himself, away from the danger of emotional breakdown. At least, the Baroness helps him until she falls in love with him; partly out of pity, partly out of fascination with physical ugliness, Luxulyan takes her as his mistress. By the time the journal ends he has lost his reason.

Like Roserra's aesthetic detachment, Luxulyan's uneasiness with women was a safeguard as well as a barrier. It is also a state of mind which Symons says he himself never quite escaped. Uneasiness, he writes, "creeps over me stealthily, perfidiously, in-sidiously, when I am most unaware of its existence: even in the presence of those I am passionately fond of." Then, continuing his self-analysis, he gives the reason: "I except from this cate-gory neither my mother nor my mistress—whose names were identical—Lydia[36]—for, in spite of my fondness for the one, and the intolerable vehemence and violence of my passion for the other, the most consuming, the most animal passion I ever had, there were times when my uneasiness, either in their presence or their absence, became exasperating."[37] One might say that every woman Symons loved or tried to love had his mother's name. And just as his repudiation of his father made it impossible for him to find an ideal outside himself in religious faith, so his emo-tional dependence upon his mother—an imprisoning emotion which he could not escape but which he bitterly resented—destroyed the hope of release from himself through love of a woman. He thought women mysterious and terrible because his own emotions toward them were confused and terrifying; he believed all sexuality essentially cruel because he used it cruelly, as a way of expressing the resentment he could not conquer. And, like the religion in which he could not believe, the love which he could not feel convinced him nevertheless of his own damnation:

> Annihilation awaits me, or some more infamous peril,
> Shot from a mad girl's eyes, as if some one behind me
> Stood in the midnight to stab me, and I was forsaken
> Even of myself, lost in caresses, lost in sedition,
> Saved in no sense, but hurled halfway down to Perdition.[38]

"Interludes of wholesome air, as through open doors, upon those hot, impassioned scenes": with this image Pater describes those passages in *Days and Nights* which make art alone the changeless, the enduring ideal in an otherwise meaningless world —"though," Pater adds, "on what grounds we hardly see, except his own deep, unaffected sense of it."[39] Symons, who had told his father he would not soil his hands with trade and had set himself to become an aristocrat of letters, described his ideal of the artist in his first book: Aprile in *Paracelsus* is, he says, the supreme artistic type, "the lover of beauty and beauty alone," so much a type indeed that he is scarcely a "realisable human being,"[40] yet an ideal, nonetheless, and one to which the young Symons clearly aspired as a way of salvation. In choosing this ideal Symons seems never to have questioned the necessity of separation between artist and society nor to have hoped that each might be of use to the other. He takes it as given that the artist is isolated and that he should be so, for society can never understand his work. Even further, if society does understand and accept his art, either his art is bad, or society has accepted it for the wrong reasons. There are those who may compromise, but any compromise is dangerous, for artist and society are always at war.[41]

There is no real need to linger over these doctrines or even over their application in the praise of Mallarmé's deliberate attempt to bewilder any bourgeois readers who might stumble upon his

works, or of Villiers de l'Isle-Adam's haughty disdain for the
world in which he unfortunately found himself; they are by now
very familiar, are, in fact, clichés whose validity is perhaps once
again a question—we have circled back to the point where the
role of the artist in society might be debated in a new "Palace
of Art." In Symons' time, however, although these ideas had been
in the air for years, there was still something a little brazen and
daring about this manifesto: "It is for their faults that any really
artistic productions become popular: art cannot appeal to the
multitude. It is wise when it does not attempt to; when it goes
contentedly along a narrow path, knowing, and caring only to
know, in what direction it is moving."[42]

Supported by the violently anti-bourgeois tradition of the
French, Symons separates the artist as completely from society
as a monk is separated from domestic life: his is to be a different
world. So he states in his essay on Verlaine, and there he gives
as well the duty of the artist, the narrow path along which he is
to walk, holding up Verlaine as his example of one who lived the
perfect artistic life. Verlaine, Symons says, was a great poet because "he got out of every moment all that that moment had to
give him," and his whole art was "a delicate waiting upon
moods."[43] His ideal poet lives by the doctrines of Pater's *The
Renaissance.*

For in Symons' early years in London his ideas on "the perfect
moment" all showed the influence of Pater's *The Renaissance.*
Symons describes himself as one who devoutly practiced "the
religion of the eyes," looking into every omnibus, watching faces
in the crowds which passed him in Piccadilly lest he miss a sudden, gracious gesture, a beautiful face;[44] he found in his eyes a
way of turning himself from "that strict tedious world within."[45]
This was also the pleasure that the music halls gave him: backstage especially he enjoyed, like Dégas, the vision of a world in
flux—moving shapes and shadows; sudden, unreal glimpses of the
dancers on stage; profiles of the spectators. And if he watched
carefully, the flux might momentarily resolve itself into an arrangement. He describes such a moment, one in which he suddenly caught a glimpse of the ballet at the Alhambra as he was
passing on the street outside: "In the moment's interval before

the doors closed again, I saw in that odd, unexpected way, over the heads of the audience, far off in a sort of blue mist, the whole stage . . . . It stamped itself on my brain, an impression caught just at the perfect moment, by some rare felicity of chance."[46] On that occasion the doors closed, ending the impression at the moment it was realized, but had they not done so, Symons would have turned quickly away: "When I have seen a face, an aspect of the sky, pass for a moment into a sort of crisis, in which it attained the perfect expression of itself, I have always turned away rapidly, closing my eyes on the picture which I dread to see fade or blur before me. I would obtain from things, as from people, only their best."[47]

Put this way, his philosophy sounds almost altruistic, though in fact (as Symons often realized himself) to take from things and people "only their best," to find that anything but that best is tedious or disgusting, reflects the coldest possible egoism. And Symons' concept of the artistic vision often has a certain coldness; since the artist is isolated from the world around him, he tends to be more interested in people's gestures than in their personalities; he resembles the actress Esther Kahn in one of Symons' stories: "At night, after supper, the others [her family] used to sit around the table, talking eagerly. Esther would get up and draw her chair into the corner by the door, and for a time she would watch them, as if she were looking on at something, something with which she had no concern, but which interested her for its outline and movement."[48] Pushed to its extreme, the habit of watching life from the outside can so reduce life's emotional content and its significance that one may come to the point of saying, as Symons says, "I have always been apt to look on the world as a puppet show . . . ."[49]

Yet there is no need to preach at Symons about the dangers of his "impressionist" philosophy; he knew them well enough himself, recognized them, one feels, from the very beginning, for his religious background had made it impossible for him ever really to be amoral. When he writes, for instance, of Gabriele D'Annunzio, praising him as a man who is an "artist in life itself," because he can feel more passionately than others "the heat of sunlight, the juicy softness of a ripe fruit, the texture of women's hair," Symons suddenly turns just in the midst of his praise to point out that all D'Annunzio's books are tragedies which end in gross, material horror: "And they are tragedies because no man has yet found out a remedy against the satiety of pleasure, except the remedies hidden away somewhere in the soul. Youth passes, desire fades, attainment squeezes the world into a narrow circuit; there is nothing left over, except dreams that turn into nightmares, or else a great weariness."[50] To attempt to free oneself from the circle of the inner world by enjoying every possible sensation of the physical world will end, paradoxically, only by making the circle of the trap narrower. Pater was not the only one who found that the life of sensation, the life spent grasping at exquisite passions, beautiful sights, delicious odors which might serve "to set the spirit free for a moment," was bound to end in failure. At the end of Symons' "A Prelude to Life," the sadness and frustration underlying Pater's "Conclusion" rise to the surface and the murmur of Heraclitus' stream becomes a roar in which all other sounds are lost. After he has described his "religion of the eyes," Symons continues:

This search without an aim grew to be almost a torture to me; my eyes ached with the effort, but I could not control them. At every moment, I knew, some spectacle awaited them; I grasped at all those sights with the same futile energy as a dog that I once saw standing in an Irish stream, and snapping at the bubbles that ran continually past him on the water. Life ran past me continually, and I tried to make all its bubbles my own (p. 50).

To realize that the search is aimless and that the moments enjoyed during it are meaningless is fearful; and Symons' vision of the horror may have been the quality in him which deepened Yeats' desire for a "sacred book" that would bring the supernatural back into the world. Yeats says that Symons had this effect upon him "without ever being false to his own impressionist view of art and life," and yet his next sentence makes it seem likely that it was Symons who turned to Yeats for help and that together they hoped to find in Symbolism a way in which the "perfect moment" might be considered something more than a photograph kept in the album of the mind. Yeats writes: "It seems to me, looking backward, that we always discussed life at its most intense moment, and that moment which gives a common sacredness to the Song of Songs, and to the Sermon on the Mount, and in which one discovers something supernatural, a stirring at the roots of the hair."[51] If the moment were a symbol pointing toward some divine reality, or, coming at it from the other direction, if it were a breakthrough of divine energy into the material world, then its appreciation need not make one aware always of its passing; rather the moment "in time and out of time" would serve as a reflection of the permanence behind it, and in identification with that permanence, discovered through the moment, might lie the possibility of finding the true self.

In the letter with which he dedicates *The Symbolist Movement in Literature* to Yeats, Symons mentions the talks that he and Yeats had together, and says, like Yeats, that they were not arguments, nor was one teaching the other, but both were engaged in a common exploration of the doctrines of Symbolism. Yeats, nevertheless, was the leading spirit, for, says Symons, "You have seen me gradually finding my way, uncertainly but inevitably, in that direction which has always been to you your natural direction." In fact, Symons appears a little self-conscious and shamefaced over the fact that he has changed from his old, "impressionist" position: "I speak often in this book of Mysticism, and that I, of all people, should venture to speak, not quite as an outsider, of such things, will probably be a surprise to many."[52]

Indeed the book which Symons had intended in 1896 to call *The Decadent Movement in Literature* would probably have had a very different focus from the book which appeared in 1899 as *The Symbolist Movement.* Certainly in 1893, when Symons wrote an article called "The Decadent Movement in Literature," his emphasis was on appreciation of the moment for its own sake: "To fix the last fine shade, to fix it fleetingly; to be a disembodied voice, and yet the voice of a human soul; that is the ideal of Decadence."[53] By 1899 Symons dismissed even the term "Decadence" as descriptive only of an "interlude, half a mock-interlude" held before the scenes while preparations were being made backstage for the dramatic appearance of Symbolism; if the term "Decadence" meant anything at all, it might be applied only to style, to "ingenious deformation of language."[54]

But when Symons, having set Decadence to one side, attempts to define the meaning and purpose of Symbolism, his writing loses some of the clarity, the precision of thought, that so often makes it a joy to read. Clearest, perhaps, is his discussion of the negative value of Symbolism—as a weapon against materialism— and that may have been the area in which Symons felt on his surest footing. He ends his "Introduction" to *The Symbolist Movement* with a ringing—and very Yeatsian—denunciation of "exteriority," "rhetoric," and the "materialistic tradition." And he adds that in its capacity to create symbols imaginative literature becomes "a kind of religion, with all the duties and responsibilities of the sacred ritual" (pp. 8–9). The conclusion of his essay on Mallarmé further explains the religious function of Symbolism; Symons has been describing the imprisoning self-consciousness of modern times and the impossibility of escaping it through a false—a necessarily false—attempt to be "natural." Yet there is an escape: "Symbolism, implicit in all literature from the beginning, as it is implicit in the very words we use, comes to us now, at last quite conscious of itself, offering us the only escape from our many imprisonments. We find a new, an older sense in the so worn out forms of things; the world, which we can no longer believe in as the satisfying material object it was to our grandparents, becomes transfigured with a new light" (p. 134).

This passage echoes the positive definition of Symbolism which appears at the beginning of Symons' book. There he makes the artist's creation of symbol analogous to God's creation of the world, both kinds of creation being forms of expression "for an unseen reality apprehended by the consciousness" (pp. 1–2). Later, when discussing Gérard de Nerval, Symons links this theory with the doctrine of "correspondences": since the visible world is the symbolic expression of the divine imagination, then every part of it is filled with divine energy and is divinely significant—all is bathed in a "light overflowing from beyond the world" (p. 30). It is this doctrine which makes it possible for Symbolism to offer an "escape from our many imprisonments"; the summarizing paragraph on the work of Mallarmé concludes: "And it is on the lines of that spiritualising of the word, that perfecting of form in its capacity for allusion and suggestion, that confidence in the eternal correspondences between the visible and the invisible universe . . . that literature must now move, if it is in any sense to move forward" (pp. 134–35).

These attempts at definition are inadequate, being themselves necessarily symbolic, but even Yeats' very beautiful definition of symbol, formulated in the years when he and Symons were discussing these things, is given only in an image: "A symbol is indeed the only possible expression of some invisible essence, a transparent lamp about a spiritual flame."[55] And Symons' words do give a feeling, an emotion more than an idea, of freedom and clear light for the soul in the vision of a world suddenly made significant because it reflects pure being. There remains, however, a question: is the unseen reality mirrored by symbols a reality discovered or one imposed? In *The Symbolist Movement* Symons does not come to any decision, but he was, of course, aware of both possibilities: one of the book's essays is on Villiers de l'Isle-Adam, who said: "Know once for all that there is for thee no other universe than that conception thereof which is reflected at the bottom of thy thought," and "Thou art but what thou thinkest: therefore think thyself eternal." On the page in which he quotes these lines from Villiers' *Axël*, Symons adds a note: " 'I am very far from sure,' wrote Verlaine, 'that the philosophy of Villiers will not one day become the formula of our century' " (pp. 41–42).

The philosophy was one that fascinated Symons—as, indeed, it fascinated Yeats—for it was something of which he had long been aware. Even as early as 1886, when he wrote of Browning's dramatic monologue, Symons notes of the speakers that "life exists for each as completely and as separately as if he were the only inhabitant of our planet."[56] Symons noted too that Meredith "carries the world behind his eyes, seeing, wherever he goes, only his own world,"[57] and he made Wilde's psychological theory that nature copies art into a mystical doctrine: "It is one of the privileges of art to create nature, as according to a certain mystical doctrine, you can actualise, by sheer fixity of contemplation, your mental image of a thing into the thing itself."[58]

The theory that the human imagination creates its own world and is its own eternity is very ancient, but its age does not make

it any less dangerous if it strike forcefully upon a mind not
properly balanced. When Symons wrote about Gérard de Nerval,
his own mind, one can see, was reeling from the force of thoughts
like these:

Who has not often meditated, above all what artist, on the slightness,
after all, of the link which holds our faculties together in that sober
health of the brain which we call reason? Are there not moments when
that link seems to be worn down to so fine a tenuity that the wing of a
passing dream might suffice to snap it? The consciousness seems, as it
were, to expand and contract at once, into something too wide for the
universe, and too narrow for the thought of self to find room within
it. Is it that the sense of identity is about to evaporate, annihilating all,
or is it that a more profound identity, the identity of the whole
sentient universe, has at last been realised? (pp. 23–24).

The doctrine which began by making each individual a reality
entirely to himself can leave him ultimately unsure of any
identity whatsoever. Worse still, the symbols of man's imagination
become terrifying and menacing as he loses control over them
and as they begin to reflect his own fear of himself.[59] All this
Symons saw and described in his essay on Gérard de Nerval;
later, when he tells of his own period of insanity, it is this essay
to which he most often alludes. He writes almost as if he were
appalled that, having understood so well, he could still have gone
mad. Quoting sentence after sentence from the essay, he keeps
saying, "It was I who had done all this, I in that madhouse":
"I . . who had quoted from *La Rêve et la Vie*—a madman's
narrative—such sentences as these. 'First of all I imagined that
the persons collected in the garden of the madhouse all had
some influence on the stars, and that the one who always walked
round and round in a circle regulated the course of the sun.' "[60]

Symons and Yeats, as they discussed and put into practice the
doctrines of Symbolism, may well typify the two kinds of artists
whom Symons describes in "Gérard de Nerval." Yeats was one of
those who could look fearlessly into the darkness of the self and
see, for "with him, imagination is vision," while Symons suffered
the fate of "the vague dreamer, the insecure artist, and the un-
certain mystic" who, when he gazes, sees only shadows, terrifying
reflections of his own imagination (p. 25).

Always, however, Symons had at hand two possible escapes from self, which, though he knew them to be purposeless, were nevertheless very useful in holding off the darkness that pressed in upon him: walking alone through crowds and travelling in foreign countries. To take country walks would not help him, for Symons says that he could walk for hours without hearing or seeing anything at all, with no sensation save the physical delight of walking.[61] In "Christian Trevalga" he describes this withdrawal into self in a very dramatic image: "And outward things, too, as well as people, meant very little to him, and meant less and less as time went on. What he saw, when he went for long walks with his father, had vanished from his memory before he returned to the house; it was as if he had been walking through underground passages, with only a faint light on the roadway in front of his feet."[62] But in a crowd the noise, the confusion and movement, demanded attention: Symons tells of seeing Coventry Fair in his late teens, his first plunge into "the bath of the multitude," which "seemed, for the first time in my life, to carry me outside myself."[63] During his first years in London, there was never an evening in which he did not go out, sometimes just to walk among the crowds in the Strand or in Piccadilly, and in his *Confessions* he identifies his feelings about the crowd with those of Gérard de Nerval: "The real world seeming to be always so far from him, and a sort of terror of the gulfs holding him, in spite of himself, to its flying skirts, he found something at all events realisable, concrete, in those drinkers of Les Halles."[64] Christian Trevalga also walks in Piccadilly "that he might take hold of something real," but as he succumbs to madness his doing so only adds to his sensations of unreality; the disorder and noise of the crowd bewilder and horrify him, having become the reflection of his own confused consciousness, and at the same time they rob him of any remaining sense of his individual existence: " 'I can see no reason,' he said to himself, 'why I am here rather than there, why these atoms which know one another so little, or have lost some recognition of themselves, should coalesce in this particular body, standing still where all is movement.' "[65] For the sense of reality which a crowd can give is a tenuous one at best, and Symons' pleasure in walking through crowds was a dubious therapy.

Symons' other escape lay in travelling for its own sake. Just as the crowd at once heightens and dissolves the sense of individuality, so a winding white road both symbolizes and negates all sense of time and space. In "The Wanderers" Symons writes:

> . . . life, a long white road,
> Winds ever from the dark into the dark,
> And they [the wanderers], as days, return not.[66]

The vision of the road whose whiteness shines out in a surrounding darkness resembles the tunnel in which Trevalga walked, so little thought is there of the scenes past which the road may wind. Defiantly, too, Symons takes pleasure in the very fact that on the road time's passage has no more meaning than the spatial surroundings have. The road is its own world, caught between past and future, yet without present:

> Because life holds not anything so good
> As to be free of yesterday, and bound
> Towards a new tomorrow; and they wend
> Into a world of unknown faces, where
> It may be there are faces waiting them,
> Faces of friendly strangers, not the long
> Intolerable monotony of friends.[67]

It was while he was travelling in Italy that Symons went insane; he says that on his way there, he was curiously unaware "that past and future are continually with us; only the present flies continually from under our feet."[68] Perhaps at that time he was unaware of it, had lost the sense of it, but ordinarily the consciousness of the present flying continually from under his feet was always with him. The desperation with which he tried to hold the present moment, like the feverish activity with which he attempted to make himself believe in his own reality, only made matters worse; finally, like Henry Luxulyan, Symons could say: "The world, ideas, sensations, are all fluid, and I flow through them, like a gondola carried along by the current: no, like a weed adrift on it."[69]

Confessions, Symons' account of his madness, begins in Venice, moves to Bologna, and then to Ferrara, where his breakdown became complete. It is a strange book, made up as it is of long quotations from Symons' earlier works, of sudden images which came to him in his madness, and of descriptions which have an almost preternatural lucidity. Images of imprisonment dominate the book. Symons quotes, for instance, from an article he wrote while in Venice on the music of that city; it begins by describing the harsh sounds, the cries and songs heard on the Venetian canals, but soon becomes a fascinated meditation on the dungeons under the Bridge of Sighs: "They are dark cells, a torture-room, rusty chains and bolts and bars, chains just long enough to enclose an ankle or two wrists, chains long enough to enclose the body in permanent inaction against the wall."[70] When he came to Ferrara, already close to insanity, Symons was suddenly terrified by the sight of the grim Castello Vecchio, black in the moonlight, its moat glittering around it, and by the thought again of the dungeons lying beneath its battlements (p. 18).

He was discovered a few days later wandering helplessly outside Ferrara, and he was thrown into one of the prisons of the Castello where he was chained and cruelly beaten by the guards: "Fettered on both ankles and both wrists I dragged myself with painful steps round and round the stone walls of my cell, gazing hopelessly at the barred window that let in but a little light, and at the Judas, which was continually opened and shut, showing me the grimacing faces of those inhuman beasts" (p. 25). Rescued at last by the English consul, he was brought back to England and placed in an asylum, where, two years later, he recovered.

That scene in the Castello Vecchio lies at the end of the mind's darkest passages. The prison of the self, which was an image to Rossetti and a philosophical abstraction to Pater, became a terrifying reality in the mind of Symons. He tried to escape it in every way which was open to him—religious belief, the love of woman, the artistic and ordering imagination—but each of these passages, for him at least, led only the more directly down into the prison at the very center of his mind.

Whether the dream now purposed to rehearse
Be Poet's or Fanatic's will be known
When this warm scribe, my hand, is in the grave.
John Keats

Chapter VII

The Decadent Consciousness

Pater's "Conclusion" to *The Renaissance* is answered by two sentences in *I and Thou*. Martin Buber writes: "We only need to fill each moment with experiencing and using, and it ceases to burn. And in all the seriousness of truth hear this: without *It* man cannot live. But he who lives with *It* alone is not a man."[1] The man who lives with It alone is the man subscribing to the "Conclusion"'s central doctrine: that each consciousness is totally isolated and that all contacts with the world are experiences within that consciousness and nothing more. Every man, according to this theory, dreams his life.

Marius the Epicurean describes Pater's eventually successful struggle to escape the theory and its effects. When Marius finds it possible to believe that he is, in fact, not alone but is in the presence of "an eternal friend to man,"[2] he comes to know the world of relation as well as the world of experience. But such a faith never came to the men of "the Tragic Generation," partly perhaps because the interpretation they gave to the lives of such models as Rossetti and Swinburne made total isolation a tenet of their artistic faith.

Keats' account of a dream at the beginning of *The Fall of Hyperion* prophesies the outcome of that creed. He writes of finding himself in a beautiful garden before the remnants of a feast. Even those remnants are delicious, and the poet eats them gratefully but becomes thirsty as he does so. Then he sees a "vessel of transparent juice" and pledging "all the mortals of the world,"[3] he drinks from it. In that moment he undergoes the experience of all mortals: Paradise is taken from him. After a period of unconsciousness, he comes to himself in a great temple, an awe-inspiring human construction set up to the east of Eden.

At the temple's west end stands an image, flanked by steps, toward which the poet walks. When he reaches the steps, he is warned suddenly by a voice from the shrine that unless he can mount them he will die. At that moment a coldness grips his limbs and then his body so that only with pain and difficulty does he struggle to the lowest step and safety. Then the goddess explains:

> "None can usurp this height, . . .
> But those to whom the miseries of the world
> Are misery, and will not let them rest.
> All else who find a haven in the world,
> Where they may thoughtless sleep away their days,
> If by a chance into this fane they come,
> Rot on the pavement where thou rotted'st half."
>   (ll. 147–153)

There are, however, many who are conscious of the world's misery yet are not present before the goddess. These are, so to speak, the "once-born," those whose awareness of life's sufferings impels them immediately to work at alleviating as much misery as they can; their way of salvation is clear. But Keats' concern in the parable is with those who, in Henry James' phrase, are burdened with "the oddity of a double consciousness," those men of imagination caught between their awareness of life's actualities, their dream of life's potential:

> "Every sole man hath days of joy and pain,
> Whether his labours be sublime or low—
> The pain alone; the joy alone; distinct:
> Only the dreamer venoms all his days,
> Bearing more woe than all his sins deserve.
> Therefore, that happiness be somewhat shar'd,
> Such things as thou art are admitted oft
> Into like gardens thou didst pass erewhile,
> And suffered in these temples."
>
> (ll. 172–80)

The imagination, source of his suffering, is also the dreamer's only means of salvation. Through his imagination he must come to the vision of reality.

Every poet, every person of imagination from Keats' time to the present, stands at some point in his life before Moneta's steps. And the poets of the nineties perished there, not because they "found a haven in the world" but because in the specious haven of their own imaginations they slept away their days. They desired moments of heightened consciousness, of imaginative insight, "simply," as Pater advised in the "Conclusion," "for those moments' sake." By doing so, they robbed such moments of all significance, narrowed them into the circle of the individual consciousness, and, destroying the possibility of vision, brought them wholly into the realm of dream.

At the same time, to speak practically, they left themselves without a subject for poetry. There is very little to be said about a moment when it is treated purely as experience, and what is said can be saved from banality only by tricks of style. The revelatory moment, the moment of meeting, on the other hand, offers a fruitful subject—as the works of Henry James attest. Nevertheless, it is in the area of subject rather than of form that a consistent poetic tradition exists from Keats through Rossetti and Pater, Symons and Johnson, to Yeats, Pound, Eliot, and Wallace Stevens. All are centrally concerned with the moment of heightened consciousness, but there is a crucial difference between the attitudes of the modern poets cited and those of the Decadents: either, as in the work of Yeats and Eliot, the poet has found a belief which will give significance to the moment, or, as in the work of Stevens

and Pound, the poet's subject is his very search for that belief—
the series of orderings, abandonments, and re-orderings with
which he strives to make his imagination "adhere to reality."[4]

The Decadents failed in their lives and in their art. But our
recognition of that failure and its accompanying bewilderment,
loneliness, and frustration should evoke not pity, that patronizing
emotion, but rather compassion: since the problems that the
Decadents faced have still no generally accepted solution, and
since every man must still make his own way, hoping only that
his inevitable mistakes may at least be remediable ones, then each
of the Decadents is in very truth one of us.

Notes

Introduction

1 Graham Hough, *The Last Romantics* (London, 1961), p. xix.
2 George H. Mead, *Movements of Thought in the Nineteenth Century* (Chicago, 1938), p. 375.
3 Walter Pater, *Studies in the History of the Renaissance* (London, 1873), p. 197.
4 George Santayana, *Scepticism and Animal Faith* (New York, 1955), p. 15.
5 Arthur Symons, "The Decadent Movement in Literature," *Harper's New Monthly Magazine*, LXXXVII (November, 1893), 862.

i *Dante Gabriel Rossetti*

1 D. G. Rossetti, *Collected Works*, ed. W. M. Rossetti (2 vols.; London, 1897), I, 384. Hereafter the *Collected Works* will be cited within the text as *CW*.

2 Oscar Wilde, "A Cheap Edition of a Great Man," *Reviews*, Vol. XII of Robert Ross's edition of Wilde's collected works (14 vols.; Boston, [1910]), p. 151.

3 Arthur Symons, "Dante Gabriel Rossetti," *Figures of Several Centuries* (London, 1917), p. 203.

4 William M. Rossetti, ed., *Dante Gabriel Rossetti: His Family Letters* (2 vols.; Boston, 1895), II, 328.

5 Walter Pater, "Dante Gabriel Rossetti," *Appreciations: With an Essay on Style* (London, 1889), p. 234.

6 S. T. Coleridge, *The Complete Poetical Works of Samuel Taylor Coleridge*, ed. Ernest Hartley Coleridge (2 vols.; Oxford, 1912), I, 456.

7 W. B. Yeats, *The Autobiography of William Butler Yeats* (New York, Macmillan, 1938), p. 267.

8 Rossetti, *Family Letters*, I, 418.

9 It was, according to Symons, from Madox Brown that the Pre-Raphaelites learned to focus their attention upon capturing the moment on their canvases.—Arthur Symons, *Dante Gabriel Rossetti: L'Art et le Beau*, Quatrième année, II (Paris, n.d.), 10.

10 Prosper Mérimée, "Les Beaux-Arts en Angleterre," *Revue des Deux Mondes*, II, Seconde Période (15 October 1857), 869.

11 Rossetti, *Family Letters*, II, 212.

12 Pater, *Appreciations*, p. 235.

13 Symons, *Figures of Several Centuries*, p. 204.

14 *Purgatorio*, XXX, ll. 76–78.

15 William Bell Scott, *Autobiographical Notes* (2 vols.; London, 1892), II, 112.

16 Yeats, *Autobiography*, p. 267.

17 D. H. Lawrence, *Studies in Classic American Literature* (New York, 1953), p. 86.

18 A. C. Swinburne, "D. G. Rossetti," *Essays and Studies* (London, 1875), p. 100.

ii *Algernon Charles Swinburne*

1 Cited by Georges Lafourcade in *La Jeunesse de Swinburne* (2 vols.; Paris, 1928), I, 137.

2 This source material is admirably gathered and used in Oswald Doughty's account, "The Jovial Campaign," *Dante Gabriel Rossetti: A Victorian Romantic* (New Haven, 1949), pp. 226–42.

3 Reproduced in *Memorials of Edward Burne Jones* by G[eorgiana]

B[urne]-J[ones] (London, 1906), p. 164.

4 A. C. Swinburne, "Dedicatory Epistle," *The Poems of Algernon Charles Swinburne* (6 vols.; New York, 1904), I, vii.

5 A. C. Swinburne, "Charles Baudelaire," *The Complete Works of Algernon Charles Swinburne,* ed. Sir Edmund Gosse and Thomas James Wise (The Bonchurch edition, 20 vols.; London, 1926), XIII, 419. Future references to this edition will be incorporated within the text under the title *Works.*

6 Letter by John Ruskin printed in A. C. Swinburne, *The Swinburne Letters,* ed. Cecil Y. Lang (New Haven, Yale University Press, 1959), I, 182. Future references to the letters will be incorporated within the text under the title *Letters.*

7 Georges Lafourcade, *Swinburne: A Literary Biography* (London, 1932), p. 228.

8 Swinburne wrote to Paul Hamilton Hayne on June 22, 1875: "Mr. Stedman's comparative depreciation of my Songs before Sunrise—at least his preference of my other books to this one—could not but somewhat disappoint me. For my other books are books; but that one is myself."—*Letters,* III, 35.

9 Proof, as C. Y. Lang points out, lies in Swinburne's letter to Watts on February 7, 1878: "Please don't on any account send any part of the MS [*Lesbia Brandon*] hither; but if you have by you the proofs of the chapter where the heroine (waiting to hear of her lover's death) sings songs (French and North-English) to her children, please send them at once."—*Letters,* IV, 40.

10 A. C. Swinburne, *The Novels of A. C. Swinburne: Love's Cross-Currents: Lesbia Brandon* (New York, 1963), p. 269.

11 The sincerity of this and other passages from *Notes on Poems and Reviews* has been questioned by critics, but Clyde Kenneth Hyder proves in *Swinburne's Literary Career and Fame* (New York, 1963), pp. 57–60, that one must take the *Notes* seriously.

12 Swinburne, *Lesbia Brandon,* pp. 202–3.

13 W. B. Yeats, "A Dialogue of Self and Soul," *The Collected Poems of W. B. Yeats* (New York, Macmillan, 1956), p. 232.

14 T. S. Eliot, *Selected Essays* (New York, 1950), p. 285.

15 Walter Pater, *Studies in the History of the Renaissance* (London, 1873), p. viii.

iii *Walter Pater*

1 William Sharp, "Personal Reminiscences of Walter Pater," *The Atlantic Monthly,* LXXIV (December, 1894), 810.

2 William Sharp, *"Marius the Epicurean: His Sensations and Ideas,"* *The Athenaeum,* No. 2992 (February, 1885), p. 273.

3 John Pick in "Divergent Disciples of Walter Pater," *Thought,* XXIII (March, 1948), 114–28.

4 Walter Pater, *Studies in the History of the Renaissance* (London, 1873), p. 205, and *Plato and Platonism: A Series of Lectures* [London, 1901], pp. 5–6—hereafter cited as *Plato.*

5 Walter Pater, *Marius the Epicurean: His Sensations and Ideas* (2 vols.; London, 1885), I, 143.

6 Walter Pater, "Coleridge's Writings," *Westminster Review,* n.s., XXIX (January, 1866), 108.

7 Pater, "The Doctrine of Plato," *Plato,* p. 158.

8 Pater, "The Genius of Plato," *Plato,* p. 135. These lectures on Plato are a fine summary of Pater's thought, though they may well leave the student rather bewildered about Plato's. The little jingle "Whatever Miss T. eats / Turns into Miss T." applies delightfully to Pater's treatment. Any Platonic theories which do not fit into Pater's world scheme are explained as unworthy of him, and like bits of gristle, left on the plate: "Generalisation, whatever Platonists, or Plato himself may have to say about it, is a method, not of obliterating the concrete phenomenon, but of enriching it, with the joint perspective, the significance, the expressiveness of all other things beside."—"The Doctrine of Plato," *Plato,* p. 157.

9 S. T. Coleridge, "On the Principles of Genial Criticism concerning the Fine Arts," *Criticism: The Major Texts,* ed. W. J. Bate (New York, 1952), p. 373.

10 Pater, "Preface," *The Renaissance,* p. viii.

11 Ruth Child, *The Aesthetic of Walter Pater* (New York, 1940), p. 111.

12 Pater, *Marius,* I, 149.

13 Pater, *The Renaissance,* p. 196.

14 Ernest Lee Tuveson, *The Imagination as a Means of Grace* (Berkeley, 1960), p. 88.

15 John Locke, *Essay Concerning Human Understanding,* Bk. II, Ch. xi, Section 17.

16 Pater, *Marius,* I, 149–50.

17 *Ibid.,* I, 154.

18 Friedrich Wilhelm von Schelling, "Concerning the Relation of the Plastic Arts to Nature," 1807, tr. Michael Bullock in Herbert Read's *True Voice of Feeling* (London, n.d.), pp. 333–34.

19 Bernard Bosanquet, tr., *The Introduction to Hegel's Philosophy of Fine Art* (London, 1886), p. 15.

20 Pater, *The Renaissance,* p. 196.

21 Pater thought the change a wise one for others as well. Oscar Wilde in his review of *Plato and Platonism* says that Pater suggested to him that he too should write in prose rather than verse (*Reviews,* p. 544). And Arthur Symons quotes a letter written to him by Pater in 1888 in which, after praising Symons' poetry, Pater tactfully makes his point: "You know I give a high place to the literature of prose as a fine art, and therefore hope you won't think me brutal in saying that the admirable qualities of your verse are those also of imaginative prose. . . . I should say, make prose your principal *métier,* as a man of letters, and publish your verse as a more intimate gift for those who already value you for your pedestrian work in literature."–Arthur Symons, "Walter Pater," *Figures of Several Centuries* (London, 1917), p. 327.

22 Pater, *Marius,* I, 165.

23 T. S. Eliot, "Burnt Norton," *Four Quartets* (New York, Harcourt, Brace, 1943), p. 5. Jean Sudrann in "Victorian Compromise and Modern Revolution" also recognizes a likeness between *Four Quartets* and *Marius,* comparing the latter's "fresh starts" to Eliot's spiritual journey.–*ELH,* XXVI (September, 1959), 443.

24 Thomas Wright has already noted closely the reflections of Pater's early years in his work (*Life of Walter Pater* [2 vols.; New York, 1907], I, 19–30). He points out, however, that "The houses in 'Emerald Uthwart' and 'The Child in the House' are less the Paters' house at Enfield than what, in Pater's opinion, that house ought to have been. And this is the key to all the quasi-autobiographical elements in his works."–*Ibid.,* I, 19–20.

25 Walter Pater, "The Child in the House," *Miscellaneous Studies: A Series of Essays* (London, 1895), p. 147. The story appeared originally in *Macmillan's Magazine,* XXXVIII (August, 1878), 313–21.

26 Pater, "The Child in the House," *Miscellaneous Studies,* p. 159.

27 Pater, *Marius,* II, 244.

28 *Ibid.,* I, 154.

29 Quoted in Arthur Symons, *A Study of Walter Pater* (London, 1932), p. 29.

30 Pater, *Marius,* I, 166.

31 *Ibid.,* I, 168.

32 Walter Pater, "Imaginary Portraits 2. An English Poet," ed. May Ottely, *Fortnightly Review,* n.s., CXXXV (April, 1931), 446.

33 Pater, *Plato,* pp. 36–37.

34 Pater, *Marius*, II, 145.

35 *Ibid.*, II, 16.

36 Wright says that Pater's favorite amusement as a child was playing at being a clergyman and that "he preached regularly and with unction to his mother, grandmother, and his admiring Aunt Bessie."—*Life of Walter Pater*, I, 21.

37 B. A. Inman, "Organic Structure of *Marius the Epicurean*," *Philological Quarterly*, XLI (April, 1962), 491.

38 Pater, *Marius*, I, 167–68.

39 One might consider his withdrawal of the "Conclusion" in the second edition a kind of answer, if only a negative one. Pater writes, "This brief Conclusion was omitted in the second edition of this book, as I conceived it might possibly mislead some of the young men into whose hands it might fall." However, Jerome Buckley's supposition that the actual motivation for the withdrawal was probably provided by the description of Mr. Rose in Mallock's *New Republic* is a shrewd one.—"Pater and the Suppressed Conclusion," *MLN*, LXV (April, 1950), 247–49.

40 Pater, *Marius*, II, 24–25.

41 Walter Pater, "Prosper Mérimée," *Fortnightly Review*, LIV (December, 1890), 852–53.

42 Symons, "Walter Pater," *Figures of Several Centuries*, p. 335.

43 Walter Pater, *Gaston de Latour* (London, 1896), p. 51.

44 Pater, *Marius*, II, 72.

45 *Ibid.*, II, 70.

46 *Ibid.*, II, 81–82.

47 Pater, "Conclusion," *The Renaissance*, p. 211.

48 Pater, "Prosper Mérimée," pp. 853–54.

iv *Oscar Wilde*

1 W. B. Yeats, *A Vision* (New York, 1938), p. 148.

2 Arthur Symons, *A Study of Oscar Wilde* (London, 1930), p. 50.

3 *Ibid.*, pp. 84–85.

4 Arthur Nethercot, "Oscar Wilde and the Devil's Advocate," *PMLA*, LIX (September, 1944), 843.

5 Oscar Wilde, *The Letters of Oscar Wilde*, ed. Rupert Hart-Davis (New York, Harcourt, Brace, 1962), p. 352. Future references to this work will be cited in the text under the title *Letters*.

6 Oscar Wilde, "Art and the Handicraftsman," *Miscellanies*, Vol.

XIV of Robert Ross's edition of Wilde's collected works (14 vols.; Boston, [1910]), p. 307. This edition of Wilde's works will be referred to hereafter as *Collected Works.*

7 Oscar Wilde, "The Grovesnor Gallery," *Miscellanies* (*Collected Works,* Vol. XIV), p. 23.

8 *Ibid.,* p. 11.

9 Yeats remembers hearing Wilde say of *The Renaissance:* "It is my golden book; I never travel anywhere without it; but it is the very flower of decadence: the last trumpet should have sounded the moment it was written."—W. B. Yeats, *The Autobiography of William Butler Yeats* (New York, 1938), p. 114.

10 Robert Sherard, discussing the statement, "For years Dorian Gray could not free himself from the influence of this book [*A Rebours*]," says sharply, "This is, of course, silliness. Yet Oscar Wilde used to make the same silly self-deceiving statements about himself, and attributed to some 'poisonous book' which he had once read [*The Renaissance?*] many of the abnormalities of his conduct." —Sherard, *The Life of Oscar Wilde* (New York, 1928), p. 66.

11 Arthur Symons, "Introduction," *The Renaissance* (Modern Library Edition, New York, [1919]), p. xv.

12 Wilde, *Dorian Gray* (*Collected Works,* Vol. IV), p. 27.

13 Henry James, *The Ambassadors* (2 vols.; New York, 1909), I, 217.

14 Walter Pater, "Conclusion," *Studies in the History of the Renaissance* (London, 1873), p. 211.

15 Walter Pater, "A Novel by Mr. Oscar Wilde," *Uncollected Essays* (Portland, Maine, 1903), p. 127.

16 In the Introduction to his edition of Wilde's reviews Robert Ross comments: "The great men of the previous generation, Wilde's intellectual peers, with whom he was in artistic sympathy, looked on him askance. Ruskin was disappointed with his former pupil, and Pater did not hesitate to express disapprobation to private friends; while he accepted incense from a disciple, he distrusted the thurifer."—*Reviews* (*Collected Works,* Vol. XII), p. xii. Ross is not reliable in his interpretation or even his presentation of facts—it seems unlikely, for instance, that Ruskin thought about Wilde one way or another—but here he may be giving at least a partial truth.

17 André Gide, *Oscar Wilde,* tr. Bernard Frechtman (New York, 1949), pp. 3–4.

18 Wilde, *Miscellanies* (*Collected Works,* Vol. XIV), p. 27.

19 Oscar Wilde, "L'Envoi, an Introduction to *Rose Leaf and Apple*

Leaf," Miscellanies (Collected Works, Vol. XIV), pp. 31–32. In the Widener Collection there is a copy of *The Happy Prince and Other Tales* (London, 1888) which bears the autograph inscription: "To John Ruskin in all love and loyalty from Oscar Wilde. June '88."

20 A manuscript letter in Houghton Library from Walter E. Ledger to Thomas B. Mosher, written from Wimbledon, England, on February 12, 1906, says that "Sir Rennell Rodd quarrelled with Wilde when the latter published Rose Leaf and Apple Leaf, for it was without Rodd's permission. The original title of the work was 'Songs in the South' and it was dedicated to Rodd's father. Two of the poems in it were omitted in the American edition."

21 *The Athenaeum* reviewed the poem, listing the imitations from Shakespeare, Milton, Tennyson, and Swinburne, and concluding that "there is scarcely a poet of high mark in this century whose influence is not perceptible."—*The Athenaeum,* No. 2804 (July 23, 1881), p. 103.

22 A letter from Wilde to Reginald Harding, sent from Merrion Square, Dublin, in July, 1877, shows that Wilde's "Romish leanings" moved a wealthy cousin virtually to strike him from his will.—Vyvyan Holland, *Son of Oscar Wilde* (London, 1954), p. 243.

23 Oscar Wilde, "The Burden of Itys," *Poems (Collected Works,* Vol. I), p. 83. Future references will be made in the text under the title *Poems.*

24 Oscar Wilde, *Salomé (Collected Works,* Vol. VI), p. 67. Sometimes Wilde's inability to efface himself in a poetic reverie has very amusing consequences. In "The Burden of Itys," for instance, he adopts Baudelaire's lines on Michelangelo's "Night":

> Ou bien toi, grande Nuit, fille de Michel-Ange,
> Qui tords paisiblement dans une pose étrange
> Tes appas façonnés aux bouches des Titans!

(Charles Baudelaire, "L'Idéal," *Les Fleurs du Mal*)
and makes them:

> "O . . . that I could charm
> The Dawn at Florence from its dumb despair
> Mix with those mighty limbs and make that giant breast my lair!"
> (*Poems,* p. 92.)

25 Manuscript letter from George E. Woodberry to Charles Eliot Norton, written from Lincoln, Nebraska, April 25, 1882. Charles

Eliot Norton Collection, Houghton Library, Harvard University.

26 Charles Baudelaire, "De L'Eclectisme et du Doute: Salon de 1846," *Curiosités Esthétiques (Oeuvres Complètes de Charles Baudelaire* [Paris, 1868–73], Vol. II), p. 165.

27 Charles Baudelaire, "Éloge du Maquillage: Le Peintre de la Vie Moderne," *L'Art Romantique (Oeuvres Complètes,* Vol. III), p. 100.

28 Oscar Wilde, "The English Renaissance," *Miscellanies (Collected Works,* Vol. XIV), p. 258.

29 Matthew Arnold, "The Study of Poetry," *Essays in Criticism,* Second Series (London, 1898), p. 1.

30 Wilde, "Critic as Artist," *Intentions and The Soul of Man (Collected Works,* Vol. III), pp. 164–65.

31 Wilde, "Decay of Lying," *Intentions (Collected Works,* Vol. III), p. 33.

32 *Ibid.,* p. 34.

33 This was at the first meeting of Yeats and Wilde, just after the latter had written a review praising *The Wanderings of Usheen.* —Yeats, *Autobiography,* p. 118.

34 W. B. Yeats, *The Collected Poems of W. B. Yeats* (New York, Macmillan, 1956), p. 322.

35 *Ibid.,* p. 342. Yeats also echoed Wilde's idea in his prose when he wrote in 1937: "Somebody saw a woman of exuberant beauty coming from a public-house with a pot of beer and commended her to Rossetti; twenty years later Mrs. Langtry called upon Watts and delighted him with her simplicity. . . . Two painters created their public; two types of beauty decided what strains of blood would most prevail."—W. B. Yeats, "Introduction," *Essays and Introductions* (New York, 1961), p. xi.

36 Oscar Wilde, "The Letters of a Great Woman," *Reviews (Collected Works,* Vol. XII), pp. 49–50.

37 The discussion between Wilde and Woodberry on form touched upon the Grand Canyon: "He spoke of Colorado Canyons; 'but are they beautiful in form,' I said, and he said 'Oh yes!' and gave a description to convince me, that was pure color without one line in it."—Woodberry, manuscript letter to C. E. Norton, Charles Eliot Norton Collection, Houghton Library, Harvard University.

38 Wilde, "The Soul of Man," *Intentions (Collected Works,* Vol. III), p. 300.

39 Wilde, "The English Renaissance," *Miscellanies (Collected Works,* Vol. XIV), p. 251.

40 Charles Baudelaire, "Eugène Delacroix: Salon de 1846," *Curiosités Esthétiques (Oeuvres Complètes,* Vol. II), p. 102.
41 Wilde, "Pen, Pencil, and Poison," *Intentions* (*Collected Works,* Vol. III), pp. 88–89.
42 Wilde, "The Critic as Artist," *Intentions,* (*Collected Works,* Vol. III), p. 144.
43 Charles Baudelaire, "A Quoi Bon la Critique?: Salon de 1846," *Curiosités Esthétiques (Oeuvres Complètes,* Vol. II), p. 82.
44 Wilde, "Decay of Lying," *Intentions* (*Collected Works,* Vol. III), p. 21.
45 Wilde, "The Critic as Artist," *Intentions* (*Collected Works,* Vol. III), p. 145.
46 *Ibid.,* p. 197.
47 Wilde, "The Soul of Man," *Intentions* (*Collected Works,* Vol. III), pp. 274–75.
48 Wilde, "The Critic as Artist," *Intentions* (*Collected Works,* Vol. III), p. 184.
49 *Ibid.,* p. 185.
50 *Ibid.,* p. 183.
51 Baudelaire's dandy is the last representative of an old aristocratic order: "Le dandysme est un soleil couchant; comme l'astre qui décline, il est superbe, sans chaleur et plein de mélancolie. Mais, hélas! la marée montante de la démocratie, qui envahit tout et qui nivelle tout, noie jour à jour ses derniers représentants de l'orgueil humain et verse des flots d'oubli sur les traces de ces prodigieux mirmidons."—"Le Dandy: Le Peintre de la Vie Moderne," *L'Art Romantique (Oeuvres Complètes,* Vol. III), p. 95.
The link between aristocracy and dedication to poetic form had been made by Alexis de Tocqueville: "Prise dans son ensemble, la littérature des siècles démocratiques ne saurait présenter, ainsi que dans les temps d'aristocratie, l'image de l'ordre, de la régularité, de la science et de l'art: la forme s'y trouvera, d'ordinaire, négligée et parfois méprisée."—*De la Démocratie en Amérique* (2 Vols.; Paris, 1951), II, 83.
In De Tocqueville's opinion, however, there was to be a gain as well as a loss. The Parnassians saw only the loss and set themselves to proving De Tocqueville false. The fear of democracy that they felt in doing so is obvious in the violence with which Théophile Gautier "explains" his principles: "Non, imbéciles, non, crétins et goîtreux que vous êtes, un livre ne fait pas de la soupe à la gélatine."—"Preface," *Mademoiselle de Maupin* (Paris, 1873), p. 18.

52 André Gide, *The Journals of André Gide,* tr. Justin O'Brien (4 vols.; New York, 1947–51), II, 400.

53 Frank Harris, *Oscar Wilde: His Life and Confessions* (2 vols.; New York, 1918), I, 299; Yeats, *Autobiography,* p. 245; Hesketh Pearson, *Oscar Wilde: His Life and Wit* (New York, 1946), p. 271; Sherard, *Life of Oscar Wilde,* pp. 354–57.

54 Arthur Nethercot's study "Oscar Wilde and the Devil's Advocate" uses a similar method in analysing *The Picture of Dorian Gray* and Wilde's plays, though he insists too much perhaps on the truth of the "moral" Wilde, saying, "He [Wilde] knew that the truth about the man Oscar Wilde was preserved in his writings" (p. 850). Is it really clear, however, that Wilde ever came to so good an understanding of himself?

55 When describing Lord Henry, Wilde writes: "And so he had begun by vivisecting himself as he had ended by vivisecting others" (p. 68); this is the sin of Roger Chillingworth and of Ethan Brand. Julian Hawthorne reviewed *The Picture of Dorian Gray* for *Lippincott's Magazine;* there he compares it with Balzac's story "La Peau de Chagrin" and with Stevenson's *Dr. Jekyll and Mr. Hyde,* but, disappointingly, he makes no parallels between his father's stories and *Dorian Gray;* yet there are enough similarities in thought and even in method to make such a comparison very interesting.—Julian Hawthorne, "The Romance of the Impossible," *Lippincott's Magazine,* XLVI (September, 1890), 412–15.

Vincent O'Sullivan says that Wilde did not take American literature seriously except for the works of Poe, Whitman, and Hawthorne, "not really liking any of them, I think, but Hawthorne—the Hawthorne of *The Scarlet Letter*."—*Aspects of Wilde* (New York, 1936), p. 133.

56 H. Montgomery Hyde, ed., *The Trials of Oscar Wilde* (London, 1948) p. 128. This is also the version printed in *Lippincott's Magazine,* XLVI (July, 1890), 1–100, but its repetition at the trial is cited here because in the course of the questioning the point was made that through Pater's influence this passage was changed.

57 Gide, *The Journals of André Gide,* II, 409.

58 *Ibid.,* pp. 409–10.

59 Wilde, "The Critic as Artist," *Intentions* (*Collected Works,* Vol. III), p. 221.

60 Wilde, *Miscellanies* (*Collected Works,* Vol. XIV), pp. 139–40.

61 Aubrey Beardsley drew a delightful cartoon which serves as frontispiece for Stuart Mason's *Bibliography of Oscar Wilde* (Lon-

don, 1914). The picture is entitled "Oscar Wilde at Work '(Il ne faut pas le regarder)' "; it shows Wilde at his desk surrounded by those works on which he is particularly dependent: books by Gautier, Flaubert and Swinburne, a copy of *French Verbs at a Glance,* and, largest of all, a well-thumbed family Bible.

62 Oscar Wilde, *A House of Pomegranates (Collected Works,* Vol. II), p. 74.

63 *Ibid.,* pp. 128–29.

64 Frank Harris gave Wilde the central idea for the plot when he told him of an event in the life of Benjamin Disraeli that had been described to him while he was in Cairo: there a Mr. Cope White-house told Harris that Disraeli had made money by entrusting the Rothschilds with the purchase of Suez Canal shares. The story is substantially true, though Frank Harris was not himself convinced. "It seemed to me strange that this statement, if true, had never been set forth authoritatively; but the story was peculiarly modern and had possibilities in it. Oscar admitted afterwards that he had taken the idea and used it in 'An Ideal Husband.' "—*Oscar Wilde: His Life and Confessions,* I, 182.

65 Oscar Wilde, *An Ideal Husband (Collected Works,* Vol. IX), p. 46.

66 André Gide recalls Wilde's saying to him: "I don't like your lips; they're straight, like those of someone who has never lied. I want to teach you to lie, so that your lips may become beautiful and twisted like those of an antique mask."—*Oscar Wilde,* p. 6.

67 "Never speak disrespectfully of Society, Algernon," says Lady Bracknell. "Only people who can't get into it do that."—Oscar Wilde, *The Importance of Being Earnest (Collected Works,* Vol. VII), p. 163.

68 In another letter Wilde also has a very sensible technical discussion on the difficulty there is in describing a prison within the objective, impersonal ballad form: "With regard to the adjectives, I admit there are far too many 'dreadfuls' and 'fearfuls'; the difficulty is that the objects in prison have no shape or form. To take an example: the shed in which people are hanged is a little shed with a glass roof, like a photographer's studio on the sands at Margate: for eighteen months I thought it *was* a studio for photographing prisoners. There is no adjective to describe it. I call it 'hideous' because it became so to me after I knew its use. In itself it is a wooden, oblong, narrow shed with a glass roof.

"A cell may be described psychologically with reference to its effect on the soul: in itself it can only be described as 'whitewashed' or 'dimly lit.' It has no shape, no contents; it does not exist from the point of view of form or colour.

"In point of fact, describing a prison is as difficult artistically as describing a water-closet would be. If one had to describe the latter in literature, prose or verse, one could say merely that it was well or badly papered; or clean or the reverse. The horror of prison is that everything is so simple and commonplace in itself, and so degrading and hideous and revolting in its effect" (*Letters*, pp. 654–55).

69 Oscar Wilde, "The Grave of Keats," *Poems*, p. 157.
70 Yeats, *Autobiography*, p. 244.
71 Sherard, *Life of Oscar Wilde*, p. 40.
72 Charles Baudelaire, "De L'Essence du Rire," *Curiosités Esthétiques* (*Oeuvres Complètes*, Vol. II), p. 369.
73 George Woodberry, manuscript letter to C. E. Norton, Charles Eliot Norton Collection, Houghton Library, Harvard University.

v *Lionel Johnson*

1 W. B. Yeats, *The Autobiography of William Butler Yeats* (New York, 1938), p. 242.
2 *Ibid.*, p. 259.
3 Lionel Johnson, "Incurable," *The Pageant*, I (1896), 131–33.
4 Letter from Rhual, December 29, 1884, in *Some Winchester Letters of Lionel Johnson* (London, 1919), p. 168. Russell himself edited the letters and published them anonymously.—George Santayana, *The Middle Span* (New York, 1945), p. 57.
5 Rhual, January, 1885, *Winchester Letters*, p. 170. According to Arthur Patrick it was allusions like these to the Johnson family that caused the edition to be withdrawn from circulation.—Arthur Patrick, *Lionel Johnson, Poète et Critique* (Paris, 1939), p. 9.
6 Lionel Johnson, *"Barrack-Room Ballads and Other Verses* by Rudyard Kipling," *The Academy*, XLI (May 28, 1892), 509.
7 *Winchester Letters*, p. 176.
8 *Ibid.*, p. 50 and p. 53. On July 19, 1884, Captain Johnson wrote to Russell permitting the resumption of the correspondence and explaining that he had stopped it "having been warned that it might tend to the unsettling of his [Lionel's] mind on religious matters" (p. 124).
9 Yeats, *Autobiography*, p. 165.

10 *Winchester Letters,* p. 105.
11 W. B. Yeats, "William Blake and the Imagination," *Essays and Introductions* (New York, 1961), p. 111. In "The Tower" Yeats wrote:

> Now shall I make my soul,
> Compelling it to study
> In a learned school.
> —W. B. Yeats, *The Collected Poems of W. B. Yeats*
> (New York, Macmillan, 1956), p. 197.

12 Santayana, *1 he Middle Span,* p. 55.
13 *Winchester Letters,* p. 111.
14 *Ibid.,* p. 15.
15 William Rossetti writes that Browning delighted Rossetti because in his poems were "passion, observation, aspiration, mediaevalism, the dramatic perception of character, act, and incident."—*Dante Gabriel Rossetti: His Family Letters* (2 vols.; Boston, 1895), I, 102. Largely through Rossetti's influence Browning became very popular at Oxford and by Johnson's time a devotion to him was part of the aesthetic tradition.—M. B. Cramer, "Browning's Literary Reputation at Oxford," *PMLA,* LVII (March, 1942), 232–40.
16 *Winchester Letters,* p. 20.
17 Lionel Johnson, *The Academy, XLII* (August 6, 1892), 103.
18 *Winchester Letters,* pp. 182–83.
19 Lionel Johnson, *The Art of Thomas Hardy* (London, 1894), p. 162.
20 W. B. Yeats and Lionel Johnson, *Poetry and Ireland* (Churchtown, Dundrum, 1908), p. 19.
21 Lionel Johnson, "Cardinal Newman," *Post Liminium: Essays and Critical Papers,* ed. Thomas Whittemore (London, 1911), p. 301.
22 *Ibid.,* pp. 297–98.
23 Lionel Johnson, "Walter Pater," *The Complete Poems of Lionel Johnson,* ed. Iain Fletcher (London, 1953), p. 269.
24 *Winchester Letters,* p. 165.
25 Katherine Tynan, *Memories* (London, 1924), p. 113.
26 Yeats, *Autobiography,* p. 165. Yeats' amusing pretense of bewilderment over Johnson's methods of punctuation (which he describes, nonetheless, with perfect accuracy) shows that he had his own methods of counter-attack: "He [Johnson] punctuated after the manner of the seventeenth century and was always ready to spend an hour discussing the exact use of a colon. 'One should use a colon where other people use a semi-colon, a semi-colon where other people use a comma,' was, I think, but a condescension to my ignorance, for the matter was plainly beset with many subtleties."

—*Ibid.*, p. 262.

27 Johnson, *Post Liminium,* p. 165.

28 *Ibid.*, p. 160.

29 John Henry, Cardinal Newman, "The Second Spring," *Sermons Preached on Various Occasions* (London, 1891), pp. 171–72.

30 Santayana, *The Middle Span,* pp. 61–62.

31 Harold Frederic, *The Damnation of Theron Ware* (New York, 1896).

32 Johnson, "The Church of a Dream," *Complete Poems,* pp. 82–83. A poem written in 1891, the very year of Johnson's conversion, and dedicated to Ernest Dowson, shows a very similar feeling:

> Leave we awhile without the turmoil of the town;
> Leave we the sullen gloom, the faces full of care:
> Stay we awhile and dream, within this place of prayer,
> Stay we, and pray, and dream: till in our hearts die down
> Thoughts of the world, unkind and weary.
> —"Our Lady of France," *ibid.*, p. 15.

33 Yeats, "In Memory of Major Robert Gregory," *Collected Poems,* p. 130.

34 Johnson, "Mystic and Cavalier," *Complete Poems,* p. 29.

35 Johnson, "To Passions," *ibid.*, pp. 174–75.

36 Johnson, "A Dream," *ibid.*, p. 143.

37 Johnson, "The Dark Angel," *ibid.*, p. 67.

38 T. S. Eliot, "The Waste Land," *Collected Poems, 1909–1935* (New York, Harcourt, Brace, 1936), p. 89.

39 *Winchester Letters,* p. 147.

40 Wilde, "Critic as Artist," *Intentions and The Soul of Man,* Vol. III of Robert Ross's edition of Wilde's collected works (14 vols.; Boston, [1910]), pp. 164–65.

41 Johnson, *Post Liminium,* pp. 217–18.

42 Lionel Johnson, "*Eighteenth Century Vignettes* by Austen Dobson," *The Academy,* XLII (December 19, 1892), 531.

43 Johnson, *Complete Poems,* p. 85.

44 Arthur Symons, ed., *The Poems of Ernest Dowson* (London, 1915), p. viii.

45 Johnson, "At the Cheshire Cheese," *Complete Poems,* p. 259.

46 Yeats, *Autobiography,* p. 260.

47 Johnson, "Winchester," *Complete Poems,* p. 227.

48 Johnson, "Lines to a Lady upon her Third Birthday, 1889," *ibid.*, p. 45. "At Eton" (pp. 201–2) and "A Dream of Youth" (pp. 53–57), both also written in 1889, have similar themes. A nostalgia for childhood is not, of course, peculiar to Johnson; so widely were

his feelings shared by others of his generation that England seems
almost to have become one of the "nurseries of Heaven."

49 Johnson, *Post Liminium*, p. 218.
50 Lord Francis Russell, *My Life and Adventures* (London, 1923),
pp. 90–91.
51 Johnson, *Post Liminium*, p. 247.

VI *Arthur Symons*

1 An unpublished letter to Arthur Moore from Dowson in the
Morgan Library gives the latter's first impression of Symons: "I met
Arthur Symons last night: do you know him? He is a standing
dish with the 'Academy' and knows his Paris well; but on the
whole I was not greatly impressed."–Quoted by Thomas J. Gar-
baty, "The Savoy, 1896: A Re-edition of Representative Prose and
Verse" (unpublished Ph.D. thesis, University of Pennsylvania,
1957), p. 201.
2 Paul Verlaine, "My Visit to London (November 1893)," tr. Arthur
Symons, *The Savoy*, No. 2 (April, 1896), pp. 119–35.
3 W. B. Yeats, *The Autobiography of William Butler Yeats* (New
York, 1938), p. 272.
4 Unpublished letter from Arthur Symons to William Rothenstein
[1893–1894], in the Rothenstein Collection, Houghton Library.
5 Vincent O'Sullivan, *Aspects of Wilde*, (New York, 1936), p. 77.
6 Arthur Symons, ed., *The Savoy*, No. 8 and last (December, 1896).
     1) "Mundi Victima," pp. 13–27.
     2) "Walter Pater," pp. 33–41.
     3) "The Childhood of Lucy Newcome," pp. 51–61.
     4) "Hérodiade," pp. 67–68.
     5) "The Isles of Aran," pp. 73–92.
     6) "A Literary Causerie: By Way of Epilogue," pp. 91–92.
7 Arthur Symons, "Dieppe: 1895," *The Savoy*, No. 1 (January,
1896), p. 85 and p. 93.
8 On the first page of *Confessions: A Study in Pathology* (New
York, 1930), Symons mentions the strain of insanity in his family.
Roger Lhombreaud, although he emphasizes Symons' battle against
debt, mentions reports of witnesses which suggest that during the
last years of her life Symons' mother was not completely sane.–
Arthur Symons: A Critical Biography (London, 1963).

9 Arthur Symons, "Conclusion," *Studies in Prose and Verse* (London, [1904]), p. 290.

10 Arthur Symons, *A Study of Oscar Wilde* (London, 1930), p. 50.

11 Symons, "Prosper Mérimée," *Studies in Prose and Verse*, p. 32.

12 *Ibid.*, pp. 37–38.

13 Wilde, *Dorian Gray*, p. 5.

14 Symons, "Walter Pater," *Studies in Prose and Verse*, p. 76.

15 Arthur Symons, *The Symbolist Movement in Literature* (New York, 1908), p. 134.

16 Lhombreaud, *Arthur Symons*, p. 5.

17 Arthur Symons, "A Prelude to Life," *Spiritual Adventures* (London, 1905), p. 4.

18 Symons, "Fact in Literature," *Studies in Prose and Verse*, p. 3.

19 Symons does not use this phrase in "A Prelude to Life" but gives himself the title in *Confessions*, p. 48.

20 Frank Harris, *Contemporary Portraits*, Third Series (New York, 1920), p. 73.

21 Typical of Harris' slap-dash reporting is his account of Symons' attack of insanity, as garbled a piece of gossip as the story of H. C. E.'s crime in *Finnegans Wake*. Harris tells the story given him by a friend: "He [Symons] was walking with his wife one day in Genoa, I think it was, when he suddenly lost control of himself and began to break shop windows, muttering wildly all the while, 'Lost! Lost!' Lost, indeed, I'm afraid, down and out."—Harris, *Contemporary Portraits*, Third Series, p. 82.

    According to Symons' own account he was alone in Ferrara. He does not mention the shop windows.—*Confessions*, pp. 18–23.

22 Yeats, *Autobiography*, p. 272.

23 In *Confessions* Symons makes an explicit comparison between himself and this character described in *Spiritual Adventures*. See *Confessions*, p. 1.

24 Symons, "Christian Trevalga," *Spiritual Adventures*, p. 96.

25 Arthur Symons, "A Woman," *Days and Nights* (London, 1889), p. 143. Late in his life Symons put Rossetti's "The Orchard Pit" into verse, using the latter's outline and, at times, his phrasing, in a poem called "The Pit of Hell."—Arthur Symons, *Jezebel Mort and Other Poems* (London, 1931), pp. 9–34.

26 Arthur Symons, "Renée," *London Nights* (London, 1895), p. 6.

27 Arthur Symons, "In the Oratory," *Silhouettes* (London, 1896), p. 19.

28 Symons, "Perfume," *Silhouettes*, p. 41.

29 Arthur Symons, "New Year's Eve," *The Savoy*, No. 2 (April, 1896), p. 25. Lionel Johnson has a parody of this sort of Symons' poem, which he calls "an attempt at the sensuous love-lyric":

> Sometimes in very joy of shame,
> Our flesh becomes one living flame:
> And she and I
> Are no more separate but the same.
>   —Johnson, "Incurable," *The Pageant*, I (1896), 131.

The parody is so close to many genuine poems that Symons must have winced.

30 Symons, "Paris," *London Nights*, p. 87.

31 Arthur Symons, "An Epilogue to Love, VI," *The Fool of the World* (London, 1906), p. 102.

32 *Ibid.*, p. 103.

33 Symons, "Walter Pater," *Studies in Prose and Verse*, p. 67.

34 Luxulyan's sudden moments of terror are described so vividly that they may also have been Symons'. Luxulyan describes a cab-ride home from a concert; when the cab turns out of narrow streets into a broad road, the fear of death suddenly possesses him: "One enters into it as into a long dimly lighted alley, and at the end of the road is the sky, with one star hung like a lantern upon the darkness; and it seems as if the sky is at the end of the road, that if one drove right on one would plunge over the edge of the world. All that is solid on the earth seems to melt about one; it is as if one's eyes had been suddenly opened, and one saw for the first time."—Symons, "Extracts from the Journal of Henry Luxulyan," *Spiritual Adventures*, pp. 254–55. In "A Prelude to Life," p. 17, Symons uses the last sentence to apply to his own fear of death.

   At another time, Luxulyan wakes suddenly in great terror: "I had the sensation of a world in which the daylight had been blotted out, and men stumbled in a perpetual night, which the lamps did not make visible."—*Ibid.*, p. 262.

35 Symons, "Henry Luxulyan," *Spiritual Adventures*, p. 251.

36 The bride's name in "An Autumn City" is worth remembering; it is Livia.

37 Symons, "Unspiritual Adventures in Paris," *Wanderings* (London, [1931]), p. 103.

38 Arthur Symons, "For Des Esseintes. VI, Perdition, " *Love's Cruelty* (London, 1923), p. 31.

39 Walter Pater, "A Poet with Something to Say," *Uncollected Essays* (Portland, Maine, 1903), pp. 83–84.

40 Arthur Symons, *An Introduction to the Study of Browning* (London, 1886), p. 35.

41 Symons, "Paul Verlaine," *Symbolist Movement*, p. 81.

42 Symons, "A Literary Causerie," *The Savoy*, No. 8 (December, 1896), p. 92.

43 Symons, "Paul Verlaine," *Symbolist Movement*, p. 76 and p. 80.

44 Symons, "Prelude to Life," *Spiritual Adventures*, pp. 49–50. In *London*, he adds a few very interesting details: "I am able to remember how I used to turn out of the Temple and walk slowly towards Charing Cross, elbowing my way meditatively, making up sonnets in my head while I missed no attractive face on the pavement or on the top of an omnibus, pleasantly conscious of the shops yet undistracted by them, happy because I was in the midst of people, and happier still because they were all unknown to me." —Arthur Symons, *London: A Book of Aspects* (Minneapolis, 1909. Printed privately for Edmund D. Brooks and his friends), p. 22. The circumstances under which they were written may help to explain the casual organization of many of Symons' poems.

45 Symons, "Songs of the Poltescoe Valley," *Fool of the World*, p. 29.

46 Arthur Symons, "At the Alhambra: Impressions and Sensations," *The Savoy*, No. 5 (September, 1896), p. 75.

47 Symons, "The Magic of Auxerre," *Wanderings*, p. 178.

48 Symons, "Esther Kahn," *Spiritual Adventures*, p. 55. Symons noted Hawthorne's similar tendency to "watch life from a corner, as he watched the experimental life at Brook Farm."—Symons, "Nathaniel Hawthorne," *Studies in Prose and Verse*, p. 55.

49 Symons, *London*, p. 28.

50 Symons, "Gabriele D'Annunzio," *Studies in Prose and Verse*, p. 140.

51 Yeats, *Autobiography*, p. 273.

52 Symons, *Symbolist Movement*, p. vi.

53 Arthur Symons, "The Decadent Movement in Literature," *Harper's New Monthly Magazine*, LXXXVII (November, 1893), 862.

54 Symons, "Introduction," *Symbolist Movement*, p. 6.

55 Yeats, "William Blake and his Illustrations to the *Divine Comedy*," *Essays and Introductions* (New York, 1961), p. 116. This essay first appeared in *The Savoy*, No. 3 (July, 1896), pp. 41–57.

In his description of the trip he took with Yeats to the Aran Islands, Symons writes: "We talked of Parnell, of the county families, of mysticism, the analogy of that old Biblical distinction of body, soul, and spirit with the symbolical realities of the lamp, the wick, and the flame."—Arthur Symons, "The Isles of Aran," *The Savoy*, No. 8 (December, 1896), p. 73.

56 Symons, *Introduction to Browning*, p. 5.

57 Symons, "A Note on George Meredith," *Studies in Prose and Verse*, p. 143.

58 Symons, "Prosper Mérimée," *Studies in Prose and Verse*, p. 33. The doctrine appears in *Axël:* "For in your own pure will you hold the essence of all things and are the god you have it in your power to become. Such is the dogma and prime secret of true knowledge." —Auguste, Comte de Villiers de l'Isle-Adam, *Axël*, tr. H. P. Finberg (London, 1925), p. 214.

59 His understanding of the power of the imagination gave Symons this splendid insight into the later paintings of D. G. Rossetti: "Yet, as his intentions overpower him [Rossetti], as he becomes the slave and no longer the master of his dreams, his pictures become no longer symbolic. They become idols. Venus, growing more and more Asiatic as the moon's crescent begins to glitter above her head, and her name changes from Aphrodite to Astarte, loses all the freshness of the waves from which she was born, and her sorcery hardens into a wooden image painted to be the object of savage worship. Dreams are no longer content to be turned into waking realities, taking the color of daylight, that they may remain visible to our eyes, but they remain lunar, spectral, a dark and unintelligible menace."—Symons, "The Rossettis," *Dramatis Personae* (Indianapolis, 1923), pp. 130–31.

60 Symons, *Confessions*, pp. 86–87.

61 Symons, "Prelude to Life," *Spiritual Adventures*, p. 16.

62 Symons, "Christian Trevalga," *Spiritual Adventures*, p. 91.

63 Symons, "Prelude to Life," *Spiritual Adventures*, p. 42.

64 Symons, *Confessions*, p. 86, and "Gérard de Nerval," *Symbolist Movement*, p. 18.

65 Symons, Christian Trevalga," *Spiritual Adventures*, p. 107.

66 Symons, "The Wanderers," *Amoris Victima* (London, 1897), p. 34.

67 *Ibid.*

68 Symons, *Confessions*, pp. 10–11.

69 Symons, "Henry Luxulyan," *Spiritual Adventures*, p. 311.

70 Symons, *Confessions*, p. 8.

vii *The Decadent Consciousness*

1 Martin Buber, *I and Thou* (New York, 1958), p. 34.
2 Walter Pater, *Marius the Epicurean: His Sensations and Ideas* (2 vols.; London, 1885), II, 74.
3 John Keats, *The Poetical Works of John Keats,* ed. H. W. Garrod (Oxford University Press, 1956), p. 408, ll. 40–45.
4 Wallace Stevens uses the phrase when discussing the necessity and the difficulty of bringing together imagination and reality in "The Noble Rider and the Sound of Words," *The Necessary Angel* (New York, 1951), pp. 1–36.

Index

Alighieri, Dante. *See* Dante Alighieri

Aristippus of Cyrene, 40–41, 46–48

Arnold, Matthew: social thought of, xiv, 6, 16, 68, 69, 95; influence on Wilde of, 67, 68; influence on Johnson of, 85, 87–88, 89, 94; mentioned, 47, 64, 79

Art for art's sake: Rossetti's interpretation, 4; Swinburne's interpretation, 21–23; Pater's interpretation, 42; Wilde's interpretation, 65

Artist, isolation of: accepted by Decadents, xiv, 33, 95, 109–10,

exemplified by Rossetti, 4–6, 9, 17; symbolized by Lady of Shalott, 5, 82; attitude of Pater toward, 49

Badley, J. H., 83, 85

Balzac, Honoré de, 79, 84

Barbey d'Aurévilly, Jules, 62, 98

Bastien–Lepage, Jules, 84

Baudelaire, Charles, 20–21, 63, 66, 68, 69, 79, 84, 134*n24*, 136*nn40,51*

Beardsley, Aubrey, xvi, 97, 137–38*n61*

Blake, William, 11, 32, 36

Brown, Madox, 128*n9*